THE JEWISH ECONOMIC ELITE

GERMAN JEWISH CULTURES

EDITORIAL BOARD:

Matthew Handelman, Michigan State University
Iris Idelson, Goethe Universität Frankfurt am Main
Samuel Spinner, Johns Hopkins University
Joshua Teplitsky, Stony Brook University
Kerry Wallach, Gettysburg College

Sponsored by the Leo Baeck Institute London

THE JEWISH ECONOMIC ELITE

MAKING MODERN EUROPE

CORNELIA AUST

Indiana University Press

This book is a publication of

Indiana University Press
Office of Scholarly Publishing
Herman B Wells Library 350
1320 East 10th Street
Bloomington, Indiana 47405 USA

iupress.indiana.edu

© 2018 by Cornelia Aust
All rights reserved

No part of this book may be reproduced or utilized in any form or by any means, electronic or mechanical, including photocopying and recording, or by any information storage and retrieval system, without permission in writing from the publisher. The Association of American University Presses' Resolution on Permissions constitutes the only exception to this prohibition.

∞ The paper used in this publication meets the minimum requirements of the American National Standard for Information Sciences—Permanence of Paper for Printed Library Materials, ANSI Z39.48-1992.

Manufactured in the United States of America

Library of Congress Cataloging-in-Publication Data

Names: Aust, Cornelia, author.
Title: The Jewish economic elite : making modern Europe / Cornelia Aust.
Description: First edition. | Bloomington, Indiana : Indiana University Press, [2017] | Series: German Jewish cultures | Includes bibliographical references and index.
Identifiers: LCCN 2017042564 (print) | LCCN 2017043345 (ebook) | ISBN 9780253032171 (E-book) | ISBN 9780253032157 (cloth : alk. paper) | ISBN 9780253032164 (pbk. : alk. paper)
Subjects: LCSH: Europe—Commerce—History—19th century. | Jews—Europe—Economic conditions—19th century. | Jews—Commerce—Europe—History—19th century. | Jews—Social networks—Europe—History—19th century. | Jewish capitalists and financiers—Europe—History—19th century. | Jewish businesspeople—Europe—History—19th century. | Jewish merchants—Europe—History—19th century.
Classification: LCC HF3495 (ebook) | LCC HF3495 .A97 2018 (print) | DDC 381.089/92404—dc23
LC record available at https://lccn.loc.gov/2017042564

1 2 3 4 5 23 22 21 20 19 18

For my parents—für meine Eltern mit großer Dankbarkeit

CONTENTS

Acknowledgments	ix
Note on Spelling, Transcription, and Translation	xiii
Introduction	xv
1. Amsterdam: A Center of Credit	1
2. Frankfurt an der Oder: Central European Middlemen	37
3. Borderlands: Legal Restrictions, Army Supplying, and Economic Success	80
4. Praga: A Stepping Stone	110
5. Warsaw: The Rise of a Jewish Economic Elite	137
Conclusion	176
Abbreviations	187
Bibliography	189
Index	209

ACKNOWLEDGMENTS

It has been a long journey to complete this book. It is a great pleasure to thank those individuals and institutions that have supported me at different stages of my research. Without their help, I could not have written this book.

At the initial stage of my research, I received generous support from numerous institutions: a Benjamin Franklin Fellowship from the University of Pennsylvania; an International Dissertation Research Fellowship from the Social Science Research Council and a doctoral fellowship from the Memorial Foundation for Jewish Culture (both 2006–2007) supported my archival research, as did multiple Goldfein Research Awards from Jewish Studies at the University of Pennsylvania and a Pew Summer Fellowship from the University of Pennsylvania. The Louis Apfelbaum and Hortense Braunstein Apfelbaum Fellowship at the Katz Center for Advanced Judaic Studies in Philadelphia in 2008–2009 provided me not only with time to write but also with the opportunity to meet and engage with an amazing group of scholars interested in various aspects of Jewish economic history and its cultural implications. I also wish to express my gratitude to the staff of the Van Pelt Library and especially the Interlibrary Loan department, which found even the most obscure books and articles. Moreover, I am grateful to the staff at the Katz Center for Advanced Judaic Studies and its library for making the Center a place to read and write.

In revising my thesis into a book, my gratitude extends to the Martin Buber Society of Fellows at the Hebrew University in Jerusalem and the Leibniz Institute of European History in Mainz. In Mainz, I am especially grateful to the library staff for providing me with some hard-to-find titles, to my student assistant Alessa Schummer for proofreading the complete manuscript, and to Vanessa Weber, who helped me to find my way through the art submission guidelines. My colleagues at both institutions offered constant advice and support.

My very special gratitude goes to François Guesnet, who introduced me to the study of Jewish history twenty years ago and has remained a mentor and friend ever since. I wish to thank my advisor, Benjamin Nathans, who not only read patiently through multiple chapter drafts, but his questions and suggestions stimulated me to conceptualize my topic within a wider framework. Similarly, I thank David Ruderman, Adam Teller, and Francesca Trivellato.

Acknowledgments

I wish to acknowledge the help and support that I experienced in the multiple archives I visited throughout Europe and their staff. Most time I spent in the Secret State Archives (Geheimes Preußisches Staatsarchiv) in Berlin, the Central Archives of Historical Records (Archiwum Główne Akt Dawnych) in Warsaw, and the Central Archives for the History of the Jewish People in Jerusalem. Shorter visits to the city archives in Warsaw, Gdańsk, Wrocław, Frankfurt an der Oder, and Leipzig; the Main State Archives of Saxony in Dresden, the Main Archives of the State of Brandenburg in Potsdam, and the Amsterdam City Archives were equally fruitful. In Warsaw, I am grateful to the late Krzysztof Teodor Toeplitz for providing me with access to material concerning the history of his family; in Jerusalem, Moshe Mossel shared his knowledge about the genealogy of Ashkenazic families in eighteenth-century Amsterdam.

I would like to thank Glenn Dynner, François Guesnet, Debra Kaplan, Jonathan Karp, Adam Mendelsohn, Shaul Stampfer, and Francesca Trivellato for reading and commenting on parts of the manuscript. My thanks also go to the participants of the conference on "Jewish Commercial Cultures in Global Perspective" in 2015, whose comments on the final part of the manuscript were extremely helpful. Adam Teller and an anonymous reviewer read through the complete manuscript and supplied thoughtful feedback. Marc Friede (Marburg) helped with maps, Oliver Ihlow with the family graphics, and Ruth Ebenstein did a first round of copy-editing the manuscript. Any remaining errors are, of course, mine.

I am grateful to Brill for allowing me to publish chapters 4 and 5 of this book, a much shorter version of which appeared as an article titled "Merchants, Army Suppliers, Bankers: Transnational Connections and the Rise of Warsaw's Jewish Mercantile Elite" in the volume *The Jewish Metropolis*, edited by Glenn Dynner and François Guesnet (2015). A German version of chapter 3, "Von Itzig Jacob zu Izaak Flatau. Transregionaler Handel im preußisch-polnischen Teilungsgebiet," appeared in the *Jahrbuch für Regionalgeschichte* in 2016; Franz Steiner Verlag kindly gave permission for its publication here.

For insights and support at various stages of the book coming into being, I also want to thank Karen Auerbach, Israel Bartal, Maria Cieśla, Bernard Cooperman, Jonathan Dekel-Chen, Jürgen Hensel, Manfred Jehle, Judith Kalik, Rebecca Kobrin, Stefan Litt, Evelyne Oliel-Grausz, Derek Penslar, Andreas Reinke, Gideon Reuveni, Rotraud Ries, Jessica Roitman, Moshe Rosman, Veronica Santarosa, David Sorkin, Rolf Straubel, Claudia Ulbrich, Veerle Vanden Daelen, Hanna Węgrzynek, and Marcin Wodziński.

I extend my gratitude to the editors of the German Jewish Cultures Series, and especially Iris Idelson-Shein, for including my book in their series, and Dee Mortensen and Paige Rasmussen at Indiana University Press for their advice and enthusiasm in bringing this book to publication. I thank Irina Burns, copyeditor, and Deborah Grahame-Smith, production editor.

Finally, and most important, I want to thank my friends and family, who have supported me in every possible way. There are many friends and fellow researchers, spread across the United States, Israel, Germany, and Poland, who have supported me along the way: Rainer Barzen, Elisheva Baumgarten, Ruth von Bernuth, Sarah van Beurden, Rebecca Cutler, Saskia Dönitz, Sharon Gordon, Claudia Jarzebowski, Denise Klein, Karolin Machtans, Daniel Mahla, Vanessa Mongey, Anna Novikov, Michal Pagis, Rami Regavim, Yael Rice, Merav Shohet, Manfred Sing, Mirjam Thulin, Rebekka Voß, and Kerry Wallach. You have helped me with getting through the emotional strains of writing a book, diverted my thoughts to more important things in life when necessary, housed and nourished me in many ways.

My greatest gratitude goes to my family. I wish to express my love and gratitude to my parents, Ursula and Bodo, who gave me all the love and support I could have wished for on a journey that took me far from home. If they ever had doubts about my choosing the path of becoming a historian, they hid it well and believed in me with all their hearts. They supported me in every possible way as parents and, later on, as grandparents, for which they traveled near and far. My parents-in-law, Hans, who left us too soon, and Inge, were equally supportive in all ways possible. My deepest gratitude goes to Johannes for his support, patience, and, most of all, love; and to Selma and Jonathan, who are the joy of my life.

NOTE ON SPELLING, TRANSCRIPTION, AND TRANSLATION

The very complex geography of east central Europe is mirrored in the fact that many places had multiple names—in German, Polish, and sometimes Yiddish. Moreover, in the time under consideration political borders and thus names of places changed. I have tried to consistently use names current at the time discussed; that is Posen rather than Poznań, and Lemberg not L'viv, but also give the official name used today at the first mention. Where English equivalents exist, as in the case of Warsaw, I have used them. The same goes for personal names. Most of my protagonists were known by more than one name, often an official name used with the Christian administration and a Hebrew one that appears in internal Jewish documents. Some used a German, Polish, or Yiddish name depending on the language of the document in question. I usually settled on one version of the name, also in terms of spelling, which I use throughout the text, while pointing to the existence and usage of other forms of an individual's name in specific contexts.

For different coins, currencies, and units of measurement, I mostly stayed with the original terms, like thaler or złoty, and added explanations when necessary. For the transliteration from Hebrew, I followed the system of the Library of Congress in a slightly simplified form, except for words used commonly in English, like Hasidism, not Ḥasidism. For Yiddish I followed the widely used YIVO Romanization system.

All translations within the text are mine unless otherwise noted.

INTRODUCTION

How did Jewish bankers rise to prominence in central and east central Europe during the nineteenth century? This question, long untouched by historians and fraught with simplistic notions about Jewish proneness to business and money, lies at the core of this book. *The Jewish Economic Elite* is a study of the commercial connections of members of the Jewish mercantile elite across Europe, from Amsterdam in the west to Warsaw in the east between the second half of the eighteenth and the first decades of the nineteenth centuries. It uncovers largely unknown networks of Jewish merchants and entrepreneurs across the northern part of the European continent and tells the human stories behind these networks. Subverting the east-west dichotomy deeply rooted in the Jewish historical narrative, it explores the formation and shifting of commercial networks and the rise and decline of commercial undertakings of individual Jewish families following them from west to east. There, in Warsaw, a new Jewish economic elite rose to success around the mid-nineteenth century. Though this was the case elsewhere in Europe as well, this development contradicts a too simple notion that contrasts an underdeveloped east with a modernizing west. Rather, these merchants and entrepreneurs, who were connected via family, community, and commerce, partly sought to escape restrictive legal conditions in central Europe and saw new opportunities in the markets of the east.

Moreover, the book adds to our understanding of the relationship of Jewish economic actors and the emerging of the capitalist economy in Europe. It explains the transition from the flourishing of Court Jews of the absolutist regimes of central Europe to the rise of a new Jewish commercial and banking elite by the mid-nineteenth century. Unlike often assumed, the rise of the latter is not connected to the success of the former in a linear fashion. The economic, political, and social shifts of the period contributed to the decline of the commercial undertakings of some Jewish families whereas others profited and climbed to new success. Many of those who rose to success in Warsaw moved from trade in agricultural goods into army supplying and from there into banking, though during the time under consideration, these merchants and entrepreneurs usually relied on multiple sources of income. Occupational flexibility, a willingness to take entrepreneurial risk, and migration were major factors in the rise of this new economic elite.

Finally, the importance of diaspora communities in transcultural and transnational commerce has been noted repeatedly by historians and it is no surprise that Jews are often seen as paradigmatic in this area of economic activity. However, regarding the early modern period, the focus has often been on the far-reaching networks of Sephardic merchants and their converted brethren in western and southern Europe, Spain, and the New World, most recently in the works of Francesca Trivellato and Jessica Roitman.[1] The movement of Jews across the European continent has mostly been seen in scholarship as one of poor and often desperate Ashkenazim migrating westward because of persecution and economic hardship. That mass stood in contrast to a small number of wealthy and well-connected Court Jews, who supplied the courts across central Europe with money, army supplies, and luxury goods. However, the common narrative, first established by Jonathan Israel in his laudable and successful attempt to examine Jewish economic history in the early modern period as a European phenomenon, suggested a decline of the Jewish economic situation in the first decades of the eighteenth century.[2] Though such a development did occur, the picture is somewhat distorted by a strong focus on western and partly central Europe and a focus on the decline of the fortunes of central European Court Jews. Including east central and eastern Europe more closely into the picture does provide a correction to the assumption of economic decline caused by a relatively peaceful period between the Peace of Utrecht (1713) and the beginning of the Napoleonic Wars at the end of the eighteenth century.

Until the mid-1990s, historians have paid only marginal attention to the economic aspects of Jewish life in Europe and beyond. The hesitation among many scholars of Jewish history to touch on the question of Jews and their economic profiles in general and the link between Jews and the emergence of capitalism in particular is partly related to heated debates during the nineteenth and early twentieth centuries that identified and often criticized Jews as the harbingers of capitalism. Despite early rejections, arguments like those of Werner Sombart about Jews as "internal strangers" and bearers of a thoroughly rational and contractual religion who pioneered international trade and subsequently capitalism have influenced historians for nearly a century.[3]

Max Weber's thesis about the close linkage between the Protestant ethic and the emerging spirit of capitalism seemed to turn religious identification into a central feature for economic success in the capitalist economy of the modern world. Sombart's subsequent claim that it was not Protestantism but rather Judaism that contained the seeds of the capitalist rationale, moved Jews to the center of this debate.[4] Sombart's rejection of capitalism, modernity, and what he perceived to be the decline of Western civilization made him susceptible to anti-Jewish argumentation. Together with his followers, Sombart used his arguments to blame Jews for their supposed alienating role within the national state and for Jewish cosmopolitanism, be it in the form of capitalist entrepreneurs or socialist and communist revolutionaries. To escape these debates, many historians have avoided questions of Jewish economic activities. Moreover, the focus in Jewish history on specific regional and national contexts may have blurred historians' vision for distinctively transregional and transnational phenomena like commerce.[5]

It was not until the early 2000s that historians have engaged more vividly in the question of the role of Jews in commerce in early modern and modern Europe. The renewed interest in Jewish commercial activities and networks joins together with a broader turn toward Jewish economic history. This new interest in Jewish economic activities or perceptions of these activities among Christians and Jews alike is manifested in an increasing number of publications.[6]

In this book I apply the awareness of the importance of transcultural and transnational commercial connections to explore the changing economic activities and networks of members of the Jewish mercantile elite in Europe in the period of transition between the Seven Years' War (1756–1763), the Congress of Vienna (1815), and the first years of the Kingdom of Poland (established in 1815), also known as Congress Poland. In this period the geographic and the mental map of Europe changed significantly. The partitions of Poland, the French Revolution and its impact across Europe, as well as the Napoleonic Wars fomented a period of political, social, and economic uncertainty. The book clarifies the role of Jews and more precisely the Jewish mercantile elite in central and east central Europe in the larger economic system of their time. A transnational approach to Jewish history is central in this endeavor and aims to overcome the common application of political boundaries of early modern principalities, empires, and later nation-states to Jewish history.

Jewish Economic Activity and the Rise of Modern Economy

The book tackles two sets of questions. The first deals with the place of Jewish merchants and entrepreneurs within the economic sphere in general and commerce in particular across the European continent at the turn from the eighteenth to the nineteenth century. The second set of questions approaches the mechanisms of building and maintaining commercial networks among Ashkenazic merchants.

First, the book asks how the changing economic and political fate of cities like Amsterdam, Frankfurt an der Oder, and Warsaw influenced the Jewish mercantile elite. The narrative trails the changes over time from around the mid-eighteenth century, a period described by Jonathan Israel as a time of Jewish economic decline, to the second decade of the nineteenth century, which is often perceived as the century of Jewish banking. Thus the period is perched between the end of the phenomenon of the Court Jews, which was closely tied to the flourishing of absolutism, and the rise of a new Jewish banking elite, exemplified by the Rothschild family and others, in an emerging capitalist society. The narrative moves from Amsterdam in the west through central Europe eastward to Warsaw to tie together the commercial decline of Amsterdam with the rise of a new Jewish banking elite in Poland in general and in Warsaw in particular. It explains how political and economic developments influenced the choice of merchandise Jews traded in, the impact of these and other changes on the geographical composition of commercial ties, and how this transitional period influenced Jewish commerce. It thus challenges Israel's narrative of a general economic decline rooted in relative peace prevailing in eighteenth-century Europe and argues that a new wave of army suppliers emerged in central and east central Europe in the period of the Seven Years' War and the partitions of Poland (1772, 1793, 1795). Thus, decline and revitalization of Jewish economic life did not follow one after the other, but they were parallel processes, differing according to time and place.

Jewish economic activity and the rise of a new economic elite in nineteenth-century central Europe has usually be seen through the lens of the economic success of Court Jews. Their emergence, serving at and supplying princely courts during the seventeenth century, was indeed central to the Jewish economic profile.[7] Though small in number, their supply networks supported a large number of Jewish families as sub-contractors and fostered the (re)emergence of Jewish communities. According to Jonathan Israel, the Thirty Years' War was a pivotal point insofar as the crucial role Jewish merchants assumed in army contracting and regional and transregional commerce ensured their settlement in early modern Europe.[8] In the historiography, attention has focused on the phenomenon of the Court Jew and his relation to the emergence of the modern state and early capitalism in the German states of the seventeenth and eighteenth centuries.[9] Selma Stern characterized Court Jews as a product of a transitional period toward court absolutism and early capitalism. Implicitly rejecting Sombart's thesis, Stern argued that despite the modern character of the phenomenon, "the Court Jew was never a *homo capitalisticus*."[10] The phenomenon of Court Jews or similar arrangements of wealthy Jewish individuals with close ties to the respective rulers has been discussed in various geographic and chronological settings.[11] Their trans-European connections have often been stressed as well as their particular position within the Jewish community.[12] Research on German Court Jews since the 1990s has shed new light on the phenomenon and raised questions regarding their social and familial context and their role within Jewish society—questions that are also applicable to the privileged Jewish wholesale merchants of the second half of the eighteenth and early nineteenth centuries. This intermediate generation of merchants and entrepreneurs is often overlooked in the historical narrative, thereby creating a seemingly straight line from Court Jews to nineteenth-century bankers and entrepreneurs. This book is particularly interested in this generation of merchants and entrepreneurs and sheds new light on their rise to being part of the Jewish commercial elite of nineteenth-century central and east central Europe.

Although most Jewish historians were reluctant to study Jewish economic history, Jewish historians from eastern Europe were an exception. Similar to Simon Dubnov's partial rejection of the German-Jewish historiographic focus on intellectual history and his particular interest in the history of the Jewish community and its autonomy, there was a group of Polish-Jewish historians of the interwar period that was specifically interested in the economic history of east European Jewry. These historians charted various issues of Jewish economic history from the Middle Ages to their own lifetimes, though they were often driven by strong ideological convictions, such as Marxist traditions and a particular interest in labor history.[13] Other historians, like Ignacy Schiper, were strongly influenced by attempts to disprove Sombart's claims. Many of these works on Jewish commerce and Jewish merchants were tied to contemporary debates about the usefulness or harm of Jewish economic activities, and were often limited to the Polish context. Ultimately, this tradition was cut short by the Holocaust and the destruction of Polish Jewry.

Nevertheless, the scholarship of these Polish-Jewish historians found some continuation in the studies of those who survived, like Artur Eisenbach, and Jacob Goldberg.[14] Most of these scholars were less interested in Jewish merchants and mercantile activity than in the middlemen function of Jews in the feudal economy or the location of a Jewish working class. Although their work was deeply attuned to economic aspects of Jewish history, it focused primarily on Poland and the Polish-Lithuanian Commonwealth.

Since the 1990s, studies of Polish Jewry have shown the close relationship between Jews and the Polish nobility, and specifically between the great magnate-aristocrats and their Jewish leaseholders. They demonstrate the important role Jews played in the feudal economy in general and in commerce in particular in the Polish-Lithuanian Commonwealth until its dissolution at the end of the eighteenth century. Adam Teller demonstrated how successful Jews were integrated into the feudal estate economy of eighteenth-century Poland-Lithuania. Moreover, he identified Jewish society's economic flexibility as a key point to Jewish economic success in the estate economy, an observation that seems equally true for those Jewish merchants and entrepreneurs who rose to economic power around the turn from the eighteenth to the nineteenth century.[15]

However, the period from the dissolution of the Council of the Four Lands (*Va'ad 'arba' 'aratsot*) in 1764 to the foundation of the Kingdom of Poland in 1815 has received relatively little attention. Most works on Jews in early modern Poland are concerned with the various aspects of Jewish life in the seventeenth and the first three quarters of the eighteenth centuries, whereas historians of the modern period usually begin their inquiries around 1815, when political borders and conditions became more stable again.[16] An exception is the period around the Four Year Sejm (1788–1792), although these studies are primarily concerned with the debates about the emancipation of the Jewish population.[17] Despite the ever changing political conditions and borders between the first partition of Poland in 1772 and the establishment of the Kingdom of Poland in 1815, this period was formative in terms of the eventual emergence of a new Jewish mercantile elite in nineteenth-century Poland.

Kinship and Ethnicity in Ashkenazic Commercial Networks

The second set of questions that resurface throughout the chapters revolves around the ways commercial ties were built and maintained, the ways conflicts were solved, and to which legal measures merchants resorted. Although these questions are common in works on a wide variety of commercial networks from India to the New World, they have yet to be applied to the economic history of Ashkenazic Jewry in the early modern period.[18] This study of social and economic networks of diaspora communities examines the quality and importance of kinship, shared ethnicity, and religion in the formation of business ties. It examines how relations between individual actors within commercial networks were formed as well as how and when non-Jewish business partners joined the commercial webs of Jewish merchants. Although familial and ethnic ties among business partners could strengthen trust, they were not foolproof insurance against failure caused by outside circumstances or actions of business partners. Thus, this book also pays attention to the failures of individual merchants and larger business undertakings to examine how they came about and how close-knit familial or communal ties could or could not prevent them. Nevertheless, it takes issue with Trivellato's central argument stating that Jewish networks allowed non-Jews to participate closely as these networks were connected largely by a shared business ethos.[19] As valuable as this conclusion is and certainly it applies to many Sephardic commercial networks, its validity needs to be verified for the Ashkenazic case.

A decade ago, David Landes pointed out the importance of family and kinship as bases for economic activity and even for entrepreneurial success in the modern period.[20] This is even more applicable in the early modern period. Moreover, beyond family ties, commercial success has often been attributed or at least closely linked to ethnic solidarity and the employment of kinship and ethnic ties in commercial networks in general and in long-distance trade in particular. The belief in the importance of ethnic solidarity is based primarily on two classical works on "trade diasporas," an expression coined by Abner Cohen in 1971.[21] Cohen and Philip Curtin were most influential in creating a picture that mostly equated "trade diasporas" with trust based on kinship and ethnic or religious belonging.

According to these considerations, commerce in general and long-distance trade in particular was based on mutual trust among business partners. The issue of trust and risk points not only to the importance of ethnic solidarity but also to its limitations. In a society with relatively weak state institutions, it was not, as Gunnar Dahl formulated in his work on commercial culture in late medieval Italy, "the goods, the harbours, the bills of exchange, or the insurance that made business grow—it was the entrepreneurs, the individuals, who saw the opportunities and took the calculated risks."[22] In order to manage risk, trust in business partners was crucial. Economists' studies have shown that trust among members of the same ethnic group or even within the close or extended family was not a given.[23] Although familial and ethnic ties among business partners could strengthen trust, they did not constitute an insurance policy against failure caused by outside circumstances or actions of business partners.

Only in the last decade, scholars studying commercial networks anchored in ethnic/religious communities have criticized this model and sought to describe the mechanisms behind the creation of mutual trust among commercial traders of the same ethnic/religious background and other merchants as well. Francesca Trivellato speaks of "networks of mercantile trust" that were not necessarily ethnically or religiously homogenous.[24] Sebouh David Aslanian describes social capital generated within social networks as a "key factor . . . to generate and maintain trust, trustworthiness, and uniform norms," in this case, among early modern Armenian Julfan merchants.[25] Based on these insights, trust can be defined as belief in the positive outcome of future business undertakings with a specific and regular business partner. It is based on the assumption that repeated business transactions with a specific business partner create an atmosphere that implies meaningful economic and even social consequences if a business partner's expectations are not matched. Commercial networks are defined in this case as regular connections and repeated commercial interactions among multiple individuals. It is important to underscore that even if one explores Jewish commercial networks, they were hardly ever limited to Jewish merchants. Non-Jewish merchants, clients, or in some cases state officials were often involved on a regular basis. The position of a merchant within a network was defined by the distribution of different resources, meaning his/her access to commodities, capital, and knowledge. Commercial networks always kept a dynamic character and were exposed to change due to political events, bankruptcy of individual merchants, strife among merchants, and changing familial, political, and economic constellations.[26] The repeated interactions implied not only familiarity but also that misconduct in business could have serious consequences for those concrete commercial connections, as well as for a businessman's reputation.

To examine these different dynamics among Jewish merchants, brokers, and entrepreneurs lies at the core of this work. This approach will allow me to conceptualize social (and economic) patterns, while positioning them within general economic developments.[27] In recent decades, the literature on early modern trading networks has grown tremendously. These trading networks were never self-contained and always involved members of more than one religious, ethnic, or national group. However, the expression "cross-cultural trade" cannot hide the fact that exchange between these different groups in general and in between Jews and non-Jews in particular was often limited to the commercial sphere.[28] In the case of the members of the Jewish mercantile elite in early modern Europe, commercial ties with non-Jews allowed Jewish merchants and entrepreneurs to gain access to locations that generally restricted Jewish settlement, to link them to the general world of commerce and to facilitate the creation of much-needed ties with the local and state administration.

As in any commercial or social network, the social and economic relations depicted here are neither closed nor complete. There are always more ties that extend relations further geographically and into other social groups. The question emerges whether networks and even ethnic networks can substitute for other social categories, such as class. The merchants and entrepreneurs examined here belonged to the Jewish mercantile elite. Although they were connected economically and socially to other members of Jewish society, they nevertheless constituted a social group of their own. Moreover, the source basis hardly allows detailed descriptions of their connections to members of a lower social stratum involved in subcontracting or transportation. As such, my analysis of commercial connections illustrates the transnational dimension of these connections and the ways these ties transcended political borders but nevertheless remains limited in displaying only part of the social reality, given that many connections remain invisible.

The growing body of literature on commercial and communal networks in the Sephardic world has made it clear how important it is to avoid facile assumptions about Jewish commercial networks. This research has shown the importance of the integration of non-Jewish business partners as well as the limits of ethnic solidarity in diaspora networks. Here, the focus has been on the Sephardic world of southern and western Europe, the communities of Sephardic traders primarily in Italy, Amsterdam, and London, whose wealthiest members were involved in transcultural trade from the Mediterranean and western Europe to the Americas as well as to India.[29] In the Ashkenazic case, however, we find that etic networks, often based on additional close marital ties, retained their central importance well into the nineteenth century. This does not mean that Ashkenazic commercial activity took place in a void and independently of the general economy. Ashkenazic merchants and entrepreneurs did business with Christians, they had Christian clients and business acquaintances, and used similar channels to transfer goods and credit, but we do not see shared business or any formal business partnerships. This does not mean, however, that being Jewish or a family member was sufficient to become part of a specific commercial network. Social capital, shared notions of business behavior, prior experience in the trade, and access to information were different parameters that played an important role within Ashkenazic networks.

Amsterdam, Frankfurt an der Oder, Warsaw

The book is based on rich archival material from Poland, Germany, the Netherlands, and Israel, as well as some published sources in Polish, German, French, Dutch, Hebrew, and Yiddish. This corpus of source material includes state records on the financial situation of Jewish communities as well as individual merchants, a large sample of bills of exchange, petitions by Jewish merchants that often detail their economic and social position, as well as internal Jewish material like communal record books (*pinkassim*).

As the map shows, the commercial networks covered large parts of northern Europe stretching from Amsterdam in the west to Warsaw in the east. Beginning in the west, the first chapter describes the role of Amsterdam as a commercial center and of the city's Ashkenazic brokers as important suppliers of credit to Jewish merchants in central and indirectly eastern Europe until at least another decade after the end of the Seven Years' War in 1763. Constituting a counterbalance to the customary focus on the local Sephardic community, it traces the business undertakings and commercial connections of the Symons family, their building of commercial connections via marriage ties, and the role of bills of exchange in transregional trade. This implies a shift of attention to the Ashkenazic community of Amsterdam and its mercantile elite. Their economic endeavors were often smaller in scale and none attained the wealth of their affluent Sephardic brethren or of the successful Protestant merchant-bankers of the eighteenth century. Nevertheless, they were an important part of Amsterdam's commercial life, and took a central role in the brokerage of credit to central and east central Europe. Although they shared the economic fate of the declining financial center of Amsterdam, they also provided the preconditions for the rise of a new Jewish economic elite in nineteenth-century Europe.

Chapter 2 focuses on Frankfurt an der Oder. The city serves as an example for a central European hub, crucial for the commercial exchange between east and west due to its geographic location and its fairs. Tracing the family connections of the Symons family from Amsterdam to members of the Jewish mercantile elite in Frankfurt an der Oder in general and the Schlesinger family in particular, the chapter follows the fate of the city's Jewish mercantile elite from their relative economic success around the Seven Years' War to the economic decline of the city in general and the Jewish community in particular toward the end of the eighteenth century. Migration—and here especially the eastward migration—was a central strategy to adapt to legal restrictions and changing economic conditions.

Jews were readmitted to Prussia only at the end of the seventeenth century and a new group of successful entrepreneurs emerged who were active in wholesale

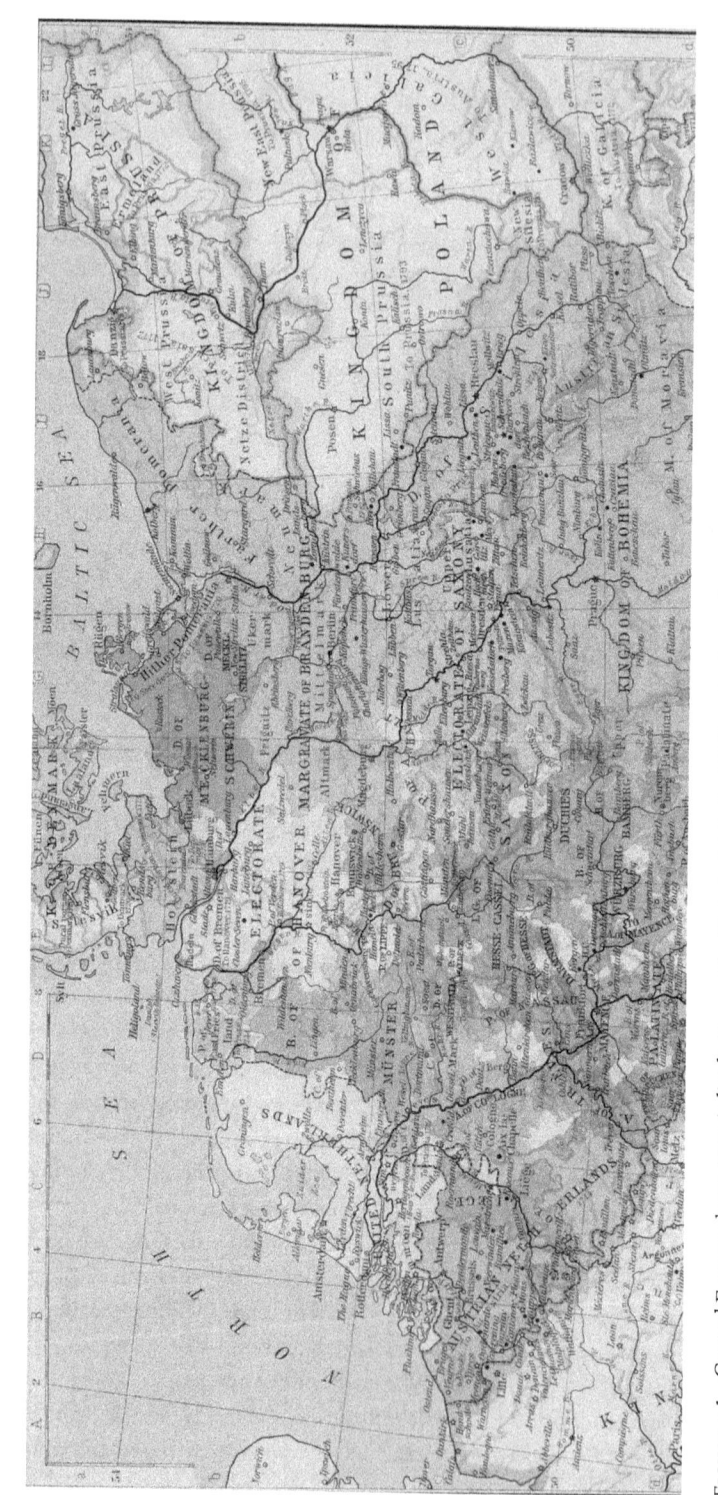

FIGURE 1.1. Central Europe about 1786 (edited). From: *The Historical Atlas* by William R. Sheperd, 1926. Digitalized by University of Texas Libraries.

trade, alongside a smaller group that was involved in minting and manufacturing. Though some performed similar tasks as did Court Jews, a new mercantile elite began to emerge that was less closely bound to the princely courts. Many of these merchants and entrepreneurs earned their riches in the Seven Years' War. Concurrently, a wide gap developed between a very small mercantile elite and a majority of relatively poor Jews, who were primarily involved in retail trade.[30]

The chapter focuses on members of the new mercantile elite that emerged largely in the second half of the eighteenth century. Although most of them enjoyed legal status as privileged and protected Jews (*Schutzjuden*), they were not Court Jews in the classical sense. They usually did not have close ties to a specific princely court, especially when living in commercial cities like Frankfurt an der Oder, Königsberg (Kaliningrad), or Breslau (Wrocław). Nevertheless, they usually were the wealthiest members of their respective Jewish communities, fulfilled important functions within the communal administration, enjoyed close ties to the local non-Jewish administration, maintained transregional commercial connections, and more often than not they showed at least a certain affinity to the Jewish enlightenment in its early stages.

Chapter 3 analyzes the rise of a new group of Jewish army suppliers in the borderlands between Prussia and Poland. It argues that similar to developments in the area of Alsace-Lorraine, the political shifts and the specific economic conditions allowed Jewish merchants to become important army suppliers. The chapter traces the fate of the Jewish sub-supplier Itzig Jacob from West Prussia, who over two decades became an important army supplier and banker, while moving eastward and eventually settling in Warsaw. It argues that it was prior experience in commerce, transregional connections, willingness to take entrepreneurial risk and ability to extend credit when supplying more than one army that allowed for a successful path east and socially upward.

Chapters 4 and 5 finally turn to Warsaw and Praga, a small town on the opposite side of the Vistula River, and the rise of a new Jewish economic elite in the Polish capital. Chapter 4 shifts the focus to Jewish merchants and entrepreneurs who developed, alongside commercial ties with the Polish nobility, close ties to the last Polish king Stanisław August Poniatowski and his administration as well as to the subsequent state administrations in Warsaw. Though most of them did not relinquish ties to the nobility, their focus shifted in particular when living in and around Warsaw. These members of the Polish-Jewish elite as well as Jewish immigrants from central Europe began to form a new mercantile elite in Warsaw and the Kingdom of Poland from the first decades of the nineteenth century. They profited from their partly close integration into the feudal economic system of the Polish-Lithuanian Commonwealth, their occupational flexibility and their willingness to take entrepreneurial risk. At the same time, they had to maneuver through politically instable times, in which not only their business ventures but also their legal position was at stake. The ensuing political debate forced those members of the mercantile elite to position themselves between Jewish corporate identity and the ideas of Jewish emancipation.

Chapter 5 demonstrates how the transition from army supplying into two fields of economic activity—banking and leaseholding of state monopolies—led eventually to the rise of a Jewish economic elite in nineteenth-century Warsaw and Poland more generally. The chapter traces the careers of the extraordinary female merchant, Judyta Jakubowiczowa, of Frankfurt an der Oder, who became one of the most important bankers in Warsaw by the 1820s; her example also demonstrates the crucial role of women in Jewish commerce. Her example shows the transition from army supplying to banking, while her stepson, Berek Szmul (Sonnenberg/Bergson), will provide an example for the move into state monopolies and the salt monopoly in particular as well as for the economic activities of Hasidic entrepreneurs. The contrary cultural and religious orientation of these two figures further leads to the question how closely these orientations were linked with economic success and which role they played in the formation and maintenance of commercial networks.

The broad range of sources in multiple languages reflects the transregional and transcultural nature of the familial and commercial connections of members of the Jewish mercantile elite across continental Europe. Kinship and ethnic belonging remained central for the establishment and maintenance of commercial networks among Ashkenazic Jews far into the nineteenth century. By addressing the transregional connections of members of the Jewish mercantile elite, the book demonstrates that the decline of Amsterdam as a (Jewish) financial center did not only go along with the rise of London but also—at least in the case of the Jewish mercantile elite—with the rise of Warsaw, though on a much more modest scale. It suggests that commercial networks were not ever stable entities and in the period under consideration, the economic decline of Amsterdam in the west and the rise of Warsaw in the east affected these commercial connections in fundamental ways. The focus on Warsaw and Polish lands also shows that the history of Polish Jewry is an integral part of European Jewish history, not just because of their sheer numbers, but because the rise of a modern Jewish economic elite in east central and eastern Europe is inseparable from the general economic and social developments elsewhere in Europe.[31]

Notes

1. Trivellato, *The Familiarity of Strangers*; Roitman, *The Same But Different?*
2. Israel, *European Jewry*, 195–215.

3. See Muller, *Capitalism and the Jews*, 1–5.

4. Sombart, *Die Juden und das Wirtschaftsleben*; Weber, "Die protestantische Ethik und der Geist des Kapitalismus," vol. 20, 1–54, vol. 21, 1–110. On the debate around Max Weber, Werner Sombart, and Georg Simmel's *The Philosophy of Money* (1900), see Muller, *Capitalism and the Jews*, 46–61.

5. Rosman, "Jewish History across Borders," 15–29.

6. An exception to this is Israel, *European Jewry*. His pathbreaking work, which emphasizes the transregional character of Jewish commerce and also defined an early modern period in Jewish history for the first time, was first published in 1985. His study highlighted the importance of promoting commerce by early modern states for the readmission of Jews in western and central Europe. Israel has been criticized for his primary focus on the economic sphere and marginalization of cultural aspects of Jewish history, yet his work has been crucial in creating a stronger awareness among historians of both the importance of economic questions within Jewish history and the centrality of transnational aspects of that history. For a critique of Israel's approach, see Ruderman, "Review: Israel's European Jewry in the Age of Mercantilism," 154–159. See also Karp, "It's the Economy, Shmendrick!," 8–11; Reuveni and Wobick-Segev, *The Economy in Jewish History*, 1–20; Kobrin and Teller, *Purchasing Power*, 5–17.

7. Israel, *European Jewry*, 29, 37. See also Karp, "Economic History and Jewish Modernity," 252.

8. Israel, *European Jewry*, 72, 101. However, the phenomenon of the Court Jew passed its peak and mostly disappeared in its classical form after 1750. Ries, "Hofjuden," 21.

9. The two most important early historians on the phenomenon were Selma Stern and Heinrich Schnee, though the latter's work remains problematic due to his apparent anti-Semitic convictions. Schnee, *Die Hoffinanz und der moderne Staat*, 3:265–266. On Schnee, see Laux, "Ich bin der Historiker der Hoffaktoren," 485–513.

10. Stern, *The Court Jew*, xiii, 4, 11–12 (quote).

11. Graetz, "Court Jews in Economics and Politics," 27; Kaplan, "Court Jews before the Hofjuden," 11–12, 25.

12. For a more recent definition of Court Jews, see Ries, "Hofjuden," 15–16, 21, 27–29. Most historians of Polish-Jewish history assume that a parallel phenomenon of Court Jews did not exist in eastern Europe: Hundert, "The Role of the Jews in Commerce in Early Modern Poland-Lithuania," 252; Hundert, "Was There an East European Analogue to Court Jews?," 68–75. Moshe Rosman has argued that certain Jewish individuals who served Polish magnates in the Polish-Lithuanian Commonwealth fit into one group with the Court Jews of central Europe as they were involved in similar commercial and administrative activities and assumed similar roles as founders and patrons of Jewish communities. However, they were less involved in politics. Rosman, *The Lords' Jews*, 147–153, 183–184; Rosman, "Izrael Rubinowicz," 497, 506.

13. The most prominent among them were Ignacy Schiper, Emanuel Ringelblum, Raphael Mahler, Majer Bałaban, and Bernard D. Weinryb. Ringelblum, *Żydzi w Warszawie*; Schiper, *Dzieje handlu żydowskiego*; Schiper, *Onhoyb fun kapitalizm bey yuden in mayrev Eyrope*; Bałaban, *Historja i literatura żydowska*; Mahler, *Yidn in amolikn Poyln in likht fun tsifern*; Mahler, *A History of Modern Jewry*; Weinryb, *Neueste Wirtschaftsgeschichte der Juden in Russland*

und Polen. See also Léon, *Judenfrage & Kapitalismus*, 10, 65. Jürgen Hensel adopted a similar approach. Hensel, "Polnische Adelsnation und jüdische Vermittler 1815–1830," 13–14.

14. Among their most important works are Goldberg, *Jewish Privileges in the Polish Commonwealth*, 156–158; Eisenbach, *The Emancipation of the Jews in Poland*, 206–212.

15. Teller, *Money, Power, and Influence*, 189. See also Hundert, *The Jews in a Polish Private Town*; Rosman, *The Lords' Jews*.

16. A look at the works of Majer Bałaban's students shows mostly interest in Jewish communities in the seventeenth century. More recent studies like that of Moshe Rosman and Adam Teller focus primarily on the eighteenth century until the first partition of Poland. Gershon Hundert, by contrast, has stressed the importance of the eighteenth century for Polish-Jewish history: Hundert, *Jews in Poland-Lithuania*, 4. For works on the Kingdom of Poland after 1815, see Guesnet, *Polnische Juden im 19. Jahrhundert*; Dynner, *Men of Silk*; Wodziński, *Haskalah and Hasidism*.

17. On Jews during the Four Year Sejm, see Gelber, "Żydzi a zagadnienie reformy Żydów na Sejmie Czteroletnim," 326–344, 429–440; Goldberg, "Pierwszy ruch polityczny wśród Żydów," 45–63; Michalski, "Sejmowe Projekty Reformy Położenia Ludności Żydowskiej w Polsce," 20–44.

18. On the usage of the terms "trade diaspora," "entrepreneurial networks," and "diaspora networks," see Baghdiantz McCabe, Harlaftis, and Pepelasĺe Minoglou,, *Diaspora Entrepreneurial Networks*, xviii–xix. See also Sheffer, "A Profile of Ethno-National Diasporas," 359–370. For the most recent work on the Armenian diaspora, see Aslanian, *From the Indian Ocean to the Mediterranean*. For northern Europe, see Murdoch, *Network North*; Müller, *The Merchant Houses of Stockholm*; Bull, "Merchant Households and their Networks in Eighteenth-Century Trondheim," 213–231. On contemporary ethnic networks, see Light and Gold, *Ethnic Economies*.

19. Trivellato, *The Familiarity of Strangers*, 273–278.

20. Landes, *Dynasties*, ix–xvii.

21. Cohen, "Cultural Strategies in the Organization of Trading Diasporas," 266–281; Curtin, *Cross-Cultural Trade in World History*, 7.

22. Dahl, *Trade, Trust, and Networks*, 299.

23. From an economist's perspective, Oliver E. Williamson suggested to substitute the term "trust" with "calculativeness": Williamson, "Calculativeness, Trust, and Economic Organization," 453–486. For a discussion, see Craswell, "On the Uses of Trust," 487–500.

24. Trivellato, *The Familiarity of Strangers*, 273.

25. Aslanian, *From the Indian Ocean to the Mediterranean*, 167–168.

26. Davern, "Social Networks and Economic Sociology," 287–302.

27. For a general introduction to social network analysis, see Wasserman and Faust, *Social Network Analysis*, 3–4. Notably, the nature of the source material does not provide dense enough data to apply social network analysis in its most rigorous form, as business archives and merchant correspondence are largely lacking. For a more rigid application in a historical context, see Padgett and Ansell, "Robust Action and the Rise of the Medici," 1259–1319. On the historical application of network theory, see also Wellman and Wether-

ell, "Social Network Analysis of Historical Communities," 97–121. Both rather assume or suggest the study of local not transregional or transnational communities.

28. For a detailed discussion, see Trivellato, *The Familiarity of Strangers*, 16–20.

29. Trivellato, "The Port Jews of Livorno," 31–48; Oliel-Grausz, "Networks and Communication in the Sephardi Diaspora," 61–76; Roitman, *The Same But Different?*, 1–6.

30. Jersch-Wenzel, *Juden und "Franzosen,"* 154–155, 248. Jonathan Karp has argued that one of the reasons Wilhelm von Dohm and other Prussian proponents of Jewish emancipation were so concerned with the Jewish occupational structure and the "productivization" of the Jewish population was indeed an economic decline in the last decades of the eighteenth century. Karp, *The Politics of Jewish Commerce*, 98. On the emergence of the Jewish elite in Berlin, see Lowenstein, *The Berlin Jewish Community*, 25–32.

31. Hundert, *Jews in Poland-Lithuania*, 1–4. The numerical strength of Polish Jewry has been one of the reasons Hundert brought forward to underpin the importance of the Jewish experience in eighteenth-century Poland. This argument is certainly valid, but should not let us lose sight of the close connections between Polish Jewry and other Ashkenazic Jews further west.

THE JEWISH ECONOMIC ELITE

ONE

Amsterdam: A Center of Credit

In her memoirs, Glikl bas Juda Leib (also known as Glückel of Hameln), a Jewish female merchant of Hamburg, relates that her husband traveled for business to Amsterdam twice a year. Though in her narrative she is more concerned with her daughter's prestigious wedding to the Ashkenazic Cleve family, she mentions in passing that in three weeks in Amsterdam her husband was able to earn half the dowry for their daughter.[1] By that time, the last quarter of the seventeenth century, Amsterdam had long assumed its position as the commercial and financial center of Europe and the world. In 1701, an observer stated: "Amsterdam is the place where very nearly all the bills payable within Europe are drawn, remitted or otherwise discounted and traded."[2] Instead of providing special privileges to distinct merchant groups like many other early modern commercial cities, Amsterdam had "created inclusive institutional arrangements to protect all merchants, regardless of their origin, wealth, religion, or economic specialization."[3] By the early seventeenth century, Amsterdam had replaced Antwerp as the center of trade in bills of exchange; stable exchange rates made the city an attractive, and in certain periods, even the only possible place for such trading. Throughout the seventeenth century, merchant-bankers of all denominations gravitated to Amsterdam, a trend that continued for much of the eighteenth century.[4]

This chapter is the departing point for our journey to the east. When exploring the role Jewish merchants, brokers, and entrepreneurs played in the emergence of the modern economy, I move away from central European Court Jews, who are often perceived as the precursors of the Jewish economic elite in modern Europe. Rather, I examine the role of a hitherto neglected group of Jewish economic actors. Ashkenazic merchants and brokers involved in the trade in bills of exchange in Amsterdam did inhabit an important place in trade and credit operations across Europe, even though they played a relatively minor role in international banking in Amsterdam during the eighteenth century.[5] They assumed a central position in integrating different European markets, especially those in central and eastern Europe.

Unlike in the Sephardic world, the operations of these Jewish merchants and brokers were heavily rooted in Jewish familial and ethnic networks. Francesco Trivellato argued in her work on Sephardic Mediterranean networks that familial and ethnic networks did not generally play a major role and that especially in the long-distance trade trust was rather governed by "social norms, legal customs, and rules for communication."[6] However, the example of Amsterdam's Ashkenazic traders shows the persistent importance of ethnic- and family-based networks among Ashkenazim, though they obviously did not operate outside and apart from general commerce and banking. Despite the fact that the literature on Jews in early modern commerce features Sephardic merchants more prominently, the importance of Amsterdam's Ashkenazic merchants and brokers and their commercial networks for the expansion of trade and the provision of credit toward central and eastern Europe cannot be overestimated.

By the eighteenth century, central and eastern Europe had integrated considerably into the west European credit market. Thus, Amsterdam was also a stronghold of merchant banking, financing large parts of central and east European trade via bills of exchange, which were not only an instrument of payment for goods but also a commodity in and of themselves, commonly used for credit operations. Notably, Amsterdam's time did not last; the shift from Amsterdam to London as the international center of finance was already fully under way in the second half of the eighteenth century. Yet the Dutch city did remain the backbone of credit and trade in bills of exchange for northern, central, and eastern Europe until the last quarter of the eighteenth century.[7]

Jewish merchant bankers—Sephardim and Ashkenazim alike—were prominent in Amsterdam's merchant and banking community, yet they were neither the wealthiest nor did they run the largest merchant and banking houses in the city. None of them could compare in wealth and trade volume to the most affluent Christian houses.[8] Nevertheless, Ashkenazic merchants, brokers, and a few bankers constituted a crucial link to the general banking world of Amsterdam as providers and brokers of credit for Jewish and non-Jewish merchants in central and eastern Europe.

When Amsterdam rose to be the center of commerce and finance in the early modern world, it also stood out as one of the most tolerant cities in Europe. After breaking from Spanish rule in 1581, the Reformed Church soon became the "privileged" church in the newly formed Dutch Republic. Although there were legal restrictions on public worship, especially for Catholics, personal freedom of religion was mostly honored by the state; these environs of liberty drew many religious refugees to the Dutch Republic in general and to Amsterdam in particular. The first Portuguese New Christians to settle in Amsterdam sought new commercial opportunities, but profited equally from the city's religious freedom. They arrived as Christians, but in the first decades of the seventeenth century an increasing number of them declared their return to the Jewish faith. Over the first two decades of the seventeenth century, these Portuguese Jews founded three different Jewish congregations. By 1616, Amsterdam's city council recognized the right of Jews to practice their religion publically. Around the same time, the first Ashkenazic Jews began to settle in Amsterdam, though in much smaller numbers than their Sephardic brethren. Following the Thirty Years' War (1618–1648), the Khmel'nyts'kyi uprisings in the Polish-Lithuanian Commonwealth (1648–1650) and the war between Sweden and Poland (1655–1660), larger numbers of Ashkenazic immigrants poured into Amsterdam. In the main they were not welcomed by Amsterdam's Sephardim, who encouraged them as well as poor Sephardim to leave the city, partly by allotting money for their re-emigration to Poland and Germany, partly by sending them to Dutch colonies such as Curaçao. Nevertheless, a large number of Ashkenazim stayed in Amsterdam.

Organizationally, the first Ashkenazim were dependent on and marginalized within the Sephardic community until they became a fully independent community in 1639. The split into a German Ashkenazic and a Polish Ashkenazic congregation ended in 1673 when municipal authorities called for uniting the two. The community continued to grow, eventually outnumbering the Sephardic population in Amsterdam.[9] Despite unceasing attempts on the part of the government and the Sephardic community to keep poor Ashkenazim away from the city, the number of Ashkenazim grew from about 3,600 at the beginning to about 22,000 by the end of the eighteenth century.[10]

Over the seventeenth and early eighteenth centuries, Amsterdam had turned into a center of Jewish life for both Sephardim and Ashkenazim. It became a center of rabbinical and intellectual debate as well as a center for printing Yiddish tomes, with authors, publishers, printers, and book dealers traveling to and from the city.[11] For about a century and a half Amsterdam grew into one of the most important hubs for Sephardim and Ashkenazim in terms of intellectual exchange, print, business, social encounters with Christians, and Jewish involvement in commerce and financing.

Despite this plethora of activity of Ashkenazim, historical research has paid little attention to the history of Amsterdam's large Ashkenazic population in general and to their commercial activities in particular.[12] It was particularly those Ashkenazic merchants and brokers who built and maintained the commercial connections on the European continent and who kept the credit flowing to central and, indirectly, eastern Europe. Many Sephardim and most Ashkenazim in Amsterdam remained rather poor; the number of wealthy Jewish families was small. Out of about 3,000 Sephardim and 10,000 Ashkenazim in 1743 only 442 earned more than 800 guilders a year, most of them as merchants, brokers, and money changers, or from interest on capital. Out of these 442 only 159 were Ashkenazim.[13] While they were indeed excluded from some occupations, Jews were free to engage in international commerce, securities trade, maritime insurance, banking, and some branches of industry. Many specialized in the distribution of Indian goods across Europe, although they were excluded from trading certain goods, or acted as intermediaries between English importers and continental merchants; goods from Spanish and Portuguese colonies were handled primarily by Sephardim. Jews were active in commerce and in international exchange services. In the exchange trade they created novel ways of financing both business and government activities, but were rather hesitant about moving into banking proper. In 1760, 60 registered and many more unregistered Jewish brokers of bills of exchange were active in the city; Ashkenazim were more prominent among the latter. Illustrative of the disparity in number of non-Jews to Jews is the fact that a letter of sixty-one Amsterdam and Rotterdam bankers to the State General on matters of the circulation of inferior coins in 1746 bore the signature of only one Jewish banker: Tobias Boas. Three years later, the breakdown differed in a petition to withdraw a resolution that prohibited the payment of a commission to merchants importing precious metals: that bore the signature of forty-one Christian and thirty-eight Jewish merchants, among them Benjamin, Samuel, and Berent Symons, Philip Levy Gompertz, and two members of the Keijzer family.[14]

Jewish merchants were heavily involved in commerce, especially the import of stones and metals, in brokering and the exchange trade, but hardly in banking proper. Their important role in the exchange trade can also be gleaned from the fact that the 1753 edition of Isaac LeLong's *De koophandel van Amsterdam* (The Commerce of Amsterdam) includes a calendar noting the hour of the starting and ending times of Shabbat; he explained that commerce with Jews was so widespread that a Christian had to be aware of when Shabbat began on Friday night and ended on Saturday night.[15] Among those so vividly involved in exchange trade was the Symons (Pollack) family.

The Symons Family

The Ashkenazic community in Amsterdam had only a few wealthy members whose families were active in international trade and finance. Benjamin and Samuel Symons (Pollack), two brothers whose ancestors had lived in Amsterdam since the early seventeenth century, were primarily involved in trading diamonds and bills of exchange but also provided other financial services. The Symons family belonged to the community's small affluent elite, although the volume of their business activity was incomparable to that of the most affluent Sephardic merchants and bankers. In 1743, Benjamin Symons was listed as one of the ten wealthiest taxpayers in the Ashkenazic community, with an annual income of 2,500 guilders; the wealthiest community member was registered with an annual income of 8,000 guilders.[16] Benjamin Symons also used his wealth to benefit the community. In 1757, he and his wife Martha donated a curtain to cover the Torah Ark (*paroẖet*) as well as covers for the *bimah*, from which the Torah is read, and the *amud*, the lectern, from which the prayer is led.[17] We know little about the family's involvement in communal affairs, but its economic status does suggest some communal influence. Benjamin Symons served as one of the officers (*parnas*) of the Ashkenazic burial society (*Ḥevrah Kadisha*).[18] The prominent family never made it into the ranks of the best-known Ashkenazic families in Amsterdam, such as the Gompertz, Norden, or Keijzer families, but its commercial activities did span from the Ottoman Empire, Russia, and the Baltic in the east through all of central Europe to England, Italy, France, and as far as Suriname in the west. After Benjamin Symons died in 1763, his sons Abraham and Emanuel joined the firm and became partners with their uncle Samuel Symons six years later.[19] In the following decade, when the company operated under the name Benjamin & Samuel Symons & Sons, it was Benjamin Symons's son Abraham who traveled to Warsaw and Danzig and took over the business in central and east central Europe. Emanuel Symons extended the family's business to the Mediterranean. In their attempts to consolidate and extend their business, their choice of marital partners played a central role. The central economic tool in their commercial endeavors was the trade in bills of exchange.

The Role of Bills of Exchange in Central European Commerce

Institutional conditions to facilitate commerce varied greatly between Amsterdam in the west, central European cities in the Holy Roman Empire, and eastern Europe. Formal institutions of commerce were of crucial importance for transregional trade, especially in the case of bills of exchange, which by the eighteenth century were considered the most important means of facilitating this trade.[20] Though bills of exchange had existed since the Middle Ages, they became more suitable for long-distance trade and the provision of credit in the early modern period with the general acceptance of the system of endorsement. Endorsing the back of a bill of exchange allowed for its transfer from one merchant to the next before the bill was due (see figures 1.1 and 1.2). After considerable resistance it was slowly accepted in central Europe from the mid-seventeenth century on. Leipzig allowed its usage in 1682; Danzig (Gdańsk), one of the most important commercial cities on the Baltic Sea, ratified their practice only in 1701, even if merchants in central Europe had already used it for many decades. Endorsement allowed a bill of exchange to circulate beyond its initial signatories, providing greater flexibility in the trade in bills of exchange. Because there were neither international banks nor international courts that could enforce debts against foreign agents, bills of exchange proved the most effective means to transfer funds or loans abroad. Moreover, the

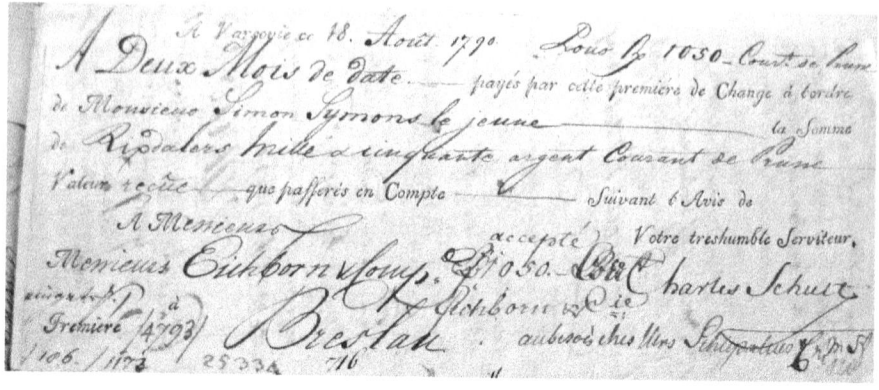

FIGURE 1.1. Bill of exchange, issued in Warsaw for Simon Symons and drawn to the banking house of Eichborn in Breslau, 1790. APW, Oddział Kamieniec Ząbkowicki, Dom Bankowy Eichborn, no. 4084, 120. Credit: Archiwum Państwowe we Wrocławiu.

flow of bills of exchange helped establish international currency exchange rates, as they determined the demand for national or territorial currencies.[21]

The endorsement came into usage later in central and eastern Europe than in western Europe; similarly, specific regulations regarding bills of exchange and the quotation of exchange rates were introduced later by a century or more. Depending on the geographic location, codifying regulations regarding exchange law grew an urgent necessity. Often these regulations were part of city or fair regulations, but by the seventeenth century, commercial centers in central Europe had begun to introduce particular municipal exchange regulations, although there was a clear time lag between cities in the west and those further east. Thus, Frankfurt am Main introduced an exchange regulation in 1578, Hamburg in 1601, and Nuremberg in 1621, whereas cities further east followed more than half a century later: Riga in 1671, Breslau in 1672, and Leipzig in 1682. Only in the eighteenth century were exchange regulations introduced into general state laws: in Prussia this happened in 1724 and in Russia in 1729.[22] Other innovations in commercial law followed.

Introducing the joint liability rule was of even greater importance, and it was fully developed by the eighteenth century. Veronica Aoki Santarosa indicated that the joint liability rule "put in place a formal mechanism that linked otherwise distinct personal networks"[23] in eighteenth-century France. With long chains of transmission and long distances between the issuer and the payer of a bill, the former had to be sure that the latter would honor his bills of exchange. The joint liability rule added an additional incentive to discipline the payer. It ensured that in a case of default, all endorsers as well as the issuer and payer "could be held liable for the full amount of the bill." Once a payer refused to honor a bill of exchange

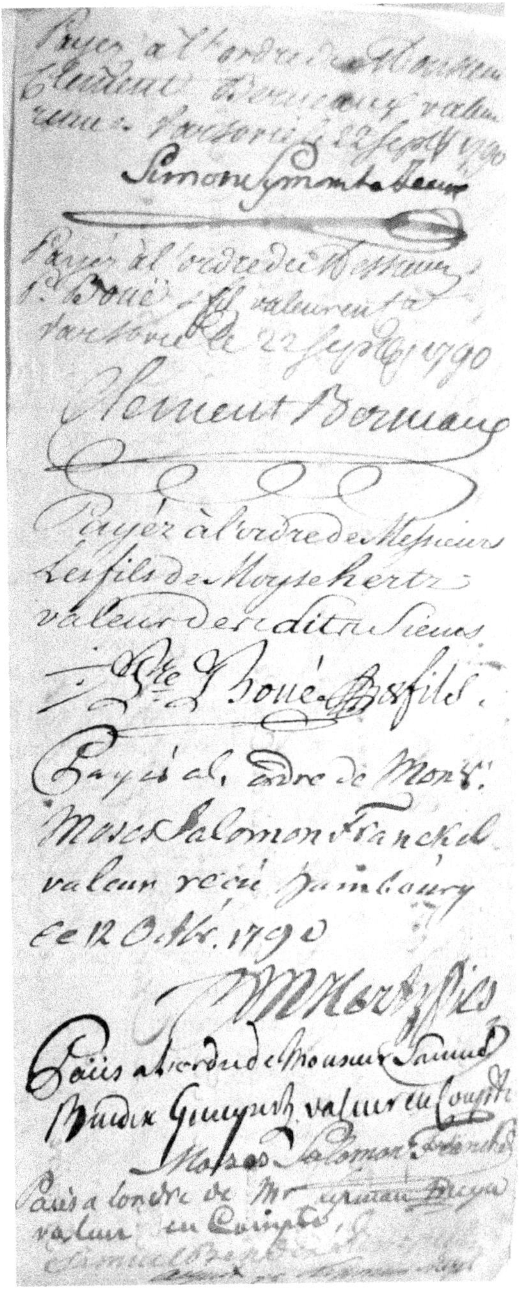

FIGURE 1.2. Back of the bill of exchange with endorsement, 1790. APW, Oddział Kamieniec Ząbkowicki, Dom Bankowy Eichborn, no. 4084, 120v. Credit: Archiwum Państwowe we Wrocławiu.

and a notarial office recorded a protest, the holder of the bill of exchange could demand payment from any endorser or from the issuer by drawing a re-exchange bill or by suing. Whoever received a demand of payment could turn to another endorser with the same claim. Moreover, when a protest was issued, copies of it had to be distributed to all endorsers and to the issuer, thereby endangering the reputation of a defaulted payer.[24]

The city of Leipzig was one of the new players in international trade in bills of exchange from the late seventeenth century on. From the end of the seventeenth to the first half of the eighteenth century, the fairs were focused on the commodities trade; bills of exchange were used primarily as a means of payment, and exchange rates with Amsterdam were listed only during the fairs. The Leipzig regulations of 1682 introduced the joint liability rule, stating that the creditor of a protested bill of exchange needed first to turn to the last endorser from whom he had received the bill. If the endorser could not pay off the creditor, the latter could turn to the earlier endorser after issuing a contra protest, and so on. The comments on the regulation state clearly that the creditor did not have to take the endorser to court before turning to the earlier endorser in the chain. He then should follow the order of the chain and cannot turn to any endorser out of sequence. However, the annotations note that it was common among merchants to turn to any endorser they thought would be most likely to pay and that their appeals elicited good results.[25] Although the joint liability rule enabled merchants to turn to an endorser's domestic jurisdiction rather than a payer's foreign court to enforce debt, the existence of courts in market places was of great importance, especially when those marketplaces wanted to attain greater international recognition. In Leipzig, exchange regulations were issued together with additional state interventions, the most important being the foundation of a commercial court (*Handelsgericht*) in 1682, the first in a German city. Prior to that effort, the city court had been responsible for all trade disputes and found itself habitually overwhelmed by this task in a city that held three annual fairs. Despite these measures, the regular listing of exchange rates with Amsterdam and other centers of commerce occurred all year long only during the second half of the eighteenth century. Amsterdam then became the central place of brokerage of bills of exchange from Leipzig to northeastern Europe.[26]

It is not surprising then that introducing the commercial court came with new regulations on trade in general and on brokers in particular, as well as with a revised *Judenordnung*, a set of regulations concerning Jews.[27] The latter regulated the entry of Jews into the city, the documents they needed to attend the fairs and to leave, taxes levied on Jewish merchants, and the necessity of special passes. Although these regulations discriminated against Jewish merchants, they were part of a concerted effort to draw precisely those merchants, and thus more commerce, to

Leipzig. Such efforts were not specific to Leipzig; they can be found in commercial cities across Europe. This legislation recognized the importance of Jewish merchants for international trade, and especially for the exchange between western and eastern Europe; thus it sought to attract Jewish merchants to Leipzig despite strict Saxon regulations that forbade their settlement in the state.[28]

Still, the limitations of formal commercial institutions within Europe remained enormous. Until the mid-eighteenth century, for example, bills of exchange issued in St. Petersburg could only be drawn to Amsterdam. Institutionally, Amsterdam housed more than one hundred notarial offices by the mid-eighteenth century, which also registered protests of bills of exchange. In comparison, the first eight notarial offices in Warsaw were opened only in 1808. The rulers of the Polish-Lithuanian Commonwealth had not introduced any specific regulations regarding the trade in bills of exchange in the country or in its larger commercial cities. This lag in trade regulations is probably the key reason why most payments by east European (Jewish) merchants in Frankfurt an der Oder or Leipzig were made in cash. Bills of exchange that were issued in eastern Europe were usually directly drawn on west European banking houses in Amsterdam or Hamburg, and in a few cases, in Breslau.[29] A lack of legal security did not allow for the enforcement of payments of bills of exchange in eastern Europe. Thus, the fairs in Frankfurt an der Oder and Leipzig—where bills of exchange were traded—turned into important places of brokerage.

The use of bills of exchange as a new instrument for credit and commerce also had implications for the more traditional forms of it in Jewish society, which seemed to fade. In the Polish-Lithuanian Commonwealth, a kind of debt bill—a so-called *membrana* in Polish or a *mamran* in Hebrew, derived from the Latin word for parchment, had been in use since the sixteenth century and "displayed distinct commercial and legal advances over [medieval] bearer notes."[30] Employed by Jews and non-Jews alike to raise credit and facilitate commerce, *membrany* were often issued in Latin or Polish but also sometimes in Hebrew. They could be circulated by leaving the name of the creditor on the back of the bill blank, but without an endorsement they could not be circulated as widely as bills of exchange.[31] Although this type of bill was used in the Polish-Lithuanian Commonwealth as well as in Silesia and Prussia and is, for example, mentioned in Glikl bas Juda Leib's memoirs, it did not gain any significance for trade across Europe and probably ceased to exist during the first decades of the nineteenth century.[32] In Amsterdam, J. G. Heineccius emphasized in his 1774 Dutch work on exchange law that Jews were active in the exchange trade and that they did not write their bills of exchange in old rabbinic letters, meaning Hebrew, which Christians obviously would not understand.[33] Thus, Jewish merchants and brokers used the same instruments for credit and commerce as did Christians.

For both, Christians and Jews access to courts and trust in these legal institutions were of great significance, despite the joint liability rule. The uneven developments of legal instruments become apparent, when we find Simon Symons from Amsterdam struggling with the Polish legal system, in which he had little trust. He did not believe that Polish courts would help him to gain justice. In trying to recover various debts in 1767, Simon Symons and his business partner, Levin Pincus Schlesinger, did not turn directly to Polish courts, or did so only initially. Rather, they submitted a request to the Prussian government in which they pleaded for unspecified support from the Prussian resident Gideon Benoît in Warsaw regarding various debts, including those from bills of exchange. They argued thus: "we cannot hope for any particular effect without the highest assistance due to the usual local *modo procedendi*."[34] We do not know how this case ended or what kind of support the merchants received, if any, but their entreaties highlight some of the challenges of trading across borders.

Even with the introduction of increasingly "sophisticated financial instruments such as double-entry bookkeeping, bills of exchange, bank to bank transfers, and insurance,"[35] not all of these instruments were available at the same level across Europe. Communication between places remained particularly slow, legal support was not always available, and international law was still underdeveloped or nonexistent in central and eastern Europe. Therefore, highly personalized trust and closely-knit networks based on family and ethnic belonging remained important in order to overcome these obstacles and the fragmentation in jurisdictional sovereignties.

The Business of the Symons Family

The trade in bills of exchange of the Symons family is just one example of its extensive business activities across Europe and beyond, which were strongly even if not exclusively linked to family ties. In the main, historians have abstained from using bills of exchange as a source, primarily because they provide only narrow glimpses into commercial networks, the flow of money and goods and merchant behavior. As an article of daily use for early modern merchants, bills of exchange have sometimes survived in substantial numbers in business archives.[36] In this case, account books and collections of business letters offer a much better source for studying questions of business, commercial ties, international trade, trust, and reputation. However, these sources are not always available, especially from firms or merchants in the early modern period. The smaller the business, the less likely it is that such documents survived. This is also the case for the Symons family and most other Ashkenazic merchant families in Amsterdam throughout the eighteenth century.[37] Therefore, I have based my study of the business connections of Benjamin and Samuel Symons and other family members on protested bills of exchange, which were entered into notarial record books, and some contracts, which were also preserved in equal measure. The information protested bills of exchange hold for the historian is more limited than information that can be drawn from business letters. Without the accompanying business correspondence, the exact nature of the business behind these bills of exchange can often not be determined; still bills of exchange do allow some glimpse into an otherwise closed world of early modern business practice.

Of course, protested bills of exchange constitute only a small part of all bills of exchange that were traded and accepted by any given merchant, banker, or broker.[38] When a bill of exchange arrived in Amsterdam and was not accepted by its payer, it had to be taken to a notarial office. There the payer had to announce his refusal officially and the notary entered the protest into the record book, together with a copy of the bill of exchange. The notary entered this copy on the front page and recorded the protest on the back of the page, sometimes including the reason of refusal (see figures 1.3 and 1.4). The protest of a bill of exchange was in many cases unrelated to the unreliability of a drawer or to the illiquidity of the payer. Often the payer had not yet received a letter accompanying the bill of exchange and advising the payment (*avis*); sometimes the reasons for not accepting a bill of exchange remain obscure. In many cases, it was not a sign of default, and one can assume that most bills were paid by the time of their maturity. This finding is commensurate with the findings of Santarosa regarding the usage and handling of bills of exchange in the Christian banking house Maison Roux in Marseille.[39]

The bills of exchange examined for this study were usually written in Dutch, German, or French; some originated in the Mediterranean, England, or the Americas and were drafted in Italian or English; a good number bore more than one language. Hardly any of these bills of exchange circulated exclusively among Jewish merchants. Jews issued bills of exchange to non-Jews, received them from Christians, and relied on non-Jewish banking houses in Amsterdam to pay their bills.

Though Benjamin Symons was registered in Amsterdam as a jeweler, he and his brother were heavily involved in the trade in bills of exchange. In general, a growing number of Jewish and Christian merchant houses in Amsterdam ceased trading in commodities in favor of accepting and trading in bills of exchange during the second half of the eighteenth century. I have analyzed 389 protested bills of exchange that were entered into the record books over the course of the three decades between 1747 and 1777; each one involved one or more members of the Symons and the Schlesinger family, as drawers, payees, payers, endorsees and endorsers, primarily Benjamin and Samuel Symons, Simon Symons, and their relatives in Frankfurt an der Oder, Levin Pincus Schlesinger and Pincus Moses Schlesinger.[40] The fact that many of the bills were issued in Leipzig during fairs, where credit was extended from Amsterdam to Leipzig allude to the usage of these

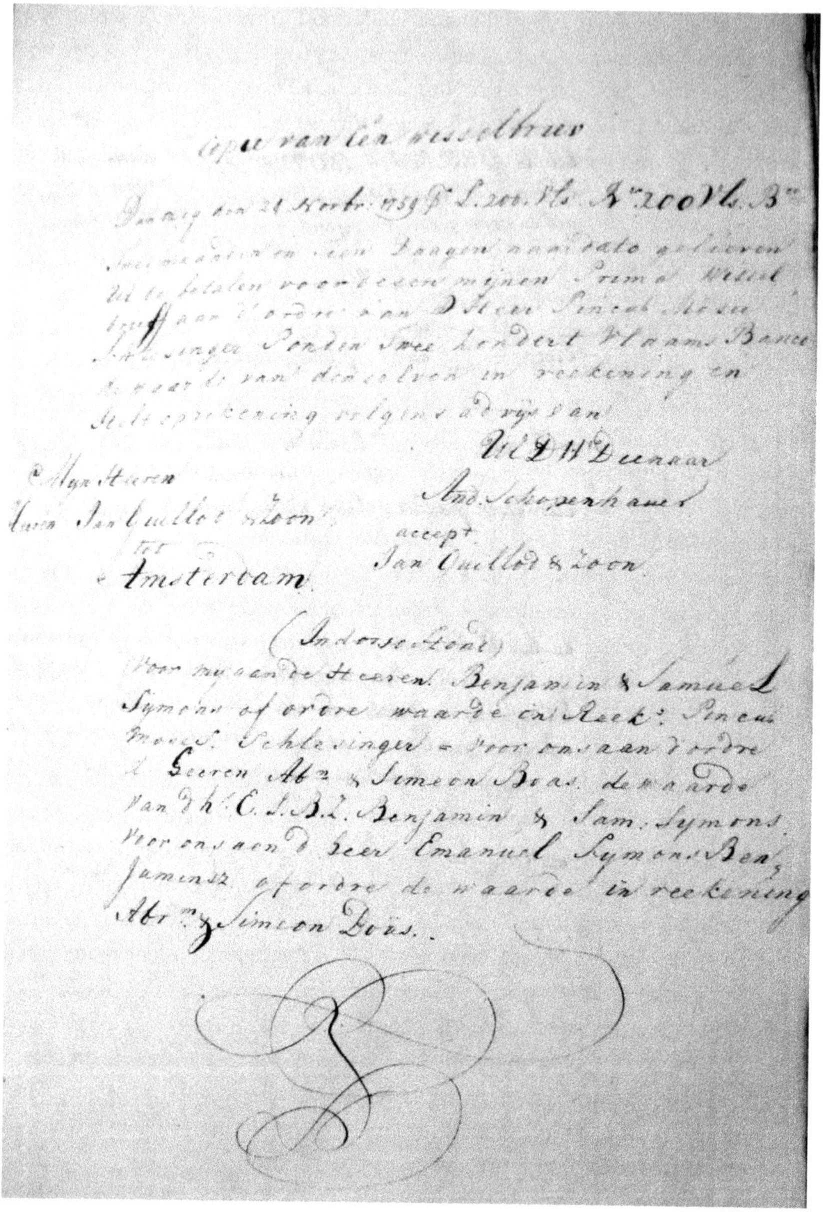

FIGURE 1.3. Bill of exchange copied into the notarial book of the Amsterdam notarial office Gerrit Bouman, 1760. Notarielle Archieven van Amsterdam, no. 5075, Notariat Gerrit Bouman, file 12600, no. 77. Credit: Amsterdam City Archives.

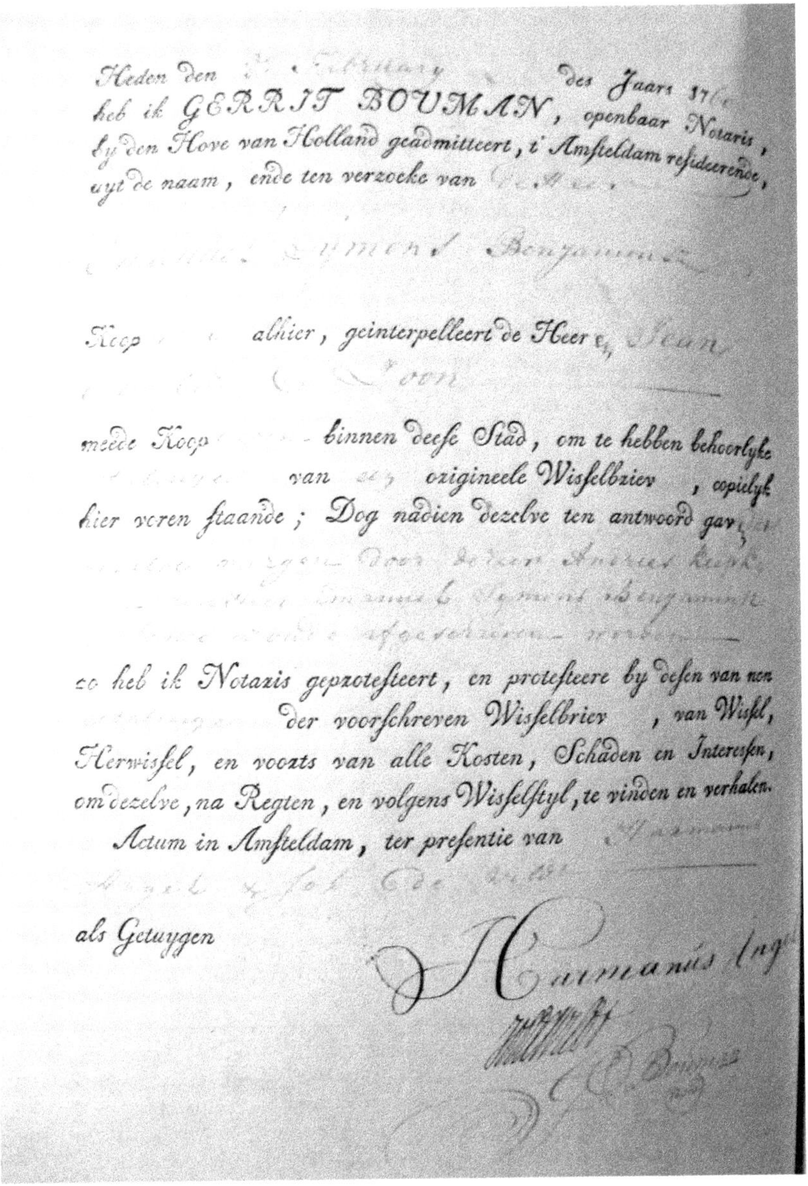

Heden den [...] February [...] des Jaars 176[...]
heb ik GERRIT BOUMAN, openbaar Notaris,
by den Hove van Holland geadmitteert, t' Amsteldam resideerende,
uyt de naam, ende ten verzoeke van [...]

[...] *Symens Benjamin* [...]

Koop [...] alhier, geinterpelleert de Heer [...] *Jean*
[...] *Zoon* [...]

meede Koop [...] binnen deese Stad, om te hebben behoorlyke
[...] *van [...] origineele Wisselbrier, copielyk*
hier voren staande; Dog nadien dezelve ten antwoord gav [...]
[...] *Door Doctor Andries Kuyk* [...]
[...] *Emanuel Symens Benjamin* [...]
[...] *afgeschreven werden* [...]

So heb ik Notaris geprotesteert, en protesteere by desen van non
[...] *der voorschreven Wisselbrier, van Wissel,*
Herwissel, en voorts van alle Kosten, Schaden en Interessen,
om dezelve, na Regten, en volgens Wisselstyl, te vinden en verhalen.
Actum in Amsteldam, ter presentie van [...]
[...]

als Getuygen

FIGURE 1.4. Protest of bill of exchange, 1760. Notarielle Archieven van Amsterdam, no. 5075, Notariat Gerrit Bouman, file 12600, no. 77v. Credit: Amsterdam City Archives.

Table 1.1. Distribution of functions of members of the Symons, Nijmegen, Boas, and Schlesinger family in bills of exchange.

Function regarding bill of exchange Merchants/Bankers	Drawer	Beneficiary payee	Drawee acceptor	Endorsee	Presenter	Acceptance "in honor"
Benjamin & Simon Symons		19	33	145	220	70
Barend Symons (brother of B&S Symons)			8	9	11	10
Simon Symons & Levin Pincus Schlesinger	31	11				
Simon Symons	14	4		1		
Isaac Symons (nephew of B&S Symons)	4					
Emanuel Symons	1			16	31	1
Levin Pincus Schlesinger		1				
Pincus Moses Schlesinger	22	19		9		
Elias Moses Daniels Nijmegen			22			
Tobias Boas	1			24		
Abraham & Simon Boas		4		30	1	
Alexander Pincus Schlesinger	1					
Jacob Moses Schlesinger		6				

Sources: Stadsarchief Amsterdam, Notarielle Archieven (no. 5075), Notariat Gerrit Bouman, files 12592, 12594–12608, 12611–12617, 12619, 12620, 12622, 12623, 12625, 12627; Notariat Daniel Brink, files 10391, 10394, 10424, 10427, 10430, 10432, 10433, 10435, 10443, 10445–10453, 10460–10462, 10464, 10468, 10470, 10471, 10505, 10511, 10527, 10590. Notariat Salomon Dorper, files 10819, 10827; Notariat C. van Homrigh, files 12361, 12393; Notariat D. Geniets, files 13641, 13644, 13647, 13654, 13655, 13660, 13669, 13672, 13682, 13697, 13747. Simon Symons und Levin Pincus Schlesinger wegen ihrer in Pohlen ausstehenden Wechsel und Forderungen, I. HA, Rep. 9, Polen, no. 28-7C, GStA.

bills of exchange as payment for commodities. Moreover, Benjamin and Samuel Symons functioned in the main not as providers of credit but as presenters of bills of exchange to other Jewish and Christian merchant or banking houses in Amsterdam (see table 1.1).

The intricate marriage patterns of the Symons family created a wide web of connections. These connections and their interplay with commercial undertakings are reflected in a large number of bills of exchange that were drawn to, endorsed to, paid or redeemed by the Symons brothers. The 389 bills of exchange analyzed here point to the centers of their trading activities that were located primarily in central and northern Europe, especially Danzig, Frankfurt an der Oder, Leipzig, Hamburg, and Königsberg (see table 1.2). In western Europe, most bills of exchange drawn to Amsterdam were issued in Paris. The Symons also received bills of exchange from as far away as Suriname through their business partners and relatives Tobias, Abraham, and Simon Boas from The Hague. The large number of small Dutch and North German towns also point to involvement in the local trade with bills of exchange. The number of bills of exchange issued at a given place provides a good impression of the extension and focal points of Benjamin and Samuel Symons's networks, although they do not precisely reflect the Symonses' business activities due to their different roles in the transactions and the greatly varying amounts drawn on different bills of exchange.

As table 1.1 shows, more than half of the bills of exchange that arrived in Amsterdam were presented to a payer by Benjamin and Samuel Symons, emphasizing their role as brokers rather than as providers of credit. In more than one third of the cases they are not noted as endorsees on the back of the bill, rather having received the bill from a business partner who requested that they redeem it in his name. In comparison, only thirty-three bills of exchange were drawn to Benjamin and Samuel Symons; most of those were issued by close relatives. In many cities, those bills of exchange were issued exclusively by Christian merchants; that fact is unsurprising in St. Petersburg, Paris, or Dresden, yet far more surprising in Surinam, Livorno, or Prague, all cities with a considerable Jewish population.

Kinship, Ethnic Networks, and Commercial Success

Although we know that family ties did not always suffice to create trust and that commercial relations based on family ties did not always succeed, relatives by birth or marriage were, nevertheless, in many cases regarded as more trustworthy than people from outside the family.[41] Women in the early modern period disposed of social and financial capital and were able to bring into a marriage wealth or family connections, and in some instances, both. The establishment of relatives—usually sons—in places that were central to a merchant's business was a very common strategy to geographically extend commercial networks. Among Christian merchants,

Table 1.2. Distribution of bills of exchange related to the Symons family in Amsterdam according to their place of issue (1747–1777).

Western Europe	Amount	No. of bills	Central Europe	Amount	No. bills
Low Countries			**German Lands**		
The Hague	55,440 G	8	**Prussia**		
Amsterdam	3,439 G	4	Frankfurt an der Oder	44,040 G	34
Nijwegen	2,590 G	5		5,311 Rt	
Utrecht	10,913 G	3	Königsberg	6,000 G	17
Bruxelles/Brüssel	1,860 G	2		6,318 fl.P.	
Groningen	3,200 G	2	Berlin	14,310 G	14
Akkrum	1,000 G	1		3,000 Rt	
Deventer	961 G	1		977 P	
Dorum	1,100 G	1	Crefeld/Krefeld	1,500 G	2
Heerenveen	500 G	1	Emden	50 G, 62 Rt	2
Leeuwarden	1,200 G	1	Minden	1,500 G	2
Mechelen	90 G	1	Wesel	900 G	2
Middelburg	6,000 G	2	Billerbeck (?)	289 G	1
Ockenburg	1,435 G	1	Memel	200 fl. P	1
Vlissingen	3,000 G	1			75
		34	**Silesia**		
France			Hirschberg	600 Rt	2
Paris	40,370 Fl	20	Breslau	200 Rt	1
Bordeaux	1,441 Fl	4			3
	2,700 P		**Saxony**		
Bayonne	1,900 Fl	1	Leipzig	14,502 G	34
Nantes	200 Fl	1		14,154 Rt	
Strasbourg	1,873 Fl	1	Dresden	1,156 Rt	4
		27			38
England			**Remaining German Lands**		
London	613 P	3	Hamburg	46,613 G	29
				1,500 Rt	
Italian Cities	7,848 Fl	8	Frankfurt am Main	9,282 Rt	9
Livorno	6,511 Fl	5	Cassel/Kassel	7,900 G	7
Florence	1,000 Fl	1		1,200 D	
Genoa	1,300 Fl	1	Hannover	14,000 G	7
Milano		15	Brunswick/Braunschweig	5,200 G	1
			Elberfeld	1,200 G	1
Portugal	?	3	Liege/Lüttich	502 G	1
Lissabon			Osnabrück	500 G	1
			Remscheid	500 G	1
			Solingen	200 G	1
			Stolpe	300 G	1
					59
			Habsburg Empire		
			Vienna	12,335 Rt	17
			Prague	2,269 Rt	9
					26
			Switzerland		
			Genf/Geneva	1,402 Fl	1

Sources: Stadsarchief Amsterdam, Notarielle Archieven (no. 5075), Notariat Gerrit Bouman, files 12592, 12594–12608, 12611–12617, 12619, 12620, 12622, 12623, 12625, 12627; Notariat Daniel Brink, files 10391, 10394, 10424, 10427, 10430, 10432, 10433, 10435, 10443, 10445–10453, 10460–10462, 10464, 10468, 10470, 10471, 10505, 10511, 10527, 10590. Notariat Salomon Dorper, files 10819, 10827; Notariat C. van Homrigh, files 12361, 12393; Notariat D. Geniets, files 13641, 13644, 13647, 13654, 13655, 13660, 13669, 13672, 13682, 13697, 13747. Simon Symons und Levin Pincus Schlesinger wegen ihrer in Pohlen ausstehenden Wechsel und Forderungen, I. HA, Rep. 9, Polen, no. 28-7C, GStA.

Note: D=ducats; Fl=florin; fl. P=Flemish pound; G=guilders; P=pound; R=Rubel; Rt=Reichsthaler.

Eastern Europe	Amount	No. of bills	Northern Europe	Amount	No. of bills	Others	Amount	No. of bills
Poland			**Denmark**			**Ottoman Empire**		
Danzig	7,486 fl.P	33	Copenhagen	6,250 Rt	6	Smyrna	8,590 G	6
	10,100 Rt							
Warsaw	11,275 G	5	Altona	4,015 Rt	3	Constantinople	6,000 G	1
		38			**9**			**7**
Russia			**Sweden**					
St. Petersburg	800 G	9	Stockholm	2,202 Rt	7	Surinam	4,934 G	**11**
	9,532 R							
Riga	2,545 Rt	8	Gothenburg Göteburg	800 Rt	1	**Others**		
Reval	400 Rt	1	Stralsund	500 Rt	1	Eulenburg (?)	5,200 G	2
		18			**9**	Liebau (?)	300 Rt	2
			Norway			St. Anna	1,100 G	1
			Bergen	1,425 G	3	(unclear)	3,334 G	4
			Trondheim	150 Rt	1			**9**
					4			
sum		**56**			**22**			**27**

marriage into local merchant families often also played an important role in enhancing a family's geographic mobility and strengthening commercial ties. However, it seems that merchants were more often sent as agents to important commercial centers without marrying into a local merchant family.[42] Historians have often noted the importance of marriage among members of the Jewish mercantile elite within the borders of specific political territories such as Prussia and in central commercial cities like Berlin, Königsberg, and Breslau.[43] Yet marital ties often transcended political borders. As noted before, it appears that in the world of central European Ashkenazim those familial and ethnic ties carried a greater weight than in the world of early modern Sephardic commerce.

Jewish merchants and entrepreneurs usually employed a variety of strategies of mobilizing familial connections that were driven not only by economic consideration. In the case of the Symons family in Amsterdam, where legal restrictions on settlement did not exist, economic considerations were central in shaping the bolstering of familial and commercial networks. That does not mean, however, that kinship played an exclusive role. Connections between Jewish merchants were usually closer than those between those same merchants and their Christian counterparts. Yet close commercial and especially familial ties between Ashkenazic and Sephardic merchants were rare, even in Amsterdam. Thus, it seems legitimate to give preference to the term ethnic over religious to describe these networks.[44] Within this web of relations, male and female spheres of economic activity were closely interrelated and complementary. Women constituted an important element in constructing commercial networks when families fostered new connections by marriage. Moreover, their dowries traditionally constituted an important part of a new couple's financial assets and business capital. Based on the example of Glikl bas Juda Leib and from archival evidence about the economic activities of widows, we can assume that most women were closely involved in their husbands' business. In cases of the untimely passing of a spouse, women could not have continued the business without any prior experience.[45]

The marital alliances of Ashkenazic merchants in the early modern period reveal a variety of geographic patterns. In the world of central European Court Jews, kinship relations played a crucial role; marital choices were made based on social status and economic ability. Various examples from seventeenth- and early eighteenth-century Court Jews and the Jewish commercial elite show that familial connections were central to commercial cooperation and often provided opportunities for social and economic advancement. The distinction between Court Jews and the mercantile elite during the seventeenth century had in the main disappeared by the second half of the eighteenth century.[46] Close connections to Christian rulers remained central for many Jewish merchants settling in cities with a court, yet, central European cities holding transregional fairs gained increasing importance for Jewish commerce and were crucial meeting places for merchants.

In the case of Glikl bas Juda Leib we have already seen that Amsterdam was an important hub for Jewish merchants from German-speaking lands, providing them with access to the credit market in Amsterdam. Glikl's choice of spouses for her children shows her strategy of extending the geographical reach of her commercial connections. The choices for marital unions display a pattern that connected important centers of (Jewish) commerce in the Holy Roman Empire from north to south with Amsterdam as the most important commercial and financial spot outside the empire.[47]

Similarly, the Symons family in Amsterdam sought to extend their business contacts into central Europe. Their goal included extending and strengthening existing commercial networks. To do so, they sought out marriages among close relatives in the same or nearby locations so as to enhance the business at a specific place via new business partners and additional capital. Marriages were also arranged with prospective suitors who lived a long distance away, because they could create new business opportunities and broaden commercial networks. Like other mercantile families, the Symons family combined these different approaches.

Although the Symons were linked by marriage to more than one family, their connection to the Boas family in The Hague, probably the most notable Ashkenazic family in Dutch trade and finance, was of particular importance. Here the strengthening of commercial ties and the increase of capital was at the core of the arrangement. The Boas family quickly rose to prominence after their initial immigration to the Netherlands. Settling in The Hague in 1701, Hyman Boas (1662–1742), a Jewish immigrant from Poland, specialized in trading textiles, precious stones, and gold. His son Tobias Boas (1696–1782) rose to be one of the leading Jewish merchants and bankers in The Hague and the Netherlands, marrying his children off to members of other outstanding Jewish entrepreneurial families in the Netherlands, such as the Gompertz family, and in the Holy Roman Empire, such as the Oppenheim and Wertheimer families. Tobias Boas succeeded in turning the family's business into a large-scale banking house of international repute.[48]

Thus, it must have been a prestigious match for the Symons family when Sara Symons (b. 1704) married Tobias Boas in 1722. Sara Symons was the sister of three successful merchants and brokers, the aforementioned brothers, Samuel and Benjamin Symons, and Berent Symons (b. 1708).[49] After the death of his first wife, Samuel Symons married Mietje Boas, Tobias Boas's daughter. In the following generation, two more children of Tobias Boas married children of the other Symons brother, Benjamin. His daughter, Veronica Symons (1733–1809), married Abraham Boas (1728–1798) in 1748. Emanuel Symons entered the branch of the

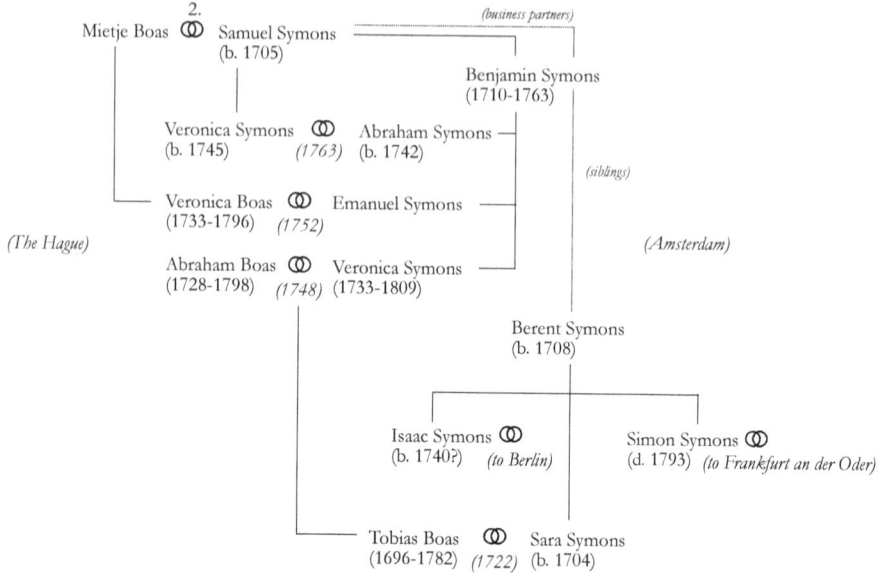

FIGURE 1.5. The marriage ties between the Symons family in Amsterdam and the Boas family in The Hague. Credit: Oliver Ihlow.

family business that reached the Mediterranean and Atlantic, when he married Veronica Boas (1733–1796) four years later (see figure 1.5). These close connections also found expression in the business ties of the two families. Bills of exchange issued to or received by Tobias Boas, and later by Abraham and Simon Boas, from Surinam, the Ottoman Empire, Italy, and France were usually redeemed by Emanuel, their son-in-law and brother-in-law, respectively, in Amsterdam.

Geographically the bills of exchange confirm that Benjamin Symons's son, Emanuel Symons, assumed responsibility for the business ties with the Boas family in The Hague. Tobias Boas as well as his sons Abraham and Simon Boas occasionally sent bills to Benjamin and Samuel Symons to present them to a payer in Amsterdam and to be deposited into the Boases' account. However, twenty-five of thirty bills that Emanuel Symons received from his father-in-law or brothers-in-law he presented under his own name. More than half of all bills of exchange were issued by Christian merchants and presented to Christian banking houses or merchants in Amsterdam.

Marrying into a prominent local Jewish family in the Netherlands was a way to raise the assets of the family's business, consanguineous marriage was a way to keep the family's business together. Thus, Samuel Symons married his daughter

Veronica (b. 1745) to Abraham (b. 1742), the son of his business partner and brother, Benjamin Symons, who had passed away half a year earlier in January 1763.[50] Consanguineous marriages were not uncommon; among Sephardic Jews, they were the norm rather than the exception. In the seventeenth century, the Amsterdam Rabbi Menasseh ben Israel even recommended marriages between cousins or between uncles and nieces.[51] For Benjamin and Samuel Symons, the cohesion and strength of their shared business was surely the most important incentive for marrying their children to each other, though similar marital arrangements were probably not uncommon in families where capital played a lesser role. The Dutch premarital contract between Abraham and Veronica Symons and their parents, which was entered into notarial records prior the wedding, offers some details about the marital arrangements. Presumably, it was a Dutch version of the most important matters stipulated in the Hebrew marriage contract (*ketubah*). Jews in Amsterdam had to register their marriages and have them publically announced on the steps of the Town Hall prior to the actual Jewish ceremony; it may have been in this context that they drew up a contract in Dutch to supplement the Hebrew-language *ketubah*. However, it is likely that the measure was also taken in order to make the contract recognizable in a non-Jewish court in case of a possible business dispute.[52]

The marital contract of Abraham and Veronica Symons stipulates a clear division of the couple's assets, but it also alludes to the expectation that they would share their business and the income it brought in. Veronica Symons's dowry and the resulting interest as well as all movable goods that she would bring into the marriage were to remain in her possession. In addition, the contract detailed provisions in case of one passing away. The contract points to the wealth of the family and to the importance of dowries for raising liquid capital. Veronica Symons brought a dowry of 17,000 Dutch guilders in cash plus additional clothing and her movable goods into the marriage. It is unclear whether the marriage contract comprised two particular payments: that of a dowry paid by the bride's family and a dower paid by the groom's family, as was the custom among Sephardim.[53] However, the stipulations for the case of the husband's death, point to a rather Sephardic custom. Veronica would receive 10,250 guilders from her husband's family if he were to die after the second year (20,500 guilders after the third) of their marriage, in addition to everything she had brought in, his movable goods, and everything they had inherited or earned jointly in their business during the marriage. According to Ashkenazic tradition that abided by the stipulations (*takkanot*) of R. Tam, a twelfth-century French Talmudic commentator, and the medieval communities of Speyer, Worms, and Mainz (*kehillot Shum*), the dower was to be returned to the husband's family in the case of his death in the first year of marriage. In contrast, the Sephardic tradition awarded the wife up to half of her husband's dower.[54] This

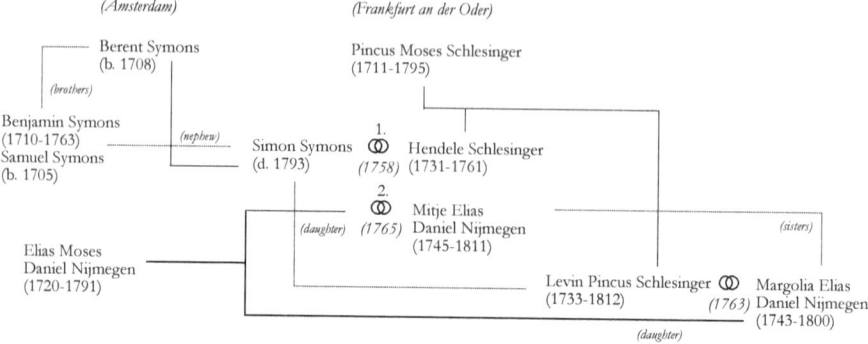

FIGURE 1.6. The marriage ties between the Symons and the Nijmegen family in Amsterdam and the Schlesinger family in Frankfurt an der Oder. Credit: Oliver Ihlow.

tradition may also have been a means to protect portions of the business capital from claims in case of insolvency, since dowries were at least theoretically excluded from creditor's claims.[55]

For the commercial venture into central and east central Europe, the Symons family employed an additional marriage strategy, as illustrated in figure 1.6. The third brother, Berent Symons, sent two of his sons away: Simon, one of the two, was sent to Frankfurt an der Oder, where he married Hendele, the daughter of the affluent merchant Pincus Moses Schlesinger, in 1758.[56] This marital tie was advantageous for both sides. Simon Symons began a shared business with his brother-in-law, Levin Pincus Schlesinger. While the Schlesingers gained easier access to the Amsterdam credit market, the Symons family extended its ties into one of the most important Jewish families in the textile trade in Prussia.

The Schlesingers' familial ties to Amsterdam were further bolstered with an additional marital arrangement. In 1763, Levin Pincus Schlesinger traveled with his father to Amsterdam, where he married Margolia Elias Daniel Nijmegen (1743–1800).[57] Two years later, Levin's business partner, Simon Symons, went to Amsterdam to marry Mitje Elias Daniel Nijmegen (1745–1811), a sister of Margolia. Symons' first wife Hendele died at the age of thirty after only three years of marriage, presumably in childbirth; their only son passed the following year.[58] Perhaps it was the additional financial capital that these weddings brought into the shared business of Levin Pincus Schlesinger and Simon Symons that provided them with the financial power to offer their services to the Polish king Stanisław August Poniatowski, who appointed them court suppliers in 1765, the same year as Simon Symons's marriage to Mitje Elias Daniel Nijmegen.[59] The father of the two young women, who moved to Frankfurt an der Oder after their marriages, was Elias Moses Daniel Nijmegen (1720–1791) of the Daniel Nijmegen family from Amsterdam, which enjoyed a similar financial standing to that of the Symons family.⁶⁰ As such, Benjamin and Samuel Symons gained access to new markets in central and east central Europe whereas the connection provided the Schlesinger family with easier access to capital that was crucial for financing their trade in textiles and bills of exchange.

The business relationships between the Symons brothers, Elias Moses Daniel Nijmegen, Simon Symons, and the Schlesinger family continued for several years. Their commercial connections were rooted primarily in trade in bills of exchange. The business partners also met in person when traveling to the Leipzig fair. Since 1729, both Benjamin and Samuel Symons traveled regularly to the Easter and the Michaelis fair; two of the three annual fairs in Leipzig. There they would meet with Pincus Moses Schlesinger, whose daughter later married their nephew Simon Symons. Pincus Moses Schlesinger came to Leipzig for two of the three annual fairs each year from 1737 until at least 1775.⁶¹ The Symons brothers also brought young relatives or relatives-to-be to the fair as servants, probably to train them in business and to introduce them to their business partners. In 1743, Benjamin Symons brought fifteen-year-old Abraham Boas, who married his daughter five years later. In 1746, Benjamin was accompanied by his sixteen-year-old nephew, Simon Boas.⁶²

The bills of exchange examined here confirm the importance of family relations as well as the fact that these Jewish merchants and brokers operated within the general economy of credit and commerce. In cities like Berlin, Danzig, Königsberg, Vienna, Leipzig, and Frankfurt am Main we discover equal numbers of Jewish and Christian drawers of bills of exchange; places to which the Symons and the Schlesinger family had close commercial ties. In Frankfurt an der Oder and Warsaw, though, bills of exchange were issued exclusively by Jewish drawers, primarily members of the Symons or Schlesinger family. Similarly, in Hamburg more than two thirds of the bills of exchange were issued by Jewish merchants, though not only by family members.

In the German states, Benjamin and Samuel Symons received the largest number of bills of exchange to present and redeem in Amsterdam from Pincus Moses Schlesinger, who had an account with them. Particularly close and regular business ties can also be traced to Mayer Alexander Traub of Mannheim, whose family hailed originally from Amsterdam; to Abraham Isaac Wallach, a community elder in Königsberg; to Hertz David Wallach of Hamburg, and to Moses Wessely, a merchant and *maskil* (Jewish enlightener) of Hamburg.⁶³ In their cases, it seems that the Symons cashed the bills of exchange on behalf of the respective payees and held on to the money for them, probably in an account they had with the Symons; however, the evidence is too sparse to draw conclusions regarding their exact business relations.

This preponderance of Jewish drawers again alludes to the importance of Hamburg as a hub between Amsterdam and Prussia, in particular for networks that were ethnically heavily based on Ashkenazim. Thus, the Symons brothers and their sons functioned primarily as middlemen between Jewish and non-Jewish merchants throughout Europe, on the one hand, and banking houses in Amsterdam, on the other. The number of bills processed through Hamburg points to the prominent involvement of the Symons and the Schlesinger families in the credit business, and to the fact that these bills of exchange were not used solely as payment for goods. Hamburg played a crucial role in the business between Amsterdam's merchant-bankers and merchants and entrepreneurs in Prussia, who needed capital for manufacturing and trade. Direct loans from Amsterdam were not an option because the different jurisdictions did not allow for enforcement of direct loan contracts; thus Prussian merchants would not have been incentivized to repay loans. The use of bills of exchange to raise credit was a convenient alternative because it was based on established commercial ties and because unreliability in payment would have jeopardized long-standing commercial connections. Moreover, goods that were traded along the same channels could serve as collateral. Hamburg enjoyed the additional advantage that merchants and bankers could exploit the difference in interest rates, which were much higher in Prussia than in Amsterdam and Hamburg.[64]

Trust and reliability remained crucial in the business with bills of exchange. Only in a few cases did unreliability of a drawer or illiquidity of a payer lead to the protest of a bill of exchange. The reasons for not accepting a bill of exchange often remain obscure; in a case from 1760, the brothers Neufville, well-known bankers in Amsterdam, refused to accept a bill for over 3,400 guilders that had been issued by the banker Gotzkowsky in Berlin to a certain Isaac Hirsch. The bill had then been endorsed to Pincus Moses Schlesinger and was eventually protested by Benjamin and Samuel Symons in Amsterdam, when the Neufville brothers explained that they were not (yet) willing to accept the bill because "both endorsers are negligent."[65] Moreover, less than two months earlier, Simon Symons had issued three bills of exchange to Isaac Hirsch and seven to Pincus Moses Schlesinger to be drawn on Simon Moses Levy in Amsterdam. Neufville had heard that Simon Moses Levy did not accept any of the bills and that the bills were not covered. This example suggests the importance of information exchanged between bankers and brokers in Amsterdam, and how it shaped their decisions.

In the case of nonacceptance and protest of bills of exchange, close commercial networks and established trust between business partners could provide some security. Brokers like Benjamin and Samuel Symons had the means to prevent the holder of a protested bill of exchange from turning to any of the endorsers or the issuer. When, for example, the Amsterdam banker Simon Moses Levy refused to accept bills of exchange issued by Simon Symons and the bills of exchange were protested, his uncles Benjamin and Samuel Symons stepped in to accept the bills "per honor." In such a case, a person or firm that was not named in the bill of exchange would accept it after its rejection in order to protect the good name and credit of the drawer, payee, or one of the endorsers. Of the 389 bills of exchange surveyed that involved Benjamin and Samuel Symons, the brothers acted as acceptant "per honor" in seventy cases (18 percent; see table 1.1).

In addition to concerns regarding the reputation of business partners, who in the Symons's case were often family members as well, the acceptance "per honor" might also have been a means to profit from the re-exchange process by saving transaction costs. The Symons brothers were the payers on whom the bills of exchange were drawn in one-third of the seventy bills of exchange they accepted "per honor." After they initially refused to honor them, the Symons brothers accepted them "per honor" the same day either for the issuer or for one of the endorsers. Many of these cases involved their close and regular business partners and family members—Simon Symons, Pincus Moses, and Levin Pincus Schlesinger. It seems plausible that these bills were used to speculate on exchange rates and arbitrage by using a counter bill or redraft. In such cases, the protestor of an unaccepted bill of exchange borrowed money at the place of payment, issued a new bill of exchange for this new creditor, and drew it to the drawer of the original bill. In a redraft, the costs of protest, provision, and the agio (surplus from currency exchange) were added to the original sum.[66] For example, in June 1767, Simon Symons and Levin Pincus Schlesinger issued thirteen bills of exchange to different individuals in Danzig with a total value of 11,000 thaler to be drawn on the Symons in Amsterdam. Six were issued to Hertz Wulff Friedburg, who sent them directly to the Symons. When the bills arrived, the Symons initially did not accept them, but then accepted them later "per honor" for Friedburg. While the notarial records do not allow for any conclusion as to why this was done, one can surmise that the Symons may have issued a bill in Friedburg's name to themselves and drawn it back to Simon Symons and Levin Pincus Schlesinger with a higher sum. Yet the exact nature of this business cannot be established without the accompanying business letters.

Despite this example, accepting a bill of exchange "in honor" was primarily a means to protect close business partners, including family members. These sorts of mechanisms grew even more important during times of crises, such as in 1763 when numerous banking houses in Amsterdam failed. The crisis also revealed the limits and dangers of the far-flung system of trade in bills of exchange. The Seven Years' War had yielded an economic boom to central Europe, and the provision of credit through bills of exchange grew significantly. Merchants increasingly drew bills of exchange that were not sanctioned by any commercial transaction. These merchants, and the Symons brothers among them, relied on making profit with drawing and redrawing bills of exchange. However, by the end of the war, inflation and rapid price fluctuations—the drop of grain prices in particular—led to a breakdown of the whole system and to the bankruptcy of banking houses first in Amsterdam, and then in Hamburg and Berlin. Falling prices and a scarcity of new loans prevented bankers and entrepreneurs from rolling over existing debts. The crisis left clear traces in the bills of exchange handled by Benjamin and Samuel Symons. In general, the number of protested bills was higher in 1763 than in previous and later years. Payment for some bills was rejected by a liquidator after the bills had been originally accepted by Aron Joseph & Co. and Juda Jacob & Sons prior to their bankruptcy in early 1763. The much more serious failure was that of the Neufville brothers in July 1763, which dragged many others behind until by August 1763 about fifty bankruptcies had been registered in Amsterdam.[67]

The following case demonstrates the importance of mechanisms among merchants and brokers that could preserve their reputation. On August 1, 1763, Pincus Moses Schlesinger in Frankfurt an der Oder issued three bills of exchange for Simon Symons drawn to the large Christian banking house Hope & Co. in Amsterdam; their combined value amounted to 4,800 guilders. The bills arrived in Amsterdam via the hands of the Hamburg merchant Moses Wesseley; on August 9, Benjamin and Samuel Symons protested after Hope & Co.'s refusal to honor them; the protest does not detail the reason for the default.[68] Apparently, Pincus Moses Schlesinger relied on the payment of his bills of exchange covered by silver coins he had sent to Hope & Co. in Amsterdam earlier that year. Still, prior to the maturity of the bills of exchange, Samuel Symons and Elias Moses Daniel Nijmegen, the father-in-law of Pincus Moses Schlesinger's son and of Simon Symons, appeared in Gerrit Bouman's notarial office. There, they declared that they were willing to take the silver, which had been melted into sixty-five bars, and accept bills of exchange up to the sum of at least 60,000 guilders.[69] On September 16, when the bills reached maturity, Hope & Co. again refused to pay, and the Symons brothers and Elias Moses Daniel Nijmegen agreed to accept these bills of exchange.[70] Most likely, the general financial difficulties related to the financial crisis of 1763 in Amsterdam caused Hope & Co. to refuse: the obligation only mentions that they "faced difficulties" in honoring the bills.[71]

Jewish merchants' outstanding debts after the Seven Years' War brought Simon Symons and Levin Pincus Schlesinger into financial difficulties of their own. At least two Jewish merchants, Baruch Aron Levi of Berlin and Joseph Benjamin of Halle, turned to the Prussian government with a request against Symons and Schlesinger in 1768. They had received ten bills of exchange that were issued by Symons and Schlesinger in Leipzig in May 1767 and two in Königsberg in July of the same year. Five had been originally issued to the latter's father, Pincus Moses Schlesinger, and then passed on to Baruch Aron Levi as a first endorsee. The payers for the majority of bills were supposed to be two Christian banking houses in Amsterdam, Joost van Eyck and Jacob Philip Bock. In addition, one bill was drawn on Benjamin and Samuel Symons, and one on Elias Moses Daniel Nijmegen. All bills were protested and returned to their payees or first endorsees Baruch Aron Levi and Joseph Benjamin, though the reason for this action is no longer evident. Eventually, Baruch Aron Levi demanded 9,700 guilders, and Joseph Benjamin sought over 1,500 guilders, including interest on the unpaid bills of exchange. Both claimed that Simon Symons and Levin Pincus Schlesinger had left Frankfurt an der Oder intentionally and moved to Warsaw in order to escape their bill debts. As jewelers under the protection of the Polish king, Joseph Benjamin argued, they would be nearly impossible to prosecute. Benjamin and Levi appealed to the Prussian government for support since, as Levi stated: "I can hardly expect any effect without Your Royal Majesty's highest protection and support in the light of the well-known distinctive administration of justice in Poland."[72] As in other cases, it seems rather unlikely that turning to the Prussian government had any effect. The case shows that legal options were rather limited when it came to conflicts concerning bills of exchange. Particularly in instances regarding international connections to eastern Europe, only a choice of reliable business partners could provide some—but never full—protection from loss.

The general introduction of endorsements and the joint liability rule across central Europe eased long-distance trade, bridged differences between commercial institutions in various political settings, and increased legal security for traders. In locales where the authorities aspired to turn a fair into an international marketplace, as in Leipzig, they sought to create additional formal institutions such as commercial courts that would enhance the city's appeal to merchants across Europe, Jews and non-Jews alike. However, none of these formal commercial institutions could replace the import of personal connections rooted in family and shared religion or ethnicity, as we have seen in the specific case of the Symons family in Amsterdam and the Schlesingers in Frankfurt an der Oder.

The Decline of the Symons' Family Business

In the years following the end of the Seven Years' War, credit activities in Amsterdam began to shift to state financing and away from financing commerce.[73] Trade and brokerage in bills of exchange and financing credit had been the primary business areas for Jewish merchants and brokers in Amsterdam, who rarely entered the field of providing government loans. Benjamin and Samuel Symons made a small and eventually unsuccessful foray into the field of state loans when they provided credit, via the Saxon Court Jew Moses Ephraim Levy, to the Saxon crown at the beginning of the Seven Years' War. The Symons issued a one-year loan of more than 300,000 guilders on 5 percent interest and received as pledge parts of the Saxon silver from the "Green Vault" (*Grünes Gewölbe*), the treasury of the Saxon rulers. A year later, however, the loan was transferred to an Ashkenazic banker in Amsterdam and eventually to the Christian banking house Frege in Leipzig.[74] This episode seems to mark the entire and rather brief excursion of Benjamin and Samuel Symons into state loans.

By contrast, Christian bankers began to provide more and more government loans, extending credit to various German states, Sweden, Poland, and Russia.[75] None of the Ashkenazic merchant or banking houses were involved in large state loans provided by the large Christian banking houses in Amsterdam and issued to Poland between 1777 and 1792. The only Jewish banking house in the Netherlands involved in state loans during that period was the Symonses' relatives in The Hague, Abraham and Simon Boas, who issued small loans to Austria, Denmark, Spain, Sweden, and Bohemia.[76] On a much smaller scale, Simon Symons in Warsaw was also involved in brokerage and extending credit to Polish nobles; he provided financial services in the 1770s and 1780s. Yet akin to his relatives in Amsterdam, his loans were fairly minor in comparison to those Polish noblemen obtained from the large Christian banking houses in Warsaw.[77]

Thus, by the last quarter of the eighteenth century, a whole array of reasons seems to have converged to result in the decline of the Symons' family firm, which more or less disappears from archival records by the late 1770s. In addition to an increasing move of banking houses in Amsterdam into state loans, for which the Symons lacked the financial means, the collapse of the Anglo-Indian diamond trade after 1765 probably also contributed to the economic decline of the Symons' family business; Benjamin and Samuel Symons had been prominent in the diamond trade.[78] Further to the east, Prussia was hit by another wave of bankruptcies in 1766. Archival documentation suggests that members of the Symons and Schlesinger families also felt the impact of this crisis, especially when taking into account the considerable drop in the estimated assets of Pincus Moses Schlesinger, Simon Symons, and Levin Pincus Schlesinger in Frankfurt an der Oder between 1765 and 1774.

Though we lack data on the further fortune of the family, some family members might have chosen emigration as a means to improve their economic lot. For example, members of the Daniel Nijmegen family moved to London during the last quarter of the eighteenth century.[79] Similarly, the house of Prager, studied by Gedalia Yogev, had maintained business branches in both Amsterdam and London from the mid-eighteenth century. However, the merchant house did eventually cease to exist by the end of the century, despite London's rise in status as a financial center.[80]

Further east, the fortune of Simon Symons also took a bad turn. We find him in Warsaw as an active merchant, broker, and banker in the last two decades of his life, trading in bills of exchange and lending money to Polish nobles, especially Adam Poniński and Antoni, Vincent, and Ignacy Potocki. These ties lasted up to 1793. Symons signed contracts with Jozef Lubomirski over trade in forest products and purchased large amounts of potash from the noble's manufactory, which he shipped to Elbląg. Nevertheless, to keep a perspective on his business, Ignacy Potocki returned more than 8,000 ducats to Simon Symons between 1787 and 1789. However, the prominent Warsaw banking house Tepper, in comparison, received more than 43,000 ducats from Potocki in the same period of time.[81] It was probably this close connection to Polish nobility, especially to Antoni Potocki, head of the Black Sea Trade Company, and to Warsaw banking houses that caused Simon Symons' bankruptcy in 1793. Rumors about unreturned loans took down the banking house Tepper and subsequently all other banking houses in Warsaw. Concurrently, Moses Boas and Abraham Symons from Amsterdam were, like most creditors, unable to recover their debts. Both turned to the former Polish king Poniatowski in Grodno in 1797 in an attempt to recover a royal obligation of more than 8,500 ducats that they had received from Frideric Cabrit, yet another Warsaw banker who went bankrupt in 1793.[82] It is unlikely that they ever saw a single ducat of it. Their relative Simon Symons passed away the same year, thus, ending the venture of the Amsterdam Symons family expanding business eastward.

Conclusion

Despite the rise of Warsaw as a new center of Jewish trade and finance in east central Europe, the Symons family could not profit from these new developments. Rather, after two generations of successful commerce and financial business, their fate followed the same trajectory as that of the city of Amsterdam. The decline of Amsterdam as a commercial and financial center greatly affected the commercial and financial elite, Christian and Jewish, which had flourished there over the previous two centuries. Though some retained and adapted their business to the new circumstances, for example, by relocating to London, many others left the stage of international business.

Although we can detect a decline in the economic fortunes of Ashkenazic merchants and brokers in Amsterdam toward the end of the eighteenth century, Jonathan Israel's narrative of economic decline needs some qualification. The specific conditions of Amsterdam did not lead to a decline of economic fortunes in the first half of the eighteenth century, at least not for the wealthier strata of the Ashkenazic community. Rather, their commercial expansion eastward provided them with ample economic opportunities, especially in the third quarter of the century, including in financing the Seven Years' War. Only toward the end of the century a decline alongside Amsterdam as a center of finance occurred. Some economic players found revitalization elsewhere, like in London, while the economic fate of Ashkenazim in Amsterdam improved only slowly toward the mid-nineteenth century.

Nevertheless, for about a century, Ashkenazic merchants and brokers from Amsterdam had played a central role in providing or transferring credit to central and east central Europe, primarily by financing commerce. Though the money was usually channeled through Christian and Jewish firms and provided in the main by the large Christian banking houses in Amsterdam, close family ties were at the core of Jewish merchant houses. The inquiry into the trade in bills of exchange also provides a clear picture of how closely members of the Jewish mercantile elite were integrated into the general, non-Jewish world of business. These ordinary Ashkenazic merchants and brokers were of vital importance to central European commerce. They functioned as intermediaries between the financial center of Amsterdam and Jewish merchants in central and indirectly in eastern Europe. As brokers in Amsterdam, they channeled loans from the larger and primarily Christian merchant and banking houses to Jewish merchants in central European cities like Frankfurt an der Oder, Königsberg, Danzig, Berlin, Leipzig, or Breslau. They also constituted a crucial link between Jewish and Christian merchants, brokers, and bankers.

When the French army conquered the Dutch Republic in 1795, the revolutionaries who proclaimed the Batavian Republic also declared all its inhabitants to be equal citizens. In 1796 the Dutch National Assembly confirmed the emancipation of the Jews, although the abolition of economic restrictions did not induce major changes in the occupational profile of Dutch Jewry.[83] Among the Jewish merchants examined here, those in Amsterdam were—in contrast to those in Prussia or Poland—the first to receive legal equality. It did not save them from their fate of economic insignificance on the European stage.

Notes

1. Turniansky, *Glikl: Zikhronot*, 266–269.

2. Quoted from De Vries and Woude, *The First Modern Economy*, 136. See also Spufford, "From Antwerp and Amsterdam to London," 160.

3. Gelderblom, *Cities of Commerce*, 1 (quote), 39–40.

4. Spufford, "From Antwerp and Amsterdam to London," 163.

5. On Ashkenazic migration to Amsterdam, see Kaplan, "Amsterdam and Ashkenazic Migration in the Seventeenth Century," 22–44. On the economic activities of Jews, Ashkenazim and Sephardim, see Bloom, *The Economic Activities of the Jews in Amsterdam*; Israel, "The Republic of the United Netherlands until about 1750," 85–115; Fuks-Mansfeld, "Enlightenment and Emancipation," 170–175.

6. Trivellato, *The Familiarity of Strangers*, 275. Jessica Roitman comes to similar conclusions regarding the Sephardim of Amsterdam in the first half of the seventeenth century: Roitman, *The Same but Different?*, 269–276.

7. Schnabel and Shin, "Liquidity and Contagion," 933–934; Spufford, "From Antwerp and Amsterdam to London," 166.

8. De Vries and Woude, *The First Modern Economy*, 139–140; Cassis, *Capitals of Capital*, 8, 10. On Hope & Co., one of the most important Christian banking houses in Amsterdam, see Buist, *At spes non fracta*.

9. Swetschinski, "From the Middle Ages to the Golden Age," 64–70; Israel, "The Republic of the United Netherlands until about 1750," 87–89, 92; Kaplan, "The Jews in the Republic until about 1750," 121, 125–128.

10. Tal, *The Ashkenazi Community of Amsterdam*, 86.

11. On Yiddish print in Amsterdam, see Berger, *Producing Redemption in Amsterdam*.

12. Some general works deal with both Sephardim and Ashkenazim in Amsterdam, and numerous works deal with the communal, social, economic, and intellectual history of Amsterdam's Sephardim. For recent English monographs, see Bodian, *Hebrews of the Portuguese Nation*; Kaplan, *An Alternative Path to Modernity*; Swetschinski, *Reluctant Cosmopolitans*; Saperstein, *Exile in Amsterdam*; Levie Bernfeld, *Poverty and Welfare*.

13. Bloom, *The Economic Activities of the Jews in Amsterdam*, 70–71, 212–213. Among the wealthiest Sephardim were nine with an income between 10,000 and 50,000 guilders and twenty-two with an income of 5,000 to 10,000 guilders, while the best earning Ashkenazic merchant made 8,000 guilders a year.

14. Yogev, *Diamonds and Coral*, 15–21; Bloom, *The Economic Activities of the Jews in Amsterdam*, 177, 183.

15. LeLong, *De koophandel van Amsterdam*, 157.

16. Bloom, *The Economic Activities of the Jews in Amsterdam*, 213. The jeweler Jochem Mozes was registered with an annual income of 8,000 guilders, followed by the widow of Salomon van Norden and Salomon Philip Gompertz, both merchants, with 6,000 guilders, and the money changer Herman Abraham Keijzer with 4,000 guilders.

17. Tal, *The Ashkenazi Community of Amsterdam*, 167.

18. Van Straten, *De begraafboeken van Muiderberg 1669–1811*, 131.

19. Notariat D. Geniets, file 13654, StAA, NAA, nos. 217–219.

20. On the importance of institutions and the distinction between informal and formal institutions, see North, *Institutions, Institutional Change and Economic Performance*, 4, 46–47.

21. Schneider, "Messen, Banken und Börsen," 150–151; Schnabel and Shin, "Liquidity and Contagion," 934. The most concise history of bills of exchange is De Roover, *L'Evolution de la Lettre de Change*, 82–84, 119–122, 140. See also Pannwitz, *Die Entstehung der Allgemeinen Deutschen Wechselordnung*, 31–32, 263–275. For Leipzig: Beachy, *The Soul of Commerce*, 36.

22. Schneider, "Messen, Banken und Börsen," 146, 168. See also Ludovici, *Grundriß eines vollständigen Kaufmanns-Systems*, column 1790.

23. Santarosa, "Financing Long-Distance Trade," 716. On the introduction of the joint liability rule, see Van der Wee, "Monetary, Credit, and Banking Systems," 325–327. See also Schnabel and Shin, "Liquidity and Contagion," 338–339.

24. Santarosa, "Financing Long-Distance Trade," 693.

25. Püttmann, *Die Leipziger Wechselordnung*, 47–48.

26. Denzel, "Die Integration Deutschlands in das internationale Zahlungsverkehrssystem," 96. No records from the Commercial Court in Leipzig have survived.

27. Beachy, "Fernhandel und Krämergeist," 135–147; Beachy, *The Soul of Commerce*, 32–35.

28. The *Leipziger Wechselordnung* mentions Jews in specific only once, stipulating that a Jewish debtor had to bring the repayment to his creditor; otherwise the creditor had to pick up the money from the debtor: Püttmann, *Die Leipziger Wechselordnung*, 29.

29. Denzel, *Geld- und Wechselkurse der deutschen Messeplätze Leipzig und Braunschweig*, 5, 13–16; Denzel, "Zahlungsverkehr auf den Leipziger Messen," 152, 156–162.

30. Fram, *Ideals Face Reality*, 132.

31. On the halakhic discussions surrounding the permissibility of debt bills that were circulated and sometimes issued without a set sum (so that creditors later could add the expenses that incurred while handling goods) and the ways in which creditors had to be satisfied by debtors, see Fram, *Ideals Face Reality*, 129–143.

32. Philipp Bloch presents three *mamranoth* from the second half of the eighteenth century from Posen (Poznań); all three mention that the *mamran* can be redeemed anywhere, but preferably in Breslau or Frankfurt an der Oder. Bloch, "Der Mamran (ממרן), der jüdisch-polnische Wechselbrief," 62–63; Turniansky, *Glikl: Zikhronot*, 402. In the inventory of assets of the Jewish merchant and banker Judyta Jakubowiczowa in Warsaw from 1829, among hundreds of bills of exchange, only three were in Hebrew (issued in 1804 and 1815), and they were debt obligations rather than widely circulating bills of exchange. See Eisenbach and Kosim, "Akt masy spadkowej Judyty Jakubowiczowej," 133, 136.

33. Bloom, *The Economic Activities of the Jews in Amsterdam*, 195.

34. Simon Symons und Levin Pincus Schlesinger wegen ihrer in Pohlen ausstehenden Wechsel und andere Forderungen, I. HA, Geheimer Rat, Rep. 9 (Polen), no. 28-7C, GStA.

35. Dahl, *Trade, Trust, and Networks*, 17.

36. One example for large amounts of preserved bills of exchange is the Christian banking house Eichborn in Breslau, which also did business with Simon Symons from Amsterdam. Bezahlte Wechsel und Anweisungen 1776–1826, syg. 4081–4086, APW, Oddział Kamieniec Ząbkowicki, Dom Bankowy Eichborn.

37. An exception is the Prager family, from which about 1,300 Yiddish letters, sent from Amsterdam to London in the second half of the eighteenth century, survived because they were submitted to the Public Record Office following a court case. The firm was studied by Yogev, *Diamonds and Coral*, 183–274.

38. An additional problem is rooted in the fact that during the second half of the eighteenth century, well over a hundred notarial offices existed in Amsterdam, often producing up to four bulky volumes of entries every year. Although I was able to find the notarial offices used most frequently by Benjamin and Samuel Symons and their business partners, it is not inconceivable that more bills were protested at other notarial offices. Thus the sample only provides a glimpse into the business in bills of exchange of the Symons family.

39. Santarosa has shown that 44 percent of bills of exchange in her sample from Marseille in the 1780s were protested. As was the case with protested bills of exchange in Amsterdam, in Santarosa's sample the most common reason for a refusal to honor a bill of exchange was the lack of an *avis*. Santarosa, "Financing Long-Distance Trade," 703, 714.

40. The bills of exchange are from the following archival collections: Notariat Gerrit Bouman, files 12592, 12594–12608, 12611–12617, 12619, 12620, 12622, 12623, 12625, 12627, StAA, NAA. Notariat Daniel Brink, files 10391, 10394, 10424, 10427, 10430, 10432, 10433, 10435, 10443, 10445–10453, 10460–10462, 10464, 10468, 10470, 10471, 10505, 10511, 10527, 10590, StAA, NAA. Notariat Salomon Dorper, files 10819, 10827, StAA, NAA. Notariat C. van Homrigh, files 12361, 12393, StAA, NAA. Notariat D. Geniets, files 13641, 13644, 13647, 13654, 13655, 13660, 13669, 13672, 13682, 13697, 13747, StAA, NAA. Simon Symons und Levin Pincus Schlesinger wegen ihrer in Pohlen ausstehenden Wechsel und andere Forderungen, I. HA, Rep. 9 (Polen), no. 28-7C, GStA.

41. This assumption held true for Jewish as well as non-Jewish merchant families. See, for example: Bull, "Merchant Households and their Networks in Eighteenth-Century Trondheim," 220; Müller, *The Merchant Houses of Stockholm*, 245–248; Veluwenkamp, "Familienetwerken binnen de Nederlandse koopliedengemeenschap van Archangel," 660.

42. Bogucka, "Dutch Merchants' Activities in Gdańsk in the First Half of the 17th Century," 19–32.

43. On the marriages among Jewish families in Prussia, see Straubel, *Die Handelsstädte Königsberg und Memel in friderizianischer Zeit*, 473, 699.

44. On the relative separation of Ashkenazim and Sephardim in terms of business, see Trivellato, *The Familiarity of Strangers*, 43–45. Of course, Ashkenazim and Sephardim did business with each other, especially where they lived in proximity as in Amsterdam or London. Yogev, *Diamonds and Coral*, 258–259, 326. However, these ties did not lead to intermarriage between Sephardim and Ashkenazim. On the relationship between Sephardim and Ashkenazim in Amsterdam, see Kaplan, "The Self-Definition of the Sephardic Jews of Western Europe," 122–125, 128–132, 141–142. On the usage of the term "ethnic," see Stow, *Theater of Acculturation*, 24. According to Stow the usage of the term *natio* in its early modern meaning referring to a group of origin would be more appropriate, but I prefer the term "ethnic" as, unlike Sephardim, Ashkenazim did not use the term *natio* for their self-description.

45. On the question of separate male and female spheres in Jewish history and the limited usefulness of this approach, see Rosman, "The History of Jewish Women in Early Modern Poland," 25–56. For Jewish women's economic role, see also Toch, "Jewish Women Entrepreneurs in the 16th and 17th Century Economics and Family Structure," 254–263.

46. Ries and Battenberg, *Hofjuden*, 18. See also Ries, "Status und Lebensstil," 292–295.

47. Turniansky, *Glikl: Zikhronot*, 616–617. On the marriages in Glikl's family, see also Ries, "Status und Lebensstil," 283–287. On the structure of Glikl's commercial networks, see Israel, "Handelsmessen und Handelsrouten," 268–279.

48. Israel, "The Republic of the United Netherlands until about 1750," 102; De Vries, *From Pedlars to Textile Barons*, 41.

49. The marriage registers in Amsterdam provide evidence only that Sara was a sister of Berent (also Barend, Berend, Barent), but according to archival records in Berlin, Isaac Symons, a son of Berent Symons, was the nephew of Benjamin and Samuel Symons. Acta betr. den Prozeß zwischen dem Juden Barend Simon / Amsterdam und seinem Sohn Isaac

Simons hierselbst, 1754–1759, I. HA, Rep. 9 (Allgemeine Verwaltung), Y2, Fasz. 123, GStA; Akte betreffend die Auseinandersetzung zwischen Abraham Hirschel und Benjamin & Samuel Symons, I. HA, Rep. 49, Lit. K, 1759–1769, no. 16213, GStA, 815v. I assume that Mitje Boas was Samuel Symons second wife because she was too young to have been the mother of his daughter Veronica Symons. Notariat Gerrit Bouman, file 12608, StAA, NAA, no. 409.

50. D.T.P. Ondertrouwen, StAA, mf. 729, 408; mf. 732, 273; mf. 739, 444.

51. Trivellato, *The Familiarity of Strangers*, 134. It is noteworthy that consanguineous marriages seem common in the Symons family, yet there are no examples of it in the Ashkenazic families in central and eastern Europe that are examined here. There is, however, not enough evidence to conclude that such marriages were more common among Ashkenazim who lived in close proximity to Sephardim. On marriage law, see Elon, *The Principles of Jewish Law*, 356–360.

52. The public announcement of marriage applied to all Christian denominations (Catholics, Anabaptists and others) equally, save members of the Dutch Reformed Church. Prior to the ceremony, intended marriages had to be registered and announced on three successive Sundays. In addition, a civil ceremony legalized the marriage. Verdooner and Snel, *Trouwen in Mokum*, 11. Notariat Gerrit Bouman, file 12608, StAA, NAA, no. 409. The contract was entered in the notarial records on July 21, 1763, two weeks after the public announcement of the marriage.

53. On this practice among Sephardim in Livorno, see Trivellato, *The Familiarity of Strangers*, 135–136.

54. Epstein, *The Jewish Marriage Contract*, 140–142.

55. According to Trivellato, this was the case for Livorno. It was also not uncommon for a bride to demand a guarantee for her dowry from the groom's father so that she would be able to collect her *ketubah* from her father-in-law. Epstein, *The Jewish Marriage Contract*, 248. On Ashkenazic marriage traditions, see Klein, *Das jüdische Ehegüter- und Erbrecht der Frühneuzeit*, 130–147.

56. Juden Acta betreffend die jährlich einzureichenden Juden Tabellen (1748–1759), Abteilung 1, VII, 107, StAF, 325v–326. His marriage with Hendele is mentioned in D.T.P. Ondertrouwen, StAA, mf. 741, 420. Since it took place in Frankfurt an der Oder the names of Simon Symons' parents are not noted. In another record a son of Berent Symons is called Simon Barents but referred to as Symons Junior. Simon Symons was regularly referred to as junior, le Jeune, or der Jüngere. Notariat Daniel Brink, file 10430, StAA, NAA, no. 1653. Ignacy Schiper erroneously referred to Simon Symons as a brother of Benjamin & Samuel Symons. Schiper also mentions a fourth brother, Jacob Symons, who does not appear in any primary source. Schiper, *Dzieje handlu żydowskiego*, 302.

57. D.T.P. Ondertrouwen, StAA, mf. 739, 402.

58. Ibid., mf. 741, 420. Acta Subhastationis des hies. Schutz-Juden Pincus Moses Schlesinger zu auf der Schmiede-Gasse belegenes Wohn-Haus, 1779, Abteilung 1, VII, 437, StAF, 80v.

59. Metryka Koronna, 1764–1780, KK 18 (mf. A-6083), AGAD, 171. However, from 1760 on, Simon Symons is eliminated from the registry lists of Frankfurt an der Oder and listed as absent. Juden Acta betreffend die jährlich einzureichenden Juden Tabellen (1760–

1770), Abteilung 1, VII, 108, StAF. The fact that Levin Pincus Schlesinger is listed constantly in the Frankfurt an der Oder registers suggests that he remained in Frankfurt. The same might be true for Simon Symons's wife since he is listed in a 1778 registry of inhabitants of the Potocki estates outside of Warsaw as Simon Symonowicz from Frankfurt an der Oder together with only a servant. Konskrypcia Żydów 1778, APW, syg. 93, (mf. 17867), AGAD.

60. Bloom, *The Economic Activities of the Jews in Amsterdam*, 213.

61. Although Benjamin and Samuel Symons alternated their visits, each traveled with the same servant. Judenverzeichnisse 1726–1742, Geheimer Rat, Loc. 9482/4, SHstA DD; Judenverzeichnisse 1742–1764, Geheimer Rat, Loc. 9482/3, SHstA DD.

62. Judenverzeichnisse 1742–1764, Geheimer Rat, Loc. 9482/3, SHstA DD, 14v, 66v. Simon Boas (1730–1795) was the son of Tobias Boas and Sara Symons, a sister of Benjamin and Samuel Symons.

63. Löwenstein, *Beiträge zur Geschichte der Juden in Deutschland*, 224, 266; Krüger, *Die Judenschaft von Königsberg in Preußen 1700–1812*, 16; Spalding, *Elise Reimarus (1735–1805)*, 268.

64. Schnabel and Shin, "Liquidity and Contagion," 930–936.

65. Notariat Gerrit Bouman, file 12600, StAA, NAA, no. 36. Isaac Hirsch(el) was a brother-in-law of Isaac Symons, who was taken to court by his father Berent Symons and uncles Benjamin and Samuel Symons a few years earlier. Back then, Gotzkowsky had vouched for Berent Symons. Acta betr. den Prozeß zwischen dem Juden Barend Simon / Amsterdam und seinem Sohn Isaac Simons hierselbst, 1754–1759, I. HA, Rep. 9 (Allgemeine Verwaltung), Y2, Fasz. 123, GStA. The Berlin merchant-banker Gotzkowsky was later involved in speculative grain deals with Neufville from Amsterdam. Schnabel and Shin, "Liquidity and Contagion," 941–942. On Isaac Symons and Isaac Hirschel and their business ventures in Berlin, see Aust, "Daily Business or an Affair of Consequence?," 71–90.

66. Ludovici, *Grundriß eines vollständigen Kaufmanns-Systems*, 183. The agio had to be paid by the side that exchanged a weaker currency into a stronger one.

67. Notariat Gerrit Bouman, file 12608, StAA, NAA, no. 468, 571, 520. The Christian banking house Neufville had invested in highly speculative and risky transactions, including some with the Berlin banker Gotzkowsky. Schnabel and Shin, "Liquidity and Contagion," 940–946; Rilcy, *International Government Finance*, 32–33. See also Bloom, *The Economic Activities of the Jews in Amsterdam*, 197–198.

68. Notariat Gerrit Bouman, file 12608, StAA, NAA, no. 550. Unfortunately, the archives of Hope & Co. at the municipal archives in Amsterdam do not provide any more details as to why the company refused to pay in this specific case. I wish to thank Barbara D. Consolini for helping me to go through the relevant material of the Hope & Co. archives.

69. Notariat C. van Homrigh, file 12361, StAA, NAA, no. 886.

70. Notariat Gerrit Bouman, file 12611, StAA, NAA, no. 942.

71. Though Hope & Co. was not directly affected by the downfall of the banking house of the Neufville brothers, the ensuing crisis led to the freeze of credit in Amsterdam, and bills of exchange were widely refused. Archief van de Firma Hope & Co., file 103, 2, StAA. In October 1763 Hope & Co. paid the Symons brothers 2,088 guilders for Pincus Moses Schlesinger, though it is unclear whether the payment was related to the prior incident.

72. Acta die Forderungen des Schutz-Juden Pincus Moses Schlesinger an den Simon Simons zu Warschau betr., I. HA, Geheimer Rat, Rep. 9 (Polen), no. 28-12B, GStA; Simon Symons und Levin Pincus Schlesinger wegen ihrer in Pohlen ausstehenden Wechsel und andere Forderungen, I. HA, Rep. 9 (Polen), no. 28-7C, GStA.

73. De Vries and Woude, *The First Modern Economy*, 674–687; Cassis, *Capitals of Capital*, 9–14. See also Schnabel and Shin, "Liquidity and Contagion," 929–933.

74. Notariat Gerrit Bouman, file 12597, StAA, NAA, no. 331. Bloom, *The Economic Activities of the Jews in Amsterdam*, 172, 178. See also Schnee, *Die Hoffinanz*, 240–244. Acta die in Holland gegen verpfändetes Herrschaftliches Silber Geschirr und Juwelen, durch den Geheimen Rath Grafen von Bolza und nachhero durch den Cammer Rath Fregen, aufgenommene Capitalia und Zinsen, 1764–82, 10036 Finanzarchiv, Loc. 33709, Rep. XI, Sect. II, Lit H, no. 25, SHstA DD; Die in Holland auf das grüne Gewölbe negociirte Anleihe betr. 1764 u. 1768, 10025 Geheimes Konsilium, Loc. 5286, SHstA DD.

75. De Vries and Woude, *The First Modern Economy*, 142–143.

76. Riley, *International Government Finance*, 139, 151, 165, 183, 248, 295.

77. Metryka Koronna, MK 283, AGAD, 175, 182v, 183v; Metryka Koronna, MK 284 (mf. 2192), AGAD, 44v–45; Metryka Koronna, MK 286 (mf. 2194), AGAD, 107–112; Metryka Koronna, MK 297 (mf. 2205), AGAD, 74v–75, 135–135v, 184v–186, 218v, 235, 240v–241, 256v, 284–290; Metryka Koronna, MK 299 (mf. 2207), AGAD, 189–189v, 211v–212; Metryka Koronna, MK 300 (mf. 2208), AGAD, 86v, 119v–120v; Metryka Koronna, MK 301 (mf. 2209), AGAD, 4–4v, 11, 61v; Akta interezu z Symonem junior, AGW, Dział Archiwum Główne Potockich zesp. 342/ II, AGAD; Rachunek wierzycieli 1783–1788, AGW, Anteriora, zesp. 342, syg. 221, AGAD, 23, 31; Tabelle des dettes sur les Billets de Sa Majesté restées a la Charge de Sa Cassette Royale, 1793, AKP, syg. 354, (mf. 26745), AGAD, 32. Buist, *At spes non fracta*, 112, 114.

78. Yogev, *Diamonds and Coral*, 169.

79. We know that the only son of Margolia Elias Daniel Nijmegen and Levin Pincus Schlesinger from Frankfurt an der Oder moved to London—probably following his maternal uncles—where he drowned in a sea accident around 1800. Acta vom Erlaubnisgesuch des Juden Levin Pincus Schlesinger zu Franckfurth an der Oder zum Ankauf des Keesebierschen Hauses, Rep. 2, S 4233, BLHA.

80. Yogev, *Diamonds and Coral*, 183–274.

81. Akta interezu z Symonem junior, AGW, Dział Archiwum Główne Potockich zesp. 342/II, syg. 485, AGAD; Rachunek wierzycieli 1783–1788, AGW, Anteriora, zesp. 342, syg. 221, AGAD.

82. Korespondencja Stanisława Augusta 1792–1797, syg. 3a, AGAD, 110–110v.

83. Prince William of Orange confirmed the equal status of Jews after Napoleon's defeat against Russia in 1813. Fuks-Mansfeld, "Enlightenment and Emancipation, from c. 1750 to 1814," 167, 171, 173–174. For a more cautious assessment of the Jews' legal position, see Sonnenberg-Stern, *Emancipation and Poverty*, 33–37, 50.

TWO

Frankfurt an der Oder: Central European Middlemen

In 1758 Simon Symons arrived in Frankfurt an der Oder from Amsterdam and married the daughter of a wealthy and successful local Jewish merchant named Pincus Moses Schlesinger. That union seemed like a promising familial connection. Right after the wedding, Simon Symons entered into a business partnership with his brother-in-law, Levin Pincus Schlesinger, extending their business eastward to Warsaw. Nearly two decades later, however, the elder Schlesinger complained bitterly about his son-in-law in a letter to the Prussian ruler. He claimed that upon his arrival Symons "found himself in bad financial circumstances, but now he is a rich person and the court-jeweler of the king of Poland."[1] Since Schlesinger was seeking legal support against Symons from the Prussian administration, it seems natural that he would try to cast his former son-in-law in a bad light. It is difficult to assess, much less reconcile, the different accusations these merchants lodged against each other. Documents from a highly complex court case in Danzig and other correspondence with the Prussian government support the impression that Schlesinger's problems with Simon Symons contributed to his economic difficulties, which eventually ended in his bankruptcy by the time he passed away in 1795. Simon Symons had died two years earlier in Warsaw; he, too, had lost everything.[2]

Despite this sad demise, the beginning of their business partnership shone with promise. As was explored in the previous chapter, the Symons family of Amsterdam was a central player in the brokerage of credit from Amsterdam to central Europe, especially to Prussia. This chapter examines the critical role of the Schlesinger family in particular and the Jewish merchants in Frankfurt an der Oder in general as middlemen between east and west. It argues that it was them who built and maintained close ties to Polish Jewish merchants and were one determinant of the rise of a new Jewish mercantile and financial elite in the nineteenth century.

The Schlesingers were middlemen between Jewish and non-Jewish merchants, brokers, and bankers in the west and Jewish merchants in the east. They possessed less wealth and influence than the tiny group of central European Court Jews, but played a crucial role in the economic developments in central Europe from the second half of the eighteenth into the nineteenth century. While exploring how they filled their role as middlemen, this chapter also addresses how important familial and ethnic networks were in their economic endeavors. Moreover, it shows the influence of the Jews' legal position on the life of these Jewish merchants, who had to grapple with strict Prussian legislations toward Jews. As David Sorkin argued, central Europe—unlike the west and the east—most dramatically restricted the political status of the Jewish population in the early modern period. The granting of privileges largely to individuals or groups of individuals not Jewish communities as such kept Jews in the German lands in a politically inferior position.[3]

After establishing ties to Amsterdam, Pincus Moses Schlesinger's son, Levin Pincus, entered into a formal business partnership with Simon Symons, and both moved on to Warsaw, actively extending the business of both families eastward. Notably, the contacts between the two families were established in the mid-1750s at the brink of the Seven Years' War, which was likely a lucrative time for both families. Following the war, the extension of business relations eastward seems to have increased their fortunes temporarily. The aforementioned business partnership was dissolved in the early 1770s amid quarrels. The story of these two families underscores that commercial and familial relations were not always harmonious; kinship ties did not necessarily guarantee successful business.

The Schlesingers were one of the wealthiest and most influential merchant families in the Jewish community of Frankfurt an der Oder for much of the eighteenth century. Although they enjoyed the benefits of Prussian privilege, they did not belong to the group of Court Jews who were most influential in Prussia and other German and central European states into the first half of the eighteenth century. They did not live close to the Prussian Court; rather, they settled in Frankfurt an der Oder, a town with an important commercial fair connecting eastern and western Europe. Textile trade was one of the strongholds of Jewish merchants in central Europe, and especially in Frankfurt an der Oder. They traded textiles such as raw drapery, linen, cotton, silk, and ready-made clothing. Whereas Jewish merchants were overrepresented in commerce as compared to the general population numbers, they did not monopolize or even dominate the textile trade.[4] Still, these Jewish merchants played a crucial role in the commercial exchange with eastern Europe and especially in providing the credit necessary in this trade. Particularly in the eastern parts of Prussia, their business focused on the east; together with Jews from Poland and later Russia, they dominated this part of the market by utilizing their transregional connections.

The familial, communal, and business connections of the Schlesinger family developed around the Frankfurt fair and extended to other commercial cities within and outside of Prussia. My focus here is on how they constructed and maintained their familial and commercial connections but also how general economic measures and specific local circumstances such as protective trade regulations, the partitions of Poland, and the subsequent decline of the fairs in Frankfurt an der Oder undermined the economic stability of previously successful merchant families such as the Schlesingers. After some relative economic success around the Seven Years' War, the city and its Jewish merchant community slipped into a slow decline toward the end of the eighteenth century. These developments eventually caused Jewish merchant families to shift their economic activity and networks away from Frankfurt.

Beyond the field of commerce, the Schlesinger family was also part of the communal leadership, in line with the practice of Jewish communities being headed by members of the mercantile elite in eighteenth-century Europe.[5] Within the community, the Schlesinger family, along with some others, was drawn to enlightenment ideas, without following the more radical forms of the Haskalah, the Jewish enlightenment, that developed in the Prussian capital of Berlin. Here too, these merchants capture an encounter between east and west, this time, intellectual in nature. We, thus, need to exercise some caution toward the notion of the Jewish enlightenment and its close linkage to economic success and the assumption that those members of a wealthy Jewish mercantile elite were necessarily ardent followers of the Haskalah.

The Schlesinger family, the Jewish community of Frankfurt an der Oder, and the city itself with its three annual fairs exemplify the central role this triumvirate fulfilled in the commercial connections between western and eastern Europe during the eighteenth century. This case equally illustrates the turning fortunes of individual merchants, families, and cities in the shifting economic system in central Europe toward the end of the eighteenth century.

Prussia's Policy toward Jews

Following the Thirty Years' War (1618–1648), a new centralist state began to emerge in central Europe. Based on the intermarriage of the Hohenzollern family of Brandenburg and the Duchy of Prussia, the rulers of Brandenburg-Prussia integrated new territories and sought to centralize its administration after the end of the Thirty Years' War. This process continued after Frederick III, Elector of Brandenburg, succeeded in elevating his status to King, and the Kingdom of Prussia emerged in 1701. The promotion of large-scale immigration was part and parcel of this policy, especially under his predecessor, Frederick William (known as The Great Elector). Central to these measures was the Edict of Potsdam (1685) that encouraged French Huguenots to immigrate to Brandenburg-Prussia, driven by demographic and economic consideration after the devastations of the war. Jews too became part of these immigration measures, though on a much smaller scale.

After the medieval expulsions, Jews began to resettle in central and western Europe in the final quarter of the sixteenth century, but it was only the Thirty Years' War that marked a real turning point in their readmission. Many German states already used Jewish army providers and court factors during the war to supply their courts with goods and credit. The new phenomenon of central European Court Jews arose as a result of these services and their continuation after the war.[6] Prussia, however, came late to this development. It was only in 1671 that Brandenburg-Prussia allowed Jews to resettle. Frederick William invited wealthy Jewish families who had been expelled from Vienna to settle in Berlin and a few other Prussian towns. He aimed at drawing inhabitants who could provide fiscal income and economic advancement to the state, though he placed severe restrictions on the economic, religious, and personal freedom of Jews.[7]

These newly admitted Jews were thought to generate fiscal income and contribute to the creation of a Prussian manufacturing industry, despite the fact that most of them remained primarily active in commerce. Typically, the focus in historiography remains on Jews in Berlin, Königsberg, and Breslau, the development of their Jewish communities, and the emergence of the Haskalah in Prussia.[8] However, Jews settled in a number of smaller Prussian cities as well. Due to legal restrictions and as intended by state policy, the number of Jews in the Prussian provinces remained very small. Ten Jewish families from Austria were allowed to settle in Frankfurt an der Oder in 1671, and in 1688 more Jews lived in that town than in Berlin or Königsberg. The growth of the community slowed down during the eighteenth century. In 1718, forty additional families were admitted. Among the latter was Moses Jacob Schlesier/Schlesinger (1683–1757), a drapery and silk merchant, who according to his name may have arrived from Silesia. Additional Jews, like the later communal elder Levin Buko (also Levin Jacob Elias), were admitted in the first half of the eighteenth century together with their families on an individual basis.[9]

In the second half of the eighteenth century the rights of individual Jews were based on the Revised General Code (*Revidiertes Generalprivilegium und Reglement*) of 1750 that imposed severe restrictions on Jews settling in Prussia. The earlier General Code of 1730 had already transferred the policy toward Jews from royal decrees, still the legal basis of Polish Jewry at the time, to state law. As such, the direct relationship between the monarch and the Jews as his subjects was abolished. Jews were integrated into state law, thereby "marking the victory of the centralized absolutist polity over the corporative state."[10] Still, the Revised General Code of 1750 was extremely restrictive. Jews were divided into six different categories: from a very small group of "generally privileged" (*Generalprivilegierte*) to "privileged protected Jews" (*Ordentliche Schutzjuden*), and "unprivileged protected Jews" (*Außerordentliche Schutzjuden*), down to community employees and "tolerated" Jews registered via the privilege of a "protected Jew," and finally servants employed by Jews of the first group. Jews of the latter three categories were completely dependent on their communal or individual employer, but even Jews of the second and third category could not choose their place of residence freely and were limited to transferring their settlement privilege to only one child.[11] In contrast to their counterparts in

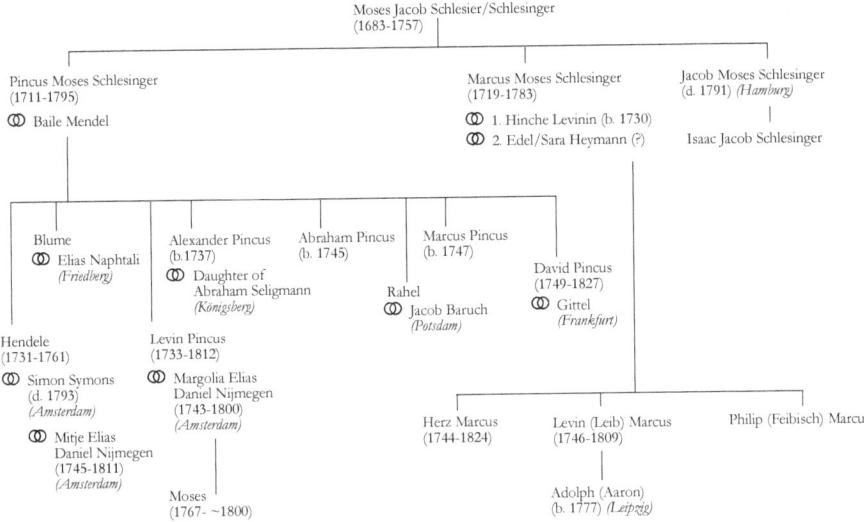

FIGURE 2.1. Family tree of the Schlesinger family in Frankfurt an der Oder.
Credit: Oliver Ihlow.

Berlin, Königsberg, and Breslau, none of the community members in Frankfurt an der Oder received a general privilege for their services to the state.

Among the most affluent members of the community were Pincus Moses (1711–1795) and Marcus Moses Schlesinger (1719–1783), sons of Moses Jacob Schlesinger, who had arrived in the city in 1718 (see figure 2.1). They were listed in the city's records in the 1760s as discount brokers (Wechselhändler) and merchants with various goods, trading especially with Poland and Russia.[12] They lived in the center of Frankfurt an der Oder; some family members owned houses along the city's main streets.[13] They were also able to employ servants; in the early 1750s Moses Jacob Schlesinger had a maidservant, a cook, and a boy. His son Marcus Moses also had three servants whereas his son, Pincus Moses Schlesinger, is listed as employing five: a boy for trade, a boy, a teacher, a cook, and a maidservant.[14] One has to be mindful of the fact that employing servants was sometimes a ruse for keeping relatives or acquaintances without a privilege of residency in the city. Nevertheless, it illustrates the family's comparative wealth within the Jewish community of Frankfurt an der Oder.

Frankfurt an der Oder: A Commercial Hub

Situated on the Oder River, about 80 kilometers (50 miles) east of Berlin and 450 kilometers (280 miles) west of Warsaw, Frankfurt became a hub between western and eastern Europe already in the Middle Ages. Located on the medieval trade route Paris-Aachen-Berlin-Warsaw-Moscow, it received its town charter in 1253. By the mid-fifteenth century, the three annual local fairs turned into transregional fairs, drawing merchants from east and west. The university, founded in 1506, and the printing press initiated around the same time made the city more attractive to students and scholars from across Europe. By the mid-eighteenth century Frankfurt had turned into a town of nearly 10,000 inhabitants with commercial importance for the exchange of merchandise between east and west.

Although a small medieval Jewish community was expelled in the fifteenth century, Jewish merchants continued to visit the town's fairs until they returned to settle in Frankfurt an der Oder at the end of the seventeenth century. Most Jewish inhabitants were actively involved in commerce. As most Polish fairs declined due to the politically unstable and bellicose decades from the second half of the seventeenth century into the first half of the eighteenth century, the fairs in Breslau, Frankfurt an der Oder, and Leipzig grew into important hubs for the exchange of commodities between western, central, and eastern Europe.[15] The town's three annual fairs drew large numbers of merchants; each fair—the first held between Ash Wednesday and Easter (Reminiscere), the second in July or August (Magarethen), and the third in November (Martini)—spanned three weeks; each began with a week of stalls, another week for wholesale commerce, and the third for payment.

Polish Jews wielded a large influence on the fair throughout the eighteenth century. In the 1730s, Christian and Jewish merchants complained about the behavior of custom officials in Frankfurt an der Oder. A royal decree of the Prussian king Frederick William I ordered to ease access to the fair for all merchants, but explicitly mentioned Jewish merchants, thus, hinting at their importance for the fairs. The fair continued to thrive, particularly in spring and summer during the second half of the eighteenth century. Polish Jews frequented the fairs in large numbers; they exchanged raw products such as hides, fur, wax, and honey for manufactured goods, primarily textiles. At its height up to 1,500 men, 400 wagons, and 1,000 horses reached the town from Poland for a single fair.[16]

Like fairs across Europe, the fairs in Frankfurt an der Oder also proved to be a market for marriage, discussions of Jewish regional communal issues, or the hiring of communal servants, in particular for Polish Jews who sought positions in Jewish communities in Prussia.[17] In the 1780s, Moses Wasserzug, a Polish Jew, recounts: "And after I finished my training [as a *shoḥet*], I traveled to Frankfurt an der Oder in the month of Tammuz to find a communal function; it was the custom of the land that during the fair in Frankfurt an der Oder in the month of Tammuz fellow Jews asked and searched for teachers and butchers for all their places of living."[18] Moreover, the printing press and the university also drew Jews to Frankfurt an der Oder around the year. Jewish students, printers, and rabbis arrived from across

Europe to study medicine at the local university or to make use of the Hebrew printing press that had been there since the late seventeenth century. Christian Hebraists set up the Hebrew printing press, but employed Jewish printers; it became renowned for the first Talmud edition printed in Germany (1697–1699). In 1678 the university became the first in Germany to admit Jewish students to study medicine. That same university first issued doctoral degrees for Jewish students in 1721, although the atmosphere for Jews was according to physician Tobias Cohen less than welcoming, at least in the early years. Nevertheless, the city with its university, the Hebrew printing press, and its fairs drew a substantial number of Jews, who chose to either reside there or travel there to pursue their studies or for business.[19]

Government officials were well aware of the importance of Jewish merchants and especially of their role in exporting manufactured textiles to eastern Europe. Prussian officials regularly invited representatives of Polish Jews from Little and Great Poland after 1774 to answer questions regarding the domestic textile products, the variety of these goods, their price and quality. Moreover, these officials inquired about the conditions of travel, whether Jewish merchants were held up when arriving to and departing from Frankfurt an der Oder, about the quality of the roads as well as the taxes and fees charged from Jewish merchants.[20] Representatives of Jewish merchants from Poland complained primarily about the high prices for Prussian textile products, the delays upon entering Frankfurt an der Oder during fair time, and about the treatment they suffered in some inns along the way. Though it is doubtful that these inquiries led to considerable improvements, they demonstrate an awareness of the role Jewish merchants played at the fairs.

The fairs closely linked Jewish merchants from across central Europe. A register from 1756 lists twenty-eight Jewish merchants from Berlin, eight from Hamburg, six from Frankfurt am Main, three from Amsterdam, two from Königsberg and Fürth, and one from Leipzig, Magdeburg, and Halberstadt, including three female widowed merchants listed under their own names. Among these fifty-two merchants, only three were listed as trading in tobacco, gold, silver, books, spices, and furs; the rest traded primarily in textiles. Comparable numbers from the Leipzig fair show that Polish Jews purchased primarily textiles.[21]

Familial and Commercial Networks of the Schlesinger Family

As elsewhere in central Europe, Jewish merchants were certainly overrepresented among the merchants of Frankfurt an der Oder compared to their percentage population, but they were neither the wealthiest nor did they dominate the top of the merchant class. Most Jews in the city, where they constituted less than seven percent of the overall population, were involved in either retail or wholesale trade.[22] In 1765, the city's classification according to account books shows that most Jewish

Table 2.1. Assets of Jewish and Christian merchants in Frankfurt an der Oder, 1765.

Assets (in thaler)	Jewish merchants	Christian merchants
20,000		1
18,000		1
15,000		2
13,000	2	
12,000		5
10,000	1	3
≥10,000	3	11
8,000		2
5,000	2	3
4,000		1
3,000	1	4
2,500	1	
2,000	3	5
1,500	2	3
1,200	2	
1,000	7	11
≥1,000	18	29
900	1	
800	1	4
700	2	
600	3	
500	9	2
400	17	1
300	7	
200	12	1
100	4	
≥100	56	8
<100 (poor)	5	
Total	82	49

Sources: Acta wegen Classificierung hiesiger Handlung treibender Personen, zu Paraphirung ihrer Handlungs-Bücher 1765 bis Junii 1766, Abt. 1, X, 220, StAF, 21, 25–31, 72; Straubel, *Frankfurt (Oder) und Potsdam*, 75, 83, 268–269.

merchants were retail merchants. Altogether, only twenty-one held assets of 1,000 thaler and above whereas the number rises to forty-one for Christian merchants (see table 2.1). The classification does not list a single Jewish merchant with a fortune of more than 20,000 thaler. The table shows the unequal distribution of assets among Jewish and Christian merchants and that most of the former lived humbly as retail traders. The small wealthy Jewish elite that did not consist of more than three to five families lagged behind the more than fifteen Christian merchants with comparable assets.

By the end of the Seven Years' War in 1763 only members of the Schlesinger family are found to have a fortune of more than 10,000 thaler. Marcus Moses and his brother Pincus Moses Schlesinger were each assessed at 13,000 thaler, and the latter's oldest son Levin Pincus Schlesinger in company with Simon Symons from Amsterdam was assessed at 10,000 thaler. Two more merchants, Juda Herz Beer and Levin Buko, had comparable assets of close to or over 10,000 thaler. Although only one Christian trading firm had a fortune over 20,000 thaler, eleven Christian firms fell into the category of more than 10,000 thaler in assets, while the large majority reached assets over 1,000 thaler in 1765. Among Jewish merchants, the majority fell into the lowest group, with assets of less than 1,000 thaler.

The commercial activities of the members of the Schlesinger family stretched from London and Amsterdam in the west to Hamburg, Leipzig, Danzig, Königsberg, and Warsaw in the east. Settling family members in various important commercial cities and nodes for financial activities was crucial. The connections of the Schlesinger family exemplify the far-reaching networks of central European Jewish merchants and their role as middlemen between western and eastern Europe. To build, maintain, and extend these networks, members of the Schlesinger family employed three central strategies to connect individual family members to a number of commercial centers: first, the establishment of close familial ties by sending family members to important commercial cities and via strategic marital unions; second, traveling to fairs constituted a valuable means for establishing and maintaining contact; third, although Jewish merchants were constantly in contact and did business with Christian merchants, the establishment and maintenance of close ties to non-Jewish merchants was crucial in particular in locations where Jews were legally restricted in terms of settlement and trade. Each of those strategies was employed at different cities, though often we also find a combination of these measures.

Family Ties

The placement of family members in important commercial hubs was intended to broaden existing business connections or establish new ones. As was already stated, Hamburg played a central role as intermediary between Amsterdam and Prussia.[23] Though Hamburg is better known for its community of Portuguese Jewish merchants, Ashkenazic merchants, brokers and bankers constituted a crucial link to Amsterdam for Jewish merchants in Prussia. The first Ashkenazic families settled permanently in Hamburg around the 1620s, although they initially lived legally under Danish protection in Altona, which is today part of Hamburg. The three Jewish communities of Altona, Hamburg, and Wandsbek eventually constituted a common federation in 1671 under the leadership of the Altona rabbinate. Hamburg's Ashkenazic Jews did not differ in terms of occupational structure from

Jews in other German cities; most of them were involved in commerce and finance in one way or another.[24]

For the Schlesingers, Hamburg constituted an important link in their commercial activities. The most important connection to Hamburg was Jacob Moses Schlesinger, a brother of Pincus Moses and Marcus Moses Schlesinger in Frankfurt an der Oder. He owned his own trading firm, was involved in the trade with bills of exchange, and was among the elders of the Jewish community in Hamburg from the 1760s on.[25] He maintained close ties to his two brothers and must have entered a formal business partnership with Marcus Moses Schlesinger because the latter's will could only be opened and his assets divided after his death in 1784 when his brother Jacob Moses Schlesinger arrived from Hamburg. Marcus Moses Schlesinger's two older sons, Leib and Feibisch, entered into a partnership with their uncle Jacob Moses Schlesinger, an arrangement to which Marcus Moses Schlesinger's widow agreed and related according to the protocol in the communal *pinkas* (record book) that she trusted her brother-in-law and her sons to support her adequately. After Jacob Moses Schlesinger's own death, his firm continued under the name J. Schlesinger Sohn & Comp.[26] Together with the marriage into the Symons family of Amsterdam, this familial connection to Hamburg allowed the Schlesingers to successfully trade in bills of exchange and to boost their credit in Amsterdam.

Economic considerations, however, were not the only motivation in choosing a partner for marriage. In particular, legal restrictions on Jewish communities in Prussia that targeted strict limitation of Jewish population growth, had to be considered by the parents of the potential grooms and brides. Although Pincus Moses and his brother Marcus Moses Schlesinger were privileged protected Jews and members of the second highest class of Jewish inhabitants, they were allowed to pass their status on to only one child each.[27] Thus, both brothers chose matches for their children—and for their sons in particular—not only because of economic consideration but also dictated by the need to secure their children's legal status. Frankfurt an der Oder's municipal records allow us to trace the paths of four of Pincus Moses Schlesinger's sons. His own privilege was passed on to his son, Levin Pincus Schlesinger, when he married Margolia Elias Daniel Nijmegen from Amsterdam. Yet for his siblings, other pathways had to be explored.[28]

The most common solution was to emigrate and secure a match in another city, preferably one that provided novel economic opportunity as well. Both Alexander Pincus and Abraham Pincus Schlesinger moved to Königsberg in the 1760s. There, Isaac Mendel, Pincus Moses Schlesinger's brother-in-law, managed an extensive wholesale trade with Poland and Russia until his death in 1765. The Baltic port city of Königsberg, in the north of the Prussian state, played a key role in the commercial exchange between western and eastern Europe. It was a hub for the exchange of primarily agricultural products from Poland and eastern Europe and salt, wine, and some manufactured products from the west. Only after the mid-seventeenth century did Jewish merchants primarily from the Polish-Lithuanian Commonwealth receive permission to settle in the city, although their numbers remained small for the following century and grew to about 300 Jews by the mid-eighteenth century. According to Prussian officials, Jewish merchants from Poland actively tried to build business ties with Jewish inhabitants of Königsberg. Nevertheless, the trade between Polish and Prussian Jews was limited, since Jews in Königsberg were legally restricted to trade in specific goods only.[29]

Alexander Pincus Schlesinger received his residence privilege by marrying the daughter of Abraham Seeligmann, a local privileged Jew and a partner in one of the most important Jewish firms in the city. Thus, Schlesinger was part of a generally large wave of immigration of Jewish men to Königsberg. In the second half of the eighteenth century nearly every second groom came from outside the city, mostly from Brandenburg but also from Silesia, Poland, and the settlements outside of Danzig, as well as from Russia after the first partition of Poland in 1772.[30] This considerable influx of Jewish grooms underlines the high degree of mobility among Jewish families. The geographic distribution of grooms also points to the commercial importance of Königsberg, and suggests a close relationship between marriage patterns and commercial activities.

Pincus Moses Schlesinger had originally organized his trade in Königsberg primarily via his wife Baile's relatives. In 1736, her father Mendel Levin received a concession from the Prussian king for wholesale trade in foreign woolen goods to Poland. A list of goods kept in his storage shows that he traded with various textiles from Saxony, Hamburg, the Netherlands, and England. In return, he was obliged to sell domestic Prussian woolen fabrics to Poland as well, which he did until his death in 1765.[31] Including the sale of Prussian manufactured goods as a condition for privileges was a common strategy employed by the Prussian government, and usually not an attractive business; the goods were judged by many merchants to be overpriced for their quality. Schlesinger regularly traveled to the Johannis fair in Königsberg and brought back mostly woolen and linen goods. The exact nature of the business partnership between Schlesinger and his father-in-law, however, remains unclear. In official letters, Schlesinger tried to diminish his relative's role in the trade to that of a mere assistant whom he provided with credit to trade with Poland in Schlesinger's name. In 1765, Mendel Levin had outstanding payments of 160,000–190,000 thaler, an amount suggesting a high trade volume. Schlesinger disagreed wholeheartedly when authorities suggested he should continue his trade through other Jewish and Christian merchants in the city instead of his son after the death of Mendel Levin. Schlesinger argued that it would be very problematic to trust outsiders with such far-flung business. Already before Mendel Levin's death, Schlesinger had been able to win the support of the magistrate of Frankfurt an der

Oder regarding his son's settlement in Königsberg; the magistrate described the success of Schlesinger's business in bright terms: "his wholesale trade, which he has been undertaking for many years with Russia, Poland and other foreign nations, still exists with desirable success; it is very important and his assets are considerable."[32]

Königsberg proved to be an important node in the commercial undertakings of the Schlesinger family, where they tried to position family members to ensure the smooth continuation of their trade. The marriage of Alexander Pincus Schlesinger also reflects the strict Prussian regulations regarding the marriage of young Jewish men and women. These restrictions led parents to search intensely for options to find marriage partners with valid privileges of residency.

Nevertheless, Pincus Moses Schlesinger did not succeed in marrying off all of his sons successfully at the appropriate age. For many the restriction on marriage meant not only an unmarried existence, but also a life of economic dependence.[33] In the Schlesinger family the youngest of the male siblings, David Pincus, remained in Frankfurt an der Oder; his marriage at forty-three is pregnant with meaning. He remained dependent on his father for many years. Neither the Prussian records nor the translation of his prenuptial contract mention any earlier marriage; he probably had to wait until a suitable opportunity arrived. When Gittel (Güttel), the only child of the privileged protected Jew Isaac Herz Reiss in Frankfurt an der Oder, turned twenty, her parents decided on the marital union with David Pincus. Thus, David Pincus Schlesinger received the privilege of the first child that had been passed on from Reiss to his only daughter, Gittel.[34] For David Pincus Schlesinger it was a prestigious marriage, but a very late one.

Fairs as Commercial Hubs and Meeting Places

The commercial activities of the Schlesinger family were based in Frankfurt an der Oder and centered on the local fair as a place of exchange. Like many non-Jewish merchants, Jewish merchants were highly mobile and traveled regularly to conduct their business. On the European continent the most important point of encounter was the fair. Although fairs took place only at specific times, their function is comparable to that of early modern ports such as Livorno and Trieste, Amsterdam, Riga, Danzig, or Königsberg. Fairs constituted important commercial hubs; they were central for merchant networks by providing possibilities for merchants to meet regularly in person, secure new business partners, introduce family members and apprentices into their business, and collect and exchange information.

For most Jewish merchants, traveling to various fairs was part of their business all year around. In a letter, Simon Symons noted that his father-in-law Pincus Moses Schlesinger was rarely at home. He traveled to the Dominici fair in Danzig, carrying along domestic drapery, and woolen and silk goods. Then he visited the Johannis fair in Königsberg, where he sustained a large repository of goods. He also travelled twice a year to the Leipzig fair. Regular travel to the Leipzig fairs was of great importance; Jews could not establish family ties to Leipzig due to the ban on permanent Jewish settlement.

In the 1740s, Saxon officials developed a growing interest in drawing Jewish merchants in particular from Frankfurt an der Oder and Breslau to Leipzig; ultimately, the efforts yielded only limited success. In 1747, the Saxon Deputation of Commerce in Dresden noticed that most Polish merchants and especially the "useful Jewish merchants" went to Frankfurt an der Oder and Breslau where Jews enjoyed better treatment. This observation led to the abolishment of the poll tax for Polish Jews traveling to the Leipzig fairs in 1747.[35] However, the constant attempts of the central Deputation of Commerce to improve the situation of Jewish merchants regarding travel, taxes, freedom during the fairs, and the occurrence of Jewish holidays during fairs were fiercely opposed by the local Leipzig government and its merchant community.[36]

Despite such obstacles, Pincus Moses Schlesinger and later his son, Levin Pincus Schlesinger, visited the Leipzig fair regularly. The primary commodities were textiles and manufactured goods that were sold in the main to Jewish merchants from Poland and Russia in exchange for raw goods, primarily furs. In addition, the Schlesingers purchased various textile products from Saxony and other places. A detailed list of products purchased by Pincus Moses Schlesinger between 1767 and 1770 includes woolen goods, Turkish yarn, Polish cloth, draperies, furs, and hare hides.[37]

Although there are some detailed records of sold and bought goods, they are too few to estimate the actual trade volume of these Jewish merchants. Efforts to improve the situation of Jewish merchants in Leipzig included new regulations that allowed every Jew who purchased goods worth at least 1,000 thaler to receive a passport of free trade (*Freypass*) and thereby be exempt, together with his wife and up to two servants, from paying the poll tax.[38] Thus, most Jewish merchants sought to register purchased goods worth 1,000 thaler even if their real amount of purchases was lower. The export lists from 1772 to 1775 show that in eight consecutive fairs four members of the Schlesinger family (the brothers Jacob Moses, Marcus Moses, and Pincus Moses, and the latter's son, Levin Pincus) registered goods worth exactly 1,000 thaler as did many other Jews; the roster shows only two insignificant exceptions. This uniformity points to the possibility that these sums intended to satisfy fair regulations and may not reflect actual trade volume. In addition, it is surprising that the three Schlesingers officially did not bring goods to sell in Leipzig. Only their brother Jacob Moses Schlesinger of Hamburg brought large quantities of goods to the fair, primarily linen and cotton cloth valued at up to 10,000 thaler.[39]

With the economic decline of the Schlesinger family in the 1780s, the family members also disappear as visitors of the Leipzig fairs. Although the importance of the fair for the trade with eastern Europe increased in the early nineteenth century, only Levin Marcus Schlesinger continued traveling there regularly until at least 1809.[40] Though Jewish merchants from Frankfurt an der Oder faced an economic downturn in the last quarter of the eighteenth century, it is difficult to speak of a general decline. The fairs in Leipzig blossomed and when the settlement of Jews became legal in the city an increasing number of Jewish merchants flocked to Leipzig.

Business Relations with Non-Jews

Although we have witnessed close-knit connections between most members of the Schlesinger family, related families and other Jewish merchants, their commercial networks were by no means restricted to Jewish merchants. Christians were their clients, often regular, sometimes temporary business partners, and credit grantors. It was particularly in places where Jewish settlement was restricted that non-Jewish merchants became regular and close business partners, even if the relationships usually were not formalized.

This was the case, in Danzig, for example, another important Baltic port city. Jewish merchants were greatly restricted in business, since the city did not allow Jews to settle within the city boundaries prior to the end of the eighteenth century. Nevertheless, Jews assumed a crucial role in the city's commerce. Most Jews who settled in the suburbs of the city (especially Langgarten and Alt-Schottland) hailed from Poland and acted as brokers for Jewish merchants from the west arriving by sea, in particular from Prussian cities, Hamburg, and Amsterdam. Those who traded goods along the Vistula River often acted as agents for Polish noblemen.[41] As Moshe Rosman has shown, Jewish merchants regularly rented space on the river boats of Polish nobles to transport raw products, including linen, flax, canvas, hemp, skins, and wood to Danzig and cloth and other manufactured goods back to the towns and villages of Poland. They "were the link between the big import and export concerns on the one hand and the small-scale consumers and suppliers on the other."[42] Many Jewish brokers, who settled outside Danzig proper, regularly appear in the proceedings of the market court (*Wettgericht*), which oversaw the dealings of brokers and non-burghers, but they were hardly involved in the larger transactions of goods and money passing through the Danzig port to western Europe.

To participate in and profit from the trade in Danzig, Jewish merchants could not rely exclusively on other Jews as business partners due to the aforementioned legal restrictions. Thus they integrated non-Jewish merchants in their networks as well. A business connection of the Schlesinger family in the 1750s and early 1760s went from Königsberg to Danzig via Isaac Mendel, the brother of Pincus

Moses Schlesinger's wife Baile. Isaac Mendel did business with Andreas Schopenhauer in Danzig, a reputable Christian merchant in the city. Schopenhauer had sent goods to Pincus Moses Schlesinger via Isaac Mendel, who had also shipped other goods to Danzig for Schlesinger.[43] City court records also show that Pincus Moses Schlesinger regularly traveled to Danzig to do business from the mid-1750s to the mid-1770s, where he visited the Dominican fair, which featured domestic fabric, woolen, and silk goods.

His sons, Levin Pincus and Alexander Pincus, and his brother Marcus Moses Schlesinger also appear now and again in the court records. For court cases that occurred regularly between trading partners, especially concerning bills of exchange, the various family members were required to provide authorized representatives in the city to be able to appear in court. These representatives were exclusively Christian merchants and burghers of Danzig. Given the circumstances, one can argue that Jewish merchants integrated Christian traders more closely into their networks when Jews were unable to fulfill certain functions. While members of the Schlesinger family did trade with different Christian merchants in Danzig, there was at least one, Andreas Schopenhauer, who constituted a regular trading partner. He also represented, and vouched for, Pincus Moses Schlesinger (1760, 1773) and Levin Pincus Schlesinger (1764) at the local court.[44]

The connections of the Schlesinger family to Danzig point to the wide range of trading activities of the Schlesingers, including raw goods and semi-finished products. Court documents reveal that Pincus Moses Schlesinger supplied cloth, leather, fur, and yarn, and purchased wood (spruce) and amber. In addition, he was involved in the trade of bills of exchange and currency, including some deals that tried to circumvent the payment of certain taxes with the assistance of Christian merchants. In 1760, Heinrich Soermann, a Christian merchant, received a few boxes of coins from Pincus Moses Schlesinger that were allegedly on transit to Lübeck. They were seized in Danzig, when authorities suspected that Schlesinger had exchanged them during the previous fair and sought to export them without permission. However, no proof for this charge could be found; the coins were then transferred to Lübeck. It is interesting, to note that in 1770, the same Heinrich Soermann was accused of accepting a shipment of linen cloth as his own even though it belonged to a Jewish merchant who was allowed to trade in Danzig only during fairs. Thus, he declared incorrectly and also assisted a Jewish merchant in using the port illegally. His fine: one-quarter of the shipment's value.[45] We learn a few critical points from these two episodes: the integration of non-Jews into Jewish trading networks; the central position of Danzig in the transnational trade between Amsterdam in the west and Poland and Russia in the east; and the involvement of Jewish merchants from Prussia in this trade.

The Jewish Community of Frankfurt an der Oder

All wealthy mercantile families examined in this book were also involved to some degree in leadership roles in their respective Jewish community. Many scholars have emphasized the important role that wealthy merchants played in the lay leadership of Jewish communities in the early modern period. In Poland-Lithuania this role was increasingly taken by wealthy leaseholders.[46] One of the still-existing *pinkassim*, which comprises more than 300 pages, of the Jewish community in Frankfurt an der Oder includes records of election procedures and results as well as myriad other communal and especially financial issues. It allows us to use the case of the Schlesinger family to gain greater insight into the role they played in the community's lay leadership. Moreover, the *pinkas* provides insights into the extent of financial pressure the community was dealing with trying to shoulder the weight of increasing taxes and fees imposed by the Prussian government throughout the second half of the eighteenth century.[47]

Those Jewish merchants with the largest assets were also the leaders within the Jewish community. In Frankfurt's community major decisions were made by a quorum of eighteen (and sometimes thirty-two) men. This quorum comprised members of different social groups within the community, though the majority hailed from the economic elite. The seven electors responsible for election of the communal leadership (*kahal*) included three wealthy men (*'elionim*), two men of average means (*benonim*), and two of the less wealthy (*paḥot 'erekh*). This structure ensured that the power rested within the upper classes of the Jewish community, despite the fact that the large majority of community members fell into the last category (see table 2.2). Though numbers changed slightly over the years, around mere ten percent of the communal taxpayers owned assets above 2,000 thaler.[48] Only they and those falling into the income group of 1,000 to 1,900 thaler took up the most important elected offices: three elders (*parnasim*), two assistants (*tovim*), two general wardens (*gaba'im*), two or three charity wardens (*gaba'e tsedakah*), a synagogue warden (*gaba'i beit haknesset*), and an accountant (*ro'eh ḥeshbon*).[49] These leadership functions were filled by members of the wealthiest families, who often held them continuously, some even for more than twenty years. Among them were the Schlesingers, and the families of Levin Buko and Juda Herz Beer.

The fiscal exploitation of Prussian Jewry reached its peak during the period from the end of the Seven Years' War in 1763 to the death of Frederick the Great in 1786. The infamous 1769 regulation that forced Prussian Jews to purchase porcelain from the Berlin manufactory and sell it abroad in order to attain a variety of concessions is the best-known example of a special charges policy that increasingly strained the Prussian Jewish communities and its members.[50] The regular protection money (*Schutzgeld*), for which Prussian Jews were jointly liable, amounted

Table 2.2. Taxpayers of the Jewish community of Frankfurt an der Oder by personal assets, 1774–1812.

Assets year	≥2,000 thaler	1,000–1,900 thaler	500–900 thaler	100–400 thaler	Total number of taxpayers
1774	10	7	25	[36]	[78]
1777	8 (7.7%)	12 (11.5%)	20 (19.2%)	64 (61.5%)	104 (100%)
1780	8 (8.2%)	9 (9.3%)	17 (17.5%)	63 (64.9%)	97 (100%)
1783	8 (8 %)	12 (12 %)	9 (9 %)	71 (71 %)	100 (100%)
1786	6	19	10	[50]	[85]
1789	6	17	10	[14]	[47]
1795	7 (7.6%)	18 (19.6%)	18 (19.6%)	49 (53.2%)	92 (100%)
1798	11 (11.7%)	13 (13.8%)	17 (18.1%)	53 (56.4%)	94 (100%)
1802	12 (12.5%)	15 (15.6%)	20 (20.8%)	49 (51.1%)	96 (100%)
1809	6 (9.7%)	16 (25.8%)	10 (16.1%)	30 (48.4%)	62 (100%)
1812	4 (4.5%)	13 (14.8%)	18 (20.5%)	53 (60.2%)	88 (100%)

Source: Listen der Schatzungen und Schutzgelder, 1774–1819, D/Fr 1, 30, CAHJP.

Note: The number of taxpayers in each group is given in absolute numbers and percent of taxpayers. In some years the second page of the assessment and thus a varying number of taxpayers from the group with assets between 100 and 400 thaler is missing, indicated with square brackets. Therefore, no percentages are given for these years. The sharp decline of numbers in 1809 and 1812 might be a result of the Napoleonic Wars.

to an annual sum that ranged from 10,000 to 25,000 thaler. Moreover, Prussian Jews and their communities had to pay numerous additional fees to travel, purchase property and on many other occasions. Frederick the Great introduced two more fiscal measures; the export of Prussian manufactured goods for the transfer of one's settlement privilege to a second child (1763/65), and three years later, the collective operation of a stocking manufactory in Templin (Brandenburg) for the same privilege. The impact of these dues on the Prussian Jewish communities was enormous; the record book of the Frankfurt community provides ample evidence, with repeat entries on taking out loans and divvying up fees among community members.[51]

Thus, one of the major tasks of the communal leadership was to raise the financial means to meet all of these obligations, mostly by taking out loans. The *kahal* first borrowed from wealthy community members, but soon credit was arranged through the merchants' commercial networks. Marcus Moses Schlesinger succeeded in acquiring a communal loan from his brother and business partner, the Hamburg merchant Jacob Moses Schlesinger. In 1767, the community in Frankfurt an der Oder received a substantial loan of 2,200 thaler (5,000 mark banco). This short-term loan was originally issued for four years. In 1769, the community repaid

Jacob Moses Schlesinger 2,700 mark banco, and issued a new bill of exchange for the remaining 2,300 mark banco. That was renewed in 1771. Only in 1775 did the community repay this bill of exchange completely after it borrowed from a non-Jewish lender. In addition to the loan from Jacob Moses Schlesinger, the community received another large loan of 3,200 mark banco from the Hamburg Jewish merchant Herz Rintel, which was also administered through Marcus Moses Schlesinger.[52] These arrangements point to the importance of commercial and familial networks that were put into use beyond the realm of just commerce. Moreover, the fact that the Jewish community began to take out loans from Christians from the 1770s on might reflect the increasing financial difficulties of the Jewish mercantile elite of the town.

Flirtation with Enlightenment Thought

Throughout the early modern period and the eighteenth century in particular, Jewish scholars across Europe had sought to educate themselves more broadly and to "integrate and reconcile this knowledge within the framework of Jewish tradition."[53] During the last two decades of the eighteenth century, the adaptation of ideas of the enlightenment and especially the strife to acquire general knowledge turned into an ideological agenda and gave birth to a specific Jewish enlightenment, the Haskalah. Beginning in the 1780s most proponents of the Haskalah lived in Prussia and especially in Berlin, where unlike elsewhere in western Europe, Jewish intellectuals felt a strong sense of intellectual inferiority and exclusion from general society. Moreover, the economic position of Jews and the economic structure of eighteenth-century Jewish society became a central issue for the *maskilim*, the Jewish enlighteners, of the Berlin Haskalah, who described Jewish economic life as dysfunctional and argued for an occupational restructuring.[54] Thus, one may ask which influence that Berlin Haskalah exerted on the Jewish mercantile elite in a town like Frankfurt an der Oder, in close proximity to Berlin.

Historians of Jews in Prussia have long linked enlightenment thought with economic success, especially when examining the centers of the Haskalah in Prussia, Berlin, Breslau, and Königsberg and the rise of their respective new economic elites. Though it is true that members of the mercantile elite were often involved in intellectual debates and that wealthy merchants and bankers increasingly patronized *maskilim* and their publications, the case of Frankfurt an der Oder indicates that the development in these three cities was rather exceptional.[55] Though Frankfurt an der Oder may seem provincial in comparison, it was not untouched by early ideas and proponents of Jewish enlightenment. Saul Levin Berlin (1740–1794) was a representative of the Jewish intellectual elite when he penned *Ktav yosher* in the 1780s, a subversive Hebrew text in support of Naphtali Herz Wessely's *Divre shalom ve'emet* (1782), which first circulated anonymously as a manuscript. At the same time, he held the rabbinical post in Frankfurt an der Oder.[56] Thus, by the 1780s for sure, ideas of the Haskalah had entered the communal elite as well. One can show, however, that whereas members of the local Jewish mercantile elite were interested in and supportive of the early proponents of the Haskalah, they did not follow the movement wholeheartedly in its more radical forms. Their close ties to eastern Europe also exerted an important influence on their attitude toward the Haskalah. The ideas of east European *maskilim* were closer to their hearts than those of the Berlin Haskalah. Most communal rabbis of the late eighteenth and early nineteenth centuries continued to arrive from eastern Europe.

The male members of the Schlesinger family were not only part of the mercantile elite and the communal leadership; they were also involved in the intellectual life of the local Jewish community and beyond. One can discern from archival documentation that religious studies were highly regarded in the family. At least, it is apparent that the older generation of Marcus Moses Schlesinger combined ideals of traditional Jewish learning and of wealth. He certainly belonged to the learned elite of his community as he became involved in the conflict between printers in Sulzbach and the Amsterdam printers Proops over the printing of the Sulzbach edition of the Talmud.[57] He also served occasionally as *mohel*, performing circumcisions, of the Jewish community.[58] After Marcus Moses Schlesinger's death in 1784, his sons Herz Marcus and Levin Marcus Schlesinger published a small book entitled *Zikaron besefer* in 1796. It contained Talmudic commentary compiled from handwritten notes left by their father, with an introduction they authored. His sons carried on the legacy of their father, most visibly his oldest son Herz Marcus Schlesinger.

The commercial connections of the Schlesinger family were also put to use for *yeshivah* studies. Following a traditional path of Jewish education, Herz Marcus Schlesinger went to Altona in 1764 to study in one of the local *yeshivot*, probably under the tutelage of his uncle, Jacob Moses Schlesinger. Afterward he returned to his hometown and enrolled at the university as a medical student in 1776. In 1780, his cousin, Isaac Jacob Schlesinger of Hamburg, also matriculated at the University of Frankfurt an der Oder to receive his doctorate in medicine, after studying medicine in Padua.[59]

Herz Marcus Schlesinger moved to Warsaw in 1779 to practice medicine. This is all the more noteworthy because his cousin Levin Pincus Schlesinger had done extensive business in Warsaw and Judyta (Judith) Jakubowiczowa, the daughter of Levin Buko, had just moved from Frankfurt an der Oder to the Polish capital. All three most likely knew each other well from their hometown.[60] Four years later, Herz Marcus Schlesinger returned to Frankfurt an der Oder and then was appointed physician of the Jewish community, which was in dire need of a physician for the *hekdesh*, the traditional Jewish hospice, and for the poor; he received a meager salary of 100 thaler per year. Surely, he also attended well-to-do patients and was active in commerce, like the rest of his family.[61]

A look at some of the works various members of the Schlesinger family subscribed to allows for an additional glimpse into their religious attitudes and paints a picture of traditional learning in Hebrew and German that was open to Haskalah ideas of Moses Mendelssohn's generation. Subscriptions included Hebrew works by *maskilic* authors as well as more traditional rabbinic works. Herz Marcus Schlesinger subscribed to the 1791 Berlin edition of Psalms with Moses Mendelssohn's German translation and commentary by Joel Brill; his brother Moses Marcus Schlesinger subscribed to the Pentateuch edition (*Ḥumesh megilot 'im tirgum ashkenazi vebi'ur*), edited by Aaron Wolfson and Joel Brill (Berlin 1789). This is not surprising when one considers that Mendelssohn's bible translation received the approbation of Isaak Joseph Teomim, rabbi of the Frankfurt community.[62] All of these books were part of Moses Mendelssohn's publication efforts and those of his students who continued to publish in Hebrew. Moreover, Herz Marcus, his brother, Levin Marcus, and their cousins, Abraham Pincus and Levin Pincus Schlesinger, subscribed to the maskil Isaac Satanow's 1798 edition of *Sefer hagedarim* (Book of Definitions), a lexicon of philosophical and scientific terms by a fourteenth-century author that constituted an effort to reprint Jewish books from the medieval and Renaissance periods.[63] The fifth subscriber in Frankfurt an der Oder was Elias Buko, a wealthy merchant and the son of Levin Buko.

In the debate concerning early burial in Judaism, which arose in the final quarter of the eighteenth century, physician Herz Marcus Schlesinger sided with the more moderate proponents of the Haskalah.[64] Though he argued against early burial in his 1797 Hebrew work *She'elat ḥakham* like Moses Mendelssohn had twenty-five years earlier, he indirectly criticized the famous German pamphlet *Concerning the Early Burial among the Jews*, published by the Berlin Jewish physician and maskil Marcus Herz in 1788 that deemed rabbinical arguments irrelevant to the question. Knowledgeable in German, Schlesinger emphasized the importance to publish in Hebrew on the matter and acquired a proper approval, a *haskamah,* by communal rabbi Judah Leib Margolioth, a native of Galicia and a forerunner of the Haskalah in eastern Europe. In addition, Margolioth volunteered his own detailed rejection of early burial to Schlesinger's book.[65]

The Schlesinger family serves as an example of successful merchants who were deeply involved in communal leadership and in the intellectual life of their community. They were closely tied to the rabbinic culture of Poland and Galicia, the home environs of the community's rabbis. Herz Marcus Schlesinger was intensely involved in rabbinical and medical debates due to his profession, but subscriptions among his relatives to similar Hebrew works point to their common attitudes. The members of the Schlesinger family in Frankfurt an der Oder can be described as conservative followers of the Haskalah, who shared Moses Mendelssohn's idea of a Hebrew enlightenment that rationalized Jewish religion without abandoning Hebrew language and Jewish law.[66] One needs to add, however, that as far as evidence allows, we do not find the merchants in the family interested or involved in the debates about the economic position and occupational patterns of the Jewish population. It seems that when these questions entered the debate with the later and partly more radical *maskilim*, the mercantile elite of Frankfurt an der Oder had first, lost interest in these currents of the Haskalah, and was struggling with its own economic position.

The Turn of Fortunes

In the early modern commercial world certain misfortunes were commonplace: the disruption of network ties, termination of business partnerships, a temporary lack of liquidity, and bankruptcy. Some of these disruptions can be ascribed to conflicts between business partners, lost merchandise, or outstanding debt, whereas others were triggered by broader economic policies and economic and political developments.[67] Smaller disruptions not necessarily caused the failure or shift of larger commercial networks, though it could have long-term consequences for individual merchants. As was true in many locations, Jewish merchants in Frankfurt an der Oder experienced both commercial disruptions and a turn of fortune due to personal economic decisions and the influence of larger economic and political developments.

In Frankfurt an der Oder, this development was closely linked to the economic policy of the Prussian state. Following the Thirty Years' War, Brandenburg-Prussia had adopted a new economic policy, which focused on population growth via immigration. It also emphasized the advancement of mining, agriculture, and manufactory production. Whereas the expansion of foreign trade was not at the center of Prussia's economic policy, the regulation of tariffs that favored the import of raw material and the export of manufactured goods affected the kind of goods Jewish merchants traded. This economic policy of import restrictions and high customs continued under Frederick II in the second half of the eighteenth century. Over time, these restrictive measures became one of the reasons for the decline of the fair in Frankfurt an der Oder, which could not compete in international trade due to these restrictions and financial burdens.[68] Despite the influence and reception of new ideas of a free market economy as propagated in Adam Smith's *The Wealth of Nations*, protective practices continued in Prussia under Frederick William II and until the breakdown of the Holy Roman Empire in 1806 and the Prussian reforms of 1812. These restrictive measures applied especially to commerce.[69]

This policy led to a decline in number of visitors and goods traded at the fairs in Frankfurt an der Oder, which was aggravated by geographical shifts after the second and third partition of Poland in 1793 and 1795. After a brief period of upswing following the Seven Years' War, the fairs drew fewer and fewer foreigners; after 1800, they ceased to attract foreign trade altogether.[70] It is not surprising then that the property assessments of the Jewish community show a considerable decline in members' assets toward the end of the eighteenth century. The steady decline among the wealthiest members of the community after 1783 (see table 2.3) was also due to the fact that many merchants or their children left the city. Eventually, not a single one of the twelve wealthiest firms in Frankfurt an der Oder was owned by a Jewish merchant, and most of the Jewish merchants were solely active in the retail trade by 1812.[71]

The economic development of the Schlesinger family fits well into this pattern of economic decline within the last decades of the eighteenth century. Communal documentation from the mid-1770s shows that Pincus Moses and his son Levin Pincus Schlesinger, who both profited from the Seven Years' War, could not retain their assets over time. Eventually, it was only Pincus Moses's brother, Marcus Moses Schlesinger, and toward the end of the century, Juda Herz Beer, who continuously maintained assets totaling around or more than 10,000 thaler. In retrospect, however, Pincus Moses Schlesinger described the time of the Seven Years' War as disastrous to his business. In a 1787 letter to the Prussian ruler he complained:

> As it is known, I once was one of the richest subjects in the lands of Your Royal Majesty, and that the many bankruptcies in Holland, Hamburg etc. in 1763, in which I lost more than 180,000 thaler, and the Seven Years' War, in which I lost so much that it makes more than 400,000 thaler altogether, ruined me completely; but I also was taken hostage during the Russian invasion of the city of Frankfurt and I provided great and important service to the public including my own losses during the events of the Seven Years' War . . . .[72]

Though his riches as well as his losses may be purposely exaggerated in this letter to persuade the Prussian officials to support his case against his former business partner and relative Simon Symons, his complaints did not lack substance. The letter points to the bankruptcies in Amsterdam and Hamburg in 1763 that did have considerable impact on Prussian commerce. In 1759, a senator and a Christian merchant of the city were indeed taken hostage by Russian troops alongside two elders of the Jewish community, Pincus Moses Schlesinger and Juda Herz Beer. The four returned to Frankfurt only after nearly a year of being imprisoned in the Russian camp and payment of a rather large sum collected from the burghers and the city's Jewish community.[73]

As we have seen, Pincus Moses Schlesinger remained active in business over at least two more decades after the end of the Seven Years' War. When he passed away in 1795, however, his sons refused to accept his inheritance, which suggests that it comprised only debts.[74] It is hard to determine what precipitated Pincus Moses Schlesinger's downfall, but one can assume that it was a combination of different factors, including the general decline of the Frankfurt fair; trade restrictions brought about by the prohibitive trade policy of the Prussian state; involvement in large and complicated credit transactions based on bills of exchange; and personal failure.

Other members of the family fared only slightly better (see table 2.3). The property assessment of the Jewish community from 1809 still lists the brothers Levin Marcus and Herz Marcus and their cousins Levin Pincus and David Pincus Schlesinger, but all of them were assessed with a property totaling between 500 and 1,500 thaler, less than what well-to-do Christian merchants owned.[75] Levin Pincus Schlesinger had returned to Frankfurt an der Oder after his business venture with Simon Symons failed, but it is difficult to judge the success of his future business. In 1798, he turned to the authorities and sought permission to acquire a house in Frankfurt an der Oder. Ownership of a house was the condition stipulated in his father-in-law's will to transfer the inheritance of his wife, Margolia Elias Daniel Nijmegen, from Amsterdam to Frankfurt an der Oder. In this correspondence Levin Pincus Schlesinger even claimed that he was not involved in any business and lived exclusively from the interest of his wife's inheritance.[76]

His cousin Levin Marcus Schlesinger had inherited his father's business after 1784 and in accordance with his father's advice, had joined a shared company with his brother Philip Marcus and his uncle Jacob Moses Schlesinger, who both lived in Hamburg. Though Levin Marcus Schlesinger stayed in business at least until 1800 and was active at the Leipzig fair in company with his uncle, the business seems to have slowly declined. Between 1802 and 1809 the Jewish community's assessment of his assets reflects a drop from 7,000 thaler to 1,400 thaler.[77]

Another sign of the family's economic decline may be found in the choice of marriage partners for some of the grandchildren of the two brothers, Marcus Moses and Pincus Moses Schlesinger. While they had tried to marry their children into families from cities central to European commerce like Amsterdam, Hamburg, and Königsberg, their grandchildren's marital matches point in a different direction. They married partners hailing from small towns in West Prussia (Stargard), East Prussia (Gumbinnen), or Silesia (Glogau); even when their partners belonged to the affluent class of these Jewish communities, they were not comparable with the matches of the preceding generation.[78] These marriages also point to a shift in the geographical orientation of this merchant family. Like others in Frankfurt an der

Oder, their view turned eastward, where they sensed new business activities, though on a smaller scale than their grandfathers expected to find in Amsterdam, Hamburg, or Königsberg. The scope of their business declined, but we may assume that at least some of their descendants entered the small-town bourgeois society of the nineteenth century.

Numbers from the community in Frankfurt an der Oder show that the whole community faced an economic downturn. If we look just at the development of the assets of the wealthiest members of the community, as shown in table 2.3, we find a decline of assets over three to four decades, with the exception of Juda Herz Beer and Elias bar Levin Buko, who increased their assets into the beginning of the nineteenth century. A similar picture evolves from the data of all taxpayers that had assets of at least 1,000 thaler at least once between 1765 and 1812. Table 2.4 shows a similar decline, only very few individuals increased their assets over time, but even then we do not see assets growing to over a few thousand thaler. These numbers, then, do not show the larger and even less wealthy part of the community, where many individuals remained in retail trade or left the city altogether.

New Opportunities

The downturn in the economic success of Jewish merchants in Frankfurt an der Oder was part of a general downturn of the city's fair and the city itself, which spread beyond the economic sphere: in 1811, its prominent university closed and moved to Breslau. Nevertheless, it is difficult to generalize and paint an exclusively dark picture of crisis and decline. A geographic shift of economic opportunity and a move of the centers of economic activity changed this city from a European market place into a provincial town of only regional importance, as other places rose to new power and influence. Over centuries, merchants reacted to such developments with mobility and occupational flexibility. These responses of adapting to changing conditions were the most successful strategies to escape economic downturn. Commercial networks did not necessarily disappear or fall apart; they often shifted when Jewish merchants relocated or entered new fields of business in search of better opportunity.

In the last two decades of the eighteenth century, Berlin, the rising capital of Prussia, increasingly drew Jewish immigrants from smaller cities. Among them were also members of the Schlesinger family, such as Lieberman Marcus Schlesinger, who continued trading in textiles.[79] Similarly and even more successfully, Juda Herz Beer's son, Jacob Herz Beer, moved from Frankfurt an der Oder to Berlin, where he rose to one of the most important Jewish army suppliers and bankers in Berlin at the turn of the eighteenth and the first decades of the nineteenth centuries.[80] This move was commensurate with a general shift from commerce to banking that took hold in Berlin and in many other European cities. In the mid-eighteenth century

Table 2.3. Assets (in thaler) of the members of the mercantile elite of the Jewish community in Frankfurt an der Oder, 1765–1812.

Name/Year	1765	1774	1777	1780	1783	1786	1789	1795	1798	1802	1809	1812
Mori ha-Cohen (d. 1733) (Marcus Moses Schlesinger)	13,000	17,000	17,000	17,000								
Edel, widow (d. 1796)					18,000	1,800	1,800	1,800				
Leib bar M. Cohen (d. 1809) (Levin Marcus Schlesinger)		5,300	5,300	5,300	7,000	9,500	9,500	7,000	7,000	7,000	1,400	
Herz bar M. Cohen (d. 1824) (Herz Marcus Schlesinger)	(10,000?)	2,000	1,300	1,000	1,000	1,400	1,400	1,400	1,400	1,200	1,200	
Marcus Moses (Schlesinger) jun.	2,500											
Pinchas Cohen (d. 1795) (Pincus Moses Schlesinger)	13,000	2,000	1,500	1,000	1,000	1,000	1,000	1,000				
Leib bar P. Cohen (d. 1812) (Levin Pincus Schlesinger)	10,000	1,000	1,000	1,000	1,200	1,700	1,800	1,800	3,000	4,500	1,000	
David bar P. Cohen (d. 1827) (David Pincus Schlesinger)								1,000	1,000	1,000	500	400
Shimeon Segal (d. 1793) (Simon Symons)	[10,000]	1,000	1,000	4,000	2,000		800					
Minke, widow (d. 1811)								2,500	2,500	1,800	1,000	

(continued)

Table 2.3. (continued)

Name/Year	1765	1774	1777	1780	1783	1786	1789	1795	1798	1802	1809	1812
Levin Jacob Elias (Buko) (d. 1776) Feigele, widow	5,000	4,000	2,000	1,000								
Elias bar L. Buko (d. 1805) (son of Levin Jacob Elias)		2,200	2,500	2,800	4,500	5,100	5,600	7,500	8,000	8,000		
Wulff Oppenheim	2,000	2,500	700	700	900	700	700	400	400	400	300	
Abraham bar Wulff Oppenheim, widow of A. Oppenheim		3,000						300	300		300	300
Herz bar Y. Beer (d. 1811)	1,000	4,000	4,400	4,800	8,000	8,000	9,000	9,300	11,000	10,000	10,000	
Herz Halberstadt (d. 1785) Elk[ele], widow		1,700	2,000	2,500	3,800	1,300						
Shaul bar A. bar Sh. (d. 1790?) (Salomon Aron) Bela, widow Shaul bar A.	1,500		3,600	3,600	6,500	6,500	4,000	4,000				
Ahron bar Sh. (d. 1781) (Aron Saul Samuel) Reizl, widow (d. 1797)	5,000	8,500	6,500	7,000		4,300	4,100	3,600				
Sum of annual assets	63,000	54,200	48,800	51,700	53,900	41,300	39,700	41,600	34,600	33,900	15,700	700

Sources: Acta wegen Classificierung hiesiger Handlung treibender Personen, Abt. 1, X, 220, StAF (for the year 1765); Listen der Schatzungen und Schutzgelder, 1774–1819, D/Fr1, 30, CAHJP. For dates of death: Frankfurt/Oder, Friedhofsreg. 1677–1866, G5/896, CAHJP.

Note: The assets of Levin Pincus Schlesinger and Simon Symons in 1765 were shared assets.

Table 2.4. Assets (in thaler) of taxpayers of the Jewish community in Frankfurt an der Oder, including all individuals who held assets of 1,000 thaler or more at least once between 1765 and 1812.

Firm/Name/Year	1765	1774	1777	1780	1783	1786	1789	1795	1798	1802	1809	1812	+/- %
Mori ha-Cohen (d. 1783) (Marcus Moses Schlesinger)	13,000	17,000	17,000	17,000									+30.7
Edel, widow (d. 1796)					18,000	1,800	1,800	1,800					−90
Leib bar M. Cohen (d. 1809) (Levin Marcus Schlesinger)		5,300	5,300	5,300	7,000	9,500	9,500	7,000	7,000	7,000	1,400		−85.3
Herz bar M. Cohen (d. 1824) (Herz Marcus Schlesinger)	(10,000)	2,000	1,300	1,000	1,000	1,400	1,400	1,400	1,400	1,200	1,200		−88
Pinchas Cohen (d. 1795) (Pincus Moses Schlesinger)	13,000	2,000	1,500	1,000	1,000	1,000	1,000	1,000					−92.3
Leib bar P. Cohen (d. 1812) (Levin Pincus Schlesinger)	10,000	1,000	1,000	1,000	1,200	1,700	1,800	1,800	3,000	4,500	1,000		−80
David bar P. Cohen (d. 1827) (David Pincus Schlesinger)								1,000	1,000	1,000	500	400	−60

(continued)

Table 2.4. (continued)

Firm/Name/Year	1765	1774	1777	1780	1783	1786	1789	1795	1798	1802	1809	1812	+/− %
Shimeon Segal (d. 1793) (Simon Symons)	[10,000]	1,000	1,000	4,000	2,000		800						−84
Minke, widow (d. 1811)								2,500	2,500	1,800	1,000		−60
Shaul bar A. b. Sh. (d. 1790) (Salomon Aron) Bela, widow Shaul bar A.	1,500		3,600	3,600	6,500	6,500	4,000	4,000					+333 +/−0
Ahron bar Sh. (d. 1781) (Aron Saul Samuel)	5,000	8,500	6,500	7,000									+40
Reizl, widow (d. 1797)						4,300	4,100	3,600					−16
Herz bar Y. Beer (d. 1811) (Hertz Baer)	1,000	4,000	4,400	4,800	8,000	8,000	9,000	9,300	11,000	10,000	10,000		+900
Levin Jacob Elias (d. 1776)	5,000	4,000											−20
Feigle, widow			2,000	1,000									−50
Elias bar L. Buki (d. 1805) (son of Levin Jacob Elias)		2,200	2,500	2,800	4,500	5,100	5,600	7,500	8,000	8,000			+264
Herz Halberstadt (d.1785)		1,700	2,000	2,500	3,800								+124
Elk[ele], widow						1,300							

Yeshaya Segal Horwitz (d. 1795)	1,200	1,300					1,400	1,400	1,100						−8.3
Mirel, widow (d. 1799)										200					
Chaim bar H. bar Ch. widow Chaim bar H.		1,200	800	1,000	1,000	800				800	800	600			−33
Wulff Oppenheim	2,500	700	700	900	700	700				400	400	300			−85
Abraham bar	3,000									300		300			−90
Wulff Oppenheim widow Abraham Oppenheim	2,000												300		
Izaak Horwitz Segal		800	1,000											(800)	+/−0
Abraham bar Y. Horwitz Segal		900	1,000	1,200	1,500	1,200	1,200			400	400	100			−89
Pinchas bar Y. Horwitz Segal		900	1,000	1,100	1,400	1,200	1,300			600	500	500		400	−55.5
Abraham bar Y. Cohen		800	1,000	1,100	1,100	1,200					500				+50
Ahron bar Y. Cohen		200	1,000	800	800	1,300	1,300			500	500			300	+50
Mordechai Katz		1,200				200	200			300				100	−83
Sharchi, widow		900					400			300					−75

(continued)

Table 2.4. (*continued*)

Firm/Name/Year	1765	1774	1777	1780	1783	1786	1789	1795	1798	1802	1809	1812	+/− %
Yusfa Buki		1,200	700	500	200								−83
Yosef Oiberschlesinger (d. 1783)		1,000	500	300									−70
Israel Frenkel Segal (d. 1782)		1,000	600	400									−60
Seeligmann Coblentz; Taube, widow (d. 1798)	1,500	500	500		300								−80
Isar Pollack						300							
Zanwill bar L.			800	800	1,800	1,800	1,800	1,800	2,500	2,800			+55
Tevli bar N. widow R. Tevli					1,200	800							+/−0
Natan bar Tevli bar N.					1,000	1,100	1,100	1,100	1,800	2,100			+110
Isar ben R. Lipman widow Isar bar L.											3,500	1,500 2,000	−42.9
Yosef bar A.					1,000	1,100	1,100	1,100	1,100	800	400	400	−27
Yakov Prostiz					5,000	1,000	5,200	4,500	6,000	1,000	600	600	+/−0
Yoel ben R. Sh.						1,200	1,100	800	800		500	400	−90
Isar bar M.		(300)	300	300	200	1,100		100					−66.7
						1,000							−91

Name										%
Leib Sabatki (d. 1796)				1,000			100			−90
Elias Cohen					500	400	800	1,000	300	−72.7
widow R. E. Cohen									200	
Meir (Oiber) Schlesinger				800	1,100	1,500	3,000	4,000	4,000	+400
David Herfurt				1,000	1,000	300	100			−90
Meir Eibshitz					1,000	1,000	1,200	2,000		+100
Shmuel Druker						1,200	1,000	1,000	1,100	−8.3
Leizer Lichtenstat							6,500	3,500	1,100	−46.2
Leib bar Avrli							2,000		300	−85
Tovim bar M. Prag							1,700	1,700	1,800	+5.9
Kalman bar M. Druker	5,000			300			1,200	1,200	1,800	−76
									1,200	
Izaak Shneitich		100		400	500	800	1,000		1,200	+100
									800	
Abraham bar L.			200				1,000	1,000		+/−0
Ziskind Segal							1,000	500		−50
Leib bar Benish Cohen							1,000	400		−60
Yakov bar A.							1,000	2,000	2,700	+170
Zelig bar L. Stargard								2,000		

(continued)

Table 2.4. (continued)

Firm/Name/Year	1765	1774	1777	1780	1783	1786	1789	1795	1798	1802	1809	1812	+/- %
Elias bar L. Stargard										2,000	1,800		-10
Yoel bar A. Buki							600	600	500	2,000			+233
widow Yoel bar A. Buki											500		
Leib Drezen										1,000	1,000		+/-0
Meir Drezen											1,000		
Moshe Frenkel										1,000	500	500	-50
Moshe bar M. Katz											1,000	500	-50
Izaak Sofer											1,000		
Hirsch bar K.											1,000	1,000	+/-0
Falk Landesberg											1,000	600	-40
Yakov bar M. Katz												1,000	
Mori bar Sh.												2,000	

Sources: Acta wegen Classificierung hiesiger Handlung treibender Personen, Abt. 1, X, 220, StAF (for the year 1765); Listen der Schatzungen und Schutzgelder, 1774–1819, D/Fr1, 30, CAHJP. For dates of death: Frankfurt/Oder, Friedhofsreg. 1677–1866, G5/896, CAHJP.

Note: The last column provides the percentage by which the assets of a taxpayer grew or declined between the years of the first and last available assessment.

the majority of bankers in Berlin were Christians; most members of the Jewish economic elite were involved in commerce. In 1814, however, Berlin counted 19 Jewish and only seven Christian banking houses. Concurrently, a new Jewish economic elite emerged in Berlin. Those who were successful before and during the Seven Years' War were replaced primarily by a new and less socially homogeneous elite between 1786 and 1812. Most of these new families made their fortunes from army supplying, brokerage, and mortgages. As such, Berlin also fits the general shift of merchants into army supplying and eventual banking. Members of the Jewish mercantile elite were much wealthier than those in Frankfurt an der Oder; many were assessed with owning fortunes numbering somewhere between 50,000 and 250,000 thaler.[81]

Concurrently, the combination of Saxon and Prussian economic politics contributed to the decline of the fairs in Breslau and Frankfurt an der Oder and the rise of Leipzig.[82] In Leipzig there was an increase in attempts to draw merchants, and especially Jewish merchants, from Poland. Jewish merchants received more passes that allowed them to enter Leipzig, a city that did not have a Jewish community. Altogether, the turnover of the three fairs soon numbered an annual total of 8,000,000–9,000,000 thaler, nearly twice as much as in Frankfurt an der Oder.[83] After the Seven Years' War, the number of Jewish visitors of the fairs increased constantly, from only a few up to 1,000 and more Jewish merchants toward the end of the eighteenth century. Often more than one-fourth of all merchants at the fair were Jewish. The shift was even more pronounced in the case of Polish Jews. The largest number of Jewish merchants usually attended the Easter fair. In 1756, 20 Christian and 8 Jewish merchants arrived from Poland. Ten years later, 94 Jewish merchants outnumbered 43 Christian merchants. In 1775, the ratio was 179 Jewish to 40 Christian merchants; in 1796 that disparity grew to 329 versus 31.[84]

The growing numbers of Jewish merchants made the Saxon administration understand the importance of ethnic commercial networks and the greater trust Jewish merchants apparently placed in their fellow Jewish businessmen in Leipzig. Thus, Leipzig offered opportunities in new business undertakings to Jewish merchants, in this case specifically banking. In general, migration apparently encouraged the move of Jews into new fields of business. Adolph (Aron), the son of Levin Marcus Schlesinger, moved to Leipzig to open a banking house with Jacob Kaskel, originally from Dresden. Michael Kaskel, the latter's brother, owned a banking house in Dresden that later turned into the Dresdner Bank.[85]

When business partners Jacob Kaskel and Adolph Schlesinger sought to establish their business in Leipzig in 1807, representatives of the conservative Retailer's Guild, which represented local retail merchants argued fiercely against accepting the request of the two Jewish businessmen. However, the central Deputation of Commerce (Commerciendeputation) that was greatly interested in developing international wholesale trade in Leipzig had good arguments to support Kaskel's and Schlesinger's request.[86] First, the trade with bills of exchange be enhanced in Leipzig in general; moreover, one should seek in particular to keep the earnings of Jewish exchange banks away from Berlin and within the borders of Saxony: "But there is no doubt that this business in Leipzig would have to be of Jewish religion, because according to prior experience the Polish and Russian Jews usually do not like to turn to Christian bankers with their financial transactions, but prefer to seek out their co-religionists, who better understand their language and their way of doing business."[87]

Further, Schlesinger and Kaskel had declared that their business activities primarily aimed at those Jewish merchants from Poland and Russia with whom they were already familiar, as the Deputation of Commerce recognized: "both supplicants, the latter via relatives in Posen, the first one through his family relations in Frankfurt an der Oder, are already well known among Jewish merchants from Poland and Russia, which promises a good success of their business."[88] Supporters of the new Jewish banking house realized exactly what advantages Kaskel's and Schlesinger's business undertaking would provide. Shared religion (or ethnicity) and family connections would make them more trustworthy for Jewish merchants from Poland and Russia.

While Schlesinger and Kaskel in Leipzig relied on their Jewish customers from eastern Europe, others preferred to move eastward to find new business opportunities. Though Jewish migration in Europe is generally described as moving westward throughout the second half of the seventeenth and the eighteenth centuries, the late eighteenth and early nineteenth centuries saw notable exceptions particularly among Jewish merchants and entrepreneurs. Members of several wealthy Jewish families from Frankfurt an der Oder turned eastward. We have already met Levin Pincus Schlesinger, who temporarily moved to Warsaw in the second half of the eighteenth century for business, while his cousin Herz Marcus Schlesinger practiced medicine in the city from 1779 until 1783. It is safe to assume that both were in close contact with Judyta (Judith) Jakubowiczowa. The daughter of the communal elder Levin Buko moved to Warsaw at the end of the 1770s. There she married and became a prominent businesswoman. Her brother, Elias Buko, moved to Grodno around the same time; and both did business with each other.[89]

Conclusion

From Frankfurt an der Oder, the commercial networks of the Schlesinger family extended to the major commercial cities of central Europe and Amsterdam. These Frankfurt merchants received most of the credit for their business from Amsterdam via Hamburg, and explored new possible extensions of their business eastward, primarily to Warsaw. Although different family members were usually listed separately in the city records in regard to their firms, assets and homes, they often combined their commercial efforts. These connections of the Schlesinger family constitute at least the skeleton of their commercial networks, which to a large extent were constructed on family relations that clearly overlapped with commercial connections. In contrast to commercial port cities like Livorno, for which Francesca Trivellato has shown the ample connections of Sephardic merchants with non-Jewish business partners near and far, central European Jewish merchants still relied heavily on ethnic and kinship networks. Though one cannot ascertain precisely why this is the case, one can assume that less developed commercial institutions as well as the inferior legal position of Jewish merchants in comparison with Christian merchants contributed to this outlook of their commercial networks.

We also saw different strategies of extending a family's business. The Schlesingers relied on close family members like in Hamburg and Königsberg, and utilized their familial connections to create new ties to expand their business undertakings, especially to attain better access to the credit market in Amsterdam. Although the lens of family networks as a basis for commercial activities might make those commercial networks look more exclusively Jewish than they necessarily were, it is difficult to trace regular and long-term connections to non-Jews. Christians, nevertheless, were integrated in such family-based networks, often over many years, when they brought financial or logistic advantages, and especially when representing Jewish merchants in cities where Jews were banned from permanent settlement like Danzig. In general, one needs to keep in mind that without the existence of commercial and familial correspondence, the networks of the Schlesinger family can only be mapped partially. The cities to which the Schlesinger family had close connections constituted the nodes of their commercial undertakings. However, one can be sure that more merchants, brokers, and bankers were involved at any level of their commercial activity.

The fortune of the Schlesinger family, other members of the Jewish mercantile elite, and the Jewish community in Frankfurt an der Oder altogether shows how closely a family's economic fate was dependent on the general economic development of a given region. Drawn to Prussian lands by economic considerations of the authorities, Jewish merchants became a crucial factor in the trade with their fellow Jews from Poland and Russia involving retailing, the purchase of raw products and the sale of cloth and textiles as well as the trade in bills of exchange and the provision of credit. Nevertheless, these merchants only played a minor role in European trade more generally. When the fortunes of Frankfurt an der Oder and its fair turned, many members of the Jewish mercantile elite sought, often successfully, to migrate to more promising places along their commercial or familial connections be it westward or eastward. Looking at general trends of Jewish migration in the eighteenth century the latter went a less usual but not less successful way.

The fate of the Jewish mercantile elite in Frankfurt an der Oder in some ways confirms the findings of Jonathan Israel of an economic decline of the Jewish population in Europe during the eighteenth century. However, this period of decline seems much shorter than presumed. At least in Prussia in general and in Frankfurt an der Oder in particular Jewish merchants and brokers still profited from the Seven Years' War. Only in the last quarter of the eighteenth century the economic situation of these merchants deteriorated more seriously. Thus, we might assume that the debates of Jewish and non-Jewish thinkers of the Enlightenment about the occupational structure and economic position of the Jewish population was not rooted only in theoretical considerations, but in an actual decline of Jews' economic position that they indeed observed. Nevertheless, some of these merchants, who successfully reacted to the changing economic situation, laid the foundation for the rise of a new economic elite of Jewish merchants and bankers in nineteenth-century central and east central Europe.

Notes

1. Acta die Forderungen des Schutz-Juden Pincus Moses Schlesinger an den Simon Simons zu Warschau betr., I. HA, Geheimer Rat, Rep. 9 (Polen), no. 28-12B, GStA.

2. Familienpapiere Schlesinger/Fersenheim, Frankfurt/Oder 1795–1875, 1,75 E, no. 587, CJB, 1.

3. Sorkin, "Beyond the East-West Divide," 247–256.

4. Straubel, *Frankfurt (Oder) und Potsdam*, 86. Straubel suggests that the Jewish share in the economic life of Prussia during this period is usually overestimated.

5. Ruderman, *Early Modern Jewry*, 95–98.

6. Jonathan Israel was among the first to highlight the readmission of Jews in the course of the Thirty Years' War and a general change in attitude toward Jewish economic activities with the rise of mercantilism. Israel, *European Jewry*, 72–118.

7. The German and particularly Prussian features of Cameralism, the theory and science of governing the state, emphasized population growth, fiscal income, the development of agriculture, mining, and manufacturing over foreign trade and a positive balance of trade, which was the most important incentive of west European mercantilism. Gömmel, *Die Entwicklung der Wirtschaft im Zeitalter des Merkantilismus*, 41–42, 44–45. On the settlement of Jews in Prussia, see Bruer, *Geschichte der Juden in Preußen*, 39–44.

8. See, for example, Lowenstein, *The Berlin Jewish Community*; Feiner, *The Jewish Enlightenment*; Reinke, *Judentum und Wohlfahrtspflege in Deutschland*; Van Rahden, *Jews and Other Germans*.

9. Moses Jacob Schlesinger's brother, Joseph Jacob (b. 1691), moved to Frankfurt an der Oder after his marriage with Rele Abrahamin (b. 1711). Judentabellen der Stadt Frank-

furt/Oder, 1748–1759, Abteilung 1, VII, 107, StAF, 2v–3. See also Meier, "Die jüdische Gemeinde in Frankfurt an der Oder," 113–114.

10. Breuer and Graetz, *Tradition and Enlightenment*, 147. For a comparison between the legal situation of Jews in the Polish-Lithuanian Commonwealth and the Holy Roman Empire, see Teller, "Telling the Difference," 109–141.

11. Breuer and Graetz, *Tradition and Enlightenment*, 1, 148–149. An English translation of the regulations is available in Marcus and Saperstein, *The Jew in the Medieval World*, 97–110.

12. Acta wegen Classificierung hiesiger Handlung treibender Personen, zu Paraphirung ihrer Handlungs-Bücher 1765 bis Junii 1766, Abteilung 1, X, 220, StAF, 21, 29v, 72. See also Straubel, *Frankfurt (Oder) und Potsdam*, 75, 83, 268–269.

13. Pincus Moses Schlesinger first bought a house in the Schmiedegasse in 1760 and sold it to his son, David Pincus Schlesinger, in 1791. Marcus Moses Schlesinger and later his widow, Sarah Heymann, owned a house, as did Levin Marcus Schlesinger (inherited from his father in 1788) and his brother, Dr. Herz Marcus Schlesinger. The house of the latter as well as the one acquired by Levin Pincus Schlesinger in 1802 was situated on the city's main street, the Richtstraße. Judenlisten Frankfurt/Oder. Rep. 19, Steuerrat Frankfurt/Oder, no. 275, BLHA, 36v–37; Acta vom Erlaubnisgesuch des Juden Levin Pincus Schlesinger zu Franckfurth an der Oder zum Ankauf des Keesebierschen Hauses, Rep. 2, S 4233, BLHA; Acta zum Haus Besitz des Schutzjuden David Pincus Schlesinger zu Franckfurth, 1796, Rep. 2, S 4232, BLHA.

14. Judentabellen der Stadt Frankfurt/Oder, 1748–1759, Abteilung 1, VII, 107, StAF, 3, 12–15.

15. In Leipzig the fairs took place around New Year's (*Neujahrsmesse*), Easter (*Ostermesse*), and in the early fall (*Michaelismesse*). On the fair in Breslau, see Weinryb, "Yehude Polin veLita veyaḥasehem le-Breslau," 25–67.

16. Philippi, *Die Messen der Stadt Frankfurt an der Oder*, 14, 54. Although not all merchants from Poland were Jews, they did constitute the majority.

17. See, for example, the description of Nathan Nata Hanover on the functions of fairs in Poland: Hannover, *Abyss of Despair (Yeven metzulah)*, 114–115.

18. In this passage, Wasserzug is referring to the Magarethen fair in the summer. Loewe, "Memoiren eines polnischen Juden," 30.

19. Targiel, "Gedruckt mit den Typen von Amsterdam," 450–481; Richarz, *Der Eintritt der Juden in die akademischen Berufe*, 29, 46–47, 54. In addition to Jewish students from Prussia and other German states, a surprisingly large number of Jewish students from Amsterdam and other towns in the Netherlands came to the city. Lewin, "Jüdische Studenten der Universität Frankfurt a.O.," 217–238, 59–96, 43–86. Tobias Cohen, who was among the first Jewish students in 1678 and received a stipend from the Prussian King, bitterly complained in his Hebrew textbook of sciences *Ma'aseh Tuviyyah*, which he published in 1708, about his treatment at the university. Ruderman, *Jewish Thought and Scientific Discovery*, 230, 236.

20. Acta die Erklärung derer zur Messe nach Frankfurt kommenden Polnischen Juden, über die ihnen vorgelegten sieben Punkte, betr., 1774–1786, Rep. 2, S 4449, BLHA, 2–8v.

21. Acta wegen Classificierung hiesiger Handlung treibender Personen, zu Paraphirung ihrer Handlungs-Bücher 1765 bis Junii 1766, Abt. 1, X, 220, StAF, 21; Register von denjenigen

Kauffleuten welche die Meßen zu Frankfurth an der Oder besuchen, Franckfurth an der Oder Anno 1756, StAF. On Leipzig, see Acta die denen Pohlnischen und Rußischen Handelsleuten zu gestattenden Freyheitten betr., 1772, LI 12b, StAL. Reinhold, "Die Leipziger Messen und die Rzeczepospolita," 80–86.

22. In 1750, Jews constituted 6.8 percent of the population in Frankfurt an der Oder. In 1786 it still was 6 percent, until their percentage fell to 2.78 percent in 1836. In 1764 the community comprised the families and servants of sixty-eight privileged protected Jews and nineteen unprivileged protected Jews. Meier, "Die jüdische Gemeinde in Frankfurt an der Oder," 114–115.

23. Schnabel and Shin, "Liquidity and Contagion," 930, 933.

24. Rohrbacher, "Die drei Gemeinden Altona, Hamburg, Wandsbek zur Zeit der Glikl," 107, 144; Marwedel, "Die aschkenasischen Juden im Hamburger Raum," 44–49, 50–53; Tiggemann, "Familiensolidarität, Leistung und Luxus," 419–422.

25. Grunwald, *Hamburgs deutsche Juden*, 23.

26. Pinkas Kehilat Frankfurt, MS 19, ML TA, 72v–73; *Der Anzeiger*, 531.

27. On the negotiations to establish a second child, see Schenk, *Wegbereiter der Emanzipation?* 103–125.

28. The register of Jews in Frankfurt an der Oder lists eight children of Pincus Moses Schlesinger, five sons (Levin, Abraham, Alexander, David, Marcus) and three daughters (Hendele, Rahel, Blume). Judentabellen der Stadt Frankfurt/Oder, 1748–1759, Abteilung 1, VII, 107, StAF, 144v–145.

29. Straubel, *Die Handelsstädte Königsberg und Memel*, 313, 381, 332–338, 669; Guesnet, "Kaliningrad," 849–850; Ajzensztejn, "Der Aufstieg der jüdischen Familie Friedländer in Königsberg," 388n26. For a detailed description of the river trade to Königsberg, see Teller, *Money, Power, and Influence*, 175–183.

30. Vertrieb und Absatz der einländischen Manufaktur-Waaren, außerhalb Landes durch den Königsbergschen Schutz-Juden Alexander Schlesinger 1766, II. HA, Abt. 7, II Materien, no. 4551, GStA, 7; Acta wegen des von dem Schutz-Juden zu Frankfurth an der Oder, Pincus Schlesinger gesuchten Schutz-Privilegii auf Königsberg in Preußen für seinen Sohn Alexander Pincus Schlesinger, II. HA, Abt. 7, II Materien, no. 4545, GStA, 3, 24. We do not know details of the fate of Abraham Pincus Schlesinger. Straubel, *Die Handelsstädte Königsberg und Memel*, 304–305, 349–350.

31. Vertrieb und Absatz der einländischen Manufaktur-Waaren, außerhalb Landes durch den Königsbergschen Schutz-Juden Alexander Schlesinger 1766, II. HA, Abt. 7, II Materien, no. 4551, GStA; Acta wegen des von dem Schutz-Juden zu Frankfurth an der Oder, Pincus Schlesinger gesuchten Schutz-Privilegii auf Königsberg in Preußen für seinen Sohn Alexander Pincus Schlesinger, II. HA, Abt. 7, II Materien, no. 4545, GStA.

32. Acta wegen des von dem Schutz-Juden zu Frankfurth an der Oder, Pincus Schlesinger gesuchten Schutz-Privilegii auf Königsberg in Preußen für seinen Sohn Alexander Pincus Schlesinger, II. HA, Abt. 7, II Materien, no. 4545, GStA, 16–18.

33. Schenk, *Wegbereiter der Emanzipation?* 82–87.

34. Acta von der Ansetzung des David Pincus Schlesinger auf das Schutz-Priv. des Isaac Hertz mit der Erbin desselben Güttel, Rep. 2, S 4287, BLHA. To secure the permission to

marry, David Pincus had to prove that he was in possession of the required liquid assets and that his age was accurate. In addition, the elders of the Jewish community confirmed the proper behavior of both partners. Two of the three daughters of Pincus Moses Schlesinger had to leave Frankfurt an der Oder. Rahel married a certain Jacob Baruch in Potsdam, and Blume married a doctor Elias Naphtali in the small Prussian town of Friedberg. Judenlisten Frankfurt/Oder, Rep. 19, no. 275, BLHA, 50v–51.

35. Hasse, *Geschichte der Leipziger Messen*, 313–314.

36. For example, the Deputation of Commerce recognized in 1780 that one of the reasons for the small number of Jews at the Easter fair in that particular year was the overlapping Jewish holidays, whereas the local government continued to try to prevent Jews from trading on Sundays during the fairs. Hasse, *Geschichte der Leipziger Messen*, 194, 200, 208, 341; Reinhold, "Die Leipziger Messen und die Rzeczpospolita," 81–82.

37. Acta die vorgeschlagene Erlassung des Leib-Zolls . . . betreffend, 10025 Geheimes Konsilium, Loc. 5409, SHstA DD, 225v–226.

38. Acta die denen Pohlnischen und Russischen Handelsleuten zu gestattenden Freyheiten betr., 1771, LI 12a, StAL, 152–154.

39. Acta die denen Pohlnischen und Russischen Handelsleuten zu gestattenden Freyheiten betr., 1772, LI 12b, StAL, 27–279. In eight fairs, Jacob Moses Schlesinger sold goods worth nearly 50,000 thaler.

40. Straubel, *Kaufleute und Manufakturunternehmer*, 81, 393. Straubel emphasizes that Levin Marcus Schlesinger's trade volume was exceptionally high compared with other Jewish merchants. Acta die auf den Leipziger Meßen sich einfindenden fremden Handels-Juden betr., Ao. 1809, LOMKD, no. 803 (Loc. 11150), SHstA DD, 10v, 43.

41. Bogucka, "Jewish Merchants in Gdańsk in the 16th–17th Centuries," 47, 49; Rosman, *The Lords' Jews*, 96; Rosman, "Ḥelkam shel hayehudim bamisḥar hashayit midrom mizraḥ Polin le-Gdansk 1695–1726," 70–83. On Jews in Danzig in general, see Echt, *Die Geschichte der Juden in Danzig*, 13–34.

42. Rosman, "Polish Jews in the Gdańsk Trade," 116.

43. Acta wegen des von dem Schutz-Juden zu Frankfurth an der Oder, Pincus Schlesinger gesuchten Schutz-Privilegii auf Königsberg in Preußen für seinen Sohn Alexander Pincus Schlesinger, II. HA, Abt. 7, II Materien, no. 4545, GStA, 10v, 12. Andreas Schopenhauer (1720–1793) was the grandfather of the Danzig philosopher Arthur Schopenhauer. He maintained close commercial ties to Amsterdam.

44. *Stadtrichter*: 300, 6, no. 95: 512; no. 96: 297; no. 99: 264–265; no. 101: 416; no. 108: 393, 416–417, 457; no 109: 114–116, APG.

45. Ibid., no. 95: 513; no. 109: 112–113. Wettgericht 300, 58, no. 26: 190; no. 27: 69, 72–73v; no. 28: 145–146v, APG.

46. Ruderman, *Early Modern Jewry*, 57–98.

47. Pinkas Kehilat Frankfurt, MS 19, ML TA. The *pinkas* records parts of the communal activities from 1754 to 1793, though the lion's share of entries spans the late 1760s to 1793. The *pinkas* is part of the R. Ahron (Armand) Kaminka collection of the Maimonides Library in Tel Aviv. Kaminka (1866–1950), originally from Berdichev, studied in Berlin and Paris. In 1893 he was ordained and received his first rabbinical appointment in Frankfurt an der Oder.

Menda-Levy, "Kaminka, Aharon," 855. He must have kept the old *pinkas* when he left the community, and presumably brought it to Palestine when he immigrated there in 1938. An additional *pinkas* was kept at the same time and is referred to repeatedly. It is located at the National Library of Israel in Jerusalem (JER NLI 6200=24), but has not been used here. In addition, some communal documents have been preserved in the Central Archives for the History of the Jewish People in Jerusalem (CAHJP, Synagogengemeinde Frankfurt/Oder, D/Fr 1).

48. The *pinkas* provides no information as to what income was necessary to belong to each of the three classes. A comparison with the Berlin *pinkas* shows that the majority of the community members was excluded, even if one assumes that the average assets of Jews in Berlin were somewhat higher. In 1760s Berlin the wealthy (*gadole 'erekh*) needed assets of 3,000 thaler; the middle ones 1,200–3,000 thaler; and the less wealthy not more than 1,200 thaler. Meisl, *Pinkas Kehilat Berlin*, lxi. In Frankfurt an der Oder, the majority of community members had assets amounting to less than 500 thaler.

49. Pinkas Kehilat Frankfurt, MS 19, ML TA, 29v, 127.

50. Schenk, *Wegbereiter der Emanzipation?*, 18–29. Schenk's extensive work on these additional dues, the bureaucratic considerations beyond them, and partly the impact on Prussia's Jewish community provides a new picture of the condition of Prussia's Jewry in the second half of the eighteenth century. See also Laux, "Zwischen Anonymität und amtlicher Erfassung," 97.

51. Meisl, *Pinkas Kehilat Berlin*, lix. The contract concerning the stocking manufactory in Templin was signed by the elders of the Jewish community in Frankfurt an der Oder in 1768. They agreed to take over the manufactory together with the Jewish community in Berlin to finance it and to sell its products at home and abroad. Eventually, the venture failed and strained the budget of both communities. Pinkas Kehilat Frankfurt, MS 19, ML TA, 8v.

52. Pinkas Kehilat Frankfurt, MS 19, ML TA, 15v, 20, 48v.

53. Ruderman, *Early Modern Jewry*, 200. On the debates concerning the beginning of the Haskalah and the distinction between an early Haskalah and the Haskalah movement, see Feiner, *The Jewish Enlightenment*, 27–35; Feiner and Sorkin, *New Perspectives on the Haskalah*, 1–8; Ruderman, *Early Modern Jewry*, 198–202.

54. On the Haskalah and economic thought, see Penslar, *Shylock's Children*, 68–81; Karp, *The Politics of Jewish Commerce*, 202–207.

55. See, for example, Breuer and Graetz, *Tradition and Enlightenment*, 1, 263–270.

56. Feiner, "Haskalah," 544–548.

57. Proops printed a Talmud edition in Amsterdam in 1752 and obtained a rabbinical approbation (*haskamah*) that included an interdiction of printing for twenty-five years. In 1755, however, Meshullam Zalman Frankel of Sulzbach set out to print another edition. The conflict involved communities across Europe; the Council of the Four Lands in Poland banned the Sulzbach edition. In 1768, Schlesinger sided with the rabbis who met in Frankfurt an der Oder and defended the printing of the Talmud in Sulzbach against the protests voiced by Amsterdam printers. Lewin, "Jüdische Studenten der Universität Frankfurt a.O.," 89 (1923); Rakover, "Amsterdam and Sulzbach," 167–175.

58. In 1791, Herz Marcus Schlesinger confirmed that his cousin David Pincus Schlesinger was circumcised by his uncle Marcus Moses Schlesinger in 1747, who had entered it in the book "in which he entered all circumcisions he performed." Acta von der Ansetzung des David Pincus Schlesinger auf das Schutz-Priv. des Isaac Hertz mit der Erbin desselben Güttel. Rep. 2, S 4287, BLHA.

59. Lewin, "Jüdische Studenten der Universität Frankfurt a.O.," 89 (1923), 43 (1924).

60. Ibid., 89 (1923). Shatzky also mentions him as R. Hirsch Schlesinger in Warsaw, though he wrongly gives Glogau as place of origin. Shatzky, *Geshikhte fun yidn in Varshe*, vol. 1, 129. Most interestingly, Shatzky also notes that Herz Marcus lived in Przejazd Street where Judyta Jakubowiczowa, who moved to Warsaw from Frankfurt an der Oder in the late 1770s, bought a house in 1809, but may have lived or done business there already in the 1780s.

61. Pinkas Kehilat Frankfurt, MS 19, ML TA, 61, 79, 134v. In addition to the 100 thaler, he received one thaler for initial visit of a new patient and 4 groschen for every following visit. His salary was partly financed with the tax on Passover flour. He did not renew his contract beyond the initial six years.

62. Teomim was rabbi of Frankfurt an der Oder from 1781 until his death in 1792. Brocke, Carlebach, and Wilke, *Biographisches Handbuch der Rabbiner*, 850–851.

63. Satanov, *Sefer hagedarim*. See also: Kagan, *Sefer haprenumerantn*, 243. On Satanow and his publishing efforts, see Feiner, *The Jewish Enlightenment*, 322–327.

64. On the Jewish debate about early burial, see Krochmalnik, "Scheintod und Emanzipation," 125–137; Wiesemann, "Jewish Burials in Germany," 19–21; Samet, "Halanat metim," 414–423; Panitz, "Modernity and Mortality," 92–118. On the general debates regarding the fear of an "apparent dead" and premature burial, see Ariès, *The Hour of Our Death*, 396–406.

65. Katz, *She'elat ḥakham*, 71–103v. The title is the term for consulting a scholar about annulment of a vow. He also subscribed to Abraham Ash's *Sefer mar'eh 'esh* (Berlin, 1803), a collection of glosses on all tractates of the Talmud. Ash compiled Talmudic and halakhic statements against early burial in his earlier work *Torah kullah* (Berlin, 1796). Herz, *Über die frühe Beerdigung der Juden*, 52, 54. On Marcus Herz, see Davies, *Identity or History?*, 200–205; Krochmalnik, "Scheintod und Emanzipation," 139–142. On this second phase of the controversy Panitz, "Modernity and Mortality," 118–135. See also Gotzmann, *Jüdisches Recht im kulturellen Prozess*, 107–124; Brocke, Carlebach, and Wilke, *Biographisches Handbuch der Rabbiner*, 645; Aust, "Conflicting Authorities," 92–96.

66. Historians disagree as to whether Mendelssohn was a radical reformer or representative of a Jewish religious enlightenment that did not seek to fundamentally reform Judaism. The second position is more plausible. For more information on the first position, see Arkush, *Moses Mendelssohn and the Enlightenment*, 289–292. On the second position, see Sorkin, *Moses Mendelssohn and the Religious Enlightenment*, 147–156.

67. See, for example, Israel, *European Jewry*, 198–205; Aslanian, *From the Indian Ocean to the Mediterranean*, 219–228.

68. Scholars of Cameralism usually distinguish between an older Cameralism of the second half of the seventeenth century and a newer form that peaked between 1740 and 1800 and was especially pronounced in Prussia. Kaufhold, "'Wirtschaftswissenschaften' und

Wirtschaftspolitik in Preußen," 54; Kaufhold, "Preußische Staatswirtschaft," 54–56; Radtke, "Preußischer Merkantilismus/ Kameralismus," 99.

69. Tribe, *Governing Economy*, 8–11, 91–92, 130–131; Kaufhold, "Preußische Staatswirtschaft," 59.

70. Straubel, *Frankfurt (Oder) und Potsdam*, 14, 44–75.

71. Ibid., 54, 74, 268–269. Listen der Schatzungen und Schutzgelder, 1774–1819. Synagogengemeinde Frankfurt/Oder, D/Fr 1, 30, CAHJP. On the demographic development of the Jewish community, see Meier, "Die jüdische Gemeinde in Frankfurt an der Oder," 114–115.

72. Acta die Forderungen des Schutz-Juden Pincus Moses Schlesinger an den Simon Simons zu Warschau betr., I. HA, Rep. 9 (Polen), no. 28-12b, GStA, 1.

73. Philippi, *Die Messen der Stadt Frankfurt an der Oder*, 35.

74. Familienpapiere Schlesinger/Fersenheim, Frankfurt/Oder 1795–1875, 1,75 E, no. 587, CJB, 1.

75. Aufstellung der Handlungstreibenden, 1808/09, Abteilung 1, X, 224, StAF, 4–7. In 1808, the Jewish community had to pay only 3,500 thaler in taxes, less than the wealthy Christian merchant Rudelius alone. Straubel, *Kaufleute und Manufakturunternehmer*, 216.

76. His wife's brothers had moved from Amsterdam to London. Acta vom Erlaubnisgesuch des Juden Levin Pincus Schlesinger zu Franckfurth an der Oder zum Ankauf des Keesebierschen Hauses, Rep. 2, S 4233, BLHA. Despite the claim to have no business, Levin Pincus Schlesinger participated in the Frankfurt fairs in 1803. Designatio aller debitirten Waaren, 1802/03, II. HA, Abt. 25, Tit. XXXII, no. 2 (vol. 45), GStA, 112–118, 178, 243–246.

77. For his activities in Leipzig and Saxony together with Jacob Moses Schlesinger, see Acta den Handelsjuden Markus Levin Schlesinger aus Frankfurt an der Oder betr. anno 1787, Tit. LI 18, StAL; Acta vom Haus-Besitz des ord. Schutz Juden Levin Marcus Schlesinger zu Franckfurth /O., 1788, Rep. 2, S 4221, BLHA, 4v; Listen der Schatzungen und Schutzgelder, 1774–1819, D/Fr 1, 30, CAHJP.

78. The son of Alexander Pincus, Moses Alexander Schlesinger, married Frommet Moses from Gumbinnen in 1801. She was a niece of Itzig Jacob from Flatow, who had moved to Warsaw in the 1790s (see chapter 3). Ansetzung des Sohnes des Königsberger Schutzjuden Alexander Pincus Schlesinger, Moses Alexander Schlesinger, als 2. Kind und dessen Verheiratung mit der Tochter Frommet des Schutzjuden Moses Jacob aus Gumbinnen 1801, II. HA, Abt. 7, II Materien, no. 4677, GStA. A daughter of the same Moses Alexander Schlesinger, Jette, married Philipp Jonas in Königsberg, but a document from 1832 attests that they left five poor daughters behind. Familienpapiere Schlesinger/Fersenheim, Frankfurt/Oder 1795–1875. 1, 75 E, no. 578, CJB, 10v.

79. Acta die auf den Leipziger Meßen sich einfindenden fremden Handels-Juden betr., Ao. 1809, LOMKD, no 803, SHstA DD, 10v, 43, 55v, 79, 91v, 144v, 218. On emigration of Jews from Frankfurt an der Oder, see Straubel, *Frankfurt (Oder) und Potsdam*, 79–80.

80. Straubel, *Frankfurt (Oder) und Potsdam*, 75.

81. Lowenstein, *The Berlin Jewish Community*, 89–95; Straubel, *Kaufleute und Manufakturunternehmer*, 202–203.

82. Straubel, *Frankfurt (Oder) und Potsdam*, 43–45; Straubel, *Kaufleute und Manufakturunternehmer*, 80–81. For the different regulations, see Philippi, *Die Messen der Stadt Frankfurt an der Oder*, 83–84; Weinryb, "Yehude Polin ve-Lita ve-yaḥasehem le-Breslau," 46.

83. Reinhold, "Die Leipziger Messen und die Rzeczpospolita," 82–85; Hasse, *Geschichte der Leipziger Messen*, 277, 300.

84. All numbers are taken from the compilations of Markgraf, *Zur Geschichte der Juden auf den Messen in Leipzig*, 13, 21–28. For some criticism of Markgraf's work, see Freudenthal, *Leipziger Messgäste*, 21. Most Jewish merchants, who arrived in Leipzig for the fairs were listed with their names until 1764. Afterward they were only counted.

85. On the efforts to set up a banking house in Leipzig, see Acta den Aufenthalt der Juden zu Leipzig betr., Ao. 1764–1816, 10026 Geheimes Kabinett, Loc. 2360/3, SHstA DD. On the Kaskel family, see Kaskel, "Vom Hoffaktor zur Dresdner Bank," 159–187.

86. The Retailer's Guild (*Kramerinnung*) and the wholesale merchants of Leipzig (*Handelsdeputierte*) were traditionally strong opponents. Beachy, "Fernhandel und Krämergeist," 137, 141–145.

87. Acta den Aufenthalt der Juden zu Leipzig betr., Ao. 1764–1816, 10026 Geheimes Kabinett, Loc. 2360/3, SHstA DD. It is noteworthy that in this case not its practitioners but the business itself is identified as "of Jewish religion."

88. Ibid.

89. Lewin, "Jüdische Studenten der Universität Frankfurt a.O.," 89 (1923).

THREE

Borderlands: Legal Restrictions, Army Supplying, and Economic Success

In his late nineteenth-century description of the history of Warsaw's Jewry, the Polish-Jewish journalist Hilary Nussbaum (1820–1895), a moderate integrationist who was a proponent of Jewish integration into Polish society, wrote about a famous figure in Warsaw's early nineteenth-century mercantile elite: "The affluent foreign Israelite Izaak Flatau settled in Warsaw and established a private synagogue at his own expense in his house on Danielewiczowska Street no. 616. He did not aim at any profit, but at the needs and convenience of his own numerous family, his friends and acquaintances who wore short European attire and spoke pure German and differed from the rest of their fellow [Polish] Jews wearing long coats and speaking jargon."[1]

According to Nussbaum, Izaak Flatau's life course was clear. We find a wealthy and foreign Jewish merchant and banker who easily moves to Warsaw for business and whilst there, clearly distinguishable in dress, language, and habitus and apparently disgusted by his fellow Polish Jews' appearance and religious behavior, founded a synagogue. Written in a time when national divides were established and colored by Nussbaum's own leanings as an integrationist, the narrative obscures the far more complicated story of Itzig Jacob, who only later became known as Izaak Flatau.

In this chapter, I argue that borderlands—in this case the Polish-Prussian borderlands—provided particular opportunities for economic success. The changing political and legal conditions called for occupational flexibility, transregional connections, and the will to take increased economic risk. In the previous two chapters, we have seen Jewish merchant families placed in a city, who sought to extend their commercial networks from there via marriage and business contacts. Itzig Jacob, by contrast, appears to be less settled for legal and economic reasons. His case shows yet another example of how Jewish merchants dealt with legal restrictions and how mobility was one way to achieve economic success.

His rise from a rather provincial merchant and small army supplier to a well-known banker and entrepreneur in Warsaw was not a straightforward trajectory. The limitation of settlement and economic rights compelled him and other Jewish merchants to develop strategies to get around those legal restrictions while concurrently ensuring their economic advancement. It was their mobility in particular and the creation and maintenance of transregional networks that allowed them to overcome legal obstacles. The moving borders and changing rules of the borderlands between Prussia and Poland in the wake of the partitions of Poland (1772, 1793, 1795; see figure 3.1) created specific challenges but also unique opportunities for at least a segment of the Jewish population. In contrast to the later portrayal of a sharp divide between German and Polish lands, the region was characterized by fluidity in terms of culture and language.

Itzig Jacob's story begins in these borderlands between Prussia and Poland, one of the many areas in eighteenth- and early nineteenth-century Europe in which political borders shifted, loyalties changed and the notion of cultural belonging encompassed multiple dimensions. Like in the French-German borderlands of Alsace-Lorraine, travelers of the time observed a rather slow change of landscape, culture, and language but no rigid borders.[2] Moses Wasserzug, born around the mid-eighteenth century in Skoki (German: Schokken) in Great Poland, hardly refers to borders, or to the crossing and changing of borders in his memoirs, even though he traveled from his hometown to Frankfurt an der Oder, Berlin and smaller places in Prussia. Skoki and Kórnik, his places of residence at the time, fell under Prussian rule in the second partition of Poland in 1793. He describes these fundamental political changes without expressing any particular strong emotion.[3]

This chapter follows the life of Itzig Jacob alias Izaak Flatau from his rather humble origins in the Polish territories occupied and annexed by Prussia in 1772 to his establishment as banker and entrepreneur in Warsaw at the beginning of the nineteenth century. It traces how the changing legal and economic conditions from the rule of the decentralized Polish-Lithuanian Commonwealth to the grip of the absolutist Prussian state affected the life of the local Jewish population. Attempts to integrate the newly occupied territories into the Prussian legal, social, and economic system had serious consequences for the population in general and the Jewish population in particular. These efforts often curtailed the rights Jews enjoyed under the rule of the Polish kings, but the status of the borderlands allowed some individuals to profit economically from these changes.

Though the scope of Itzig Jacob's success was rather exceptional, he was just one of many who turned their lives into a successful journey east. He became part of a small but influential eastward migration of Jews around the turn from the eighteenth to the early nineteenth century. This migration deviates from the common narrative of Jewish westward migration from the mid-seventeenth century on.[4] Like many other Jews in similar situations, Itzig Jacob employed a variety of strategies to turn his often difficult position into new opportunities: these included personal petitions, great flexibility in his economic endeavors and a smart combination of business and marriage connections. The war-ridden years from the partitions of

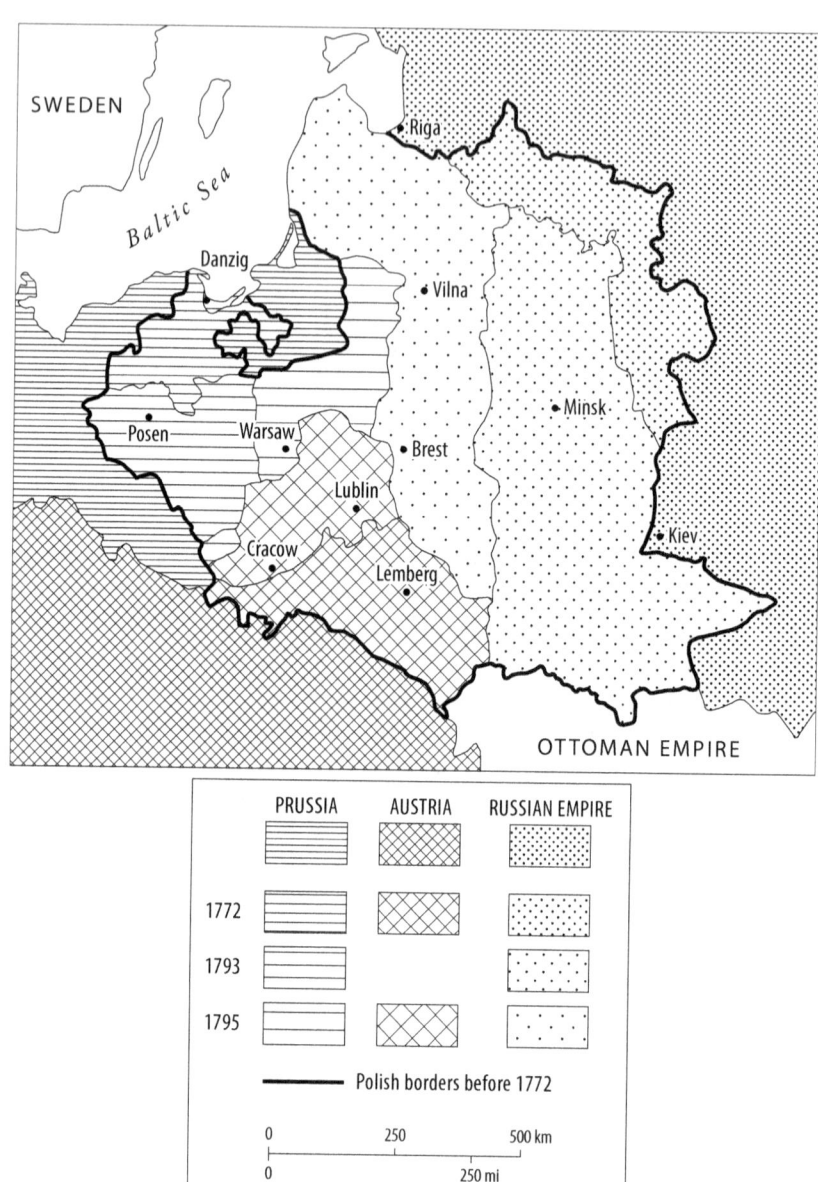

FIGURE 3.1. The partitions of Poland-Lithuania. Adapted from Bartal, *The Jews of Eastern Europe*, 28. Credit: University of Pennsylvania Press.

Poland to the Napoleonic Wars allowed him and other Jewish merchants to profit from the high need for food and feed in the armies involved. Those trading small quantities locally and those already involved in larger commercial undertakings supplied the Prussian, Polish, Russian, and later on French troops. The business of army supplying allowed Jewish entrepreneurs here and in other European border regions to enter into new business venues such as banking.

From Poland to Prussia

When Itzig Jacob was born in Flatow (Złotów), approximately a decade or more before the first partition of Poland in 1772, his family lived in a small noble town that had seen unrest and destruction from the Polish-Swedish War in the second half of the seventeenth century on. Nevertheless, a strong brewery and clothier artisan business flourished in the town, with a Jewish population of about 900 owning 106 houses. Jews constituted about half of the town's population. Itzig Jacob's family, including his six brothers, mostly lived from trade.[5] Like most Jews in the Polish-Lithuanian Commonwealth, the Jews of Flatow in Great Poland, the western part of the Commonwealth, enjoyed considerable economic freedom and communal autonomy based on royal and noble privileges.[6]

From the fifteenth century on, the number of Jewish inhabitants grew continuously, and the rights granted to Jews in Poland significantly surpassed those offered to Jews in other parts of Europe. Jews were allowed to engage in crafts and trade freely. The removal of many Jews from the royal jurisdiction in sixteenth-century Poland and their submission to noble jurisdiction did not harm their legal and economic position. While Polish magnates strengthened their power vis-à-vis the king, Jews assumed important roles in the feudal economy as leaseholders, merchants, and suppliers. By demonstrating economic usefulness, they secured their legal status and were able "to translate their economic potential into a new legal basis for their existence."[7]

By the mid-eighteenth century, Jews were an integral part of the feudal system of the Polish-Lithuanian Commonwealth, legally and economically bound to their noble lords.[8] It bears mention that Stanisław August Poniatowski, who was elected Polish king in 1764, did initiate efforts to transform Poland into a new "enlightened, prosperous and well governed" state after a period of repeated warfare and political instability, yet his attempts to reform and strengthen the Christian burgher estate had little impact on the Jewish population in small noble towns like Flatow.[9]

The legal situation of the Jewish population changed considerably when Prussia occupied the western parts of Poland in the first partition of Poland in 1772. In the old Prussian provinces, the number of Jews remained small, as intended by the state's restrictive legal policy toward Jews. The first partition of Poland in 1772 and the Prussian occupation of additional Polish territories in 1793 and 1795 posed a considerable challenge for Prussia's administration and policy makers. The Jewish population in the new territories—West Prussia and the Netze district, a narrow stretch of land along both sides of the Netze (Notec) River, in 1772, South Prussia and New East Prussia in 1793, and some additional territories in 1795 (see figure 3.2)—was much larger and enjoyed the privileges granted by Polish kings and nobles for generations. All Jews, about 3,600 in West Prussia and between 11,000 and 16,000 in the Netze district, 6 to 10 percent of the population, became Prussian subjects. In the Netze district, including Flatow, Jews often constituted up to half the population in many of the noble towns and estates; in fact, Flatow housed the highest number of Jews.[10]

The 1750 Revised General Code now applied to these new territories in 1772, which theoretically abolished the privileges of the Jewish communities and limited their economic opportunity. For all practical purposes, most areas of communal autonomy remained initially untouched as the Prussian authorities were primarily concerned with the Jewish population's economic condition. Beyond that, most Prussian administrators were unaware of the legal situation Jews had previously enjoyed under the Polish kings and nobles with regard to their economic freedom, communal structure, and juridical autonomy.[11]

Jews, active in trade and crafts, often formed the backbone of local and regional commerce, much to the surprise of the many new Prussian administrators. One of them complained about the Netze district: "It is too mad for me here with all the Jews. If I ask for a surgeon comes a Jew, a fisherman—a Jew; butcher, baker . . . all kind of craftsmen are Jews."[12] This astonishment reflects both the population structure and economic situation in West Prussia and the Netze district as well as the administrator's astonishment by that composition.

Not only did the Prussian administration have to grapple with this new situation; the Jewish population also labored hard to adapt to their new reality. In 1775, Jacob Moses, the representative of the Jewish population in West Prussia and the Netze district, submitted a request to the Prussian authorities. He referred to the Jewish population's lack of knowledge regarding new restrictions, which had been announced only orally. He requested that the Prussian administration provide a written and detailed proclamation of all regulations, especially "because the Jews of West Prussia and also those from Poland are not knowledgeable in German, and are unable to express themselves clearly and comprehensibly." He also demanded to allow the stipulation of all writings, bills of exchanges, and contracts in Hebrew as well as the jurisdiction in all matters that included Polish Jews in rabbinical courts.[13] In light of the general policy toward Jews in the newly occupied territories, it is rather surprising that the administration acceded to Jacob Moses' demands at the time.[14]

The memoirs of the aforementioned Moses Wasserzug also illustrate how difficult it was for Jews and their communities to adjust to the new Prussian administration. While Wasserzug served his community in the town of Kórnik, next to Posen (Poznań), as butcher (*shohet*), prayer leader (*hazan*), and other communal tasks, the town fell under Prussian rule in 1793. Wasserzug's familiarity with German from traveling to and living in Prussia led him to assume the task of translator between the community and the Prussian administration. He emphasized that "among all the inhabitants of the town was none who could speak in their [the German] language."[15] Moreover, Wasserzug assumed responsibility for collecting the new Prussian meat tax (*Akzise*) from the Jewish butchers, a task that turned him into a middleman between the Prussian administration and the ever poor butchers. A dispute with one of them led him to eventually leave the community. Wasserzug soon moved to Płock, which had also fallen under Prussian rule, to fulfill a similar role on the invitation of the Jewish community. Before he assumed his new responsibility, he found himself entangled in the difficulties emerging from the new Prussian rule when he was told upon arrival that he could not move from South Prussia to New East Prussia without permission from the state authorities. He received the necessary permission a few weeks later and could then fill the position of interpreter and translator.[16]

Interpreters like Wasserzug were essential to Prussia's policy. When Prussia occupied Polish territories in the first partition of Poland, it sought to strengthen its economic policies. These included implementation of protective tariffs to support manufacturing and commerce within Prussia. Another important measure was extending the military supply economy (*Magazinwirtschaft*) by creating a close net of grain depots that served the army and, in emergencies, the general population. This measure stimulated agriculture and grain trade, including the import of inexpensive grain from Poland. Concurrently, the Polish-Prussian commercial treaty of 1775, which had been forced on the Polish government, ensured unlimited import of manufactured Prussian goods to Poland and favored direct Polish-Prussian trade via low custom duties, yet also imposed high duties on Polish goods passing through Prussia. These measures evidenced less than the desired success, as the West Prussian economic system and its trade traditionally focused on the north-south axis from Danzig to the provinces in central Poland. Thus, West Prussia could not be easily integrated into the Prussian economic system. The impact of Prussian legal restrictions on economic matters for commerce in the territories occupied in 1772 was mixed. While Prussia supported some international trade, it also sought to turn Poland into a source of cheap raw material and a market for Prussian manufactured goods. These measures in West Prussia were met with resistance on the part of local nobles and the Jewish community.[17]

In particular, the large new Jewish population threatened the common approach of the Prussian authorities toward the state's Jewish subjects, as the state sought to keep the number of Jews low and to integrate the new territories into the existing legal framework of the Prussian state. Among the means that the Prussian administration employed to reduce the number of Jews, particularly in the Netze district, was the expulsion of Jewish families who could not meet the required allotment of 1,000 thaler per family. However, the implementation of these measures was often dictated by the local administration's understanding, or lack thereof, of demographic and economic realities. In some cases, local officials opposed the measures of the central government because they had greater understanding of the Jews' economic role. After the annexation of the Netze district the Prussian financial councilor Franz Balthasar Schönberg von Brenckenhoff wrote these words in reaction to the planned expulsions of Jews:

> As is known, I am not a friend nor protector of the Jews. But keeping in mind the financial concerns of the Crown, I consider it a serious disadvantage to chase so many thousands of inhabitants out of the country right now and to nearly completely depopulate some towns before other Christian inhabitants have been acquired.... Fordon, Zempelburg, Lobsens, Flatow will become wastelands at once, not even to mention the rest of the towns, in which half or a third of the inhabitants are Jews.[18]

Though the Prussian restrictions of settlement rights and the policy of expulsions caused hardship to Jews in the newly acquired Prussian territories, the administration failed to drastically alter the existing economic and settlement structure in these territories. In Flatow, Itzig Jacob's hometown, the Prussian measures of expelling poor Jews led to some decrease in the numbers of Jewish inhabitants, yet the number of Jewish-owned houses did not decline. In 1783 the town had about 1,600 inhabitants: some 700 Jews, 600 Protestants, and 300 Catholics. As the number of houses owned by Jews exceeded the number of Jewish families residing in the town, one can assume that Jews also rented out homes or apartments to Christian inhabitants of Flatow.[19]

With the creation of South and New East Prussia after 1793 and the disappearance of the Polish state, the policy of expulsion eventually came to an end. This cessation was also due to the influence of local officials who recognized the important role Jews played in the local, regional, and transregional economy, and who urgently advised the government in Berlin not to apply the same restrictions to the new territories as applied in West Prussia and the Netze district. While some officials advocated adopting a centralized administrative model, the Prussian state was ultimately willing to compromise in order to stabilize its authority.[20]

In Search of Opportunity

Jewish merchants did not passively accept the rules introduced by the new rulers. Like other subjects, they were accustomed to negotiating their conditions. In this case, that meant challenging the limitation of settlement and economic rights. The newly introduced limitations compelled members of the Jewish mercantile elite to develop specific strategies to cope with restrictions that simultaneously ensured their economic advancement. Although these strategies were not always successful, the new rulers nevertheless exhibited some interest in creating a structure of legitimacy to insure their subject's loyalty.[21] To successfully negotiate one's position under a new political power required knowledge of the new rulers' economic perceptions—or at the least, a clear picture of one's own marketable usefulness.

The case of Itzig Jacob reflects how Jewish merchants sought to negotiate their status. It also demonstrates the inconsistency of Prussian policies and measures on the one hand, and on the other it makes clear that not only poor Jews were affected by Prussian attitudes and measures toward former Polish Jews. His family belonged to those successfully involved in commerce, trading primarily in velvet, silk and other textiles, and he and his brothers traveled regularly to the fairs in Frankfurt an der Oder. In 1780, the mayor of Flatow attested to his affluence and stated that he owned merchandise from the Frankfurt fair worth at least 10,000 thaler, having amassed a fortune valued at at least 5,000 thaler. The same was said to be true of his brothers, holding settlement privileges in Flatow and Gumbinnen (Gusev in the Kaliningrad Oblast, Russia); each had at least a sales volume of 10,000 to 12,000 thaler a year.[22]

For reasons that are unknown, Itzig Jacob was unable to secure a settlement privilege like his brothers. In general, the refusal to issue settlement privileges was intended to diminish the number of Jewish inhabitants, usually the poorer strata of the Jewish population. After several failed attempts to settle—in Allenstein in the 1780s and then in Soldau, both in the old Prussian province now named East Prussia—he lived temporarily in Ortelsburg (Netze district), in Lowicz (Łowicz) near Warsaw, and in Posen in South Prussia after it was occupied by Prussia in 1793 (see figure 3.2).[23] Officially, he remained registered as a tolerated servant (*Schutzknecht*) of a certain Israel Levin in Flatow for the whole time period.[24] This was the lowest possible legal category according to the Revised General Code of 1750; thus, his legal position was completely dependent on Israel Levin, and he was not permitted to marry. Prussian authorities continued to deny him this general privilege despite the fact that Itzig Jacob was described as "a very affluent Jew originating from Flatau [*sic*] in West Prussia whose liquid funds were estimated at 50,000 thaler." The letter exchange does not provide any reason for this rejection, though an unsigned draft of a privilege is found in the file. However, the privilege was never issued, despite the active intervention by his future father-in-law, Szmul Jakubowicz, a wealthy merchant and army supplier in Warsaw.[25]

Thus, over the years, Itzig Jacob tried several times to receive settlement privileges. These attempts were accompanied by regular local travel, moving back and forth between different Prussian provinces and Poland. When he pleaded for a privilege in Soldau, a town close to the Polish border, he noted that he intended "to engage in wholesale trade in draperies of domestic and admissible foreign manufactories for export to Poland." He immediately emphasized his economic value and awareness of the fact that not all foreign manufactory products were permissible for import and export. Well aware of the common accusation of Jewish competition with Christian traders, he added: "Even though a certain merchant Schmidt trades in draperies in Soldau, he is only a retailer and handles only petty goods, so there will be no competition to my intended establishment."[26]

Still, the central government rejected Itzig Jacob's plea for settlement and for his intended trade. Granted, the government was adhering to its strict settlement regulations, yet the opposition of Soldau's burghers and merchants—who addressed the Jewish merchant using the derogative phrase "a certain Jew Itzig who has no permanent location"—probably contributed to the decision. This example shows that in addition to concrete regulations, the impact of other petitioners, often local Christian merchants and burghers, could limit the settlement and economic rights of Jewish merchants. In the case of Soldau, petitioners fiercely rejected Itzig Jacob's attempt to settle in the town and argued that even a single privileged Jew would soon bring with him servants, teachers, and other fellows: "Soldau is situated right at the border with Poland and is nearly completely surrounded by Poland—this location as well as the dense traffic from Danzig and Elbing to Warsaw is the reason why the border is completely filled with Polish Jews on the Polish side. These are just waiting to get constant access to Prussia, to the annoyance of Prussian commerce."[27] Their primary goal was to keep Jewish merchants, even the affluent ones, out of town. And in this case, they succeeded.

At an earlier point in Itzig Jacob's odyssey, the central government refused a privilege, although that decision may have worked against the state's economic interests. It was certainly counter to the interest of the local wool manufacturers in Allenstein (Olsztyn). In the early 1780s, he offered the following incentives in order to receive settlement rights in Allenstein: to provide the local textile manufactory with raw material, to purchase 4,000 pieces of cloth from it annually, and to buy Berlin porcelain valued at 300 thaler to sell abroad. Despite the Christian wool manufacturers of Allenstein submitting a number of petitions and pleading for a concession for the Jewish merchant, arguing that they had been buying wool from him for more than two years, his request was rejected. Indeed, the quality of the wool he traded was much better than that of the wool provided by state agencies or Polish estates. Moreover, it was cheaper and he granted credit or accepted payment in cloth, which he then sold in Poland. Despite the fact that his settlement would have served the interests of the local manufacturers, the central government did not abandon its restrictive policy. This case was not exceptional; weavers' guilds and local magistrates often protested the expulsion of Jews from West Prussian towns, because they were dependent on the trade provided by Jewish merchants. This example captures the contrasting mindsets of local and central powers.[28]

Jewish merchants not only argued their economic utility, they also used their mobility and transregional networks as a strategy for economic advancement and to overcome legal obstacles. It is difficult to trace all of Itzig Jacob's commercial and familial connections, but those we can sketch were crucial for his rise from smalltown merchant to army supplier and eventually banker in Warsaw. We have already seen that he, like other members of his family, traveled regularly to the fairs in Frankfurt an der Oder to trade local and primarily agricultural goods for textiles, in the main. In addition, he established close contacts to East Prussia, where we find his business partner Baruch Chemiak in the town of Neidenburg (Nidzica). Chemiak had lived there since at least 1775, though we do not know how these two business partners connected with each other. We do know that both were active in supplying meat to the Prussian army. In a petition to the Prussian administration, Chemiak pleaded for the legal status of a "privileged protected Jew" (*Ordentlicher Schutzjude*) in 1791, underscoring his great reputation among all inhabitants of the town of Neidenburg, Jews and Christians alike, but also his utility to the state by supplying meat to numerous Prussian troops passing through the area, even when it required procuring necessary cattle from more than sixty miles away. Itzig Jacob also identified himself a butcher when he requested the privilege to establish himself in the West Prussian town of Allenstein in the early 1780s; it is reasonable to assume that he entered the business of army supplying in addition to trade through this avenue. It was common that Jewish butchers sold non-kosher parts of slaughtered animals to Christians, which seems to have been the case here as well. Together they supplied storehouses for the Second Prussian Army at the local level in the vicinity of Neidenburg in the early 1790s.[29]

Though we do not know the exact form of partnership and shared business between Baruch Chemiak and Itzig Jacob, and the latter succeeded rather quickly in expanding his business as army supplier, we do know that the ties between these two business partners did not sever. They were rather strengthened via family ties. In 1798, the daughter of Baruch Chemiak, Eva, married Moses Abraham, the son of Abraham Jacob—Itzig's brother—from Flatow.[30] Itzig Jacob himself sought to extend his business and secure his legal position through marriage. Already involved in army supplying, he used contacts to Jews in Poland to acquire feed for the Prussian army. His most important contacts were Szmul and Judyta (Judith) Jakubowicz,

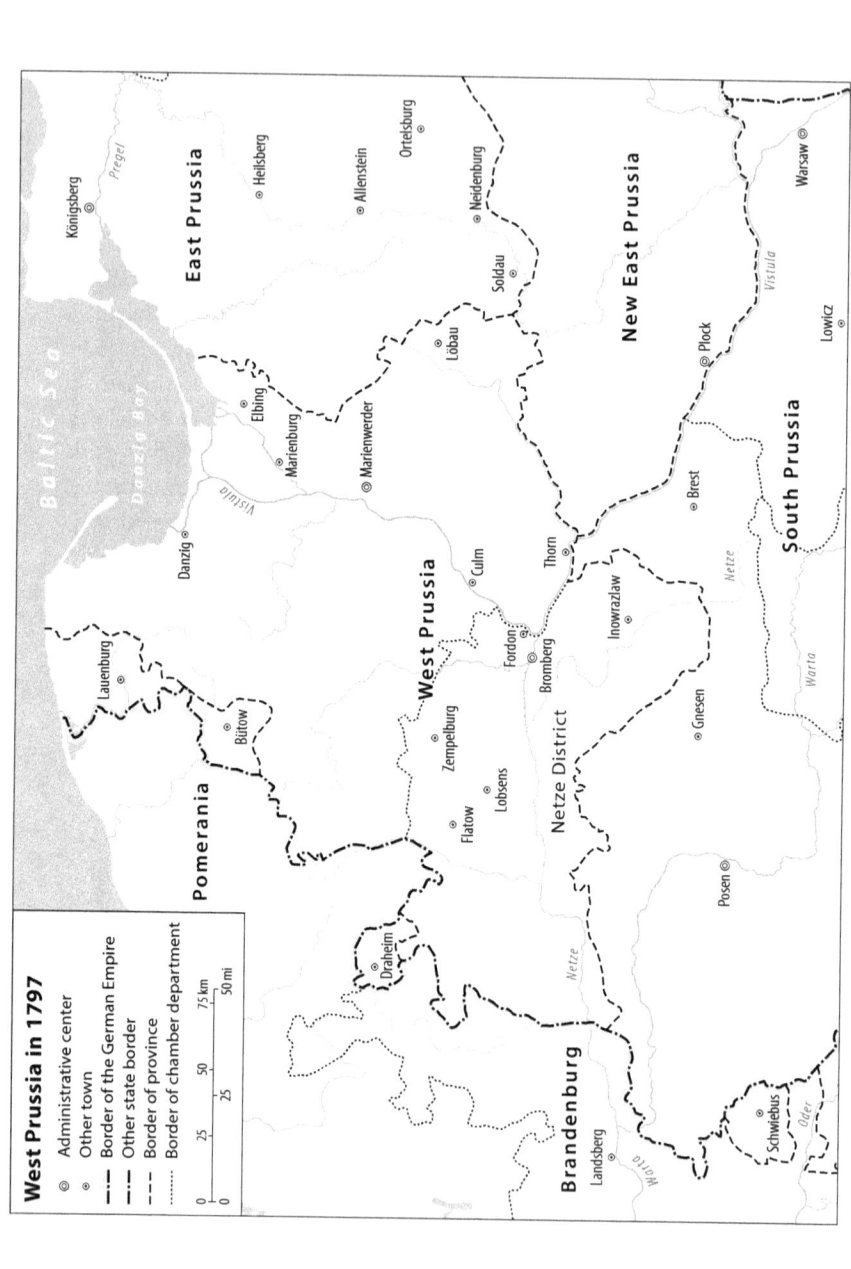

FIGURE 3.2. West Prussia in 1797. The map shows the most important stations of Itzig Jacob's life in West Prussia (Netze district), East Prussia, and South Prussia. Credit: Marc Friede, Marburg, Germany.

well-established Jewish merchants and army suppliers in Warsaw at that time. One may assume either that Itzig Jacob's family established those ties prior to the partitions of Poland or that Itzig Jacob's travels to Frankfurt an der Oder had put him in contact with Judyta and her family. However, in his aforementioned plea to settle in Soldau in 1791, he added:

> ... that the wise Polish Court-Jew Schmul in Warsaw, who owns large noble estates in the vicinity of the capital, gave me the formal agreement to marry his oldest daughter though under the condition that I will settle as *Schutz-Jude* [protected privileged Jew]—if not in Warsaw—then at least in Soldau. I received this confirmation personally in Warsaw during my recent successful business trip involving Polish leather but for good reason I fear imminent danger if my desired establishment and privilege will not be carried out soon.[31]

Itzig Jacob argued that the planned wedding would transfer a considerable fortune into the province and that the domestic manufactories would profit from his trade. Jakubowicz supported this request via a letter in which he emphasized the considerable fortune that would be transferred to Prussia via his daughter's dowry. Itzig Jacob emphasized the utility of his business and the satisfaction of the Prussian army officials with his supplies, while concurrently employing his commercial and personal connections to advance his case. Notably, both this and a later plea for a general privilege for South Prussia were rejected.[32] Eventually, it was the aforementioned marriage to Szmul Jakubowicz's daughter Ludwika that allowed him to settle in Warsaw in 1796. Until then, he rode stormy and unsteady waters.

Army Supplying as a Way to Success

Army supplying was not a new field to Jewish merchants and entrepreneurs. Rather, army supplying repeatedly played a crucial role in the rise to economic success if not political influence of small groups of Jewish merchants and entrepreneurs at different places and times. In fact, the resettlement of Jews in parts of western and central Europe around the Thirty Years' War was closely linked to their abilities as army suppliers and war financiers, two activities that were closely linked to each other. Jews in German-speaking lands enjoyed close connections to the emperor, which led to increasing help from Jewish army suppliers for imperial troops which then were often repaid with privileges and concessions. Swedish troops greatly profited from the supply of horses and other goods from Jews living in rural German areas, who were active in cattle and horse trade. The devastating consequences of the Thirty Years' War in terms of population loss and Jewish supply of various troops increased the number of settlements; thus the number of Jews living in German lands rose considerably.[33] Success in army supplying depended on a number of factors including: involvement in the relevant trades, such as textile, grain, leather, cattle and horse trade, and familiarity with trade routes, producers, and merchants across political boundaries. A detailed look at exclusively Jewish independent and dependent subcontractors of the Habsburg Court Jews—Samuel and Emanuel Oppenheimer, Simon Wertheimer and others—has shown that those factors were crucial for the successful supply of the imperial army in Hungary during the first half of the eighteenth century.[34]

Jonathan Israel argued that following the Treaty of Utrecht and the end of the War of the Spanish Succession in 1713, relatively peaceful decades across Europe was one of the causes for a decline of the economic fortunes of Jews across Europe. This argument, however, is closely linked to his implicit focus on western Europe. Supplying the military secured Jews renewed importance in central and eastern Europe throughout the second half of the eighteenth century and up to the Napoleonic Wars. The Seven Years' War, following the three Silesian Wars in the 1740s, involved not only Saxony and Prussia but drew also Russian troops westward, the latter having a particularly poor and underdeveloped supply system.[35] The Bavarian War of Succession (1778/79) involved Prussian and Austrian troops. In Poland, times were far from calm; despite efforts at reform and consolidation under the last Polish king, Poniatowski, the country became engulfed in intense political turmoil. Although the partitions of Poland in 1772, 1793, and 1795, were not wars in the strict sense of the word, they led to significant troop movement, which resulted in a need for constant supplies of food and feed. It was the need for supplies in large amounts, delivered rapidly and often across vast territories on the peripheries of the respective state, as well as the ability of Jewish entrepreneurs and their willingness to provide these supplies under difficult circumstances that gave suppliers like Itzig Jacob central importance in this business.

In the former Polish territories, the Prussian government sought to acquire grain locally and regionally through state officials and by strictly regulating any free trade with grain, though their efforts met with limited success. Like in Hungary half a century earlier, the state thought to improve and centralize the food supply and feed the army through a system of repositories.[36] The task of filling Prussian storehouses was transferred, increasingly over time, to professional army suppliers, yet this development did spur debate. In particular, Prussian administrators disputed the question whether Jewish entrepreneurs should take a prominent role in fulfilling such a sensitive task as army supplying.

Karl Georg Heinrich von Hoym, provincial minister of Silesia, supported awarding supply contracts to Jewish suppliers.[37] This inclination may have been related to his close relationship to certain Jewish entrepreneurs or to recognition that Jewish suppliers could provide supplies across borders more easily and were thus the best choice in his efforts to turn the Silesian system of grain storehouses into the best administered ones within Prussia. Other officials opposed this measure; they argued, for example, that a contract with Itzig Jacob and his partners for the supply of entire districts of South Prussia was disadvantageous to the state as well as for local inhabitants, who would have to contribute cash payments instead of produce.

Von Hoym worked on introducing a system to replace local supplies and allow for acquiring grain transregionally. Its opponents, however, claimed that Itzig Jacob had received a complete contract merely to commission subcontractors for much lower prices and that the products would be handled by three or four parties, each seeking a profit. They opined that it would be more expensive than the local supply. The eventual contract discloses that an exclusively local supply would have been inadequate. Negotiated in late May and early June 1795, the contract stipulated that Itzig Jacob and his partners were required to accept supplies from inhabitants who insisted on paying in kind, yet also had to acquire additional grain elsewhere to fulfill the contract.[38]

It is difficult to judge how these contracts were allocated. In some cases, contracts for army supplies were publicly announced. Bidding on those sorts of contracts became a common procedure.[39] One can assume that close ties with officials in the respective administrations were of great advantage in successfully bidding for these contracts. These ties to state officials were crucial in connecting Jewish merchant networks to the general economy. This way of integration is comparable to the importance Jewish merchants allotted to connections with Christian merchants in towns with settlement restrictions for Jews.

Army contracts were usually shared between business partners, primarily for logistical and financial reasons. This included close contacts between Jewish suppliers, contracts that were signed and fulfilled jointly across political borders, as well as the commissioning of local subcontractors. One such link existed between Szmul Jakubowicz from Warsaw and his future son-in-law, Itzig Jacob. Following earlier business with hides and the prospect of his marriage to one of Szmul's daughters, they joined forces in supplying the Russian army. Immediately after the 1793 partition of Poland, Itzig Jacob moved to Lowicz in newly occupied South Prussia for the years of 1793/94; from that locale he supplied Prussian troops around Lowicz. He had previously provided feed to Russian troops in Lublin in 1792. During the Kościuszko uprising of 1794 he supplied the Russian army, together with Jakubowicz, who joined him in Lowicz.[40]

By this time, Itzig Jacob had successfully moved from being a small local sub-supplier to an important supplier to several armies.[41] Over time, he "capitalized" on the expansionist policy of the Prussian state and moved eastward after the second and third partition of Poland. In 1795, after his stay in Lowicz, he moved to Posen and beat out a Jewish supplier from Breslau in negotiations for a large contract for supplying the Prussian army in South Prussia. The protocols of the negotiations show that he was the main supplier but the scale of the business was too wide to take on alone; he shared the task of providing oats, rye, flour, hay, and straw with Salomon Neumann from his former domicile Lowicz, and with Michael Schweitzer and Itzig Kempner from Breslau in Silesia. The geographic distribution of the business partners contributed to their ability to provide supplies from outside of South Prussia, in this case from Galicia, Silesia, and the area of Sandomirz. As such, army suppliers regularly received passports that allowed them to cross the borders with their goods.[42]

The protocols of the contract negotiations, however, tell yet another story about Jewish army supplying: they relate the sharp competition between suppliers. Ethnic solidarity in creating commercial networks did not eliminate competition among Jewish suppliers. On May 28, 1795, Itzig Jacob and his partners appeared before the local administration of South Prussia in Petrikau (Piotrków Trybunalski) to negotiate a new contract that had been held by a certain Nathan Abraham. They were not the only ones. The Jewish supplier Joachim Meyer from Breslau also placed a bid, cutting his prices by a few pennies per bushel or centner.[43] Eventually, the royal chamber disclosed Meyer's lower bid to Itzig Jacob and requested an even lower price. He and his partners refused and argued that the prices for grain were likely to rise before the harvest and that market prices for some of the products were already higher than their offer. They offered a deposit of 20,000 thaler in cash, which they claimed Meyer would not be able to match. Such deposits were probably offered and required to prove a supplier's good financial standing and for the state to ensure that the supplier would feel pressed to supply even under difficult circumstances in order to not lose the deposit. Moreover, Itzig Jacob and his partners claimed that Meyer: "would be at an unpleasant loss with such a large enterprise, because he is already unable to fulfill his current small delivery properly and would fail to satisfy his subcontractors who will be subjected to greatest distress."[44] They called on the officials to not pursue a minor saving via the misfortunes of multiple families, referring to Meyer's subcontractors. It is questionable whether the officials were amenable to this kind of argumentation, or whether Itzig Jacob and his partners simply had a better reputation or stronger support from some of the officials. Eventually, they were awarded the contract. In this case, defaming a competitor, be it justified or not, succeeded.

Though Jewish transregional networks were crucial in the army supply business, they did not preclude fierce competition between Jewish entrepreneurs over profitable contracts. Similar to the case described here, an anonymous pamphlet accused Berlin banker and army supplier Jacob Herz Beer of not only defaming his competitor, a certain Cohen from Breslau, but also of fraud. Cohen claimed that he had made a much lower offer but that it had been rejected due to corruption and that Jacob Herz Beer was swindling the state for more than 380,000 thaler.[45] These cases of competition appear to parallel the similarly fierce competition among Jewish lessees of noble estates and monopolies in the Polish-Lithuanian Commonwealth throughout the eighteenth century. Jewish communities tried to prevent or at least to stymie such competition by protecting a lessee's possessor's rights (*dinei hazakah*).[46] It is questionable whether any such attempts were undertaken to limit competition between army suppliers. First, these contracts were negotiated in Prussia, where Jewish communities wielded far less legal power to implement such measures. Second, as we have seen, these suppliers were highly mobile and often traveled to negotiate contracts; as such, it was even more difficult to restrict them.

Fierce competition among Jewish army suppliers, closely calculated prices, and the difficulties that arose in supplying multiple armies amid changing political circumstances were further aggravated by the payment practices of the authorities. In the second half of the 1790s, Itzig Jacob claimed outstanding payments from the Prussian authorities for various supplies to Prussian and Russian troops, including a rather large amount of accumulated interest. In the latter case, he claimed a sum of 2,000 ducats from the Prussian administration because the Russian troops had left feed behind that the Prussians confiscated.[47]

In a time of constantly shifting borders and power constellations, the ability and willingness to cross borders and incur possible risks were as crucial to army supplying as familiarity with trade in agricultural and natural goods, such as grain, cattle, and wood. These shifting political conditions strongly affected the former territories of the Polish-Lithuanian Commonwealth, and Warsaw and its surroundings in particular, from the first partition of Poland to the Congress of Vienna that finalized new borders. Late payments and the insecure political role turned army suppling into a high-risk economic venture.[48] By contrast, the political conditions allowed those merchants and army suppliers who were willing to take risks and able to maneuver successfully through challenging times to join a new Jewish elite developing in Polish lands in general and in Warsaw in particular. It also appears that this transregional feature was one factor that attracted Jews to this business. As far as records allow, we can also conclude that there were no Christian competitors in the field of army supplying in the Prussian-Polish borderlands.

Warsaw: Remaining Insecurity

We do not know whether Itzig Jacob had had his eye on Warsaw from his early days as a small army supplier and his earlier contacts and plans to wed a member of the Jakubowicz family. However, we do know that with the ever-changing political conditions, geographic mobility was central to his livelihood and that of other Jewish merchants and army suppliers. The repeated political and territorial shifts of the 1790s shaped their commercial activities and networks; the merchants had to readjust time and again to these changing conditions. With the Prussian occupation of additional Polish territories in 1793 and 1795 and of the former Polish capital Warsaw in 1796, the number of Jews living in the Prussian state again rose considerably. In 1794, Russian troops defeated a Polish uprising under the leadership of Tadeusz Kościuszko, and Warsaw initially fell to the Russian Empire in the third partition of Poland. In the final stipulations between the two partitioning powers, Russia and Prussia, Warsaw was handed over to Prussia in 1796.

Prior to the second and third partition of Poland, the Prussian administration had primarily reacted to the changing conditions rather than to develop a coherent policy toward its new territories. Now it sought to proactively establish a legal framework for the Jewish population in the former Polish territories. The restrictive Revised General Code of 1750 remained in effect in West Prussia, the Netze district and all other Prussian provinces until the Prussian emancipation edict of 1812.[49] Considering the difficulties involved in even the rudimentary application of many of the 1750 regulations onto the territories occupied in 1772, the authorities understood that applying the Revised General Code of 1750 in the new provinces South and New East Prussia would not be successful. Thus, in April 1797 the Prussian government issued a new General Code for the Jews of South and New East Prussia (*General-Juden-Reglement für Süd- und Neuostpreußen*), a mixture of reforms and regimentations that did not afford them political rights. While it retained the division of "protected" and "tolerated" Jews, it made them subject to general jurisdiction and listed a larger number of occupations permissible for Jews.[50]

Despite the shortcomings of the 1797 General Code, it eased life for many Jews. Moses Wasserzug, who still served the community of Płock at the time, was now able to leave his service position for the Jewish community and establish a hostel and inn beyond city boundaries. Notably, he was able to secure the permission with ease, and also to acquire a loan from the royal chamber toward this end. Though his success is not comparable to that of Itzig Jacob, he did ultimately profit from the Prussian occupation, advancing from communal servant to owner of an inn.[51]

On the one hand, the new General Code of 1797 sought to fashion clear guidelines for the economic activities of Jews. On the other hand, it curtailed the freedom of their cultural and religious life; and did not grant them any political rights. The General Code allegedly guaranteed freedom of religion, but the role of the rabbi was restricted and all juridical rights were abolished. The only alleviation was the abolition of the privilege *de non tolerandis Judaeis* (lit., nontoleration of Jews), which many royal towns in the former Polish territories held. The privilege was also abolished in Warsaw and, thus, Jews should have had free access to the city, but their situation remained difficult and in many ways insecure.

This was also true for Itzig Jacob. After his long-lasting though reasonably successful odyssey through the Prussian territories acquired from the Polish state between 1772 and 1795, he eventually settled in Warsaw in 1796 when the city fell under Prussian rule. He finally married Ludwika Rebekka, the second daughter of Judyta and Szmul Jakubowicz. In these years, he was only one among many Jewish merchants, army suppliers and entrepreneurs who made their way to the former Polish capital. Leib Oesterreicher, whose name suggests that he hailed from the Habsburg Empire although he also had family in Silesia, got married to Judyta and Szmul Jakubowicz's oldest daughter, (Marianna Barbara) Bona, and moved to Warsaw, where he was active in business and regularly collaborated with his father-in-law and with his brother-in-law, Itzig Jacob. Another close business partner of the latter was Moses Aron Fürstenberg, a merchant likely of Prussian origin who had also moved to Warsaw.

Despite the economic incentives that the city provided to the aforementioned merchants and many more Jews who moved to Warsaw in those years, settlement rights remained a pressing issue. The discussion about the settlement of Jews in the city peaked during the Four Year Sejm (1788–1792), but the issue was not resolved. Shortly after the Prussian administration took over the city, a new debate over the limitations of Jewish settlement in Warsaw and Praga, a town on the opposite side of the Vistula River, arose. Also after the disappearance of the Polish state these debates did not cool down. Despite demands from burghers to expel the Jews, the Prussian administration was unwilling to forgo the nearly 400,000 złoty that it received annually through various taxes applied to Jews. To exercise some form of control, Prussia introduced a system of so-called day tickets (*Tageszettel*) in 1799. This system allowed Jews who had entered Warsaw before 1796 to settle permanently; latecomers (namely, those who arrived after 1796) had to pay high taxes to receive the same right; and Jews who arrived after 1799 were obliged to pay a day-ticket charge to reside in the city temporarily.[52] Itzig Jacob and Leib Oesterreicher were fortunate that their parents-in-law had succeeded in securing a general privilege (*Generalprivileg*), the highest possible category of privileges awarded to Jews by the Prussian authorities, in 1798.[53] Still, Itzig Jacob's legal security was limited; if his wife were to die, he would be demoted to the low category of tolerated Jew. In his written exchange with the Prussian administration, he argued that the administration should grant him a general privilege based not only on his strong economic performance but also on his position as a representative of the Jewish community in Warsaw. However, the administration argued that despite some individual citizens of Warsaw who advocated on his behalf, their opinion did not reflect the wishes of all Christian inhabitants of the city and thus his appeal could not be approved.[54]

Despite those legal limitations, many wealthy Jewish merchants and entrepreneurs took advantage of the opportunity of Prussian rule to move further into the inner streets of Warsaw, which were previously off limits to Jews. Already in 1770 a large number of Jews were counted in the enclaves (*jurydiki*) of the Potocki family, which included central streets such as Senatorska Street, Krakowski Przedmieście, Długa, Przejazd, and Nalewki Street.[55] In 1801, Itzig Jacob rented the so-called Cracow Palace on Senatorska Street for ten years, together with his business partner, Moses Aron Fürstenberg. However, in 1806, the magistrate instructed the Jews of Warsaw to move from the city's inner streets to the outer ones within two years.[56] Itzig Jacob and Fürstenberg introduced three points in their correspondence to secure their right to remain in the Cracow Palace, which was situated north of the Saxon Garden (Ogród Saski), a central square near the theater. They argued that they had invested a notable sum in repairing the building. Second, they noted that according to the original contract, Jews were not allowed to reside in the building, and that they only rented spaces for trade. Their third point was the most intriguing: The petitioners suggested that the measure was taken to expel poor Jews due to their "uncleanliness" (*Unreinlichkeit*), and they assumed that those restrictions ought not apply to them. Their argument displays their clear sense of belonging to an economic (Jewish) elite despite their only partly secure legal status.[57]

Warsaw: The Entry into the Banking Business

What turned Itzig Jacob into one of the members of Warsaw's economic elite and eventually into the well-known banker, Izaak Flatau, was a flurry of economic development that started to surface in the early 1790s. Prior to that time, the important banking houses in Warsaw were run by Christian bankers, primarily of German Protestant origin, although there were a few active bankers who were Polish nobles and foreign Jews like Simon Symons from Amsterdam.

A turning point in Warsaw's banking history occurred in 1793. A general shift took place throughout Europe that undermined the durability of Protestant banking networks; in Warsaw, it was spurred by the bankruptcy of the major Christian, and mostly Protestant, banking houses in 1793. The disaster resulted from a combination of a general downturn of the European economy, including the bankruptcies of several English and Dutch banks, as well as political turmoil in Poland that led to the disappearance of the Polish state.

This historical shift also underscores the powerful effects rumors wielded on financial markets. It is instructive to keep in mind that bankruptcy was and is not easily measurable; it occurred when creditors demanded the return of their assets, usually unexpectedly and all at once, making bankruptcy "a legal, rather than an economic category."[58] When rumors spread in 1793 that the Tepper banking house was encountering financial difficulties due to unreturned loans by the Polish government, creditors began arriving in Warsaw to withdraw their capital. The bank's subsequent failure came as a shock, taking down the Warsaw banks of Schultz and Cabrit as well. In addition, that financial and political crisis similarly affected several Polish nobles who were involved in trade, banking, and industry, including Antoni Protazy Potocki, head of the Black Sea Trade Company.[59]

Only a small minority of the creditors and debtors of the large Warsaw banking houses that went bankrupt in 1793 were Jews. But, like most creditors, it is likely that they too were unable to recover their debts. Moses Boas and Abraham Symons, the son of Benjamin Symons in Amsterdam, appealed to the former king Poniatowski in Grodno in 1797 in an attempt to recover a royal obligation of more than 8,500 ducats that they had received from Frideric Cabrit. It is unlikely that they ever saw a single ducat of that debt. After the bankruptcy and death of their relative, Simon Symons, in 1793, a court commission was established in Warsaw in 1795 to deal with his assets and notify all debtors and creditors to appear before the court. Again, one can assume that little came of this, given the political circumstances and the fact that Symons had presumably been able to move a large part of his assets to Frankfurt an der Oder, where his wife Mintje lived; she was of the wealthy class of the community until her death in 1811.[60] Moreover, Symons left the Jewish community a large bequest unmatched by any other community member. This bequeathing also demonstrates the closeness of his ties to the community in Frankfurt an der Oder over the years, even after he terminated his business partnership with Levin Pincus Schlesinger.[61]

The demise of Simon Symons's (small) banking business in Warsaw in the rupture of 1793 provides a powerful symbol marking the end of the close ties to Amsterdam as a center of credit for central European Jewish merchants. Even state loans that had been administered from Amsterdam over the course of the final years of the Polish-Lithuanian Commonwealth came increasingly from bankers based in London. However, there was also a new group of entrepreneurs that took advantage of the opportunity to enter the banking business in Poland in general and in Warsaw in particular.

Like the merchant-suppliers in Alsace-Lorraine and the Rothschilds in London, Jewish bankers in Warsaw were also fortunate. Their outstanding role in army supplying afforded them an excellent position to take advantage of the bankruptcies of the eighteenth-century Christian banking houses, bankruptcies which left the field almost entirely open for newcomers. The political unrest after 1793, the second and third partitions of Poland, the Kościuszko uprising, and Prussia's takeover of the city in 1796 surely created logistical and financial hurdles for Jewish entrepreneurs, including at least some loss to their assets. Yet the political shifts and instability also helped to create opportunity for Jewish entrepreneurs to enter the banking business; they were willing to incur the inherent risks implied.

Among the first to take advantage of these new opportunities and of the Polish nobles' need for credit was Itzig Jacob. We do not know exactly when he entered the banking business after moving to Warsaw in 1796. However, contemporaneous sources and nineteenth- and twentieth-century historiography generally refer to him as a wealthy Prussian banker. Archival records mention his banking activities as beginning in 1803, though one can assume that he engaged in this business before the turn of the century.[62] In 1805, estate owner Damasius of Krajewski, in need of cash to pay off his brother in order to not split their parents' estate, decided to "travel to Warsaw to . . . the well-known merchant and banker [*Negotiant*] Itzig Jacob Flatau."[63] Thus, by the start of the nineteenth century, Itzig Jacob was already reputed to be an important banker in Warsaw.

An important income source for early nineteenth-century bankers in the former Polish territories was Polish nobles with extensive estates who needed cash to continue their lavish lifestyle or to pay off family members to not split up estates. Their estates functioned as security. Right after the second partition of Poland in 1793, the Prussian government introduced a mortgage system in its Polish territories, increasing the profitability of this business. As nobles started to record their properties into mortgage books, the system granted them the possibility of long-term loans; they were then able to mortgage their estates more systematically.[64]

Though Itzig Jacob exploited these opportunities that emerged for Jewish entrepreneurs in Warsaw, he continued to rely on various sources of income, including his business prospects in army supplying. In addition, he owned inns and leased rights to produce and sell alcohol (*propinacja*); his ownership of a brickworks factory paved the way for an attempted inroad into manufacturing. At the time of his death in 1806, his business had not yet evolved into a nineteenth-century banking house. Similarly, other Jewish entrepreneurs who had moved to Warsaw by the late eighteenth century, such as his business partner Fürstenberg, and Oesterreicher, brother-in-law of his wife, also traded in obligations and provided credit without moving fully into banking.[65] In particular, army supplying remained an important source of income for them. During the Prussian reign over Warsaw, authorities were forced to acquire grain from abroad, largely from Galicia, which had fallen under Austrian rule. In this instance too we can assume that most suppliers were Jews. Itzig Jacob supplied storehouses in Warsaw with rye from Galicia in 1801, and Oesterreicher was contracted two years later to supply the city when the authorities feared a grain shortage. Like Itzig Jacob, Oesterreicher bought the grain in Austria. Though both probably recruited Jewish sub-suppliers as they had in previous business transactions, Itzig Jacob also received some of his supplies directly from Polish nobles.[66]

The wide variety of entrepreneurial undertakings administered by Jewish immigrants to Warsaw guaranteed their economic survival in politically difficult times. The risks of army supplying were cushioned by more traditional undertakings, while the protracted payments in the supply business laid the groundwork for providing credit, thereby facilitating the move into the banking business. The economic success of a small number of Jewish entrepreneurs was rooted in two things: the willingness to incur increased risk to not only improve one's economic but also one's legal standing as well as the transregional connections across newly emerging and constantly changing borders. Though many merchants and army suppliers might have employed the same strategies, only few were as successful as Itzig Jacob. Though he traveled a long route to leave a predominantly Jewish town in the former Polish territories to head to Warsaw in search of settlement rights and economic opportunity, he was trailing the expanding Prussian state on what one might call an upward journey to the east.

A "German" Synagogue in Warsaw

As noted at the beginning of this chapter, Itzig Jacob was at least as famous for opening a synagogue in Daniłowiczowska Street as he was for being a wealthy banker. Nussbaum's description on the first page of the chapter portrays him as a German-style religious reformer, an image that resonated strongly in Polish historiography that often described Prussian Jewish immigrants as agents of Germanization.[67] It is instructive to recall that Itzig Jacob hailed from an originally Polish Jewish family, whose hometown Flatow came under Prussian occupation only when he was a young boy. By the beginning of the nineteenth century, when he had already attained the status of a well-known and wealthy figure in Warsaw's business world, he might have dressed differently than more traditional Polish Jews, clad in what was called "European attire."[68] Although we do not know exactly when he opened the synagogue, we know that he bought the house on Daniłowiczowska Street in 1800. The building was centrally located outside the city wall, close to the Theater Square. In the synagogue itself, more like a private prayer house, no significant reforms akin to those proposed by the early German reform movement were introduced; the first sermon in German was given only in 1838, more than thirty years after his death.[69] Rather, the motivation to establish a private prayer house was rooted in a general tradition not alien to Polish Jewry. With the religious freedom Jews enjoyed in the Polish-Lithuanian Commonwealth, opening a small private prayer house was not uncommon, though it grew into a touchy issue for many communities with the rise of Hasidism. In Itzig Jacob's hometown in West Prussia, it was not uncommon to open private prayer houses; under Prussian rule, one had to obtain permission to do so. His brother, Moses Jacob, requested to open a prayer house in his home in Gumbinnen in 1796, whereas his business partner Baruch Chemiak opened a prayer house and a ritual bath (*mikveh*) in Neidenburg in 1792.[70] These cases suggest that Itzig Jacob was not primarily motivated by some kind of "disdain" for his fellow Polish Jews but rather by a tradition of establishing private prayer houses for one's own family and close acquaintances. Indeed, the service in his prayer house may have differed in terms of liturgy and custom from those followed in other Warsaw prayer houses, yet it should not be readily assumed that the private prayer house was founded exclusively for that purpose. Rather, it demonstrates Itzig Jacob's interest in religious and communal matters, and it might allude to an attempt to solidify his position within the local Jewish community by increasing his reputation.

Although Jews living in Warsaw or its vicinity did maintain some form of communal organization before a communal representation was officially recognized in Warsaw in 1799, it is difficult to trace its early development. Its trajectory was unstable and closely tied to the considerations of non-Jewish authorities. Prussia recognized a communal administration (*kahal*) to ensure collection of taxes, in particular the kosher meat tax (*korobka*). Among the communal representatives elected in the following years were Itzig Jacob and his business partner, Fürstenberg.[71] Both men used their economic power to assume influence within the Jewish community and also to create economic opportunity for communal leaders, even in the unstable political circumstances of Warsaw. One such opportunity involved leasing the kosher meat tax. Even prior to creating a Jewish communal administration, the municipal administration auctioned the collection of taxes on kosher meat to cover particular expenses. In 1792 and 1793, the Warsaw newspaper *Gazeta Warszawska* announced an auction of the kosher meat tax for slaughterhouses and Jewish eateries (*garkuchni*) in Warsaw, with the proceeds to be allocated to the commission for street reconstruction. In 1801, the same newspaper announced the termination of the lease with "the Jewish banker Flatau"—that is Itzig Jacob—over the kosher meat tax used to maintain the Jewish hospital; it publicized the auction for a new six-month contract.[72] This tax may have been an additional tax, since the kosher meat tax was administered by the *kahal* and the communal lay leadership until 1809, when the Duchy of Warsaw government decided to auction off the tax publicly. Nevertheless, it remained in the hands of the elders of the Warsaw community who had the financial means as well as the necessary experience to keep competitors away.[73] Though it is unclear to what extent entrepreneurs profited financially from leasing the kosher meat tax, this example captures how closely economic and communal power were intertwined.

Conclusion

Clear regulations governed Prussian politics toward Jews and their economic activities in the old Prussian provinces; but, in the new periphery, the former Polish territories their application was uneven. Although the Prussian state applied restrictive tariffs to support the import of raw material and export of Prussian manufactured goods until the turn of the century, local policies proved irregular as administrators struggled to cope with local circumstances. Their actions were shaped by guidelines codified by the central government, their insights as local administrators and by petitions from Christian burghers, merchants, and manufacturers. Members of the Jewish mercantile elite developed their own strategies and means to counter restrictive legal and economic conditions. They sought to persuade local and central administrators of their economic utility for the state as well as for the particular region or town. They hoped that taking on especially risky business ventures for the state would pay off financially and facilitate their securing specific privileges regarding settlement and trade. Thus, the entrepreneurial strategies of members of the Jewish mercantile elite differed at least in part from those of non-Jewish entrepreneurs; Jewish entrepreneurs used their assets and services as an insurance policy of sorts to ensure or improve their legal status. The other important strategy members of the Jewish mercantile elite used to confront legal restrictions and improve their economic activities was the assembling and maintenance of transregional networks. These familial and commercial networks allowed for a greater degree of mobility, though the cooperation with local merchants also carried importance.

It was a combination of strategies—submitting petitions emphasizing one's economic usefulness, economic flexibility, close-knit networks of business and family connections, and a willingness to take risk—that led to Itzig Jacob's success and eventual transformation into the "wealthy German banker Izaak Flatau." One ought to recall that this description was filled with greater meaning by historians of later generations than it carried at the time. Though Itzig Jacob hailed from the Prussian partition territories, he was still born under Polish rule into a family of Polish Jews. Although he did open a synagogue that differed from others in Warsaw that served the local Polish Jewish population, it was first and foremost a modest prayer house for his family and acquaintances, but not part of, or an imitator of, an early German reform movement.

This chapter has shown how Jewish merchants and entrepreneurs used a combination of different strategies to circumvent legal restrictions, which encroached the social and economic life of Jews in the old and new provinces of Prussia. Though a majority of Jews, especially the less wealthy ones, suffered from the Prussian policy of diminishing the Jews economic role in the new provinces acquired in 1772, the eventual aim of creating socio-economic structures akin to the ones in the old Prussian provinces failed. Expulsions of Jews ceased after the second partition of Poland in 1793 and the example of Itzig Jacob shows that at least for some individuals the ambiguous political measures became the background for some degree of economic success, though only few became indeed forerunners of a new Jewish economic elite of the nineteenth century. The fluidity and sometimes uncertainty of the borderlands, together with the increased need for army supplies contributed to this economic success.

Notes

1. Nussbaum, *Szkice historyczne*, 92.

2. Struck, "Vom offenen Raum zum nationalen Territorium," 81–90.

3. Jersch-Wenzel, *Die Memoiren des Moses Wasserzug*, 29–30, 48. A transcript of the original Hebrew version was published by Loewe, "Memoiren eines polnischen Juden," 87–114, 440–446.

4. The classic work on the westward migration is Shulvass, *From East to West*.

5. Stern, *Der Preußische Staat und die Juden. Dritter Teil: Die Zeit Friedrichs des Großen*, vol. 2, no. 1222, 1489–1493. In a letter to the authorities from 1791, Itzig Jacob mentioned his six brothers. Acta betr. das Gesuch des jüdischen Handlungs-Bedienten Itzig Jacob, um Bewilligung eines Schutz-Privilegii auf die Stadt Soldau, 1791–1792, II. HA, Abt. 7, II Materien, no. 4717, GStA, 1.

6. On the legal situation of Polish Jewry, see Goldberg, *Jewish Privileges in the Polish Commonwealth*, 1–40; Teller, "The Legal Status of the Jews," 41–63.

7. Teller, "Telling the Difference," 109–141, esp. 119.

8. For examples of these relationships see the following works: Hundert, *The Jews in a Polish Private Town*; Rosman, *The Lords' Jews*; Teller, *Money, Power, and Influence*.

9. Butterwick, "The Enlightened Monarchy of Stanisław August Poniatowski," 193. The laws of 1768, which would have severely limited the legal and economic status of Jews in the towns of the Polish-Lithuanian Commonwealth, were never enforced. Teller, "Telling the Difference," 130–131; Hundert, *Jews in Poland-Lithuania*, 44–47.

10. Recent estimates assume that as many as 16,000 Jews lived there. Jehle, "'Relocations' in South Prussia and New East Prussia," 25. See also Bömelburg, *Zwischen polnischer Ständegesellschaft und preußischem Obrigkeitsstaat*, 422–424.

11. Jehle, "'Relocations' in South Prussia and New East Prussia," 23–47; Heyde, "Zwischen Polen und Preußen," 303–304.

12. Stern, *Der Preußische Staat und die Juden. Dritter Teil: Die Zeit Friedrichs des Großen*, 1:40.

13. Eingabe von Jacob Moses, Bevollmächtigter der Judenschaft in Westpreußen und dem Netzedistrikt, Berlin 29. Juli 1775, HA II, Abt. 9 Materien, Tit. LXVI, Sekt. 1, no. 4, vol. 1, GStA, 158–160.

14. Resolution für den Bevollmächtigten der Judenschaft in Westpreußen und dem Netzedistrikt, Jacob Moses, Berlin, 18. August 1775, HA II, Abt. 9 Materien, Tit. LXVI, Sekt. 1, no. 4, vol. 1, GStA, 166.

15. Jersch-Wenzel, *Die Memoiren des Moses Wasserzug*, 48.

16. Ibid., 49–50, 56–58.

17. Bömelburg, *Zwischen polnischer Ständegesellschaft und preußischem Obrigkeitsstaat*, 191–194, 289, 295, 462–464. On the Polish-Prussian commercial treaty, which Jerzy Lukowski calls "an exercise in piratical mercantilism," see Lukowski, *Liberty's Folly*, 206; Heyde, "Zwischen Polen und Preußen," 299–300, 306, 313–314.

18. Quoted from Bömelburg, *Zwischen polnischer Ständegesellschaft und preußischem Obrigkeitsstaat*, 434.

19. Goldbeck, *Vollständige Topographie des Königreichs Preußen*, 2:99. When Itzig Jacob's brother asked to purchase a house that other family members had already owned under Polish rule, when no restrictions applied to the purchase of property, he did eventually receive permission to do so. Despite the fact that the seventy-one Jewish families in Flatow already owned 110 houses, his request was approved. Acta betr. die Concession für den ordinairen Schutz Juden Israel Jacob zu Flatow zum eigenthümlichen Besitz eines daselbst angekauften Hauses, 1806, II. HA, Abt. 9, Westpreußen / Netzedistrikt, Stadt Flatow, Sekt. 4, no. 13, GStA, 14. The expulsions continued into the 1790s but never affected all poor Jews. Jehle, "'Relocations' in South Prussia and New East Prussia," 26–29; Bömelburg, *Zwischen polnischer Ständegesellschaft und preußischem Obrigkeitsstaat*, 441–445. Bömelburg estimates that 6,000–7,000 Jews were expelled.

20. Jehle, "'Relocations' in South Prussia and New East Prussia," 30–31; Bömelburg, *Zwischen polnischer Ständegesellschaft und preußischem Obrigkeitsstaat*, 462–464.

21. Schnabel-Schüle, "Herrschaftswechsel—zum Potential einer Forschungskategorie," 9.

22. Acta betr. das Gesuch des jüdischen Handlungs-Bedienten Itzig Jacob, um Bewilligung eines Schutz-Privilegii auf die Stadt Soldau, 1791–1792, II. HA, Abt. 7, II Materien, no. 4717, GStA, 1; Acta wegen des von dem Juden Isaac Jacob aus Flatow intendirten Etablissements in der Stadt Allenstein, 1780–1782, II. HA, Abt. 7, Ostpreußen und Litauen, II Materien, no. 4709, GStA, 4; Acta wegen der verbothenen Waaren 1765–1810, II. HA, Abt. 24, Generalakzise- und Zolldepartement B2, Tit. 24, no. 1, GStA, 60.

23. Acta das Gesuch des Itzig Jacob wegen seiner Forderungen in Pohlen betr., I. HA, Rep. 7, no. 106 i, Fasz. 62, GStA; In Sachen des Juden Itzig Jacob aus Lowitz, XX. HA, Etats-Ministerium (EM), Tit. 97j, no. 37, GStA, 1–3.

24. Das Judenwesen in Südpreußen, GDDPP I, no. 884, AGAD, 390–392, 485–490v.

25. Die Gesuche verschiedener Juden um allgemeine Privilegien und Konzessionen auf Südpreußen, GDDPP I, no. 896, AGAD, 6.

26. Acta betr. das Gesuch des jüdischen Handlungs-Bedienten Itzig Jacob, um Bewilligung eines Schutz-Privilegii auf die Stadt Soldau, 1791–1792, II. HA, Abt. 7, II Materien, no. 4717, GStA, 1.

27. Ibid., 10v, 13v.

28. Acta wegen des von dem Juden Isaac Jacob aus Flatow intendirten Etablissements in der Stadt Allenstein, 1780–1782, II. HA, Abt. 7, II Materien, no. 4709, GStA, 8–9, 17–22. His petition was ultimately rejected in 1782. On the Prussian obligation for Jews to purchase and retail hard-to-sell porcelain produced in Berlin, see Schenk, *Wegbereiter der Emanzipation?*, 250–496; Jehle, "'Relocations' in South Prussia and New East Prussia," 26–27.

29. Acta betr. die dem Juden Baruch Chemiac zu Neidenburg ertheilte Concession zu seiner Ansetzung daselbst als Extraordinarius, II. HA, Abt. 7 (Ostpreußen und Litauen), II Materien, no. 4712, GStA, 2–5v; Acta wegen des von dem Juden Isaac Jacob aus Flatow intendirten Etablissements in der Stadt Allenstein, 1780–1782, II. HA, Abt. 7, Ostpreußen und Litauen, II Materien, no. 4709, GStA, 1; Das Judenwesen in Südpreußen, GDDPP I, no. 884, AGAD, 391.

30. Acta betr. die dem Juden Baruch Chemiac zu Neidenburg ertheilte Concession zu seiner Ansetzung daselbst als Extraordinarius, II. HA, Abt. 7, II Materien, no. 4712, GStA, 92–95.

31. Acta betr. das Gesuch des jüdischen Handlungs-Bedienten Itzig Jacob, um Bewilligung eines Schutz-Privilegii auf die Stadt Soldau, 1791–1792, II. HA, Abt. 7, II Materien, no. 4717, GStA, 1v–2. Actually, Itzig Jacob married the second, rather than the oldest daughter of Szmul and Judyta Jakubowicz. By the time this letter was written, she was ten years old.

32. Acta betr. das Gesuch des jüdischen Handlungs-Bedienten Itzig Jacob, 7–7v; Die Gesuche verschiedener Juden um allgemeine Privilegien und Konzessionen auf Südpreußen, GDDPP I, no. 896, AGAD, 12–14, 17.

33. Israel, *European Jewry*, 72–87.

34. Peri, "Pe'ilutam shel safke tsava yehudim," 135–174.

35. Russian troops had to rely heavily on Jewish suppliers during the Seven Years' War. See Keep, "The Russian Army in the Seven Years War," 31–32.

36. Peri, "Pe'ilutam shel safke tsava yehudim," 171.

37. Skalweit, *Die Getreidehandelspolitik und Kriegsmagazinverwaltung Preußens*, 177–179.

38. Die allgemeine Recherche der südpreußischen Kreise und deren Kassen besonders wegen Mißbräuche beim Fouragelieferungswesen, 1795–1806, GDDPP I, no. 1028, AGAD, 110–113; Die Angelegenheiten der Entrepreneurs, 1798–1803, GDDPP IX, no. 256, AGAD, 16, 20.

39. In 1801, the administrators of South Prussia invited offers for an extensive supply of feed in an announcement in *Gazeta Warszawska*, no. 54, supplement, July 7, 1801, 956.

40. In Sachen des Juden Itzig Jacob aus Lowitz, XX. HA, EM, Tit. 97j, no 37, GStA, 1; Resolution für den Itzig Jacob Flatow zu Warschau, I. HA, Geheimer Rat, Rep. 11, 171–175, Rußland D, 1796–1797, GStA. Various sources confirm the stay of Szmul and Judyta in the Muscovite camp and the presence of Prussian suppliers. Kommissya Porządkowa X. Mazowskiego, 1794, AKP, syg. 241, mf. 10703, AGAD, 69, 88; Excerpt z Rapportu Cyrkułu Siodmego Miasta Warszawy, AKP, syg. 257, mf. 10715, AGAD, 304; Powtorna Indagacya z Zyda Boruchowicza, AKP, syg. 254, mf. 10713, AGAD, 32-33; Relacya od Łowicza 16. Maia 1794, AKP, syg. 323, mf. 3670, AGAD, 197.

41. Das Judenwesen in Südpreußen, GDDPP I, no. 884, AGAD, 391. With his first business partner, Baruch Chemiak, he had supplied storehouses on the local level in 1790/91. In the vicinity of Neidenburg, where Chemiak lived, they supplied the Second Prussian Army in Ortelsburg, Schimanen, Willenberg, Neidenburg, and Possenheim. Regarding the close links between Flatow, Ortelsburg, and the other neighboring towns, see Kossert, "Die jüdische Gemeinde Ortelsburg," 89–91, 112–115.

42. Die Angelegenheiten der Entrepreneurs, 1798–1803, GDDPP IX, no. 256, AGAD, 22, 26. In the early 1790s, a group of Prussian army suppliers received passports to travel from Silesia to Poland for a period of twelve weeks to supply horses. Szaja, "Sprawy żydowskie przed komisjami porządkowymi cywilno-wojskowymi na pograniczu wielkopolski i Śląska w latach 1789–1792," 174.

43. One centner equals about sixty-four kilograms. Hundert, *The Jews in a Polish Private Town*, 163.

44. Die Angelegenheiten der Entrepreneurs, 1798–1803, GDDPP IX, no. 256, AGAD, 11; Die allgemeine Recherche der südpreußischen Kreise und deren Kassen besonders wegen der Mißbräuche beim Fouragelieferungswesen, GDDPP I, no. 1025, AGAD, 188.

45. Grünhagen, "Eine südpreußische Kriegslieferung von 1794," 53–60. The pamphlet "Das gepriesene Preußen" was published in 1802.

46. Teller, *Money, Power, and Influence*, 111–120; Rosman, *The Lords' Jews*, 141. On the role of Hasidism in diminishing competition between leaseholders, see Shmeruk, "Haḥasidut ve'iske haḥakhirot," 182–192.

47. Die Angelegenheiten der Entrepreneurs, 1798–1803, GDDPP IX, no. 256, AGAD, 1–3; Die verschiedenen Angelegenheiten der Entrepreneurs, 1803–1805, GDDPP IX, no. 257, AGAD, 25–27, 34–40; In Sachen des Juden Itzig Jacob aus Lowitz, XX. HA, EM, Tit. 97j, no. 37, GStA, 1, 3. Some of the payments remained outstanding in 1803.

48. The same was true for earlier suppliers in the Habsburg lands. Peri, "Pe'ilutam shel safke tsava yehudim," 171.

49. Freund, *Die Emanzipation der Juden in Preußen*; Diekmann, *Das Emanzipationsedikt von 1812 in Preußen*.

50. Printed in Rönne and Simon, *Die früheren und gegenwärtigen Verhältnisse der Juden*, 292–302.

51. Jersch-Wenzel, *Die Memoiren des Moses Wasserzug*, 48, 55–57, 60. See also Heyde, "Zwischen Polen und Preußen," 331.

52. For a detailed account of the struggle during the Four Year Sejm, see Eisenbach, "The Jewish Population in Warsaw at the Turn of the Eighteenth Century," 49–58; Acta wegen der allgemeinen Gesuche und Angelegenheiten der Stadt Warschau, vol. I, GDDPP VI, no. 3565, AGAD, 12v–13, 15–15v, 192. For primary sources, see Eisenbach et al., *Materiały do dziejów sejmu czteroletniego*, vol. 6. See also chapter 4 in this book.

53. See Toeplitz, *Rodzina Toeplitzów*, 42.

54. Die Gesuche verschiedener Juden um allgemeine Privilegien und Konzessionen auf Südpreußen, GDDPP I, no. 896, AGAD, 133–138, 147–152, 157–174, 192–197.

55. Among these were two prominent Jewish businessmen. One was the army supplier and competitor of Szmul Jakubowicz, Hersz Markiewicz from Mszczonowa who lived in the court (Dworek) Ruzanowa in Mlena Street with his three servants, and two more families—16 persons altogether. In addition, a Simon Szymonowicz from Frankfurt with one servant is registered as living at Krakowski Przedmieście. He most likely was the banker Simon Symons from Amsterdam who had come to Warsaw via Frankfurt an der Oder and enjoyed close relations with both the Potocki and Poniński families. Konskrypcja Żydów 1778, APP, syg. 93, [mf. 17867], AGAD. See also Martyn, "The Undefined Town Within a Town," 27–28, 31–32; Węgrzynek, "Illegal Immigrants," 27–40.

56. See Schiper, *Dzieje handlu żydowskiego*, 369; Kieniewicz, "The Jews of Warsaw," 106. See also Bergman, "Nie masz bóżnicy powszechnej," map 2.

57. Die Umquartierung der Juden von den inneren in die äußeren Straßen Warschaus 1806, GDDPP VI, no. 3399, AGAD.

58. Steele, "Bankruptcy and Insolvency," 186.

59. Grochulska, "Échos de la faillite des banques de Varsovie," 529–540.

60. Korespondencja Stanisława Augusta 1792–1797, syg. 3a, AGAD, 110–110v; *Gazeta Warszawska*, no. 78, supplement, September 9, 1795, 896; *Gazeta Warszawska*, no. 85, supplement, October 24, 1795, 978; Listen der Schatzungen und Schutzgelder, 1774–1819, Synagogengemeinde Frankfurt/Oder, D/Fr 1, 30, CAHJP.

61. An undated compilation (probably from the later part of the nineteenth century) of the bequests administered by the Jewish community lists a bequest from Simon Symons totaling 27,154 mark with annual interest of 992 mark used for a school fund and for poor brides; the interest of another bequest over 800 mark was allocated to a fund for the poor. Verzeichnis der Legate, o.D., Synagogengemeinde Frankfurt/Oder, D/Fr 1, 93, CAHJP.

62. Prozess des Starosten Joseph von Niemojewski gegen den Landesältesten Jacob Lewin in Marienwerder wegen der letzterem übertragenen drei Obligationen in Höhe von 62 000 Rtlr. des Bankiers Itzig Jacob Flatau, I. HA, Rep. 7C, no. 6 N 10, Fasz. 16, GStA.

63. Beschwerde des Gutsbesitzers Damasius von Krajewski in seinem Prozess gegen den Juden Itzig Jacob Flatau wegen einer Obligation, 1805, I. HA, Rep. 7C, no. 34g, Fasz. 367, GStA. The term *Negotiant* was used for merchants trading in goods and money as well as for bankers. Krünitz, *Oekonomische Encyclopaedie*, 36:496–497.

64. Simsch, *Die Wirtschaftspolitik des preußischen Staates in der Provinz Südpreußen*, 208; Bruer, *Geschichte der Juden in Preußen*, 161.

65. Kancelaria Andrzeja Kalinowskiego, syg. 23, mf. S-980, APWa, 17, 23, 29, 41; Kancelaria Teodora Czempińskiego, syg. 8, no. 874, APWa; Kancelaria Przeździeckiego, syg. 7, no. 19, 23, 26, APWa; Kancelaria Aleksandra Engelke, syg. 2, no. 165; syg. 10, no. 1362, APWa.

66. Acta wegen eines in Warschau befürchteten Getreide Mangels und der deshalb getroffenen Anstalten, 1801, GDDPP VI, no. 3361, AGAD; Erwirkung eines Freipasses für Roggen für Itzig Jacob Flatow in Warschau zur Belieferung des dortigen Getreidemagazins, 1803, I. HA, Rep. 11, no. 279, Fasz. 361, GStA. In 1803, Itzig Jacob (Flatau) and Joseph Rosenthal turned to the local administration in Białystok to complain about two local nobles who did not supply for months already paid-for goods—rye, wheat, potash, and vessels for transport by boat. Vorstellung Itzig Jacob Flatau und Joseph Rosenthal an die Regierung in Bialystok, 1803, I. HA, Geheimer Rat, Rep. 7A Neuostpreußen, no. 1894, GStA.

67. Hensel, "Wie 'deutsch' war die 'fortschrittliche' jüdische Bourgeoisie im Königreich Polen?," 142.

68. Ibid., 138–141. On the role of dress for Jewish acculturation in Warsaw in the second half of the nineteenth century, see Jagodzińska, *Pomiędzy*, 80–139.

69. Bergman, *"Nie masz bóżnicy powszechnej,"* 200; Bergman, "Synagoga na Daniłowiczowskiej 1800–1878—próba rekonstrukcji," 114–115.

70. Acta wegen der von dem Schutz Juden Moses Jacob in Gumbinnen nachgesuchten Erlaubniß zur Erbauung eines Beth-Hauses, 1796–1799, II. HA, General Directorium, Abt. 7, Ostpreußen und Litauen, II Materien, no. 4767, GStA, 1-2, 10, 51; Acta betr. die dem Juden Baruch Chemiac zu Neidenburg ertheilte Concession zu seiner Ansetzung daselbst als Extraordinarius, II. HA, Abt. 7 (Ostpreußen und Litauen), II Materien, no. 4712, GStA, 41.

71. Shatzky, *Geshikhte fun Yidn in Varshe*, 1:123–127. According to Shatzky, five communal elders (*parnasim*) were appointed in Warsaw and six in Praga between 1759 and 1794.

See also Eisenbach, "The Jewish Population in Warsaw at the Turn of the Eighteenth Century," 48, 58. In addition, beadles (*shamashim*) and judges (*dayanim*) took over additional functions of communal leadership.

72. *Gazeta Warszawska*, no. 84, October 20, 1792; no. 14, supplement, February 17, 1801, 246.

73. Schiper, "Samorząd żydowski w Polsce na przełomie wieku 18 i 19-go," 518, 529. In 1806 R. Shmelke Ahron Wagner leased the tax; in 1807 it went to Berek Szmul. As on other occasions, Shatzky depicts the communal leadership as primarily profiting from the tax personally. Shatzky, *Geshikhte fun yidn in Varshe*, 1:203. In 1812, members of the communal lay leadership in Warsaw including Berek Szmul, Moses Aron Fürstenberg, and Samuel Kronenberg leased the kosher meat tax to subcontractors. Kancelaria Teodora Czempińskiego, syg.10, no. 1253, 443–446; syg. 11, no. 1268, 39–40v, APWa.

FOUR

Praga: A Stepping Stone

In the late 1770s, Judyta (also Judith or Gittl), the daughter of the affluent merchant Levin Buko from Frankfurt an der Oder, traveled to Praga. In this small town opposite Warsaw on the other bank of the Vistula (not to be confused with the Czech city of Prague, see figure 4.1), she was to marry Szmul Jakubowicz Zbytkower, a successful local army supplier and merchant. When she arrived, Warsaw, the Polish capital, was still adhering to its century-long privilege *de non tolerandis Judaeis* (lit., nontoleration of Jews), which had prevented Jews from settling inside the city walls since 1527. Nevertheless, hundreds of Jews had settled in the vicinity of Warsaw by the last quarter of the eighteenth century.

At first glance, Warsaw and Praga appear to be unlikely places for the rise of a new Jewish economic elite in modern Europe. Jewish settlement had remained gravely restricted in the Polish capital for more than two centuries; the partitions of Poland and the related political unrest seemingly made economic fortune even less likely. Nevertheless, the developments of the city drew an increasing number of Jews to the city and its environs. In unstable times, army supplying and the provision and brokerage of credit were promising business for those who were willing to take the accompanying risks. Moreover, one should not forget that in comparison with the Holy Roman Empire in general and Prussia in particular, the Jewish legal position was much advantageous in the Polish-Lithuanian Commonwealth, apart from the royal cities holding a privilege *de non tolerandis Judaeis*.

This chapter argues that Praga, and later on Warsaw, indeed provided an array of opportunities to Jewish merchants from near and far who were willing to take the risk of entering new fields of business in politically unstable times. Those coming from within the Polish-Lithuanian Commonwealth, moreover, profited from their close integration into the feudal economy of early modern Poland and could use these experiences and their personal connections toward their new businesses. With the new developments around 1800, however, not only the Polish Jews' position within the early modern Polish economy was at stake. Equally, the Jews' legal position came under negotiation. Here it was not only the fate of the individual merchant or entrepreneur, but that of Poland's Jewry as a whole that was up for debate. This often fierce debate took place first and foremost during the Four Year Sejm, which met in Warsaw from 1788 to 1792. Though no reforms of the Jewish

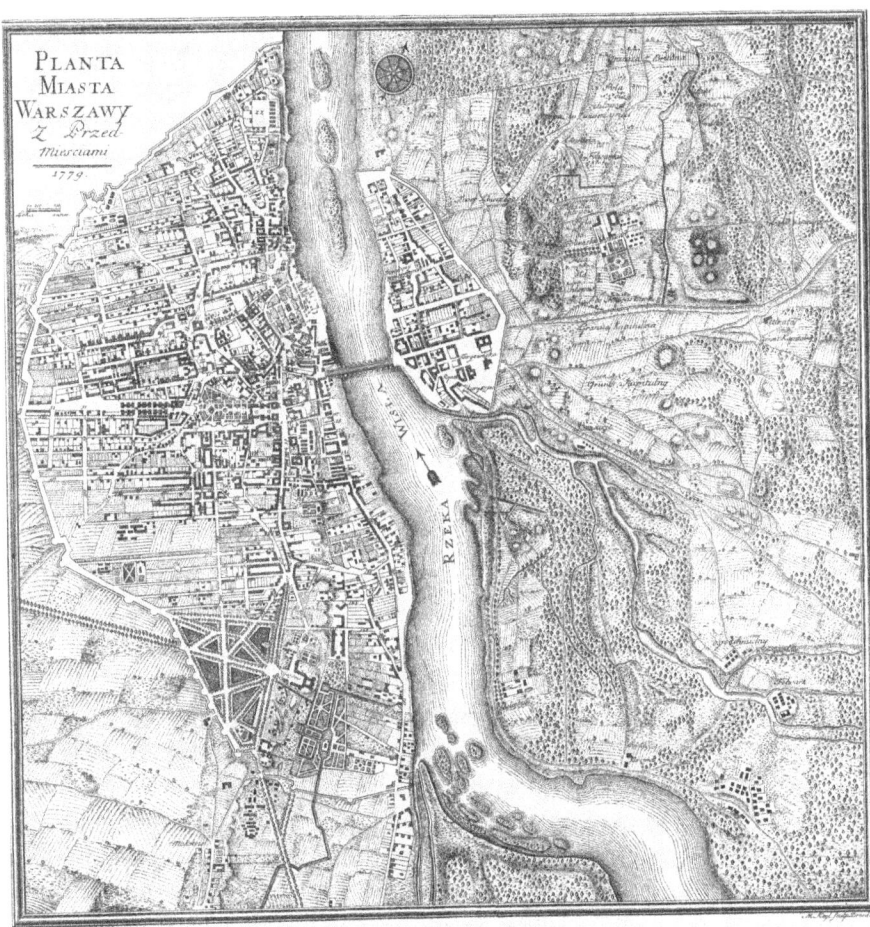

FIGURE 4.1. Historical Map of Warsaw with its suburbs, 1779. © Herder Institute Marburg, Map collection.

legal status came about, members of the mercantile elite, who often were closely engaged in Jewish communal politics, had to position themselves in the debate about the Jews' legal position between corporate identity and ideas of Jewish emancipation.

The distribution of Jews in the vast territory of the Polish-Lithuanian Commonwealth was uneven. Their settlement was based on a trend of continuous development that had taken hold since the thirteenth century, when the first royal privileges were granted to Jews who had fled eastwards from the Holy Roman Empire. These privileges—whether granted to Jews in general, to specific Jewish communities, or to individual Jews—fell into the same category as privileges granted to nobility, clergy, towns, and other minorities and individuals. The legal position of Jews in early modern Poland was generally favorable when compared to the legal standing of Jews in the Holy Roman Empire, even though Polish Jews were banned from many royal and ecclesiastical cities.[1]

For many, Praga thus became a stepping-stone to the opportunities made possible by the blossoming of Warsaw into a large European city in the nineteenth century. As this and the next chapter show, the rise of Warsaw and the evolution of a new Jewish mercantile elite in Poland in general and in Warsaw in particular were closely intertwined. The Jewish merchants, army suppliers, entrepreneurs, and bankers evolved from being a legally excluded group residing in a suburb of the capital to playing an integral role in the economic rise of Warsaw into a nineteenth-century metropolis.

The appeal that Warsaw began to develop in the second half of the eighteenth century lured a whole cadre of Jewish merchants from a varying range of geographic and socio-economic backgrounds to the city. These merchants were part of a general trend of Jewish migration to Warsaw that had boosted Jewish population in the city to nearly 7,000 in 1792. Of course, only a minority of these immigrants belonged to or became part of the Jewish mercantile elite.[2]

This chapter trails the lives of Szmul Jakubowicz Zbytkower, his third wife Judyta, and Wolfgang Heymann, his business partner and eventual adversary, to explore the very beginning of their economic rise and the challenges involved in navigating different and changing political environments. Many of these Jewish immigrants to Praga and Warsaw in the second half of the eighteenth century enjoyed a privilege of being a supplier of the royal court (*serwitorat*). Jews were allowed to remain in Warsaw during the annual meetings of the Polish Sejm (the Polish parliament), which traditionally lasted six weeks, in order to provide attending nobles with supplies and services. Banned from living in the royal city, most Jews settled on private enclaves of Polish nobles in the city (*jurydiki*) or in Praga. Settlement restrictions were not strictly enforced in Praga, which today is a neighborhood of Warsaw; in 1765, seventy Jews were counted as permanent residents. Ten years later, the settlement restrictions in Praga were abolished, thereby legalizing the existing settlement on the ground; Jews were then allowed to trade and build houses. After 1775 the number of Jews rose continually despite of political upheaval in the Polish-Lithuanian Commonwealth and the partitions of Poland. Jews used the villages and small towns in the county of Warsaw, the *jurydiki*, and Praga "as stepping stones for migration into Warsaw."[3] However, Jewish settlement in Praga did not remain uncontested. Based on arguments of economic competition, the burghers of Praga repeatedly requested the expulsion of the Jews. In 1798, when the town was already under Prussian occupation, they argued:

> ... the Jews outnumber the Christian community here by far, and therefore deprive the Christian merchants, artisans and inns of all means to sustain themselves and to progress, in addition they draw everything into their hands, settle at the best places, even established trade with spices, wine, liquor and other goods in the town hall of Praga; they own breweries and pursue all kind of professions all to great disadvantage for us, the burghers of Praga . . . .[4]

With fiscal considerations in mind, the Prussian administration ignored this request. It was precisely this large number of Jewish merchants, leaseholders, and shopkeepers that constituted an important and integral part of the local economy. It was not only that Prussian authorities could not imagine foregoing their taxes; they also grasped the negative impact removing the Jewish population would have on the town's economic fiber.

In previous chapters, we already encountered some of the individuals who made their way to Warsaw and its surroundings during the last third of the eighteenth century. Simon Symons of Amsterdam arrived together with his business partner and brother-in-law, Levin Pincus Schlesinger, from Frankfurt an der Oder in 1765; they were invited as jewelers and garnered the protection of the Polish king Stanisław August Poniatowski as court suppliers (*faktorzy*) the same year.[5] Poniatowski's reign yielded advantages to certain Jewish wholesale merchants and entrepreneurs because the Polish monarch provided protection and patronage to individuals for their services to the royal court using the institution of royal service warrants (*serwitorat*). This privilege placed Jews directly under the royal judiciary rather than under the nobility.[6] Although the number of that sort of privilege declined during the second half of the seventeenth century and the first half of the eighteenth century, it rose considerably under the rule of the last Polish monarch Poniatowski. These privileges were granted to both affluent local and foreign Jewish merchants and entrepreneurs. As Warsaw rose in status as a cultural and economic center, Poniatowksi increased his efforts to attract a mercantile elite (including Jews) to the capital; thus, economic opportunities became available. In particular, the Polish monarch invited experts such as jewel merchants, gemstone polishers, and bankers.[7]

These measures were commensurate with Poniatowski's attempts to reform political and administrative infrastructure. The king intended to develop a central government and increase the effectiveness of the taxation system. Most of Poniatowski's attempts to promote economic development, though, were hampered by the consequences of the first partition of Poland, in particular Prussia's restrictive and hostile economic policy toward Poland.

Among those who arrived in Warsaw was Wolfgang Heymann from Breslau, one of a group of wealthy merchants and entrepreneurs. Wolfgang Heymann was the son of the Prussian merchant and mint-contractor Moses Heymann of Breslau in Silesia, who held one of the few general privileges (*Generalprivileg*, the highest possible category of privileges given to Prussian Jews) issued by the Prussian monarch.[8] From the beginning of the 1770s, the younger Heymann traveled regularly to Warsaw for business, primarily in order to trade and supply the army. He was well acquainted with members of the Prussian administration, which helped his business. Heymann started out as Szmul Jakubowicz's business partner, but few years later the two became adversaries. In 1794 Heymann was found guilty of being a Prussian spy by Polish insurgents in the Kościuszko uprising in Warsaw. He was executed in July 1794 and his property was confiscated. Heymann's fate is an example of how difficult it could indeed be to negotiate one's position against the backdrop of changing political powers.[9]

Chapter 3 showed how Itzig Jacob successfully made his way from Flatow, to Warsaw, overcoming numerous legal obstacles. He belonged to a group of immigrants that moved from the partition territories to the Polish capital, converting new economic opportunities into wealth. His father-in-law, Szmul Jakubowicz, belonged to a third and probably the largest category of immigrants to Warsaw, those coming from small Polish towns and villages in the vicinity of Warsaw, though not many enjoyed that same level of economic success.

Szmul Jakubowicz Zbytkower, also known as Shmuel Yosef ben Avigdor, arrived in Praga in the late 1750s, when he was in his thirties, probably from the nearby village of Zbytki.[10] He was married three times. His first wife, Sheindl, was from Poland. His second wife, Elenora Gabriela, hailed from Breslau in Silesia; their marriage was rescinded in the 1770s. He then married his third wife, Judyta, from Frankfurt an der Oder. Nearly all of Jakubowicz's children, their spouses, and their descendants became part of the nineteenth-century Jewish elite in Warsaw. Jakubowicz himself made a fortune as a supplier for the Polish, Prussian, and Russian armies. He also leased villages and liquor concessions and traded in cattle and grain. His wealth and influence remained legendary even after his death in 1800. Indeed, even today one of the neighborhoods in Praga is called Szmulowizna in honor of its former owner.[11]

Thus Praga represents the attempts of Jewish merchants of various backgrounds to settle around Warsaw and gain access to the newly arising economic possibilities the city had to offer. In so doing, they were all confronted with widespread antipathy toward Jews and Jewish economic activity, primarily among Warsaw's burghers, but also with the challenges of ever changing political borders and rulers. Nevertheless, some Jewish merchants and entrepreneurs were indeed successful in overcoming these obstacles and in attaining wealth and amassing economic influence.

The First Years in Praga

Szmul Jakubowicz's move from a small village to Praga is representative of a process of the urbanization of Polish Jewry that gained momentum in the nineteenth century. That move translated into a step away from the close relationship between the nobility on the one and Jewish leaseholders and merchants on the other hand, and a step toward a closer connection with the state. Jews had been deeply ingrained in the Polish-Lithuanian Commonwealth's feudal economy for over two centuries, and that situation only changed in incremental steps. Some Jews moved toward a closer relationship with the state, be it as merchants or army suppliers. This process foreshadowed the tremendous economic shift to appear in the nineteenth century.[12]

Much of the early years of Szmul Jakubowicz in Praga remain in the dark. According to Emmanuel Ringelblum, Jakubowicz's father, Avigdor Jacob, was a poor innkeeper, although it seems more likely that he functioned as a sub-lessee of a liquor monopoly (*propinacja*). In eighteenth-century Poland-Lithuania, this position was typical, as was the case for the Radziwiłł estates, illustrated by Adam Teller.[13] A position as sub-lessee also would have afforded his son some capital to start his own business. Jakubowicz began trading in various agricultural goods and products; with his move to Praga, he expanded his range and established new contacts beyond the local realm of Zbytki and Praga. It is very likely that he moved from trading cattle, grain, leather, and similar goods into army supplying, similar to what we saw in the case of Itzig Jacob. On some level we also see a move away from the typically close economic connections to Polish noblemen and a turn instead toward servicing the state, first in army supplying and later on in state leases, a pattern noted among many members of the newly rising Jewish mercantile elite.

Although we do not know how Jakubowicz established his ties to Prussian Jews after his arrival to Praga, we can assume that marriage played a crucial role. It appears that Warsaw attracted not only male merchants and entrepreneurs, but also foreign Jewish women. Jakubowicz's first wife came from a traditional Polish-Jewish family; she bore him three sons. It is likely that they married before moving to Praga. After Sheindl's early death, Jakubowicz remarried sometime in the early 1770s; his second marriage brought him one daughter, Atalia, born in 1776. However, the marriage fell apart soon thereafter and in 1779 Jakubowicz remarried again. His decision to remarry around the age of fifty-five was not unusual; nor was the age difference of nearly three decades between him and his third wife considered out-of-the-ordinary.[14] On her wedding day, Judyta was twenty-five, and there is no evidence that she had previously wed or had children. Judyta's age suggests that her father was unable to find a suitable match that would have guaranteed her legal status in Frankfurt an der Oder or elsewhere in Prussia. And maybe, none of the legally possible matches would have satisfied the expectations of Judyta's family regarding social standing and economic advantage.[15]

In both cases, one can only speculate as to how this match was arranged, but it seems likely that Jakubowicz established some business contacts beforehand and used the marriages to bolster those ties. In Breslau, Jakubowicz already enjoyed close contact with Moses Heymann, holder of a Prussian general privilege, somewhere around 1770. When Simon Symons and Levin Pincus Schlesinger moved to Warsaw in the mid-1760s, they might have been crucial in establishing Jakubowicz's contact to his future wife Judyta. Both Symons and Schlesinger belonged to the economic elite of the Jewish community in Frankfurt an der Oder as did Judyta's father, Levin Buko. Linguistic skills may have played a role in Jakubowicz's choice of marrying his second and third wife. Historians have usually argued that he favored these martial ties to facilitate the enhancement of his transregional business.[16] This assumption, however, falls short in grasping the usefulness of these ties for both sides. For Judyta's family, her marriage in Praga translated into the extension of business ties eastward; it is unlikely that she would have married someone with no prospect of economic success.

Akin to the business paths of Levin Pincus Schlesinger of Frankfurt an der Oder and Simon Symons of Amsterdam, Jakubowicz made the most of the opportunities that opened with Poniatowski's ascent to the Polish throne. Since 1764, Jakubowicz served as a supplier to the royal court in Warsaw; in the 1770s, he expanded his business to supply the Polish army.[17] During those same years he began to also supply the Prussian army and to seek a legal title from the Prussian king to facilitate his business dealings with Prussia. He was aided by the aforementioned Moses Heymann. In 1771 the latter pleaded with the Prussian king to issue the title of *Commissarius* (agent) to Jakubowicz. Referring to Jakubowicz's considerable business establishment that he had already amassed by that time, and his intention to venture into new undertakings, Heymann wrote:

> I persuaded the Jew, Samuel Jaccobovicz from Warsaw, who is a general supplier of the Royal Prussian Army and a *faktor* [supplier] of His Majesty the King of Poland, to settle in this land [Silesia] and to transfer all his very considerable fortune into the land of Your Majesty, moreover he is inclined to soon get married to my respectable daughter. I also plead Your Majesty to condescend to give the above mentioned Jew Samuel the title of a *Commissarii*, since Your Majesty is aware of how difficult it is to make off from Poland with one's fortune without high protection. Thus he will be regarded as a subject of Your Majesty and there won't be any obstacles in his way out of Poland. Therefore I am also pleading for a passport for the Jew Samuel Jaccobowicz, in

order for him to travel safely to Silesia and to settle the issue of transferring his fortune.[18]

It appears that Jakubowicz thought that a petition written on his behalf by one of the most influential Prussian Jews would be more effective than filing the request himself. Indeed, about a week later, the Prussian king issued the coveted privilege of *Commissarius* as well as the passport. Although Jakubowicz was granted the privilege right away, he did not have any intention of moving to Silesia; if he did consider that, he likely abandoned those intentions soon after. Notably, he did not marry Heymann's daughter; instead he wed Elenora Gabriela of Breslau.

Jakubowicz never returned the 1771 privilege as demanded when it became clear that he had no intention of moving to Silesia, and in 1787 he was able to renew his privilege. Apparently, his services to the Prussian government and army were so significant by then that the government had no qualms about issuing the privilege to him and Judyta. After the Prussian occupation of Warsaw in 1796, Szmul and Judyta sought a *Generalprivileg*; their request met with success.[19] Jakubowicz skillfully melded together his strategy of network-building with other Jewish merchants while fostering equally good relations with non-Jewish authorities. At least initially it was Jakubowicz's relationship to members of the Jewish elite in Breslau that helped him build his relations with the Prussian administration. In addition to his Prussian and Polish titles, he was awarded the title "General Supplier of the Russian Army" by the Russian empress Catherine the Great in 1775.[20]

Along with Jakubowicz's economic success came communal honor. In the Jewish communities of the Polish-Lithuanian Commonwealth, as was the case in most Jewish communities of the early modern period, communal power was held by an oligarchic lay leadership concentrated in the hands of a handful of affluent families. In many respects, the Jewish communal government developed parallel to the non-Jewish municipal government.[21] Though it is difficult to trace the evolution of communal power and representation in Praga and Warsaw due to lack of sources and the settlement restrictions for Jews, it is clear that Jakubowicz used his economic power to also exert influence in communal matters.

Before Jews were officially allowed to settle in Praga in 1775, and before communal representation was officially recognized in Warsaw in 1799, Jews living on both sides of the Vistula did maintain some form of communal organization. Years earlier, in 1768, local Jews presented a petition to the magistrate in the "name of the whole 'congregation' of Jews from Praga," indicating that some sort of communal governing structure did exist. In addition, one communal representative (*parnas*, in this case called *syndik* in Polish) served as the representative of the Jews of Praga and Warsaw to the non-Jewish authorities. Appointed by a government official and responsible for tax collection, these representatives are often depicted rather negatively in literature. Their legitimacy was conferred upon them by non-Jewish authorities, which may explain the development of an apparent alternate power structure in the community.[22]

In the case of Jakubowicz, he was appointed *parnas* of the Praga community by the authorities in 1788. However, his communal influence was much more rooted in his purchase of a plot for a cemetery in Praga in 1780 and his role in creating the burial society (*Hevrah Kadisha*) in 1785 (see figure 4.2). The formation of the burial society provided him with power over a wide range of communal matters. Notably, Jakubowicz is often charged in the historical literature abusing his power to threaten his enemies with refusal to bury them and their families or charging outrageous fees; still, the burial society's minutes show a well-functioning oligarchy with regular elections and regular alternation of elders.[23]

The accusations about his conduct may also have been colored by Jakubowicz's leanings toward the emerging Hasidic movement. In 1781, he had arranged in Praga a famous disputation between the Hasidic *tsadik* (righteous) Levi Issac of Berdyczów and his opponent, R. Abraham Katzenellenbogen. Moreover, it seems that the separation between the Praga and the Warsaw *Hevrah Kadisha* in 1795 was also linked to the strife between Hasidim and Mitnagdim (also Misnagdim), the opponents of Hasidism.[24] Though Glenn Dynner has convincingly shown that Jakubowicz cannot be categorized a Hasid in the complete sense of the word, he was indeed strongly inclined toward this new religious movement, and his sponsorship of Hasidism was also likely part of his attempt to gain influence within the Jewish community.[25]

The close connection between communal power and relations to non-Jewish officials suggests a circulation of influence. Jakubowicz's cultivation of influence within the Jewish community, like the purchase of the burial ground, also facilitated his developing closer ties with the Christian authorities. In turn, the latter's power, like his appointment as *parnas*, amplified his influence within the Jewish community.

Judyta—the Powerful Woman

The economic success of Jakubowicz and his ample business connections seem to somewhat put into perspective the role of his third wife, Judyta Jakubowiczowa. Though she was equally involved in their shared business and turned into a successful businesswoman on her own after Jakubowicz's death, she was probably not the reason for his success. Historiography has painted a picture of Jakubowiczowa that praises her secular education, including her fluency in German and French (though her French letters that survived somewhat question her fluency), her outstanding abilities in business, and her familiarity with the latest literature.[26] Conversely, she is described as cold-hearted and miserly, dismissive of piety, and driving her children to convert to Christianity. By contrast, historians have depicted her husband rather neutrally as a pious Jew who started out small and built, step by step, a fortune as an army supplier.[27] Although it is somewhat contradictory, the Polish-Jewish historian Ezriel Natan Frenk described Jakubowicz as a victim of his simple origins, thereby imparting (probably unintentionally) considerable agency to Judyta. In short, Jakubowicz: "alone as a simple person (*a gar proster mensh*) and understanding that his large business suffered from the fact that he lacks any education and cannot even read or write, [he] decided to marry an educated woman who would help him in his business with ministers and the king."[28]

This statement does not take into account Jakubowicz's economic success as an army supplier that predated his marriage to Judyta. It is difficult to trace the extent of agency Judyta had in their shared business. Apart from her French letters, which she signed with her name, we do not know if she or a scribe penned German letters and submissions to the Prussian authorities, which were then signed by her husband. However, other evidence does show that she was indeed involved in multiple facets of their business, including business with Polish Jews. In a court record from 1794, Mendel Wulfowicz of Lublin described in detail his business dealings with both Judyta and Szmul. Knowledgeable in Polish, he had worked repeatedly as a clerk for Jakubowicz between 1788 and 1794, keeping records in Polish but also working in his tannery. After he once returned to Lublin, it was Judyta (whom he calls Szmulowa using the female form of her husband's name) who wrote to him and his father to convince him to return to Warsaw. As an incentive she offered to buy grain from the Lublin district through Mendel Wulfowicz, who accepted the offer. They renewed this cooperation in 1794 when Jakubowicz again sought to acquire grain from the Lublin district, this time to supply the Russian army.[29] Without a doubt, Jakubowiczowa firmly understood her and her husband's shared business, which she confidently continued running and expanding after her husband's death in 1800.

The Entry into Army Supplying

In their shared business, Szmul and Judyta were particularly successful in army supplying. Their accomplishments, and those of Itzig Jacob and many others as successful army suppliers, were also a result of their transregional connections. Entry into the field of army supplying, however, would have been impossible without the prior integration of Jewish entrepreneurs into the feudal order of early modern Poland and their involvement in the trade of grain and livestock. Familiarity with these goods was a precondition for entering army supplying, as was a considerable degree of flexibility and mobility.

The main goods traded by Polish Jews within and outside the country were hides, wax, grain, and other raw products. This can be explained with the economic

FIGURE 4.2. Detail from the tombstone of Berek Szmul (Sonnenberg) in Warsaw. Part of one panel depicts the Jewish cemetery of Praga. The plot of land for this cemetery was purchased by Berek Szmul's father Szmul Jakubowicz in 1780. Photo: Cornelia Aust.

position of the Polish-Lithuanian Commonwealth as a key provider of various raw materials and agricultural products to central and western Europe. Moreover, Jews were closely linked to the nobility on whose estates these goods were grown or produced. In exchange, Jewish merchants imported manufactured goods, textiles, and some luxury goods to Poland. These economic conditions also applied to the former Polish territories that came under Prussian rule during the partitions of Poland. Jews were involved in commerce in Poland on different levels, from peddling to wholesale trade; the more affluent Jewish merchants who were involved in multiple business undertakings profited in more than one way from trade with agricultural products and raw materials. First, it fostered relationships to Polish magnates; second, it diversified their economic activities; third, experience in and access to this trade was essential for successful army supplying. Although Polish nobles probably could have used their experience in the grain export trade to also engage in army supplying, as far as we know they did not gain any significance in the business. This lack of dedication might be linked to some cultural stigma vis-à-vis commerce among the Polish nobility, but also might be related to the fact that they did

Figure 4.3. Detail from the tombstone of Berek Szmul (Sonnenberg) in Warsaw. Depiction of the town of Praga on the Vistula River including the estates of Berek Szmul's father and stepmother, Szmul and Judyta Jakubowicz, including a windmill mentioned in the contract. Photo: Cornelia Aust.

not have the same multi-layered connections to traders across different political borders and lacked the geographic flexibility necessary for army supplying.

In Praga, Szmul and Judyta were closely involved in the trade in agricultural products and their processing. Although they were already involved in army supplying, their acquiring a large piece of royal land in Targówek on the Praga side of the Vistula in 1780 expanded the range of their business opportunities. They received the full right of usage, including an already existing windmill, the right to erect new buildings, and the right to produce and sell alcohol (see figure 4.3).[30] On these grounds they subsequently established a tannery, a slaughterhouse, and a textile manufactory.[31] These businesses were chosen due to their commercial value; they were closely tied to the Jakubowiczs' interests as merchants and army suppliers because meat, grain, and vodka were among the most important products that Jewish army suppliers provided to the military. Moreover, the newly established businesses in Praga also drew additional Jews from outside Praga to the city and to seek employment with Szmul and Judyta. We were already introduced to Mendel

Wulfowicz of Lublin, who worked for them in the 1790s as a clerk and was eventually promoted to a sub-supplier for grain from the Lublin area. Zelman Abramowicz, a merchant from Biała, arrived in Praga after having failed in commerce and subsequently worked for Szmul as a clerk in his slaughterhouse.[32]

The other important asset Jewish merchants brought to army supplying was their connections across borders between Russia, Poland, Prussia, and Austria, which was crucial for the supply of grain and other goods beyond local acquisition. These cross-border connections became even more relevant when Warsaw and its vicinity were cut off from the grain-growing areas in the eastern parts of the former Polish-Lithuanian Commonwealth in the 1790s after the second and third partition of Poland. Jakubowicz continued to supply the Prussian, Polish, and Russian troops for many years; however, in the 1790s and especially with the Kościuszko uprising of 1794, things grew more complicated. Although the supply of multiple troops promised increased gains, it also increased the risk of getting caught in the crossfire, literally and figuratively.

Maneuvering Business between Changing Political Powers

Though one ought to be careful to not read history through the lens of nineteenth-century nationalist considerations, there is little question that multiple allegiances posed a problem for members of groups with familial and economic connections across political borders who served more than one ruler or state. If we consider the development of early modern Jewish culture, be it the spread of books and new ideas, traveling rabbis, scholars, doctors or students, political borders were in the main ignored. The same is true for Jewish traders. In addition to members of the Jewish mercantile elite, it was primarily noblemen who formed international allegiances. Like Jews, they dealt with suspicion of disloyalty with the emergence of the nineteenth-century national movements and later nation states.[33] For army suppliers and Jewish merchants who traveled constantly across various European borders, accusations of espionage were common. In many cases, however, "dealing in news" rather than espionage was part of daily business, as fast and reliable access to information was crucial for rulers and armies and not always easily to be obtained.[34] The case of Itzig Jacob shows that this was not unusual: a Prussian general praised his services when he took on "secret tasks, which he fulfilled free of charge and at full satisfaction."[35] Though we do not know what these "secret tasks" were, Itzig Jacob's connections across borders suggest that acquisition of information was at stake.

Boundary-crossing and providing services to multiple rulers could be a fraught undertaking, as evidenced by events around the 1794 Kościuszko uprising in Warsaw. The uprising was a reaction to the second partition of Poland in 1793; the insurgents turned against Prussia, Imperial Russia, and the Targowica Confederation, a group of conservative Polish magnates who rejected the provisions of the Polish Constitution of May 3, 1791. Tadeusz Kościuszko, a veteran of the American Revolutionary War, initiated the uprising in March 1794; it was defeated in November the same year after the Battle of Praga. Legend has it that Szmul Jakubowicz used his wealth to ransom Jews and bury Jewish corpses following a massacre in Praga during this battle. As a supplier of Prussian, Russian, and Polish troops from the 1770s on, he could not have appeared more suspicious to the leaders of the Kościuszko uprising. It was well known that Jakubowicz was a supplier to the Prussian and, much more crucial in 1794, to the Russian army. Jakubowicz oversaw and supplied all storehouses in Praga for the Targowica Confederation, while he filled the storehouses of the insurrectionist government in Warsaw with rye in 1794.[36]

When the insurrection broke out, Szmul and his wife left the city, like many of their fellow inhabitants of Warsaw and Praga.[37] While Jakubowicz remained responsible for supplying the insurgent army with hay, he was also supposed to help establish a Muscovite camp north of Warsaw at today's Nowy Dwór Mazowiecki and supply it with provisions and feed. This plan was discovered by the insurgents and the supplies were confiscated. Concurrently, Jakubowicz moved to another camp near Lowicz, southwest of Warsaw, where he joined efforts with Prussian suppliers; among those suppliers was probably his (prospective) son-in-law, Itzig Jacob.[38] Switching to the Muscovite camp might have been the right move because the criminal court of the insurgent army began collecting evidence against Jakubowicz and others in October 1794. They were summoned to appear before the court in November and, as was announced by various contemporary Warsaw newspapers, they were accused of treason: of fleeing Warsaw during the insurrection and supporting the enemies of the "republic." However, the summons also evidences the important position Jakubowicz held in Warsaw; he was the only Jew brought to court with Polish nobles who had held important positions in Poniatowski's administration.[39]

Due to the soon-to-follow defeat of the insurrection, Jakubowicz never appeared before the court; still, he did temporarily lose much of his assets, including his liquor lease and property in Praga. The insurgent government confiscated and partly auctioned his tannery. The Russian government, no less, owed him and his wife about 80,000 rubles and 9,000 ducats for services from 1792 to 1794.[40] Szmul and Judyta later complained about their property loss in correspondence to Poniatowski and to the Prussian and Russian authorities. In 1796, Judyta wrote to the former Polish king, who then resided in Grodno: "Due to the disastrous revolution I am completely ruined, not only did I lose all my money and property of many years of labor but also all real property that was destroyed. When I returned with my depleted family after the siege of Praga, we sought to rebuild our destroyed household and to repair and rebuild our burned-down brewery with the help of credit."[41]

This disastrous outcome of the 1794 uprising did not last long for Szmul and Judyta; they were able to utilize their connections with the Prussian and Russian authorities to safeguard their legal and economic position. The strategies they employed did not differ from those used prior to 1794. They emphasized their service and utility to individual rulers and stressed their prior loyalty to the respective monarchs.

In an extensive exchange of letters between the couple and the former Polish king, they sought to reclaim their lost property as well as payment for supplies to Poniatowski and the Russian army in 1794. Eventually, Jakubowicz traveled to St. Petersburg to claim his outstanding payments. Despite their financial difficulties, Szmul and Judyta continued to supply the Russian troops in Warsaw in 1795 and began to supply wood to the Prussian garrison in Praga right away in 1796; in 1797 they offered to supply Poniatowski on his journey to St. Petersburg.

Concurrently, they both successfully sought the aforementioned *Generalprivileg* from the new Prussian power, although the privilege did not comprise the rights of Christian merchants.[42] Akin to their previous business ventures, these were joint attempts by Szmul and Judyta to recover from their material and financial losses and to secure their legal position. They chose carefully to invest in new business endeavors and secure privileges from the new Prussian rulers while maintaining prior connections.

Szmul and Judyta turned to the powers from which they had received their privileges, even in the case of Poniatowski, who had granted them royal privileges and remained their point of reference despite the disappearance of the Polish state. However, Szmul and Judyta knew that they had to secure their legal and thus economic status under the new Prussian rulers, a tie that they had established earlier and could thus easily employ. In their letters to the former Polish king, they repeatedly emphasized their loyalty and utility to him personally rather than to the former Polish state. This inclination highlights the importance of personal connections in the strategies of the Jewish mercantile elite. For many, it was also the connection to the Prussian ruler and administrators that proved a stepping stone and helped to ensure that these Jewish merchants and entrepreneurs succeeded economically or at least paved the path for the generation to follow.

A Less Successful Army Supplier

The dangers of acting as a transregional player between different political powers were real. The example of Wolfgang Heymann, who had turned into Jakubowicz's adversary on more than one level, demonstrates how things could go awry. Wolfgang Heymann's case also shows that business behavior did in fact play a crucial role. As the son of Moses Heymann, wealthy merchant and mint contractor in Breslau and equipped with a Prussian *Generalprivileg*, Wolfgang Heymann should have had valuable preconditions for entering and successfully continuing his father's business. Accordingly, Heymann sought to utilize his close connections to the Prussian administration to advance his business while regularly traveling to Warsaw from around the first partition of Poland.

The close ties between Moses Heymann and Szmul Jakubowicz may have also included some supervising his son Wolfgang during his business in Warsaw. However, not long after the son arrived, tensions grew between the two entrepreneurs. In 1772 Wolfgang Heymann complained that Jakubowicz was already putting obstacles in his way when he tried to acquire Polish grain to sell in Prussia. Half a year later, the Prussian resident Gideon Benoît in Warsaw reported: "Since the presence of the Jew Heymann junior in Warsaw there has been constant strife between them because of the women [*sic*]." Jakubowicz accused Wolfgang Heymann of being his wife's lover; indeed, a few years later, Elenora Gabriela divorced her husband and married Wolfgang Heymann. Concurrently, Heymann's business undertakings in Warsaw were unsuccessful. Similarly, grain acquisition in Poland for the Prussian army did not work out, leading one to wonder whether Jakubowicz contributed to this failure. Benoît complained that the growing tensions between Wolfgang Heymann and Jakubowicz led to unpleasant encounters with Russian general Alexander Bibikov. Benoît and Bibikov agreed in time to advise Heymann to leave the city, since he "had nothing to do anymore in Warsaw after his failed projects." In short, Wolfgang Heymann was expelled from Warsaw.[43]

Over the years, Heymann's business failures seem to have multiplied, though we have only sparse information about his concrete business undertakings. Despite his quasi-expulsion from Warsaw in the early 1770s, he returned regularly to the city. He traded salt from the Galician mine in Wieliczka and supplied the Russian army during the Russo-Turkish War (1768–1774). This business deal is curious; apparently, Jakubowicz did not succeed in securing a contract for supplying Russian troops during the Russo-Turkish War.[44] However, in 1775, the Russian general de Maltzow accused Wolfgang Heymann of having fled from Warsaw to Prussia with a large part of the war chest (*caisse de L'Imperatrice*) and requested that the Prussian authorities locate and arrest him.[45] However, Heymann's ties to the Polish monarch remained strong, though he had never received the title of court supplier. Only a few days after de Maltzow's request, Heymann received a moratorium from the Polish crown that temporarily freed him from financial obligations to his creditors and placed him under the protection of the Polish king. This was not unusual; the king habitually issued moratoria for affluent Jewish entrepreneurs.[46] Despite these quarrels and accusations against Heymann from various sides, his business connections were apparently lucrative enough to garner him the title of commercial agent (*Kommerzienagent*) for the Prussian state, even if he failed to be employed specifically as the commercial agent of the Prussian embassy in Warsaw. Heymann went bankrupt in 1789 and a commission was convened in Warsaw to determine the demands of the various Polish and foreign creditors.[47]

We do not know to what extent the claims of his creditors were satisfied, but it seems that he continued to do business in Warsaw into the time of the 1794 insurrection, when he was accused of being a Prussian spy and of maintaining contacts with the Russian general Iosif Andreyevich Igelström. These same accusations that were lodged at other Jews as well. Thus, in Heymann's case, the problems of serving more than one power became particularly evident; Heymann and his family's close relationship to the Prussian authorities may have made him more vulnerable during the Kościuszko uprising. Although the trial proceedings no longer exist, according to Emanuel Ringelblum who did see the records, Heymann denied the accusations and insisted that all his contacts with Prussian officials as well as with Igelström were solely of a private nature. He was unable to persuade his accusers of the private and non-political nature of his contacts. All four Warsaw newspapers printed the verdict that found him guilty of corresponding with the Prussian minister Karl Georg Heinrich von Hoym and thus transmitting information to the Prussian king and recruiting Poles for the Prussian forces in the War of the Bavarian Succession in 1778. He was sentenced to death at the height of the turmoil surrounding the Kościuszko uprising and was executed on July 24, 1794.[48]

Even in the turbulent atmosphere of Warsaw in 1794, in which many people, Jews and non-Jews alike, were accused of espionage, Heymann's case stands out. It appears authorities could tolerate commerce and supplying different and sometimes hostile powers to some extent. *Gazeta Rządowa,* a government newspaper in Warsaw, regularly announced the arrests of Jewish merchants, peddlers, and coachmen on suspicion of espionage. In most cases, however, the newspaper noted that the suspects had merely supplied the Russian or Prussian army with provisions and feed and were thus innocent and immediately released.[49] Heymann's case, was probably typical in terms of business ventures, although he was more prominent than most of the accused, yet it was exceptional in its tragic outcome.

It remains obscure to what extent Heymann's earlier business failures contributed to his misfortune by earning him a bad reputation over the years. It seems logical to assume reliability in business and the good reputation that resulted from that was crucial; a lack thereof could not be compensated by personal connections.[50] In Heymann's case, neither Jewish nor Christian business partners and clients were convinced of his business practices and thus he could not rely on advocates and relationships of trust in a dire situation. Heymann's example makes clear that despite favorably preconditions things could go wrong any time.

Moving to Warsaw?

Though the outcome of the accusations against Wolfgang Heymann and Szmul Jakubowicz was different, the accusations were closely linked to the mistrust not only lodged against merchants, army suppliers, and entrepreneurs acting across political boundaries in general but also against Jewish economic activities in particular. Like elsewhere in Europe, the debate around Jewish emancipation that ensued prior to the French Revolution was intensified by its promise of general equal rights that also took hold in Poland. This long-lasting and often harsh debate posed the question for members of the Jewish mercantile elite of how they ought to respond.

As was discussed in chapter 2, the emancipation debate was often closely linked to the question of economic utility. In Poland, the debate was framed by the arguments of the Prussian writer Christian Wilhelm Dohm on the matter of the "improvement" of the Jews.[51] "Improvement" aimed at the alleged moral and economic impairment of the Jews, which according to Dohm and others was to be attained by ameliorating the legal status of the Jewish population on the one hand and abolishing or at least limiting Jewish communal autonomy on the other. The debate about Polish Jewry's occupational distribution became central in the light of many Jews' close linkage to magnates and their service function in the rural feudal economy. In the last years of the Commonwealth, however, Jews increasingly faced displacement and dislocation at the increasing disintegration of the feudal economy.[52]

Discussion on the legal status of Jews also arose in Poland, where supporters and opponents of Dohm's arguments for Jewish emancipation discussed his ideas throughout the 1780s; the debate became most relevant for representatives of the Jewish communities during the Four Year Sejm. This remarkable Polish parliament meeting lasted four years from 1788 to 1792 to pass new laws and measures. It was the final attempt to reform the Commonwealth politically and economically to prevent further encroachment by the partitioning powers of Prussia, Russia, and Austria.[53]

Challenges to the extensive structures of Jewish autonomy in Poland, however, did in fact begin earlier. When Poniatowski was elected Polish king in 1764, he sought to turn Poland into a new "enlightened, prosperous and well governed" state.[54] One of the measures to this end occurred that year; he abolished the Council of the Four Lands (va'ad 'arba' 'aratsot), the central representation of the Jewish communities. This measure was closely related to attempts to reform the institutions of the Polish-Lithuanian Commonwealth and the government's dissatisfaction with the council's administration of the poll tax. This development also fits into a more general European picture. From the mid-eighteenth century, a number of factors threatened the old corporate order across Europe and thus also Jewish communal autonomy: the rise of increasingly centralized states, a growing capitalist economy, and the tenets of the Enlightenment. Most non-Jewish and Jewish enlighteners agreed that emancipating the Jews in Europe should bring with it abolition of Jewish communal autonomy as part of a general dissolution of corporate and estate structures. Some structures of the council, however, continued to exist informally; on the local level, in Poland Jewish self-government in the main survived.[55]

The most concentrated effort for state reform, namely, the Four Year Sejm, occurred when the state was under severe pressure from outside powers and domestic opposition. Jewish leaders throughout the Polish-Lithuanian Commonwealth understood that at the Sejm, their place within the state would be a point of discussion, even if only a minor one. Polish Jews could rely on a highly developed culture of intercession at the Sejm in Warsaw, a culture sustained primarily by paid *shtadlanim* (intercessors on the behalf of the Jewish population) sent to Warsaw from various communities.[56]

Emancipation debates also posed novel questions for members of the Jewish mercantile elite who were used to employing their economic power and networks to achieve legal security and trading privileges. To what extent would the end of communal autonomy limit their power within the Jewish setting? Would a new status of general emancipation truly mark an improvement over their sometimes far-reaching individual and communal privileges in Poland? Steps taken by members of the Jewish mercantile elite in Warsaw suggest a rather traditional pattern as well as a conservative attitude toward Jewish emancipation. In Warsaw the debate revolved around the issue of permanent settlement of Jews in the city and annulment of the privilege *de non tolerandis Judaeis*, even though many Jews had found ways to settle on this side of the Vistula by then.[57] This debate became crucial in the Four Year Sejm. Aiming for readmission into Warsaw found its first expression in a petition (*Pokorna Prośba od Żydów Warszawskich*) in 1789 in the name of the Jews of the royal provinces and Warsaw. For the right to settle 300 Jewish families within the boundaries of Warsaw and allow them free trade, petitioners offered a onetime payment of 180,000 złoty and annual payment of 3,000 thaler; they also emphasized their utility in national and international trade. The petition employed an early modern mercantile argumentation that emphasized economic utility, similar to the types of individual petitions filed by Jewish merchants and entrepreneurs for commercial rights and settlement.[58]

It is noteworthy that foreign Jews who had settled in Warsaw from the 1770s on were closely involved in interceding on behalf of Warsaw Jewry. Wolfgang Heymann of Breslau, Simon Symons of Amsterdam, and the Prussian Jewish merchant David Königsberger were among the foreign members of the Jewish mercantile elite who pleaded for settlement rights in Warsaw. When the Jewish merchants of Warsaw appointed seven plenipotentiaries in 1791, Symons and

Königsberger were among them. Both were credited with and praised for leading delegations to the king. Similar to the proposition of 1789, the delegations offered the king 20,000 thaler (360,000 złoty) for the settlement of 130 families in Warsaw and declared a willingness to pay 11,000 złoty in advance. This offer suggests that members of the Jewish mercantile elite followed traditional patterns of intervention that employed the argument of Jewish economic utility; in this case, they did not even demand general settlement rights for Jews in Warsaw, let alone general emancipation of the Jewish population.[59]

It is difficult to draw conclusions as to why members of the Jewish mercantile elite chose this strategy that seemingly aimed only at safeguarding their own position in the city. It seems safe to conclude that at least some of them were familiar with the debates concerning Jewish emancipation. Abraham Hirszowicz, a supplier to the royal court and thus part of the mercantile elite, drafted a reform project for Polish Jewry that suggested reforms in their communal organization and occupational structure. Artur Eisenbach has assumed that it was primarily Jewish merchants returning from their travels to fairs in Leipzig, Breslau, Frankfurt an der Oder, and Königsberg who imported Enlightenment ideas to Poland and thus, implicitly, an inclination to general Jewish emancipation. Even if this was true, they apparently did not apply these ideas to the political situation in the Polish-Lithuanian Commonwealth. Most likely, they were well aware that general Jewish emancipation was not among the reforms the Polish king had in mind. Moreover, most noblemen, who were generally allies of the Jewish mercantile elite, sought to preserve the political, social, and economic structures of the Polish-Lithuanian Commonwealth, including the position of the Jewish communities and their close interdependence with the nobility. They may likewise have been aware of the fact that a majority of Polish Jewry was interested in rescinding legal disabilities but much less so in full emancipation. The latter would have also meant the loss or serious limitation of communal autonomy. Jewish opponents of emancipation feared the abolishment of communal autonomy as much as a cultural acculturation toward the Christian population.[60] As such, the Jewish elite sought to preserve the estate-like nature of the relationship between the Jewish population and the state. In this, they were no different from the representatives of the Polish magnates and burghers at the Four Years Sejm who similarly sought to retain the Polish State's old structures.[61] As we have already seen around the settlement issues of Itzig Jacob, Prussian rule over Warsaw did not introduce fundamental changes to this picture.

Overall, it seems highly plausible that ideas of emancipation were only partially flowing along the commercial networks of the Jewish mercantile elite. The mercantile elite in Warsaw, though remarkably cosmopolitan in terms of their place of origin and commercial connections, generally abstained from advocating Jewish emancipation. Even if perhaps favorably disposed toward the idea, they were also well aware of the possibilities available within the political and social structure of the late Polish-Lithuanian Commonwealth. The situation did not change when Prussia assumed power in Warsaw in 1796, though Jews were officially allowed to settle in Warsaw in 1799 and the Prussian government recognized a Jewish communal administration (*kahal*) to ensure proper tax collection. Those Jewish residents, who did survive the turbulent years, literally and economically, were able to use the new opportunities in Warsaw to expand their business.

Conclusion

As I have examined the first years that led to the rise of a new Jewish economic elite in Warsaw, we have seen three groups of Jewish merchants moving to Warsaw. With the individuals named here many more arrived. There were those from afar, like the Amsterdam banker Simon Symons, who symbolized the importance of Amsterdam as a place of brokerage of credit, though the city lost its importance toward the late eighteenth century. Of much greater significance were those who arrived from close-by Prussia, the partition territories or Silesia and the third and most numerous group of Jews from the vicinity of Warsaw. It was these two groups that contributed with their occupational flexibility, their transregional connections, their risk taking, and—in the case of those from Poland—their close integration into the Polish feudal economy to the rise of a new Jewish economic elite that came to full blossom only in the nineteenth century.

Notes

1. Goldberg, *Jewish Privileges in the Polish Commonwealth*, 1. On comparative aspects, see Teller, "Telling the Difference," 114; Sorkin, "Beyond the East-West Divide," 247–256.

2. By the end of the eighteenth century, Warsaw had about 80,000 inhabitants. Different estimates regarding the number of Jews in Warsaw suggest about 3,000 in 1780. A 1792 census that included also the *jurydiki* and inhabitants on both sides of the Vistula counted 6,750 Jews. Eisenbach, "Żydzi warszawscy," 236. See also Grochulska, *Warszawa na mapie Polski "stanisławskiej,"* 25–26. On early migration to Warsaw, see Węgrzynek, "Illegal Immigrants," 19–41.

3. Eisenbach, "The Jewish Population in Warsaw," 48. A new constitution for the Jews in Mazowia from 1775 allowed them to settle on royal ground (emphyteutic ground), save Warsaw itself. Zieńkowska, "Spór o Nową Jerozolimę," 359–360. See also Eisenbach, "Status prawny ludności żydowskiej w Warszawie," 3; Eisenbach, "Żydzi warszawscy," 231–233. On the number of Jews in the Polish-Lithuanian Commonwealth in general, see Mahler, *Yidn in amolikn Poyln*.

4. Acta betr. die allgemeinen Gesuche und Angelegenheiten der Stadt Warschau, GDDPP VI, no. 3566, AGAD.

5. Metryka Koronna, 1764–1780, KK 18, mf. A-6083, AGAD, 71–72. See also Horn, *Regesty dokumentów i ekscerpty z Metryki Koronnej*, no. 51, 49–50.

6. Eisenbach, *The Emancipation of the Jews in Poland*, 52; Goldberg, *Jewish Privileges in the Polish Commonwealth*, 8–9.

7. Most of them are listed in Horn, *Regesty dokumentów i ekscerpty z Metryki Koronnej*.

8. On Moses Heymann, see Stern, *Der Preußische Staat und die Juden. Dritter Teil: Die Zeit Friedrichs des Großen*, 1:108, 213–215; Brann, "Die schlesische Judenheit vor und nach dem Edikt vom 11. März 1812," 3–44.

9. "Jugement Criminel," *Bulletin National Hebdomadaire*, July 23, 1794, 76–77; "Excerpt z raportu sądu kryminalnego Xięstwa Mazowieckiego . . . : Wyrok na starozakonnego Wolfganga Heymana," *Gazeta Rządowa*, July 25, 1794, 98. See also Tokarz, *Warszawa przed wybuchem powstania*, 99; Ringelblum, *Żydzi w powstaniu kościuszkowskiem*, 94.

10. The record book (*pinkas*) of the Ḥevrah Kadisha in Praga, which he founded in 1785, lists him as Shmuel Yosef ben Avigdor; however, most other sources refer to him as Szmul the Parnas, Szmul from Praga, and Szmul/Schmul/Samuel Jakubowicz. The secondary literature usually calls him Szmul Jakubowicz Zbytkower. Księga Bractwa Pogrzebowego na Pradze 1785–1870 / Pinkas haḥevrah kadisha de-Praga, S 63/23, CAHJP, 1. Ringelblum states that Szmul appears in the documents of the Jewish court (*beit din*) in Zbytki together with his brother Abraham. Ringelblum, "Szmul Zbytkower," 247–248. See also Michałowska, "Szmul Jakubowicz Zbytkower," 80. The year of his birth is usually given as 1727, but according to a letter he wrote to the Prussian administration in 1795, he was born in 1725. Die Gesuche verschiedener Juden um allgemeine Privilegien und Konzessionen auf Südpreußen, GDDPP I, no. 896, AGAD, 27.

11. On the genealogy of Jakubowicz's family, see Reychman, *Szkice genealogiczne*, 11–18; Ringelblum, "Szmul Zbytkower," 248. His year of death is usually given as 1801, probably a mistake that has slipped in through the Jewish calendar. Prussian records show that he passed away in the fall of 1800, probably after Rosh Hashanah, the beginning of the new Jewish year. Die Gesuche verschiedener Juden um allgemeine Privilegien und Konzessionen auf Südpreußen, GDDPP I, no. 896, AGAD, 133.

12. See Dynner, *Yankel's Tavern*, 7. The close economic relationship between Jews and Polish nobility has been intensively studied since the late 1980s. Hundert, *The Jews in a Polish Private Town*, 156–158; Rosman, *The Lords' Jews*, 206–212; Teller, *Money, Power, and Influence*, 187–199. Especially in the second half of the eighteenth century, Jews not only dominated much of the local and regional trade but also took a significant though less dominant role in international commerce that linked the Polish-Lithuanian Commonwealth to the rest of Europe. Hundert, "Re(de)fining Modernity in Jewish History," 136; Teller, *Money, Influence, and Power*, 187.

13. Teller, *Money, Influence, and Power*, 123–125.

14. Although early marriage was a religious ideal, with boys over the age of thirteen and girls over the age of twelve, these sorts of unions were less common than may be suggested by nineteenth-century narratives of *maskilim*, Jewish enlighteners. In poorer families, marriages were often delayed for financial reasons. Hundert, "Approaches to the History of the Jewish Family in Early Modern Poland-Lithuania," 20–21. Studies on the Polish-Lithuanian

Commonwealth show that although marriages around age fifteen for girls and sixteen for boys were not uncommon, they did not make up the majority. In the Polish-Lithuanian Commonwealth and in nineteenth-century Russia, husbands were usually older; for a second or third remarriage, the age gap increased; this was not uncommon, particularly for Jewish men. Goldberg, "Jewish Marriage in Eighteenth-Century Poland," 18–26; Michałowska-Mycielska, "Jewish Family Structure in the Polish-Lithuanian Commonwealth," 160–161; Freeze, *Jewish Marriage and Divorce in Imperial Russia*, 159–160. See also Guldon, "Źródła i metody szacunków liczebności ludności żydowskiej," 249–262.

15. The oldest of Judyta's four siblings, Elias, inherited his father's privilege. The second, Baruch, may have been privileged as second child; the third, Feibisch/Philip, left town. Judyta's sister Blume, who was approximately fifteen years her senior, retained her legal status in Frankfurt an der Oder via her husband, Wulff Oppenheimer. Judentabellen der Stadt Frankfurt/Oder, 1748–1759, Abt. 1, VII, 107, STAF, 114v, 132.

16. See, for example, Frenk, *Meshumadim in Poilen*, 22.

17. Schiper, *Dzieje handlu żydowskiego*, 329.

18. Der polnische Jude Jacobowicz wird Königl. Commissarius, 1771–1772, I. HA, Rep. 46B, no. 203a (Pk. 1), GStA.

19. Though privileges usually did not need to be renewed in Prussia, Jakubowicz's situation may have been different because he never fulfilled the implicit condition of the first privilege of moving to Silesia. Both Jakubowicz and Wolfgang Heymann accused each other of having the privilege in their possession; thus it was never returned. All three original privileges (1771, 1787, and 1798) remained in the hands of the Toeplitz family in Warsaw, where the late Krzysztof Teodor Toeplitz kindly allowed me to see them in 2007. All three are pictured in Toeplitz, *Rodzina Toeplitzów*, 32, 38, 42.

20. Kosim, *Losy pewnej fortuny*, 17.

21. Ruderman, *Early Modern Jewry*, 57–98; Hundert, *Jews in Poland-Lithuania*, 79–86.

22. Shatzky, *Geshikhte fun yidn in Varshe*, 1:123–127. According to Shatzky, five *parnasim* were appointed in Warsaw and six in Praga between 1759 and 1794. See also Eisenbach, "The Jewish Population in Warsaw," 48.

23. Shatzky, *Geshikhte fun yidn in Varshe*, 1:146. Prothocollum relationum, oblatarum, plenipotentarium, manifestationum, obductionum aliarumqhe in genere transactionum officii consularis C.A.V. 1789, Stara Warszawa, no. 283, AGAD, 85v, 97. Thereafter he signed documents as Szmul *parnas* (in Hebrew characters). The original *pinkas* of the Ḥevrah Kadisha in Praga no longer exists. A copy of the original Hebrew text with a Polish translation by H. Kirszenbaum and A. Fajner from 1911 is kept in the Central Archives for the History of the Jewish People in Jerusalem: Pinkas haḥevrah kadisha de-Praga/ Księga Bractwa Pogrzebowego na Pradze 1785–1870, S 63/23, CAHJP. See also Kirszenbaum, "Bractwo pogrzebowe na Pradze," 133–146. On the matter of Jakubowicz's alleged misuse of power, see Frenk, *Meshumadim*, 27–28; Korzon, *Wewnętrzne dzieje polski za Stanisława Augusta*, 1:224–225. On the elections and the organizational structure in general: Aust, *Kontinuität und Wandel in den jüdischen Gemeinden Berlins und Warschaus*, 43–48, 126–151.

24. In 1785, the *pinkas* of the burial society in Praga notes that both societies agreed to hold elections, fast days, and society meals together. Ten years later, each society went

its separate way. Pinkas haḥevrah kadisha, S 63/23, CAHJP, 5; Kirszenbaum, "Bractwo pogrzebowe na Pradze," 135.

25. Dynner, *Men of Silk*, 98–99.

26. For her letters, see Korespondencja Stanisława Augusta 1792–1797, syg. 2, 996; syg. 3b, 426-426v; syg. 7, 99–100, AGAD; AKP, syg. 363, mf. 19546, AGAD, 90–91, 155–156, 159–161. One can assume that a professional scribe might have been more accurate. Frenk, "Testament Judyty Zbytkower," 377. Similar: Shatzky, *Geshikhte fun Yidn in Varshe*, 1:142; Eisenbach and Kosim, "Akt masy spadkowej Judyty Jakubowiczowej," 88; Michałowska, "Szmul Jakubowicz Zbytkower," 81–82; Kosim, *Losy pewnej fortuny*, 264.

27. This narrative is found most vividly in the work of the Polish-Jewish historian Ezriel Natan Frenk. Frenk, *Meshumadim*, 22–32. On Frenk, see Guesnet, "Geschichte fürs jüdische Volk," 119–145.

28. Frenk, *Meshumadim*, 22.

29. Między Starozakonnemi Mendlem Wulfowiczem y Aronem Fayglowiczem, 1794, ASK, syg. 237, AGAD, 70–70v.

30. Prawe Emphiteutyczne na Grunta w Dobrach Ziemskich Targowku, AKP, syg. 357, mf. 19541, AGAD. Legally, they acquired the land under the auspices of emphiteutic law; that meant that the legal title to the land remained with the king but the right of usage was fully heritable and salable. Szmul, Judyta, and their descendants received the land for forty years in 1780, and subsequently obtained perpetual rights to the land in 1796. Protokuł Przywilejow y Konsensow na Grunta Prawem Emphiteutycznym rozdane w Dobrach Targowska, Golendzinowa y Klucza Jabłońskiego, Archiwum Potockich z Jabłonny, no. 47, AGAD, 10.

31. Ringelblum, "Szmul Zbytkower," 340–341. Because most of the archival sources were destroyed during World War II, we rely on Ringelblum. See also Michałowska, "Szmul Jakubowicz Zbytkower," 84–85. According to Ringelblum, the slaughterhouse also processed pork. The tannery was established after Poland had banned the export of untanned hides in 1789 to stimulate manufacturing within the country. The slaughterhouse was situated in proximity to the large oxen markets in Praga. In addition to trading in cattle, Jakubowicz offered to provide meat slightly below market prices in order to secure a monopoly for supplying Warsaw with meat, a request he was granted in 1789. Ringelblum, "Żydzi w świetle prasy warszawskiej," 62–63.

32. Węgrzynek, "Illegal Immigrants," 19.

33. The alleged disloyalty of Jews in Warsaw at the end of the eighteenth century became a concern primarily for later Polish historians who accused figures like Jakubowicz of supporting Russian troops and even forming a "Russian party" among the Jews of Warsaw. For example, see Tokarz, *Warszawa przed wybuchem powstania*, 194. On the shifting loyalties of Polish nobles, see Kraft, "Polnische militärische Eliten," 281.

34. Walker, de Vivo, and Shaw, "A Dialogue on Spying in 17th-Century Venice," 326. As Walker remarks, "people who travelled a lot were more likely to become spies." Nevertheless, it is problematic to assume that Jews in general were more suitable for espionage as Josef Karniel argues. Karniel, "David Michael Levy," 117. For another case, see Barber, "Isaac Bernard: Prague Jew," 131–150.

35. Die Gesuche verschiedener Juden um allgemeine Privilegien und Konzessionen auf Südpreußen," GDDPP I, no. 896, AGAD, 10.

36. Ringelblum, "Szmul Zbytkower," 255–257. "Uniwersał Konfederacyi Ziemi Warszawskiey," *Korrespondent—Kraiowy y zagraniczny (Korrespondent Warszawski)*, February 5, 1793, 202–204. In this announcement the chancellery of the confederation recommended inhabitants who had supplied hay to army purveyors and specifically to Jakubowicz without any payment, to settle the account directly with the chancellery. *Gazeta Warszawska*, no. 2, April 29, 1794, 26; Okazuiąca Expens y Zysk dla Skarbu z Zyta przez Szmula Liweranta Moskieskiego skontraktowanego, a przez Deputacyą Zywnosci zakupionego, AKP, syg. 289, mf. 10728, AGAD, 424.

37. Some were caught when they tried to leave with their assets. The Jewish merchant David Königsberger and his wife were caught together with two other Jews by an army guard when they tried to leave Warsaw in May 1794. Their four inspected suitcases contained various linen and cloths, fur, various silverware, pearls, brilliants, and bills of exchange. Kommissya Porządkowa X. Mazowskiego, 1794, AKP, syg. 241, mf. 10703, AGAD, 280–289.

38. AKP, syg. 354, mf. 26745, AGAD, no. 67, 472–472v; Korespondencja Stanisława Augusta 1792–1797, syg. 7, AGAD, 99v. Various sources confirm the stay of Szmul and Judyta in the Muscovite camp and mention the presence of Prussian suppliers. Kommissya Porządkowa X. Mazowskiego, 1794, AKP, syg. 241, AGAD, 69, 88; Excerpt z Rapportu Cyrkułu Siodmego Miasta Warszawy, AKP, syg. 257, mf. 10715, AGAD, 304; Powtorna Indagacya z Zyda Boruchowicza, AKP, syg. 254, mf. 10713, AGAD, 32–33; Relacya od Łowicza 16. Maia 1794, AKP, syg. 323, mf. 3670, AGAD, 197; Między Starozakonnemi Mendlem Wulfowiczem y Aronem Fayglowiczem, 1794, ASK, syg. 237, AGAD, 70–70v. Itzig Jacob corresponded with the Prussian administration from Lowicz before he moved to Warsaw and married Jakubowicz's daughter in 1796.

39. AKP, syg. 255, mf. 10738, AGAD, 548; "Jugement Criminel Militaire," *Bulletian National Hebdamodaire*, no. 19, October 12, 1794, 216; *Gazeta Rządowa*, no. 98, October 10, 399–400.

40. *Gazeta Wolney Warszawskiey*, no. 30, August 5, 1794, 404; no. 35, August 23, 1794, 468; AKP, syg. 285, mf. 10724, AGAD, 70; Pohorille, "Dostawy wojskowe Szmula Jakubowicza Zbytkowera," 125–135.

41. AKP, syg. 363, mf. 19546, AGAD, 90.

42. Korespondencja Stanisława Augusta 1792–1797, syg. 2, 996; syg. 3b, 426–426v; syg. 7, 99–99v, AGAD; AKP, syg. 206, mf. 19463, AGAD, 6–7, 47–47v. The Prussian *Generalprivileg* could be issued with or without the full rights of Christian merchants.

43. Der polnische Jude Jacobowicz wird Königl. Commissarius, 1771–1772, I. HA, Rep. 46B, no. 203a (Pk. 1), GStA.

44. Ostrowski, *Poufne wieści z oświeconej Warszawy*, 42–43.

45. Ringelblum, *Żydzi w powstaniu*, 94. The salt mine of Wieliczka came under Habsburg rule in the first partition of Poland in 1772. Verhaftung des aus Warschau geflüchteten ehemaligen russischen Armeelieferanten Heymann wegen Veruntreuung von Geldern, Dez. 1775, I. HA, Rep. 11, 171–175, Rußland D, 1775–1780, GStA. Ministers von Finckenstein und von Hertzberg advised six different generals of the Prussian army to arrest Heymann if found.

46. Metryka Koronna, KK 90, mf. A-6164, AGAD, 297–298. The moratorium was extended for another six months in August 1776 because Heymann had been abroad and thus could not make use of the previous moratorium. That moratorium allowed him to conduct business in all of Poland without being bothered by his creditors. Prothocollum relationum, oblatarum, plenipotentarium, manifestationum, obductionum aliarumqhe in genere transactionum officii consularis C.A.V. 1789, Stara Warszawa, no. 283, AGAD, 131–133. Among them were Simon Symons and Levin Pincus Schlesinger: Horn, *Regesty dokumentów i ekscerpty z Metryki Koronnej*, vol. II/1, nos. 204, 208, 221, 223; vol. II/2, no. 321.

47. Kommerzkollegien und Manufakturangelegenheiten 1734–1781, u.a. Bestallung des Juden Wolfgang Heymann in Breslau als Kommerzienagent, I. HA, Rep. 9, C6 a2, Fasz. 5, GStA, 128–128v; Resolution für den Commercien-Agenten Heymann, I. HA, Rep. 46 B, no. 37, Fasz. 1 (1745–1781), GStA, 73–74. He had apparently been paid in obligations by the Russian army, which he still tried to redeem in court in Warsaw in 1775. Prothocollum relationum, oblatarum, plenipotentarium, manifestationum, obductionum aliarumqhe in genere transactionum officii consularis C.A.V. 1789, Stara Warszawa, no. 283, AGAD. Emanuel Ringelblum also claims that Heymann was largely involved in banking, got involved in an affair concerning false bills of exchange, was expelled from Warsaw once again, and returned from Breslau to Warsaw only in 1788. Ringelblum, *Żydzi w powstaniu*, 94; *Gazeta Warszawska*, no. 49, June 20, 1789.

48. His father, Moses Heymann, died in 1792. Since at least the 1770s he had had close contact with von Hoym, who was a crucial player in Prussia's efforts of espionage leading the network of anti-Habsburg spies. Karniel, "David Michael Levy," 130; Ringelblum, *Żydzi w powstaniu*, 94–95; Tokarz, *Warszawa przed wybuchem powstania*, 99. According to Austrian sources, Heymann was indeed involved in espionage for Prussia against the Habsburg Empire. Karniel, "Heymann Kiewe," 42–44. According to Karniel, Heymann sent letters to various family members in Breslau that appeared suspicious and led to investigations against him by the Austrian authorities. According to Heymann Kiewe, an alleged relative of Wolfgang Heymann, the latter visited the Prussian ambassador in Vienna and contacted a number of non-Jewish spies. "Excerpt z raportu sądu kryminalnego Xięstwa Mazowieckiego . . . : Wyrok na starozakonnego Wolfganga Heymana," *Gazeta Wolney Warszawskiey*, July 29, 1794, 379–380; "Wyrok starozakonnego Wolfganga Heymana," *Korrespondent Narodowego y Zagranicznego*, July 1794, 1344.

49. *Gazeta Rządowa*, no. 63, September 5, 1794, 254; no. 76, September 18, 1794, 305; no. 86, September 28, 1794, 346; no. 90, October 2, 1794, 362; no. 98, October 10, 1794, 399–400; no. 103, October 15, 1794, 420; no. 109, October 21, 1794, 443; no. 116, October 29, 1794, 483.

50. For more on the reliability and the loss of reputation, see Aust, "Daily Business or an Affair of Consequence?," 71–90.

51. Dohm, *Über die bürgerliche Verbesserung der Juden*. On the economic issues around Jewish emancipation, see Karp, *The Politics of Jewish Commerce*, 94–134.

52. Hundert, *Jews in Poland-Lithuania*, 56.

53. On the reform projects regarding Jews, see Eisenbach et al., *Materiały do dziejów sejmu czteroletniego*, vol. 6, 78–93, 113–128, 215–227, 519–520; Gelber, "Żydzi a zagadnienie

reformy Żydów na Sejmie Czteroletnim," 326–344, 429–440; Michalski, "Sejmowe Projekty Reformy," 20–44.

54. Butterwick, "The Enlightened Monarchy," 193.

55. Bartal, "From Corporation to Nation," 19; Goldberg, "The Jewish Sejm," 164–165.

56. Guesnet, "Politik der Vormoderne—*Shtadlanuth* am Vorabend der polnischen Teilungen," 236, 239–241. On *shtadlanut*, see also Ury, "The *Shtadlan* of the Polish-Lithuanian Commonwealth," 267–299.

57. Węgrzynek, "Illegal Immigrants," 29–40.

58. Eisenbach et al., *Materiały do dziejów sejmu czteroletniego*, 129–132. See also Guesnet, "Politik der Vormoderne—*Shtadlanuth* am Vorabend der polnischen Teilungen," 251.

59. Eisenbach et al., *Materiały do dziejów sejmu czteroletniego*, 295, 340–343, 379, 382, 460. A third letter dated February 1792. See also Ringelblum, "Dzieje zewnętrzne Żydów w dawnej Rzeczypospolitej," 70–71; Schiper, *Dzieje handlu żydowskiego*, 284–285.

60. On Hirschowicz, see Schiper, *Dzieje handlu żydowskiego*, 272, 282–283, 329; Eisenbach, *The Emancipation of the Jews in Poland*, 42; Hundert, *Jews in Poland-Lithuania*, 230. See also Dynner, *Men of Silk*, 91.

61. Guesnet, "Politik der Vormoderne—*Shtadlanuth* am Vorabend der polnischen Teilungen," 253–255; Goldberg, "Pierwszy ruch polityczny wśród Żydów," 46–48; Goldberg, "The Jewish Sejm," 147–165.

FIVE

Warsaw: The Rise of a Jewish Economic Elite

Szmul and Judyta Jakubowicz first grew wealthy thanks to their business efforts in Praga, when Jewish settlement remained illegal in Warsaw. Nevertheless, in terms of raw numbers, Warsaw had seen an ever-increasing number of Jewish residents. A 1792 census counted more than 6,800 Jews in Warsaw; that figure suggests that their presence was widely accepted. Within half a century, Warsaw had attracted the largest concentration of Jews within the Polish-Lithuanian Commonwealth.[1] By the first decade of the nineteenth century, we find Judyta Jakubowiczowa, her stepson Berek Szmul, and many other members of their extended family and business partners living in Warsaw.

This chapter links economic strategies and success as well as the social life of Jewish entrepreneurs in early nineteenth-century Warsaw. It argues that alongside the general political and economic circumstances that contributed to the rise of this new Jewish mercantile elite in Warsaw, the familial and ethnic networks remained at the core of these entrepreneurial undertakings. Although these merchants, bankers, and entrepreneurs were closely integrated into the general economy and harbored no reservations about doing business with Christians, they apparently found that a wealth of mutual trust among or with their coreligionists remained an important aspect in their business. This underlying importance of family and ethnic belonging even transcended strictly religious ties. This sense of trust included entrepreneurs and bankers who spanned the spectrum in terms of their religious attitudes, from Hasidism to a rather acculturated lifestyle; some had even converted to Christianity. Thus, it is fitting to emphasize the importance of family ties and ethnic belonging, even if imagined, rather than a similar affiliation in terms of religious belonging.

The rise of a Jewish economic elite in nineteenth-century Warsaw, however, was not solely linked to those mostly well-functioning networks, but also based on the appearance of new opportunities, prior experiences in specific fields of business and the will to take entrepreneurial risk. This allowed Jewish merchants and army suppliers to rise specifically in two fields—banking and leaseholding (*arenda*) of state monopolies. Both fields followed from the traditional economic niches Jews were active in—trade and leaseholding, the lease of monopoly rights from members of the Polish nobility. This entry into new fields of business is demonstrated by first looking at army supplying during the Napoleonic Wars, following the risky but well payed-off business undertakings by Judyta Jakubowiczowa and Berek Szmul. Both also became active in banking, Jakubowiczowa much more intensely. Berek Szmul successfully entered into the leasing of the salt monopoly, which serves as a typical example for the move into leaseholding of state monopolies.

Though cultivated under the specific circumstances in the territories of the former Polish-Lithuanian Commonwealth, some of these developments went along with similar changes across central and western Europe. There, Jews equally entered the field of banking around the beginning of the nineteenth century, often creating close ties and cooperation among Jewish bankers across Europe. Unlike in western and central Europe, however, the development of a Jewish economic elite did not go along with the emergence of a strong bourgeois society, of which most Jewish entrepreneurs were part in nineteenth-century western and central Europe. Thus, the second line of argument in this chapter discerns two possibilities of cultural and religious development among the members of this newly rising economic elite. Though, in Poland in general and Warsaw in particular, it often was Jews who formed the basis for a developing bourgeois society, many coreligionists followed a different path into modernity, becoming Hasidim or following other nineteenth-century forms of orthodox Judaism. Here again Jakubowiczowa and Berek Szmul can serve as a case in point.

Army Supplying during the Napoleonic Wars

Although the Polish-Lithuanian Commonwealth disappeared from the map of Europe in 1795, the need for constant supplying of armies did not. Jan Kosim painstakingly reconstructed the economic activities of the emerging bourgeoisie in Warsaw from 1807 to 1830, including many Jewish families. Szmul Jakubowicz's third wife, Judyta Jakubowiczowa, and his son from the first marriage, Berek Szmul, were among the most important army suppliers. They were able to recoup their earlier losses and amass considerable assets during the years of the Napoleonic Wars by supplying all armies involved, including the reorganized Polish army after 1815.[2]

The example of Jakubowiczowa's one specific transaction helps us understand the importance of transregional connections and gain a glimpse into the functioning of these sorts of supply networks, paying particular attention to the role of family, locality, and the integration of non-Jews into such networks. This supply administered by Jakubowiczowa notes her ramified connections to family members, close acquaintances and business partners, Jewish or Christian, in Poland, Prussia, and Russia, across multiple political borders. During the Napoleonic Wars, which provided ample opportunity for army suppliers, Jakubowiczowa supplied French and Polish troops in Warsaw as well as others.[3] An epistolary exchange with the

Royal Lithuanian government in Gumbinnen from 1813/14 shows that she and her brother Elias Buko (signing as Levin & Bucca) were equally involved in supplying Russian troops. Although the circumstances of war did make a direct supply impossible, Jakubowiczowa was able to stock the Russian chief supplier Meyerovitz & Co with army supplies. In 1807 she also authorized the Privy Council (*Geheimrat*) Johann Simpson in Memel to charge the outstanding debts for this delivery from the Royal Prussian Army Charging Commission. This Charging Commission was responsible for payments of Prussian debts incurred during the Napoleonic Wars.[4]

This example of turning to Johann Simpson illustrates the point at which non-Jews were typically integrated into Jewish commercial undertakings. The town of Memel, where the Charging Commission resided, was closed to Jews. It was only after the Prussian edict of emancipation of 1812 that Jakubowiczowa's brother was able to move to Memel and support his sister's claims, which he delivered to the Commission directly after Simpson passed away in 1813. Upon approval of half the demanded sum, nearly 7,000 thaler, a direct transfer to Warsaw may have once again been impossible or disadvantageous for Jakubowiczowa. Instead, she authorized her agent in Berlin, the banker and army supplier Jacob Herz Beer, to collect the amount due. Beer was her closest tie to Berlin, and their relationship was likely rooted in their original acquaintance in Frankfurt an der Oder, where their families belonged to the economic and social elite of the Jewish community.[5]

This example demonstrates how different individuals were integrated into a single commercial network and the multiple steps necessary to complete a particular business venture: the process often took years, from the supply of goods to paying debts. The aforementioned case indicates the roles played by individuals ranging from Jakubowiczowa's brother, a family member; her attorney in Berlin, a Jewish business partner, and Johann Simpson in Memel, a non-Jewish business partner. Simpson was included in this business venture at least partly because of settlement restrictions that applied to Jews in Memel. Moreover, one can assume that non-Jews like Johann Simpson had better access to members of the Prussian administration, which was of great import when doing business with the state. It is more challenging to glean what Johann Simpson in particular and non-Jews in general gained from these sorts of arrangements. It seems that in places where Jews were heavily involved in all levels of trade, repeated and reliable business connections with Jewish merchants created access to transregional mercantile networks. This incentive might have been especially important for individuals who were not primarily involved in commerce or only at a local level.

The aforementioned exemplar also illustrates the difficulties in defining and tracing commercial networks, as it is difficult to judge whether these connections were single and infrequent transactions or part of a more regular cooperative effort. In the case of Jacob Herz Beer, one can easily assume that it was a regular connection, and it is entirely plausible that Jakubowiczowa did business regularly with her brother. One can only speculate the particulars of the case of Johann Simpson. The Christian merchant had been involved in transregional commerce since at least the 1760s, including connections with Benjamin and Samuel Symons in Amsterdam as well as with Simon Symons and Levin Pincus Schlesinger in Warsaw. Moreover, Johann Simpson's relatives in Danzig confirmed that he had charged Jakubowiczowa's outstanding debts "just as a favor" to her. This wording makes it likely that his business transactions with her were not an isolated singular incident, but rather spanned years.[6]

By examining army supplies during the Napoleonic Wars, we can learn a great deal as to how business was run in times of war. As shown above, the networks were at the center of interest, but supply lists from the Duchy of Warsaw illuminate other practices in the business as well. It becomes clear that Jewish suppliers prevailed in the army supplying business in terms of numbers of suppliers and in the financial volume of their supplies. In order to successfully remain in business, one had to be a merchant willing and able to reliably supply the needed provisions, acquire them at least in part from outside the Duchy of Warsaw, and extend credit by patiently waiting for payment. Thus, supplying demanded the will to take great risk and the ability to forgo payments for years, thus, to grant credit. With regard to those suppliers who matched these criteria, administrations had little wiggle room to negotiate, because the demands of multiple armies turned grain and other supplies into scarce goods. The protocols of the Duchy of Warsaw's administration between 1807 and 1811 hint at the problems that haunted them.

On September 1, 1807, an official reported in a meeting that the army was running out of food and feed and would be out of supplies within three days. He suggested seizing rye and wheat locally and negotiating a new and advantageous contract for supply of oats, hay, and straw because the contract with Jakubowiczowa was about to expire.[7] While the administration tried to acquire as many supplies as possible locally, it constantly found itself in need of additional goods. In December 1807, when it emerged that the Grand Duchy was about 1,000,000 złoty short for meat supplies, the Commission of Provisions (*Komisja Żywności*) suggested extracting the sum from the Jewish inhabitants. Notably, the plan was never realized.

Increasingly, Jewish suppliers were the ones to finance the armies by forgoing payments at least temporarily or by accepting state obligations. In 1807, the State Council negotiated with Jakubowiczowa and Berek Szmul payments for only half the amounts of 540,000 and 500,000 złoty owed by the Duchy of Warsaw. Thereafter, payments for supplies were postponed regularly; due to a lack of cash flow, the government began to soon pay its suppliers in state obligations. When Berek

Szmul requested permission in 1809 to supply oxen to the Russian army or to receive an advance of 10,000 thaler in light of the 400,000 złoty owed to him by the Polish government, he received permission. As the protocol noted that he "never caused any disappointment"; he was deemed to be a reliable supplier.[8] In November 1808, the state council noted severe problems with the supply of meat, vodka, wood, and feed to the army; many of the suppliers who remained unpaid refused to ship further supplies. Whereas the council lamented the rising prices of supplies, it also pointed to the fundamental problem. The lack of cash led to diminished competition among suppliers and thus made acquisition of goods on credit more expensive. Although there were attempts to get rid of Berek Szmul because of his allegedly overpriced supplies, the council concluded: "In the end, it will be impossible to release this meat supplier [Berek Szmul] from his contract as demanded because it would be difficult to find another one who would be willing to take on these supplies due to irregular payments. One has to try by all means to satisfy him and other suppliers, because otherwise the provision of the repositories will collapse completely."[9]

Similarly, in 1809, the State Council tried to auction the right to supply 1,000 centner salted meat for a storehouse in Toruń. Of the three bidders, Berek Szmul provided the cheapest offer, although the authorities had also solicited a bid from the local butchers. Reviewing the amounts Berek Szmul usually supplied leads one to doubt that any local supplier could have bettered his offers. A list of deliveries made between December 1810 and January 1811 (see table 5.1), offers a glimpse into the quantity of goods supplied and of the leading role Berek Szmul had assumed in the business. In three months, he delivered meat worth nearly 233,000 złoty to storehouses in Warsaw and Praga. A list of required supplies for the following month notes that he was slated to deliver meat supplies for another 213,000 złoty to fourteen additional storehouses (table 5.2). The latter sum is close to half the amount of all estimated supplies.[10]

With the increasing payment in obligations, the supply of feed and food was not only a question of logistics anymore; it was also one of credit. Indeed, it was only a select few who could afford to remain in this business: that group included entrepreneurs who either had the financial means to provide goods on credit or were able to purchase goods on credit themselves during a politically unstable time and without any knowledge of how the Napoleonic adventure would end.

Archival documents concerning the supplies of meat, vodka, wood, raw linen, and smaller amounts of salt and candles provide additional insight in the structure of army supplying (see table 5.2). The supplies of Berek Szmul and of other Warsaw-based suppliers such as Leib Oesterreicher, Judyta Jakubowiczowa, and Jakub Epstein served in the main Warsaw, Praga, and the closer vicinity of the capital. From a review of these supplies, it seems that there are two organizational patterns. One

Table 5.1. State obligations issued in March and April 1811 for army supplies provided between December 1810 and January 1811 by the army commission of the Duchy of Warsaw.

Supplier	Supply for month of	District or storehouse	Goods	Sum	
Berek Szmul	December 1810	Warsaw and Praga	Meat	85,575 zl.	232,922 zl.
Berek Szmul	January 1811	Warsaw and Praga	Meat	69,534 zl.	
Berek Szmul	February 1811	Warsaw	Meat	76,745 zl.	
Berek Szmul	February 1811	Praga	Meat	1,068 zl.	
Meysner	February 1811	Lublin district	Wood		9,365 zl.
Jakób Eyzenberg	February 1811	Lublin district	Meat	17,639 zl.	48,506 zl.
Jakób Eyzenberg	February 1811	Zamość district	Meat	14,282 zl.	
Jakób Eyzenberg	February 1811	Krasnoszów	Meat	5,639 zl.	
Jakób Eyzenberg	February 1811	Domaszów	Meat	3,952 zl.	
Jakób Eyzenberg	February 1811	Lublin district	Vodka	3,037 zl.	
Jakób Eyzenberg	February 1811	Zamość district	Vodka	1,920 zl.	
Jakób Eyzenberg	February 1811	Krasnoszów	Vodka	2,037 zl.	
Abraham Montag	December 1810	Zamość district	Meat	14,408 zl.	20,546 zl.
Abraham Montag	December 1810	Krasnoszów	Meat	1,207 zl.	
Abraham Montag	December 1810	Tomoszew	Meat	4,931 zl.	
Jakub Szper	January 1811	Zamość district	Meat	14,026 zl.	21,503 zl.
Jakub Szper	January 1811	Krasnoszów	Meat	2,407 zl.	
Jakub Szper	January 1811	Tomoszew	Meat	5,070 zl.	
Moyżesz Erlicher	Dec. 1810–January 1811	Zamość district	Wood		9,200 zl.
Bielski	March 1811	Serock	Wood		5,393 zl.
Aron Mendelsohn	December 1810	Lublin district	Vodka		1,529 zl.
Lubienski	December 1010	Lublin district	Candles		1,460 zl.

Lewek Ickowiz & Szymon Markowicz	January 1811	Modlin	Meat	5,949 zl.	44,549 zl.
Ickowicz & Markowicz	January 1811	Płock and Wyszogrod	Meat	4,887 zl.	
Ickowicz & Markowicz	January 1811	Serock	Meat	9,749 zl.	
Ickowicz & Markowicz	January 1811	Prosna and Lipno	Meat	5,653 zl.	
Ickowicz & Markowicz	January 1811	Ostrołęka	Meat	6,945 zl.	
Ickowicz & Markowicz	December 1810	Modlin	Meat	897 zl.	
Ickowicz & Markowicz	December 1810	Serock	Meat	3,130 zl.	
Ickowicz & Markowicz	December 1810	Prosna	Meat	4,193 zl.	
Ickowicz & Markowicz	December 1810	Ostrołęka	Meat	3,146 zl.	
Szmul Lewkowicz	December 1810	Międzyn	Meat	597 zl.	18,445 zl.
Szmul Lewkowicz	December 1810	Międzyn	Vodka	94 zl.	
Szmul Lewkowicz	December 1810	Siedlce district	Salt	117 zl.	
Szmul Lewkowicz	January 1811	Międzyn district	Meat	1,057 zl.	
Szmul Lewkowicz	January 1811	Międzyn district	Vodka	165 zl.	
Szmul Lewkowicz	January 1811	Międzyn district	Salt	11 zl.	
Szmul Lewkowicz	February 1811	Międzyn district	Meat	5,267 zl.	
Szmul Lewkowicz	February 1811	Międzyn district	Vodka	381 zl.	
Szmul Lewkowicz	February 1811	Siedlce district	Meat	5,522 zl.	
Szmul Lewkowicz	February 1811	Siedlce district	Candles	1,163 zl.	
Szmul Lewkowicz	February 1811	Siedlce district	Wood	3,994 zl.	
Szmul Lewkowicz	February 1811	Siedlce district	Vodka	77 zl.	
			Sum of all supplies		413,418 zl.

Source: Memorial Ministra Woyne, April 5, 1811, RMKW, serja 2-go, 115, AGAD, 80–85.

Note: zl.=złoty.

Table 5.2. Planned new supplies to storehouses after March/April 1811 by the army commission of the Duchy of Warsaw.

Supplier	Storehouses	Goods	Amount / à price	Sum
Berek Szmul	Warsaw & Praga	Meat	≈ 1,991 centner / 45 zl. 18gr.	212,992 zl.
Berek Szmul	Numerous storehouses	Meat	2,844 centner / 43 zl. 7 ½ gr.	
Jakob Epstein	Numerous storehouses	Vodka	4,444 gallon / 2 zl. 12gr.	17,420 zl. 3 gr.
Jakob Epstein	Numerous storehouses	Raw linen	177 "stones" 17 / 38 zl.	
Anton Karski	Numerous storehouses	Wood	252 fathom 60 / 16 zl. 22 gr.	4,234 zl. 12 gr.
Judyta Jakubowiczowa	Łęczyca	Meat	≈ 88 centner / 40 zl.	3,555 zl.
Leib Oestreicher	Warsaw & Praga	Vodka	3,083 gallon / 2 zl. 7gr.	6,880 zl. 10 gr.
Lineburg (?)	Warsaw & Praga	Wood	1,300 fathom / 20 zl.	26,000 zl.
Werner (?)	Warsaw & Praga	Raw linen	250 "stones" / 37 zl.	9,250 zl.
Salomon Baer	Łowicz	Meat	18 centner / 42 zl.	892 zl. 3 gr. ¾
Salomon Baer	Łowicz	Vodka	28 gallon 16 / 2 zl. 9 gr.	
Salomon Baer	Łowicz	Wood	1 fathom 45 / 18 zl.	
Salomon Baer	Łowicz	Raw linen	1 "stone" 4 / 38 zl.	
Salomon Baer	Łęczyca	Vodka	138 gallon 66 / 2 zl. 9 gr.	667 zl. 29 gr.
Salomon Baer	Łęczyca	Wood	7 fathom 55 / 18 zl.	
Salomon Baer	Łęczyca	Raw linen	5 "stones" 17 / 38 zl.	
Berek Judkowicz	Łomża, Tykocin, Szczecin	Meat	164 centner 10 / 44 zl.	8,663 zl. 21 gr.
Berek Judkowicz	Łomża, Tykocin, Szczecin	Vodka	257 gallon / 2 zl. 17 gr.	
Berek Judkowicz	Łomża, Tykocin, Szczecin	Wood	14 fathom 44 / 20 zl. 26 gr.	
Berek Judkowicz	Łomża, Tykocin, Szczecin	Raw linen	10 "stones" 8 / 46 zl. 24	
Silberstein	Storehouses in Poznań province	Meat	684 centner / 45 zl. & 36 zl. 20gr	92,040 zl.
Silberstein	Storehouses in Poznań province	Vodka	975 gallon / 2 zl. 16 gr.	
Silberstein	Storehouses in Poznań province	Wood	55 fathom 35 / 18 zl.	
Silberstein	Storehouses in Poznań province	Raw linen	39 "stones" 6 / 42 zl. 20 gr.	
Salomon Perl	Storehouses in Kalisz province	Meat	512 centner 85 / 36 zl.	18,462 zl. 18 gr.

Supplier	Location	Commodity	Quantity / Unit Price	Total
Michael Flaum	Storehouses in Kalisz province	Vodka	802 gallon / 2 zl. 20 gr.	2,183 zl. 20 gr.
Salomon Sznur	Storehouses in Kalisz province	Wood	45 fathom 44 / 13 zl. 18 gr.	2,040 zl. 8 gr.
Salomon Sznur	Storehouses in Kalisz province	Raw linen	33 "stones" 2 / 44 zl. 8 gr.	
Bielski	Storehouses in Bydgoszcz province	Meat	513 centner 60 / 50 zl.	25,680 zl.
Lewenstein	Storehouses in Bydgoszcz province	Meat	106 centner 20 / 50 zl.	5,310 zl.
Blumberg	Storehouses in Bydgoszcz province	Vodka	969 gallon / 3 zl.	5,359 zl. 1 gr.
Blumberg	Storehouses in Bydgoszcz province	Wood	55 fathom 7 / 26 zl.	
Blumberg	Storehouses in Bydgoszcz province	Raw linen	25 "stones" 26 / 39 zl. 13 gr.	
Mendel Mejorowicz	Storehouses in Siedlce province	Meat	335 centner 40 / 38 zl. 26 gr.	15,264 zl. 28 gr.
Mendel Mejorowicz	Storehouses in Siedlce province	Vodka	524 gallon / 2 zl. 6 gr.	
Mendel Mejerowicz	Storehouses in Siedlce province	Wood	29 fathom 32 / 17 zl. 25 gr.	
Mendel Mejerowicz	Storehouses in Siedlce province	Raw linen	25 "stones" 14 / 38 zl. 26	
Jakob Eisenberg	Storehouses in Lublin province	Meat	848 centner 55 / 43 zl. 25	40,509 zl. 23 gr.
Jakob Eisenberg	Storehouses in Lublin province	Vodka	1326 gallon / 2 zl. 15	
Jan Meisner	Storehouses in Lublin province	Wood	75 fathom 32 / 21 zl. 10 gr.	2,917 zl. 29 gr.
Jan Meisner	Storehouses in Lublin province	Raw linen	35 "stones" 12 / 37 zl.	
Margarth (?)	Storehouses in Radom province	Meat	358 centner 20 / 43 zl. 12 gr.	17,169 zl. 8 gr.
Margarth (?)	Storehouses in Radom province	Vodka	559 gallon 2 / 2 zl. 7 ½ gr.	
Margarth (?)	Storehouses in Radom province	Wood	31 fathom 63 / 20 zl. 27 gr.	
Margarth (?)	Storehouses in Radom province	Raw linen	14 "stones" 30 / 46 zl. 24 gr.	
Abraham Gutman	Storehouses in Cracow province	Meat	604 centner 20 / 43 zl.	25,980 zl. 18 gr.
Berek Luzenburg	Storehouses in Cracow province	Vodka	944 gallon / 5 zl.	4,720 zl.
Kazimirz Krzyztki	Storehouses in Cracow province	Wood	53 fathom 53 / 16 zl.	859 zl. 9 gr.
Jozef Mazurkiewicz	Storehouses in Cracow province	Raw linen	26 "stones" 6 / 37 zl.	931 zl. 88 gr.

Sources: Memoriał Ministra Woyne, April 5, 1811, RMKW, serja 2-go, 115, AGAD.

Note: Christian suppliers are italicized. zl.=złoty. gr.=groszy. One centner ≈ sixty-four kilograms; one Warsaw gallon (*garniec*, pl. *garnce*)=3.77 liter; a fathom (*sążeń*, pl. *sążnia*) ≈ 1.8 meters; and one "stone" (*kamień*, pl. *kamienia*) ≈ thirteen kilograms. Hundert, *The Jews in a Polish Private Town*, 163.

approach was that one supplier provided all goods, including meat, vodka, wood, and raw linen, to a smaller district or single warehouse, as did Salomon Baer. The other approach was that suppliers specialized in certain goods and provided only one or two different goods to a larger number of storehouses. That method of several suppliers, each one providing its specialty, was more common for Warsaw.

An additional finding from these supply lists from the Ministry of War is the outstanding role Jewish merchants played in the business of army supplying compared to Christian suppliers. The list of required supplies shows that the eight Christian suppliers received about 100,000 złoty, less than one-fifth of the overall sum. In comparison, the sixteen Jewish suppliers earned more than 80 percent of the overall sum. In the supplies delivered in 1810/11 the gap is even wider, three Christian suppliers out of eleven suppliers altogether provided goods worth only about 16,000 złoty from the overall volume of 413,000 złoty. Often they joined forces with each other to do so.

In Warsaw, suppliers associated with Jakubowiczowa and Berek Szmul apparently coordinated their efforts either by joining forces for certain supplies or by assigning each supplier to certain goods. These allocations were divided according to the main fields of trade that each supplier had been involved in previously. Berek Szmul was primarily involved in supplying oxen, meat, hides and feed; Jakubowiczowa provided in the main food and feed. However, she also traded in hides that she had received. For example, in 1809, she obtained hides as payment for her supplies to the Polish army and sought to export them. Jakubowiczowa's trade in hides as well as Berek Szmul's trade in meat and cattle, does not seem coincidental if one keeps in mind that one of the major business ventures of her husband and his father, Szmul Jakubowicz, was in the trade of hides, cattle, and meat. Berek Szmul also supplied salt meat to repositories on occasion, foreshadowing his further involvement in the leasing of the salt monopoly in the Kingdom of Poland.[11]

Two other suppliers closely related to or associated with Jakubowiczowa and Berek Szmul were Leib Oesterreicher, Jakubowiczowa's son-in-law, and Moses Aron Fürstenberg, an elder of Warsaw's Jewish community. Although Fürstenberger and Oesterreicher occasionally joined forces with each other, they were primarily involved in different fields of supply. Oesterreicher had moved to Warsaw during the Prussian occupation to wed Judyta and Szmul's daughter, Bona. He enjoyed close connections to the Habsburg Empire, which his family name suggested may have been the locale where his family originally resided, and to Silesia, where his father and brother lived.[12] Oesterreicher was involved primarily in the trade of wine and vodka, but also worked in grain. His grain trade was probably closely related to his trade in vodka as the fermentation into alcohol had become most lucrative when utilizing grain. Instead of shipping grain to far-away harbors, most nobles had it turned into alcohol, mostly by Jewish leaseholders. In 1805/6, Oesterreicher joined forces with his mother-in-law in a contract for acquiring grain from Abraham Liebermann, an innkeeper in Warsaw; that grain was subsequently supplied to both, the Russian troops and repositories of Jakubowiczowa. It is unclear from the source documents whether these were repositories that she supplied regularly or if she had set up her own repositories on land she owned. Anyway, this case shows that she had the means to provide supplies and store goods, when necessary, that she had acquired from sub-contractors.[13]

To reach such impressive numbers, Jewish army suppliers had to join forces as the logistic demands and financial burdens usually overstrained the abilities of any single supplier. In 1812, Jakubowiczowa joined forces with Berek Szmul to deliver a large supply of meat, wood, and wax to the provinces Poznań and Kalisz, pickaxes to Modlin, and vodka to Modlin and Toruń. Thus, they coordinated their business undertakings in order to avoid direct competition. Berek Szmul also regularly collaborated with textile merchant Moses Aron Fürstenberg.[14] The latter had undertaken various supplies for the French and Polish armies during the Napoleonic Wars, mostly providing clothing, blankets, and other textile products; he was thus operating in a different branch of army supplying. These findings support the thesis that relatives and close acquaintances divvied amongst themselves the branches of supply.[15]

These networks of the Jewish mercantile elite were not always stable and continuous. Some ties did persist into the next generation, though it is difficult to measure such continuation. For example, the economic ties between Berek Szmul and Fürstenberg span the next generation. They were involved in various mutual business undertakings, the earliest one was a partnership in 1806 to supply oxen to French troops in Warsaw. A decade later, these ties were still helpful to Fürstenberg's son, Hiel. By that time, another Jewish entrepreneur, Ignacy Neumark—who had migrated from Prussia to Warsaw at the beginning of the nineteenth century—had become the most important army supplier in the Kingdom of Poland. When Hiel Fürstenberg signed a contract with Neumark in 1817 to supply him with white cloth for coats for the Polish army, Fürstenberg's role as a sub-contractor was assured by Gabriel Bereksohn, Berek Szmul's son; Bereksohn did vouch for Hiel Fürstenberg.[16]

Jewish entrepreneurs continued to engage in army supplying in the Kingdom of Poland after the end of the Napoleonic Wars, although the business lost the crucial position it had held throughout the late eighteenth century and the Napoleonic Wars. Though one finds contracts with few Jewish army suppliers after 1815, many suppliers moved out of that risky business in the more stable era following after the Congress of Vienna and the foundation of the Kingdom of Poland. For example, in 1814 Jakubowiczowa still supplied the Russian army, but moved out of the business completely within only few years after the end of the war.[17] If one bears in mind the extent to which army supplying in the previous period appeared to be war financing (due to the substantive prolongation of payments and the usual requirement of a security deposit), it is no surprise that Jewish army suppliers moved into banking. These entrepreneurs increasingly focused on banking and other business ventures that required advancing large amounts of money.

This shifting from army supplying into banking seems to be typical for European borderlands at the turn from the eighteenth to the nineteenth century, as Michael Graetz described a similar development for the region of Alsace-Lorraine. He argued that the prolonged period of war between the 1790s and 1815 led to the rise of Jewish merchant-suppliers who were able to not only continuously supply goods in times of war and turmoil, thanks in part to their family networks, but were also able to succeed in investing their profit in banking after the war. His model suggests a particular pattern of Jewish involvement in the agricultural goods and cattle trade, transition into army supplying, and successful safeguarding of their gains. This pattern eventually fostered the move of a small Jewish elite into banking.[18]

The Move into Banking

As we have seen in the case of Itzig Jacob, the conditions for entry into banking were already laid in the 1790s and were used by a number of entrepreneurs. Across Europe, some Jewish banking houses, such as the Rothschilds in Frankfurt am Main and the Mendelsohns in Berlin, were established during the first years of the nineteenth century, whereas the turning point in territories where Jews were heavily involved in army supplying, such as Alsace-Lorraine and the former Polish territories under Prussian rule, came only with the Napoleonic Wars.[19] Army supplying was attractive during the war, but it demanded willingness to incur risks and having transregional networks to deliver sufficient supplies in place. Simultaneously, army supplying could foster close relationships to the respective administrations that remained important after the end of the war. After years of political unrest and changing rulers, the end of the Napoleonic Wars and the creation of the Kingdom of Poland yielded an era of greater stability. Although the Congress of Vienna in 1815 attenuated the dreams of resurrecting an independent Polish state and defined the borders of the partitions, the Kingdom of Poland did enjoy increased political stability. The Russian tsar became the king of Poland, and the Congress of Vienna legislated a relatively liberal constitution for the Kingdom of Poland. This stability and the diminished profitability of army supplying, coupled with several decades of a relative absence of war, bolstered the efforts of Jewish entrepreneurs to move into banking.

The move into banking was most pronounced in the case of Jakubowiczowa, who withdrew from army supplying after 1815 and then concentrated her efforts in banking. The magnitude of her business can be reasonably reconstructed from notarial records and from the inventory of her assets drawn up after her death by tax assessors. According to that inventory, her assets amounted to 2,500,000 Polish złoty, with an additional 1,000,000 in outstanding assets. Like her son-in-law, Samuel Antoni Frankel, Jakubowiczowa continued to cooperate closely with Prussian bankers, first and foremost with Jacob Herz Beer in Berlin. Nevertheless, the political changes seem to have influenced the geographical orientation of her banking business, or at least bolstered the business ties within the Polish territories and Russia that she had maintained since the last quarter of the eighteenth century. She owned obligations from the Kingdom of Poland and from a large merchant bank in St. Petersburg, but apparently her international business was limited, primarily to her connections to St. Petersburg and Berlin. In Warsaw, she enjoyed business ties to both local Jewish and non-Jewish banking houses, such as those of Epstein & Levi and Piotr Steinkeller.[20] Most of Jakubowiczowa's clients that received credit from her banking house were local Polish nobles; in general, they received loans for a period of two or three months up to one year at a rate of 5 percent interest. That most loans after 1822 were made in Russian ruble is noteworthy; it may suggest that Jakubowiczowa's business was becoming increasingly oriented toward the Russian Empire. Similarly, her debtors may have increasingly adapted to the political circumstances.[21]

By the time of Jakubowiczowa's death in 1829, two major shifts had occurred within the Jewish commercial elite in Warsaw and the Kingdom of Poland. Until 1793 all major banks were owned by Christians, mostly Protestants, but by 1843, the most important banks in Warsaw belonged to Jews or to Jewish converts to Christianity, such as Jakubowiczowa's son-in-law, Samuel Antoni Frankel.[22] Many of them were the grandchildren or great-grandchildren of Jewish immigrants, who had come to Warsaw around the late eighteenth and early nineteenth centuries from Prussia and other German-speaking lands, and their Polish-Jewish spouses.

Jewish banking houses emerged in most centers of commerce and banking in central Europe. Within the framework of the commercial and financial connections between Amsterdam and Warsaw scrutinized in this study, the rise of Jewish banking in Warsaw may be seen as a parallel to the rise of Jewish bankers in London. As Amsterdam and its capacity for providing credit for commercial activities declined, the city lost its rank not only to London but also to Warsaw. Though Jewish bankers in Warsaw operated on a much smaller scale than did their fellow Jewish bankers in England, they took over functions provided previously by Jewish merchants, brokers, and bankers in Amsterdam.

The Move into Leaseholding

Although a few Christian entrepreneurs such as Piotr Steinkeller from Cracow were involved in the salt monopoly, the business was a classic case of an economic niche taken up and successfully filled by Jewish entrepreneurs.[23] Their informal networks translated into formal contracts, without which businesses of this scale could not have operated, even within kin and ethnic networks. Jewish suppliers profited from a few different elements: the relative economic and weak social cohesiveness of Christian Polish entrepreneurs; the Jewish entrepreneurs' transregional connections to Jews in Galicia and Prussia; and their well-established ties to Polish officials, which they had built and solidified over time as army suppliers.

One of the most important fields of economic activity for Jews in the Polish-Lithuanian Commonwealth, next to trade, had been leaseholding from Polish noblemen. Though the close ties of Jews to the Polish nobility loosened somewhat in the nineteenth century, leaseholding of state monopolies was a new field of economic revenue. Thus, moving into monopoly leases did not constitute a radical occupational shift; it was rooted in one of the major occupations of Jews in the Polish-Lithuanian Commonwealth. Whereas Jews leased noble estates or specific taxes particularly in the eastern parts of the Polish-Lithuanian Commonwealth, in the eighteenth century they figured most prominently in leasing the right to produce and sell alcohol (*propinacja*). The lease of the *propinacja* meant a shift into monopoly leasing from noblemen. This form of leaseholding marked the close integration of Jews into the feudal system of the Polish-Lithuanian Commonwealth, and continued into the nineteenth century. Among the mercantile elite, a shift to leasing state monopolies occurred at the beginning of the nineteenth century. This shift suggests a move away from close connections to nobility in favor of closer connections to the state. Nevertheless, this shift also perpetuated the early modern tradition of leaseholding from the nobility.[24]

One example is the transition of Berek Szmul and his business partners into leasing the salt monopoly from the Duchy of Warsaw and then from the Kingdom of Poland. This professional move was a natural stepping-stone from Berek Szmul's prior economic activities. In addition to his involvement in army supplying, especially in the supply of salted meat, he was also involved in leasing estates from Polish nobles. For example, in 1813 he signed a six-year lease with the administrator of the Czartoryski estates for an annual sum of nearly 33,000 złoty. The lease included six estates (*folwarki*) and the attached villages, which stretched across three districts in the Warsaw and Siedlce provinces of the Duchy of Warsaw, including orchards, fruit trees, and all inns and breweries in these districts.[25]

However, in the nineteenth century, the state became a much more central actor. The political shifts of the partitions of Poland facilitated Polish Jewish entrepreneurs' move into the supply of salt, which was primarily used to preserve food. The two main sources of salt—namely, the formerly Polish mines in Sambor and Wieliczka—became part of the Habsburg Empire in the first partition of Poland in 1772. Exploitation of the salt mines was a central cameralist project for the government in Vienna. To this aim, the government established a central governmental salt administration, while in the Duchy of Warsaw and the Kingdom of Poland, the salt monopoly was still leased to private entrepreneurs. The fact that the major mines were situated outside the state is likely to have contributed to Jewish prominence in the business, as Jewish entrepreneurs were able to capitalize on their transregional networks to import salt.[26]

According to the contracts from notarial records, salt supplying was a major business; as such, the state had an interest in leasing it out completely so as to profit from high margins. The high margins resulted from the government's ability to fix the price of salt, which was not to be sold outside the monopoly, and due to high taxes the government levied on salt. Concurrently, salt supplying offered high-volume business opportunities for entrepreneurs in Warsaw and Cracow.[27] Yet the volume of the salt trade was too immense to be filled by any one individual merchant. Thus, in addition to contracts with the Polish state, we find primarily partnership agreements between various Jewish entrepreneurs from the Kingdom of Poland and Galicia in the Habsburg Empire who teamed up to supply salt to the Kingdom of Poland.

Jewish entrepreneurs in Poland had to be familiar with the administration and logistics of the salt business in the Habsburg Empire to supply salt from Galicia to the Kingdom of Poland. One way was to cooperate with Jewish entrepreneurs from Galicia. In 1811, Berek Szmul signed a contract with Izaak Wolff Rapoport, a merchant from Lemberg (L'viv; Polish: Lwów), who had a contract with the Austrian government for an annual purchase of 100,000 barrels of salt from the mines in Galicia. Berek Szmul agreed to purchase 50,000 barrels from Rapoport and then transport them to storage facilities throughout the Duchy of Warsaw for a set price of 13 to 15 złoty per barrel. Rapoport was slated to receive 45,000 złoty in advance; Berek Szmul was responsible for transporting the salt and was slated to receive 30,000 złoty from the Duchy of Warsaw. The contract, which was confirmed in June 1811 by Rapoport's agent, Joseph Zwilling from Lemberg, also stipulated that Berek Szmul was not allowed to purchase salt from any other source.[28]

However, the nature of the salt monopoly, did not rule out sub-contracting. Though the Duchy of Warsaw issued Berek Szmul a salt monopoly in 1811 and 1812, it appears that smaller suppliers continued to operate, presumably with his consent. Thus, in May 1811, Oesterreicher paid a security deposit of 30,000 złoty on behalf of three local suppliers who had secured a Ministry of Finance contract to supply 6,500 barrels of salt, a rather small amount, to their hometown in the Łowżynski province.[29]

It appears that the volume of business soon exceeded Berek Szmul's financial (and, it is likely, organizational) capacities. Attempting to anchor his business in secure financial footing and grow his operation, he joined forces with Salomon Markus Posner, who would become his closest business associate. Moreover, Berek

Szmul and Rapoport established the Southern Salt Trade Company in June 1811.[30] The long and detailed contract, written in both Polish and German, was signed in Warsaw by both entrepreneurs. Each owned two-sevenths of the company. Posner from Warsaw, and Josef Schwartzmann and Lazer Zuker from Jaroslav in Galicia also joined the Salt Trade Company and each of them owned another seventh of the company; their financial shares, losses, and benefits in the company were divided accordingly.[31] The contract, which regulated the working of the company down to the smallest detail, offers a glimpse into how this partnership was established and ran.

The contract also shows how these Jewish businessmen from different communities operated across political borders. The company was slated to buy and sell salt from the mine in Sambor in Galicia for eight years, and company associates were responsible for transporting the salt over land and water to the storages in the Duchy of Warsaw. All decisions were made according to majority vote; within the company, tasks were divvied out. Rapoport was responsible for purchasing salt from the Austrian government and with transportation costs and planning. Zuker and Schwartzmann, who had previously supplied salt on their own, oversaw the salt transport from the mines in Galicia to the storage facilities in the Duchy of Warsaw. On the other side of the border, Berek Szmul conducted business with the Polish administration; he probably knew many of the administrators from his regular army supplying. Posner became the company's primary administrator. The partners committed themselves to working for the best interests of the company at large and to preventing any other trading of salt to the Duchy of Warsaw. They set substantial fines and punishments in case of contravention; in the worst case, exclusion from the company and a hefty fine of 10,000 Dutch ducats.

This lease of the salt monopoly exemplifies an ethnic network at work that functioned transregionally and extended beyond kinship ties. What mattered in that sort of network was acquaintanceship and prior shared business interests, useful ties to non-Jewish officials, geographic location, and experience in the salt trade. One can presume that it was expected that each person was Jewish, although that was not regarded as a precondition or sole qualification for joining the contract. All company partners had experience in the salt trade; most had done business with the Polish or Austrian government. Thus, each partner brought some important expertise to the company's overall network. Although all partners were Jewish, the contract does not refer to any particular Jewish norms in terms of mutual obligations or punishment. Although ethnic belonging was important, as was expertise in the salt business, ethnicity was not reflected in business practice in the formal contract.

Although the company's connections to the Polish administration were crucial, the business was based primarily on shared ethnicity. This reliance on ethnic belonging was not limited to the members of the salt company. For example, a contract signed with the Duchy of Warsaw's government explicitly stipulated that all Jews who shipped salt on rafts from Galicia into the Duchy had to be registered, and that it was the entrepreneurs' responsibility to ensure that those Jews returned to Galicia. Thus, one can assume that most of the shipping was done by Jews and that entrepreneurs relied on ethnic networks for transporting the salt.[32]

Although ethnic belonging did play a role, business deals of this magnitude had to be based on formal contracts. Entrepreneurs joined forces via an especially detailed contract that could be enforced by the state court system. Though the notarial documents do not hint at any major strife within the company, all accounts were meticulously documented and signed in a notarial office upon the company's premature dissolution in 1816. Although the reasons for the company's termination remain unclear, they may have been related to the political changes of 1815 and the formation of the Kingdom of Poland. Having close business partners allowed wiggle room to draft less formal agreements, even if they were written. In a notarial document from 1816, dealing with the company's break-up, Berek Szmul and Posner agreed to continue their partnership which they had already "concluded and written down in a private letter" in 1813. This partnership encompassed their joined stakes in salt supplies as well other business.[33]

Founding the South Salt Trade Company was both an attempt to effectively control the import of salt to the Duchy of Warsaw as well as a step toward providing commercial activities with a more institutional framework. In January 1812, Schwartzmann and Berek Szmul signed a supply contract with the Minister of Finance to supply, via rafts and over land, 70,000 barrels of salt in three shipments, from Sambor in Galicia to thirteen different storage facilities in the Duchy. However, the price that the authorities were willing to pay—nine złoty twenty groszy per barrel, which included the cost for purchase and transport—was considerably lower than it had been previously. Nevertheless, valued at 644,000 złoty, it was a considerable deal; that was another reason why joint business partnership was necessary. The entrepreneurs only received an advance of 210,000 złoty for all three transports combined; they had to pre-finance more than two-thirds of the costs themselves. However, the Duchy of Warsaw agreed not to import any other salt and to try to prevent contraband trade. Another contract, dated 1814, entrusted Berek Szmul and his company with supplying salt from Austria to five of the six provinces of the Duchy of Warsaw.[34]

The end of the Napoleonic Wars changed not only the political landscape but also the conditions for Berek Szmul and his fellow entrepreneurs, who had supplied the relatively small Duchy of Warsaw with salt. The newly created Kingdom of Poland encompassed a far larger territory and needed much greater salt supplies. Though we cannot fully reconstruct the ensuing developments, it seems that Berek

Szmul and the banker Samuel Antoni Frankel, husband of his stepsister Atalia, sought a general salt monopoly for all of the Kingdom of Poland. Earlier, in 1813, Berek Szmul and Frankel had purchased salt from a Galician mine in Wieliczka, and in 1816 they joined forces to establish a salt monopoly in the Kingdom of Poland after the previous monopoly had been dismantled between 1813 and 1815.[35]

By June 1, 1816, the government of the Kingdom of Poland had established a new salt monopoly that discontinued the earlier ones from 1811 and 1812. The new monopoly was slated to last until 1821. Berek Szmul and Frankel signed the contract, with an option to add Posner at a later date. The contract stipulations strongly suggest why the two partners cooperated; they had both been in the business before and were unwilling to give up their profits, but the sheer volume would likely have been too high for either of them to go at it alone.[36]

Moreover, the lease added a new Prussian source for salt purchases, in addition to the existing Galician ones. This change suggests that the entrepreneurs not only had business contacts in Galicia, but could also initiate connections with other, presumably Jewish businessmen in Prussia to support their business endeavor. It is quite likely that Frankel, who had emigrated from Prussia, drew on his contacts. The lease stipulated an annual supply of 500,000 centner of salt: it was divided into 384,000 centner from the Galician mines in Wieliczka or Bochenska; 16,000 centner evaporated salt from Sambor; and another 100,000 centner of white Prussian salt. Before 1816, Frankel obtained supplies from the first two mines and Berek Szmul had supplied salt from Sambor.

Although the government set the prices for the purchase of a centner salt, it left sufficient margin to make the business profitable. In this contract, prices were set at 9.5 złoty per centner plus an additional three złoty for every centner of the Prussian salt; that translates into an annual business volume of over 5,000,000 złoty. The suppliers had to cover all the purchase and transport costs of the salt as well as all administrative fees and deposits, but they were exempt from any import taxes; in addition, the government agreed not to issue any other permits for salt transport once the monopoly went into effect. Berek Szmul and Frankel agreed to secure the monopoly to provide salt to all of the Kingdom of Poland and supply additional salt if the government deemed it necessary. The government earned a good profit from the salt monopoly; they purchased a centner of salt for 9.5 złoty and then sold it for about 24 to 30 złoty, depending on the province. In 1821, the salt monopoly yielded the state treasury a monthly profit of 150,000 złoty.[37]

Despite dissolving the first contracts for supplying the Duchy of Warsaw with salt, Berek Szmul maintained business ties with his former partners. He signed contracts with Rapoport and a certain Jozef Steinhardt from Dolina in Galicia on the matter of salt supplies. In his new cooperation with Frankel it seems that Berek Szmul could not sustain the high investments necessary, and brought in additional business partners. In 1818, Posner became an additional partner, as anticipated in the original contract. The year before, Szmul had given Posner complete power of attorney on all issues of the salt business, when he was seriously ill and unable to leave the house. Berek Szmul's frailty, however, did not keep him from running his business. In 1820, Szmul added Ignacy Neumark, one of the most important entrepreneurs and army suppliers in Warsaw, to his side of the contract.[38]

Neumark was the son of another Jewish merchant from Prussia who had come to Warsaw at the beginning of the nineteenth century. His father, Salomon Neumark, had entered the army supplying business during the Napoleonic Wars and in time dominated it after the foundation of the Kingdom of Poland.[39] Neumark's case shows the extent to which family remained an important factor, as he reserved the right to add to his part of the contract his father, Salomon Neumark, his brother Jakob Neumark and another business partner, the firm Israel Mendelsohn and Co. from Cracow. Concurrently, the company opened another office in Cracow; they sought to control the salt supply to the newly established Republic of Cracow. Berek Szmul included his son, Gabriel Bereksohn, in the salt business and took over a contract to purchase 35,000 centner of salt for storages in the Augustowski wojewodship.[40]

Yet one should not assume that networks based on kin and ethnic belonging, translated necessarily into a business that ran smoothly and sans conflict. In 1821, after the end of the five-year salt lease, strife arose between Berek Szmul and Frankel; they agreed that their conflict over the accounts had to be taken to an arbitration court.[41] However, among the factors triggering these conflicts was a shift in government policy and an internal dispute about how to run the salt monopoly appropriately. The government had decided to lease the transport of salt but not the purchase itself. At the next auction in 1820, Berek Szmul, Frankel, and a trade company named Sztamec were the three primary bidders. Berek Szmul offered a contract for 5,000 złoty less than Frankel's offer; Sztamec tendered 200,000 złoty less, but eventually proved to have insufficient capital to even take on an enterprise of this magnitude. Eventually, Berek Szmul secured the contract to transport salt to the Kingdom of Poland; he then moved into supplying the Republic of Cracow together with Neumark. This move came after Frankel was almost arrested in connection with the bankruptcy of a Christian merchant in Warsaw. A conflict later arose between Neumark and Berek Szmul, which was battled in court between Neumark and Berek Szmul's widow and children after he died in 1822.[42]

Despite these sorts of conflicts among Jewish entrepreneurs, as well as between them and the state as lessor or holder of monopolies, these endeavors were highly profitable. Thus Jewish entrepreneurs often bid against each other or joined forces when financially and logistically necessary. The lease of the salt monopoly offers a typical example of how networks based on familial connections and ethnic belonging, including Jewish converts to Christianity, empowered Jewish entrepreneurs to make the most of these opportunities. It also underscores the value of transregional connections to Galicia and Prussia and alludes to the integration of Jewish labor on a vertical scale, as Jewish boatmen were involved in the transport of salt. However, it also shows that these sorts of business endeavors were usually not accomplished solely by Jewish partners and networks. They could only succeed thanks to their close connections to government officials. Many of these ties had been established earlier by Jewish entrepreneurs, especially when they were active in army supplying; ultimately, these connections would prove to be vital in securing their access to government sources over time.

Economic Success and Religious Attitudes

Representatives of the Jewish Enlightenment in central Europe as well as non-Jewish reformers concerned with the Jews' social and economic position had perceived the restructuring of Jewish occupational patterns as central to their reform attempts. Moreover, "reforming the Jews' personality" aimed at the acquisition of European languages and secular knowledge.[43] This raises the question, how Jewish merchants and entrepreneurs integrated into general society, though they did not contribute to an imagined occupational diversification. It also makes one wonder to what extent the influx of Jewish migrants from Prussia and Silesia brought ideas of Haskalah and reform to Warsaw and how this played out especially in families of mixed backgrounds, such as in the case of Judyta and Szmul Jakubowicz.

What distinguished Warsaw from other rising commercial or banking cities was the diversity in religious and cultural terms among its Jewish entrepreneurs. Though it is true that a majority of Jewish wealthy merchants, entrepreneurs, and bankers by the mid-nineteenth century belonged to the acculturated minority of Polish and Warsaw Jewry, the beginning of the century saw an encounter of Jews from very different socio-religious backgrounds. Glenn Dynner was the first to point out very convincingly that Hasidim in the Kingdom of Poland were not simply a poor and economically backward mass; he showed that members of the Jewish mercantile elite, such as Berek Szmul and his wife Temerl, who were the most celebrated example, were also followers of the Hasidic movement and played a central role in financially sponsoring individual *tsadikim* (leaders of Hasidic communities).[44] And while many of the members of the new mercantile elite were indeed highly acculturated, this is not true for all of the protagonists. Altogether, the move into a different socio-religious milieu might not have been an exceptional case.

Though historians have usually described the marriage between Szmul and Judyta as purely a marriage of convenience, it begs the question how this arrangement worked on a practical level. When Judyta moved to Warsaw to marry Szmul Jakubowicz, she was dropped into the rather unfamiliar cultural environment of

Polish Jewry, partnered to a much older and less educated husband with leanings toward Hasidism. In Praga, he organized the famed disputation between the Hasidic *tsadik* Levi Isaac of Berdyczów and the Mitnaggdic R. Abraham Katzenellenbogen in 1781. Moreover, prayer services in his private residence in Praga were attended by at least one Hasid, and many of his visitors were said to be Hasidim.[45]

However, Jakubowicz's decision to marry Elenora Gabriela of Breslau and subsequently Judyta of Frankfurt an der Oder were motivated by desire for commercial success and business expansion. The fact that his marriage to Elenora from Breslau ended in divorce after only few years suggests the difficulties this marriage placed on both partners, alluding to diverging attitudes regarding lifestyle and religious practice. This divide continued within the family. The three sons from his first marriage—Berek, Abel, and Isaac Szmul—all became Hasidim.[46] By contrast, all four daughters from Szmul's second and third marriages belonged to the circles of acculturated Warsaw Jewry; two converted later on to Christianity. Elenora Gabriela had to leave her daughter, Atalia, behind after the divorce; she grew up together with her three stepsisters under Jakubowiczowa's tutelage. Three of the four women were married twice and out of their seven husbands two came from Prussia, one from the Habsburg Empire, and four from within Poland. We can assume that Jakubowiczowa exerted considerable influence in this matter (see figure 5.1).[47]

These arrangements raise more general questions as to what role women played as merchants and entrepreneurs, be it as wives or widows, in the framework of their familial and commercial connections. In many ways, Jakubowiczowa fits the early modern model of female economic activity. Closely involved in her husband's business from the beginning and probably trained in commercial matters by her father or other relatives, she becomes more visible in the sources only after her husband's death. As a widow she did show an incredible economic independence and unlike her peer of a century earlier, the female Hamburg merchant, Glikl bas Juda Leib, she did not remarry for nearly three decades, though we do not know if marriage was suggested to her during those years. Until her death she continued her business undertakings and moved into new economic fields.[48] At the same time she became increasingly part of a bourgeois milieu, which she knew from Prussia, and might even have been among the figures who introduced such ideas in her new hometown of Warsaw. Thus, she might be seen as a hybrid figure, who joined early modern commercial culture and bourgeois ideas of the early nineteenth century.

There is no doubt that in terms of business Jakubowiczowa was not just a nodal point in a network. Even before she was widowed, she was an active businesswoman with agency and influence. Moreover, she was also actively involved in the marriage politics of her family, as illustrated by numerous examples. In an epistolary exchange concerning the arranged marriage between her daughter, Ludwika Rebekka, and Itzig Jacob, she sought to ensure that her and her husband's privileges would be

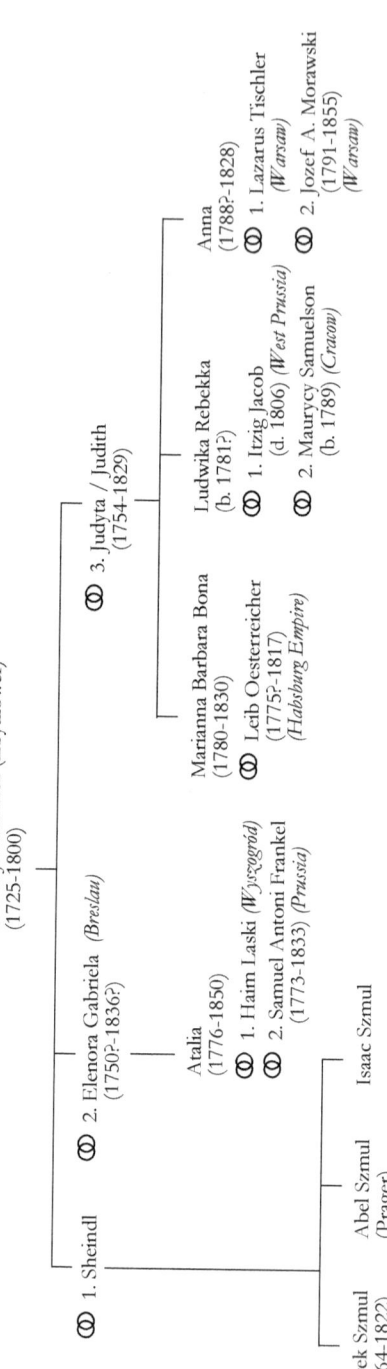

FIGURE 5.1. Family tree of Szmul Jakubowicz (Zbytkower). Credit: Oliver Ihlow.

transferred to her daughters and their husbands. When both sides agreed on the prospective marriage, the girl was only ten years old; at the time of marriage, she was fourteen or fifteen.[49] One can assume that Jakubowiczowa did agree to marrying off her daughter at that age; a letter from 1795 shows considerable influence from her on marital decisions. In this letter, Szmul Jakubowicz praised the industriousness and economic success of his son-in-law and pleaded to transfer his own Prussian privileges to him. Father of three daughters, Jakubowicz bemoaned not having a son who could support him in his old age;[50] that sentiment is curious as it disowns Jakubowicz's three sons from his first marriage, two of whom were active businessmen in Warsaw, as well as his daughter from his second marriage. It is very likely that Jakubowiczowa was the one to craft the letter, hence the mention of only her daughters.

Jakubowiczowa's personal and rather unusual decision not to remarry after her husband's death seems not to have limited her standing and influence among family members. She supervised decisions regarding her granddaughter's marriages and added to their dowry portions. At least three of her granddaughters received considerable dowry portions from their grandmother, according to their premarital contracts. In 1819, Felicya Flatau, one of the daughters of now-deceased Itzig Jacob and Ludwika Rebekka signed her premarital contract with Jakob Enoch, a physician from Kutno, while living in her grandmother's house. The contract between Jakob Enoch, Felicya Flatau, and Judyta Jakubowiczowa determined the conditions of the marriage first and foremost regarding Felicya's dowry. It stipulated that all immovable property, as well as money from inheritance, endowment, and all other sources, would remain in the possession of the future wife. The same was true for all movable goods.[51] The husband was obliged to guarantee the dowry's value by investing it either in a secure mortgage or in real estate, which were to be listed exclusively under the name of his wife. The only income that would belong to both parties would be that gained or saved during the marriage. Jakubowiczowa provided a dowry of 8,000 thaler for her granddaughter; 6,000 thaler were to be paid immediately after the wedding whereas the remaining 2,000 thaler were to be paid after three years, including 5 percent interest. The formulation of the premarital contract made clear the woman's financial independence and her right to her own assets.

Jakubowiczowa's influence did not diminish in the case of another granddaughter, Rozalia Konstancya Jozefa Oesterreicher, even though this granddaughter's circumstances were different from Felicya; she was not an orphan, and she had converted to Christianity before her wedding. Rozalia's father, Leib Oesterreicher, had passed away in 1817, so her mother, Bona, and Judyta signed the premarital contract with her daughter's future husband in 1825. The contract between Rozalia and her future husband, W. Mauricio Bethel, a lieutenant of the Russian Guard, appeared quite similar to that of her cousin Felicya's in terms of stipulated conditions and dowry amount. Rozalia Oesterreicher received 30,000 złoty from her mother; 9,000 were invested in mortgages, and the remaining 21,000 złoty were slated to be paid three years after the civil marriage. For those three years the couple would receive annual interest of 2,100 złoty. In addition, Rozalia obtained another 30,000 złoty from her grandmother; from that investment she likewise received annual interest of 2,100 złoty.[52]

Comparing the two premarital contracts allows for some very interesting observations. Both contracts followed the traditional understanding of a dowry as being the wife's possession, which the husband had to guarantee. Despite the fact that one of the granddaughters had converted to Christianity, there is no noticeable difference in the contractual structure. However, the dowry amount suggests differential treatment. Jakubowiczowa provided her Jewish granddaughter with 8,000 thaler of dowry, whereas the 60,000 złoty the converted Rozalia received from her mother and grandmother amounted to only about 3,330 thaler, less than half of her cousin Felicya's dowry. Thus, like in her business undertakings, converted family members were closely integrated, here in the transfer of capital within the family. The difference between the dowries, however, may reflect an effort by Jakubowiczowa to preserve significant portions of the family's capital within the family's Jewish side.[53]

Between Acculturation and Traditional Values

Judyta Jakubowiczowa seems to fit quite neatly into the category of an enlightened Jewish woman from Prussia who despised her husband's religiosity and anything related to it. In economic terms, she was a figure of the early modern world, closely integrated as a woman in the family's business and taking over once she became a widow. Her familial background was probably similar to that of the Schlesinger family in Frankfurt an der Oder. One can imagine that transitioning to Warsaw and to her husband was most likely difficult for Jakubowiczowa. Unfortunately, we know only little about her family background in Frankfurt an der Oder, though we saw how male members of the Jewish mercantile elite were prone to the early forms of a moderate or religious Haskalah. However, a painting supposedly portraying Judyta's mother Feigele (see figure 5.2), points to a well-off family, portraying their financial wealth not only in the dress she is wearing but also in the fact a painter depicted her; rather uncommon at the time as portraits of Ashkenazic Jews before the end of the eighteenth century are rather rare. The painting, a late nineteenth-century copy of the late eighteenth-century original, depicts a woman in elaborate headgear and collar, with ample jewelry and holding a handkerchief of presumably precious material, although dressed in appropriately dark

FIGURE 5.2. Portrait of Feigele, mother of Judyta Jakubowiczowa from Frankfurt an der Oder. Painted in accordance with the original by Maurycy Sztencel (1856–1930) in 1895. Courtesy of Bożena Toeplitz. Photo: Jacek Rajkowski.

colors. The painting, if faithful to the original, reflects the wealth and status Jakubowiczowa's parents held in Frankfurt an der Oder.[54]

Another painting, which traditionally is attributed to the Italian painter Bernardo Belloto (Canaletto), supposedly shows Judyta herself after her arrival in Warsaw with her husband Szmul (see figure 5.3). However, the picture can only provide us with some general impression of the dress and appearance of a wealthy Jewish couple around the 1770s in Warsaw. Being a small drawing of the Polish-Jewish

FIGURE 5.3. Jewish couple, drawing by Aleksander Lesser (1814–1884) after a fragment of the painting "Elekcja Stanisława Augusta Poniatowskiego" (1778) by Bernarda Bellotto (Canaletto, 1721–1780). Courtesy of Muzeum Narodowe w Warszawie (National Museum Warsaw).

artist Aleksander Lesser (1814–1884), it shows a detail of Canaletto's 1778 painting of the coronation of the last Polish king in 1764 (*Elekcja Stanisława Augusta Poniatowskiego*). Thus, this was never a portrait of the couple, though Szmul and Judyta or more likely his second wife from Breslau (as Judyta did not move to Warsaw before 1778) may have served as a model for the depiction of Jews in a larger historical painting. No matter who exactly is depicted, the drawing shows a wealthy couple but in a much more traditional dress. He is dressed in simple brownish-black coat and cloak, she wears a grayish dress with a small white collar, a brown fur coat, some golden jewelry, and a relatively simple gold-colored headwear with a red headband. Thus, the two paintings show rather a difference in style than in wealth, though no less a probably unfamiliar and more conservative environment for Jakubowiczowa.[55]

After Judyta Jakubowiczowa's husband died in 1800, she probably had more liberty to follow her own path, including her decision not to remarry. She supposedly hosted a salon in Warsaw modeled after the famous enlightenment salons of Jewish women in Berlin. These salons, which began to emerge in Berlin in the last two decades of the eighteenth century, were places of informal socialization between Jews and non-Jews; they were run by daughters and wives of wealthy Jewish merchants and bankers.[56] We can safely assume that Jakubowiczowa was familiar with the Berlin salon culture via an old and continuous commercial connection from her days in Frankfurt an der Oder. A native of the town, Jacob Herz Beer, son of the communal leader Juda Herz Beer, moved to Berlin in 1788, where he married Amalie, daughter of the wealthy Liepmann Meyer Wulff. Beer became a patron of the early religious reform movement in Berlin and opened the Beer temple in 1814, where reformed services were held with an organ and boys' choir.[57] His wife, Amalie Beer, maintained her own salon, which was most active after 1820, which is later than most salons. We know that Jakubowiczowa traveled regularly to Berlin, at least after the death of her husband in 1800 and into the second half of the 1820s. Though it is only speculation, it is more than likely that Jakubowiczowa visited Amalie Beer's salon. Similarly, she may have sat in the women's section of Herz Beer's synagogue during her visits to Berlin. One can surmise that she did subsequently run her own salon in Warsaw fashioned on the Berlin model, a model she may have transferred from Berlin into the less bourgeois atmosphere of early nineteenth-century Warsaw.

Yet one cannot describe Jakubowiczowa's attitudes toward religion as detached from tradition, acculturated to non-Jewish society, and indifferent to conversion. Although she may not have opposed the conversions of her daughters, she did personally keep ties to tradition, as can be gleaned from an examination of three documents: namely, a contract with the Ḥevrah Kadisha (Jewish burial society) in Praga; a list of her property compiled immediately after her death by the non-Jewish authorities; and her last will. The contract shows that Jakubowiczowa did not shy away from doing business with members of the burial society in Praga. After the death of her husband, the plot of land that he had purchased to establish a Jewish cemetery in Praga in 1780 remained in her possession.[58] A contract drawn between her and the Ḥevrah Kadisha in 1810 appears to codify the status quo.[59] The contract is penned in German, in Hebrew characters. The heavy German wording and spelling betray her role in drafting the contract. For the religious members of the burial society, German in Hebrew characters may have been the most appropriate way to do business with a woman. Hebrew, which was used in the *pinkas* (record book) of the burial society, was most likely not an option for Jakubowiczowa, whereas non-Jewish languages may not have been acceptable or accessible to the members of the Ḥevrah Kadisha. The contract itself left administration of the cemetery, as well as the profits from selling burial plots, to the Ḥevrah Kadisha. In return, the burial society had to pay 400 złoty annual rent to Jakubowiczowa and her descendants and maintain the cemetery. This case reflects how she carried on her and her husband's business dealings after his death, but also that she was sufficiently attached to the Praga Jewish community to remain involved with its tradition-minded leadership. Though one might argue that this arrangement was simply a business deal, her stipulations in her last will suggest otherwise. Shortly before her death, Jakubowiczowa penned two different but fairly similar versions of her will in German.[60] Her stipulations regarding her own burial suggest a close affinity to Praga and to the cemetery she had purchased together with her husband. She decided that the cemetery was to be transferred to the burial society of Praga or of Warsaw a year after her death.[61] Although a new Jewish cemetery had been opened in Warsaw in 1806 and a number of family members, including her Hasidic stepson Berek Szmul were buried there, she insisted on being laid to rest in the old Praga cemetery: "I ask to be buried quietly at my churchyard in Praga.... Moreover, three learned men shall pray for me for one year in my synagogue no. 150 in Praga; each of them will receive three hundred gulden for the year, and another three hundred gulden shall be given for the light to burn for a whole year."[62]

Her wish reflected her affinity to her and her husband's property in Praga beyond the material value; she insisted on being buried in her cemetery and being prayed for in her synagogue, though she had probably not set foot in the latter on a regular basis, if at all. She followed the Jewish tradition of having learned men pray for her after her death and light a candle in her memory. Yet her use of the word "churchyard" (*Kirchhof*) for the Jewish cemetery suggests a high degree of acculturation. Although Jakubowiczowa undoubtedly affiliated with the most acculturated group of Warsaw Jewry, she remained attached to essential Jewish customs, at least in regard to her own burial.

Jakubowiczowa's last will both complicates and confirms the image of an acculturated woman. Among her family members, she divided her assets without regard to the religion of the descendants. In the case of her deceased daughter, Annette Morawski (originally Anna), who had converted to Christianity after divorcing her first husband, Lazarus Tischler, Jakubowiczowa stipulated that the two children from Annette's first marriage and the six children from her second marriage to Józef Morawski would all receive one-eighth of their mother's share of the inheritance. Similarly, she assigned considerable amounts to charity, dividing them between Jews and Christians, although the sum for Jewish institutions was about one third higher than for non-Jewish institutions.[63] Even more surprisingly, she stipulated a gift of 5,000 gulden to be distributed to the poor "without regard to religion" during her burial. Giving to the poor in one's will was customary in Judaism but giving to Christians, much less "without regard to religion," was decidedly not. It does, however, mirror her decision to contribute to the dowries of her grandchildren, Jewish or Christian.

Upon her death in 1829, Judyta Jakubowiczowa was one of the wealthiest women in Warsaw. The state administration promptly ordered compilation of all of her property for tax purposes. This long list appears to confirm that she held highly acculturated attitudes. With the exception of "five pieces of silverware with religious depictions," not a single item is listed that appears to have been a ritual object, nor are there any books. However, one ought to keep in mind that books and ceremonial objects may have been handed down from her husband directly to his sons and sons-in-law.[64] However, she did possess a copper engraving of the Russian tsar Alexander I and a painting of the Polish prince Josef Poniatowski, items that mark her close connection to the government administration and possible admiration for Alexander I.[65] Jakubowiczowa was in many ways outstanding in her cultural attitudes, much of which probably can be accounted for by her origin. Coming from Frankfurt an der Oder, she was familiar with the early forms of the Haskalah and later on closely linked to acculturated circles in Berlin. She succeeded in fitting into a Jewish, though rather foreign environment, when she moved to Warsaw and was able to deftly pursue her own economic and cultural interests. Thus, one may describe Jakubowiczowa as a hybrid figure, who over half a century in Warsaw became economically and at least partly socially integrated into local Jewish and Christian society, while showing loyalty to the respective rulers. Culturally, however, she did transfer some ideas of cultural or religious reforms and bourgeois attitudes to Warsaw.

Jakubowiczowa's stepson and at times business partner Berek Szmul stands symbolically for the opposite path to modernity. Strongly influenced by his father's religious attitudes and his upbringing in the presumably much more traditional household of Szmul Jakubowicz's first wife, he became not only a highly successful merchant, army supplier, and entrepreneur, but also was an ardent patron of Polish Hasidism. Together with his wife, a patroness of Hasidism in her own right, he opened a Hasidic synagogue in Praga and donated books to the *beit midrash* (lit., study house). Glenn Dynner showed that Szmul was also proactive in promoting Hasidism against its *maskilic* opponents and lobbying for it with the local Polish administration.[66]

Looking comparatively at Jakubowiczowa's and Berek Szmul's case, historians have sometimes emphasized that he too allocated part of his inheritance to Christian institutions. However, in contrast to Jakubowiczowa, he did not explicitly stipulate in his last will a donation to Christian institutions; in the end, only about 10 percent of the sum dedicated to charity went to two Christian institutions. A Polish-language version of his will, which had been drawn up in Hebrew in 1818, was preserved in the files of the Kingdom of Poland's central religious authorities after his death in 1822.[67] The will stipulates only that 10 percent of his assets should be given to three Jewish trustees to be used for charity. Half the sum was to be given to the poor; the other half was to be invested, with the interest donated to those who study "holy books."[68] It is safe to assume that the reference intended exclusively Jewish religious books. When Berek Szmul died, the Polish authorities, made sure to receive their part of his tremendous assets. His heirs reached an agreement with the Polish authorities that 10 percent of the sum given to charity would be allocated to Christian institutions.[69] In contrast to Jakubowiczowa, who hardly distinguished between Jews and Christians in her posthumous charitable giving, Berek Szmul identified personally and culturally as solely part of Jewish society. These attitudes, however, mattered less when it came to the economic realm.

As illustrated earlier in this chapter, when it came to business, differences in religious attitudes were usually bridged in favor of economic considerations. Berek Szmul did business with all sorts of Jewish merchants, including those who were not his relatives, and those who were more acculturated. At the same time, he maintained close connections with the administration of the Duchy of Warsaw and the Kingdom of Poland.[70] For most of his business ventures contracts were drafted in Polish and concluded in a notary's office. However, his wealth could not compensate for the government's anti-traditionalist attitudes when it came to cultural differences.

Wealth, economic success, and proximity to non-Jewish authorities could not overcome all obstacles that Jews faced in Warsaw, particularly for those Jews who refused to dress in what was considered non-Jewish attire. At a time when settlement restrictions for Jews anywhere in central and western Europe had been abolished, residential restrictions were upheld or newly instituted in the Duchy of Warsaw and afterward in the Kingdom of Poland. As Dynner argued, these restrictions, including the designation of a number of streets at the center of Warsaw as off-limits for Jews and their businesses, were rooted in a deep fear of Jewish economic might and influence. Only those wealthy and acculturated enough in the eyes of the Christian bureaucrats were likely to receive exemptions as was the case with Judyta Jakubowiczowa.[71]

Berek Szmul, by contrast, did not fall as easily into this category. Though doubtlessly wealthy, he did not fulfill the condition of being acculturated and surely was recognizable as traditional Jew by his attire. In an 1815 petition, he claimed that he had received the right to settle anywhere in Warsaw from the Saxon king and duke of Warsaw in 1810, after a decree of 1809 had put a number of Warsaw streets off-limits for Jews, but notarial records suggest otherwise.[72] Berek and Temerl probably moved from Praga to Warsaw in the first decade of the nineteenth century. According to notarial records, Berek Szmul officially lived on Zakroczymska Street (no. 1856) until 1810; that was one of the streets north of the old city that became off-limits to Jews in 1809. These restrictions were part of the city administration's ongoing efforts to remove Jewish inhabitants from the central streets of Warsaw.[73]

The following year, Berek Szmul moved to the Bielinski Palace (no. 1066) on Królewska Street. The building belonged to the then-minister of justice Feliks Łubieński, who allowed a number of Jews to settle on his family's property, in the outbuildings of the palace situated on the part of the street permissible to Jews.[74] In 1821, more streets in Warsaw were declared off-limits, including Królewska Street; neither Berek Szmul nor his business partner Posner, who belonged to the community's conservative establishment, appear to have received an exemption; both moved away that same year, at least officially according to notarial records.[75] Though wealth was often significant in circumventing governmental legislation, the situation of Berek Szmul and others indicates that this was not always the case. Wealth and close economic relations to government circles of the Duchy of Warsaw and the Kingdom of Poland were not necessarily decisive in gaining exemptions or alleviations from government decrees.

Berek Szmul's move into Bielinski Palace may not have been completely voluntary and it seems that other Jewish entrepreneurs moved there too under similar circumstances. A review of the Jewish tenants from between 1810 and the early 1820s reveals an interesting picture. In addition to Berek Szmul, other building tenants included his regular business partners Fürstenberg, Bauererz, and Posner. Fürstenberg had immigrated to Warsaw from German lands. Registered at the location as an innkeeper, Bauererz, was also the father of Juda Leib Bauererz, known for his enlightened views.[76] Finally, Posner belonged to the Jewish community's traditional establishment.[77] After the official abolition of the *kahal*, the communal self-government, in 1822, the new official synagogue board (*dozór bóżniczy*) briefly moved its office into the building, where its longtime secretary and *maskil* Jakub Tugendhold also lived.[78]

The story of the Bielinski Palace on Warsaw's Królewska Street (no. 1066) is suggestive as it shows the proximity in which Berek Szmul lived with other business partners. This proximity was likely convenient and supportive for maintaining their business networks. The different religious attitudes of the Bielinski Palace's residents did not matter in their joint business undertakings. The same is true for the administration of the Jewish community, in which most of the residents were also involved. In terms of cultural and religious attitudes, however, the shared space had no major impact.

Berek Szmul's impressive tombstone at the Jewish cemetery in Warsaw, preserved to this day, symbolizes in a way his position within the Jewish community in Warsaw. The tombstone is designed in the form of an *'ohel* (lit.: tent); it is outstanding in size and decoration, as befitting his wealth and social status, while the inscription praises his charity and fortitude during times of trouble.[79] One side of the tombstone depicts the biblical motif of the Babylonian exile, next to an image of a distinguishably East European city, most likely Warsaw. On the other side one finds Praga on the Vistula River, displaying not exile but the wealth of Berek Szmul and his family. It shows the town of Praga, the estates his father acquired in 1780, and his father's cemetery in Praga (see figures 4.2 and 4.3). Although Warsaw may still have been a place of exile, it was also a place that brought wealth and influence and possibly some sense of belonging.

Conclusion

Finally arriving in Warsaw, we see a rising metropolis of the nineteenth century, just at the inception of industrialization. In the city, we find a new mercantile and financial elite emerge, comprising in the main Jewish immigrants from west of Poland as well as from smaller towns and villages in the vicinity of the Polish capital. They became central figures in the development of banking and eventually industrialization in the Kingdom of Poland, even though they had not yet attained the rights and liberties of emancipation. In this lack of legal equality, they differed from their fellow Jewish bankers and entrepreneurs in Amsterdam and Prussia. The first enjoyed equal rights since after the French Revolution, the latter since the Prussian reforms of 1812.

Most of these members of a new Jewish economic elite in Warsaw followed the very typical path from small-scale trader and leaseholder into army supplying and over a generation or two, into financial services and eventually into private banking. This professional trajectory moved them from very mixed sources of income into more definable fields of business. In both of these developments, they did not differ much from Jewish bankers elsewhere in Europe. They were exceptional only in that they quickly constituted a majority in the commercial and financial elite of nineteenth-century Warsaw. Moreover, we have witnessed a shift from Jews' close connections to the Polish nobility and deep integration into feudal economy toward closer ties with the state and eventually close involvement in the emerging capitalist economy.[80]

A crucial difference from the rise of a Jewish economic elite elsewhere in western or central Europe was certainly that those wealthy Jewish entrepreneurs pursued very divergent cultural or religious paths and did not unanimously fit the category of a bourgeois elite. Most Jewish entrepreneurs chose acculturation and some even conversion to Christianity. Those entrepreneurs from a Polish-Jewish context were more likely to follow Hasidism as their spiritual identity. This gulf, however, did not undermine their close familial and ethnic ties that often lay at the core of their business ventures. This does not mean at all that they had any ruminations about doing business with Christians and many even actively sought to become part of wider society. Despite this, mutual trust still proved stronger between family members in the widest sense and ethnic belonging contributed to the development of trust. Nevertheless, one needs to emphasize, that partnership required being knowledgeable and well connected in the respective business.

The exploration of the nucleus of the nineteenth-century Jewish commercial and financial elite in Warsaw has also confirmed Dynner's suggestion that leanings toward either the Haskalah and some degree of acculturation, on the one hand, and toward Hasidism, on the other hand, was closely linked to place of origin.[81] Both offered an alternative to traditional communal organizations, which one needs to add, hardly existed in Warsaw prior to the arrival of these merchants and army suppliers. Although acculturation seems to have remained attractive to those, who were influenced by early forms of the Haskalah despite the lack of emancipation, those who came to Warsaw from within Poland were much more likely to be drawn to the innovations Hasidism had to offer.

Notes

1. Węgrzynek, "Illegal Immigrants," 40–41.

2. Kosim lists nearly every transaction between Jewish (and some non-Jewish) entrepreneurs and the Polish administration in these years based on notarial records. However, he often takes at face value complaints that were raised by contemporaries of Judyta Jakubowiczowa and Berek Szmul. He accuses both of a lack of "patriotic considerations" that allowed them to accept any contract that promised gains without "any consideration of the current political situation of the country." Kosim, *Losy pewnej fortuny*, 16, 29, 32, 51–52 (quotation).

3. Ibid., 59–60. Pawłowski, *Protokoły Rady Stanu Księstwa Warszawskiego*, vol. 1, 1, 78, 88, 102, 196, 220, 315; Pawłowski, *Protokoły Rady Stanu Księstwa Warszawskiego*, vol. 1, 2, 187; Pawłowski and Mencel, *Protokoły Rady Stanu Księstwa Warszawskiego*, vol. 2, 2, 155–156, 167–169.

4. Acta betr. die rußischen Forderungen der Madame Jacobowitz, I. HA, Rep. 151 (M) IA, no. 5146, GStA.

5. Ibid., 1–2, 5, 18, 28, 51. On Beer, see Lowenstein, *The Berlin Jewish Community*, 91, 107, 137. On the Commercial Council Johann Simpson in Memel, see Straubel, *Die Handelsstädte Königsberg und Memel*, 389.

6. A bill of exchange from 1766 shows that Simpson was involved in trade to Amsterdam and Danzig. Notariat Gerrit Bouman, file 12617, StAA, NAA, no. 451. In 1771, Johann Simpson turned to the Prussian administration regarding his demands against Simon Symons and Levin Pincus Schlesinger in Warsaw. In S[achen] des Memelschen Kaufmanns Johann Simpson wegen einer an die Warschausche Juden, Simon Simons und Schlesier ex cambio habenden Forderung, XX. HA, Etats-Ministerium (EM), Tit. 111j, no. 526, GStA, 1-3; Acta betr. die rußischen Forderungen der Madame Jacobowitz, I. HA, Rep. 151 (M) IA, no. 5146, GStA, 56.

7. Rostworowski, *Materiały do dziejów Komisyi Rządzącej z roku 1807*, 381.

8. Pawłowski and Mencel, *Protokoły Rady Stanu Księstwa Warszawskiego*, vol. 2, 1, 236; Pawłowski, *Protokoły Rady Stanu Księstwa Warszawskiego*, vol. 1, 1, 48–49, 70–71, 84. Memoriał Ministra Woyne, April 5, 1811, RMKW, serja 2-go, 115, AGAD, 75, 79–80.

9. Pawłowski, *Protokoły Rady Stanu Księstwa Warszawskiego*, vol. 1, 2, 208–209. For similar later complains, see Dynner, *Men of Silk*, 99–100; Kosim, *Losy pewnej fortuny*, 16, 20–23.

Already in 1807/8, the Duchy of Warsaw faced military expenses of 35,000,000 złoty in contrast to 29,000,000 złoty of annual income. Although the general situation improved after the war with Austria in 1809 and the acquisition of Western Galicia, the problems did not cease. By 1812 the French army owed the Duchy over 12,000,000 francs, but paid only about 4,500,000. Eile, "Liweranci," 32–41.

10. Pawłowski and Mencel, *Protokoły Rady Stanu Księstwa Warszawskiego*, vol. 2, 2, 246–247.

11. Ibid., 169, 247.

12. By 1814, his father, Samuel Pinkus Oesterreicher, had passed away; his brother, Izaak Oesterreicher, still lived as a merchant in Oleśnie (Rosenberg) in Silesia. Kancelaria Jana Wincentego Bandtkie, syg. 18b, no. 1767, APWa, 41–42v.

13. Kancelaria Walentego Skorochód-Majewskiego, syg. 15, no. 353, APWa, 199–205.

14. According to notarial records, the payment for this supply was long delayed. In 1825, Jakubowiczowa signed a contract with Berek Szmul's sons. She agreed that the two brothers would receive 50,000 złoty and she 161,103 złoty of the yet unfilled demands of 211,103 złoty. Kancelaria Jana Wincentego Bandtkie, syg. 51a, no. 5032, APWa, 130–133. Schiper, *Dzieje handlu żydowskiego*, 369.

15. Notarial records allude to supplies in 1805–1808 and 1812, but one can assume that this is only a partial picture. Kancelaria Andrzeja Kalinowskiego, syg. 9, mf. S-965, nos. 2178–2180, APWa, 313–318; Kancelaria Walentego Skorochód-Majewskiego, syg. 34, mf. S-351, no. 110, APWa 190–191v; Kancelaria Jana Wincentego Bandtkie, syg. 12b, no. 1147, APWa, 96–107. Kancelaria Jana Marczyńskiego, syg. 18, mf. S-123, no. 417, APWa, 1182–1183v. See also Kosim, *Losy pewnej fortuny*, 71–72.

16. Kancelaria Walentego Skorochód-Majewskiego, syg. 32, mf. S-349, no. 453, APWa, 30–33v; Kancelaria Teodora Czempińskiego, syg. 27, no. 3405, APWa, 326–327v.

17. Kosim, *Losy pewnej fortuny*, 61.

18. Graetz, "'Aliyato ve-shkiato shel sapak ha-tsava ha-yehudi," 255–273.

19. Ibid., 257–260, 269. For Prussia, see also Straubel, *Kaufleute und Manufakturunternehmer*, 201. For the Rothschilds' role in the Napoleonic Wars, see Ferguson, *The House of Rothschild*, vol. 1, 83–110.

20. On the inventory of her house, firm, and assets, see Eisenbach and Kosim, "Akt masy spadkowej Judyty Jakubowiczowej," 88–143. In order to assess her property, the tax assessors went through eighty-five account books, which were all kept in German. The books appear to be lost today.

21. Kancelaria Walentego Skorochód-Majewskiego, syg. 101, no. 527, 21–22; syg. 104, no. 789, 9–10; syg. 106, no. 881, 21–22; syg. 107, no. 71, 163–164; syg. 110, no. 385, 245–246; syg. 149, no. 2, 240–241, APWa; Kancelaria Jana Wincentego Bandtkie, syg. 34a, no. 3309, 25–27; syg. 37a, no. 3624, 112–114; syg. 39b, no. 3869, 29–30v; syg. 41b, no. 4097, 183–184; syg. 43a, no. 4232, 108–109; syg. 46a, no. 4506, 20–22; syg. 46b, no. 4578, 105–110v; syg. 47b, no. 4681, 107–109, APWa. It was only after 1850 that the ruble became the only valid currency in the Kingdom of Poland. After the 1831 uprising, a form of hybrid coins was issued that carried dual values in kopeks and groszy. Van Wie, *Image, History, and Politics*, 96–97.

22. Guesnet, "Banking," 121. In 1843, Warsaw counted thirteen Jewish bankers. Some fifty years later, in 1897 the breakdown in ownership out of twenty-six banking houses in Warsaw was thus: fifteen were owned by Jews, three had been founded by Jewish converts to Christianity, and only eight belonged to Christians. In the provinces of the Kingdom of Poland, as many as nineteen out of twenty-one banking houses were owned by Jews.

23. Piotr Steinkeller, the older, sought to enter the salt business during Napoleonic times, but it was only in 1825 that his son succeeded in securing a contract with Konstantyn Wolicki. More Christian entrepreneurs entered the business in the later 1820s. Kołodziejczyk, *Piotr Steinkeller*, 39.

24. According to Gershon Hundert, by the 1760s more than one-half of rural and one-quarter of urban Jews earned their income primarily in this field. Jews dominated the production and sale of alcohol in villages and held leases on mills, breweries, distilleries, and taverns in towns. Hundert, *Jews in Poland-Lithuania*, 32–33, 42–43; Hundert, *The Jews in a Polish Private Town*, 64–67. On the continuation of leaseholding in the nineteenth century, see Kalik, "Leaseholding," 1003; Teller, *Money, Power, and Influence*, 107–111. On the continuous involvement of Jews in the liquor trade in the Kingdom of Poland, see Dynner, *Yankel's Tavern*, 82–102.

25. Kancelaria Walentego Skorochód-Majewskiego, syg. 36, mf. S-353, no. 2572/253, APWa, 151–160v.

26. Vogel, *Ein schillerndes Kristall*, 111–117. Vogel's work focuses on Prussia and Austria and the history of knowledge regarding salt production.

27. Kosim, *Losy pewnej fortuny*, 213.

28. Kancelaria Jana Marczyńskiego, syg. 14, mf. S-119, no. 1785/76, APWa, 187–194. One barrel (*beczek*) amounted to between seventy-seven and seventy-eight kilograms; thus the contract was for about 7,700 tons salt. See also: Kosim, *Losy pewnej fortuny*, 214; Kancelaria Jana Marczyńskiego, syg. 15, mf. S-120, no. 274, APWa, 677–680.

29. Kancelaria Walentego Skorochód-Majewskiego, syg. 21, mf. S-338, no. 1347/206, Lit. D, APWa, 236–237v. Leib Oestreicher was the husband of Berek Szmul's half-sister Bona.

30. Posner lived in the same building as Berek Szmul on Królewska Street (1066) in Warsaw. In February 1811, Berek Szmul authorized Posner to pick up 20,000 barrels of salt from Galicia as part of his contract with Rapoport. Kancelaria Jana Marczyńskiego, syg. 14, mf. S-119, no. 1813/104, APWa, 254–255.

31. Ibid., syg. 17, mf. S-122, no. 2443/64, APWa, 130a–142v.

32. Kancelaria Aleksandra Engelke, syg. 1, mf. S-523, no. 16, APWa, 58.

33. Kancelaria Jana Marczyńskiego, syg. 31, mf. S-137, no. 6102/517, 816–817; syg. 34, mf. S-140, no. 6957/322, 809–810; no. 6958/323, 811–812; no. 6960/325, 815–816, APWa; Kancelaria Jana Wincentego Bandtkie, syg. 26b, no. 2536, APWa, 1–3v. Their joined business included an older *arenda* of Posner. At that point, Posner added another 200,000 złoty into their partnership that he was supposed to receive from their dissolved salt trade company.

34. Kancelaria Aleksandra Engelke, syg. 1, mf. S-523, no. 16, APWa, 52–59v. The contract is only listed in the inventory of the notarial office but is missing. Kancelaria Andrzeja Kalinowskiego, syg. 10, mf. S-966, no. 2430/101, APWa. The provinces were Cracow, Radom, Lublin, Siedlce, and Warsaw.

35. Kancelaria Walentego Skorochód-Majewskiego, syg. 36, mf. S-353, no. 2569/250, APWa, 137–139v. Kołodziejczyk, *Piotr Steinkeller*, 37.

36. Kancelaria Jana Wincentego Bandtkie, syg. 25b, no. 2459, APWa, 41–63.

37. The price was lowest in the Cracow province with 24 złoty, 15 groszy, and highest in the Łomżynski province with 30 złoty, 9 groszy. See also Kosim, *Losy pewnej fortuny*, 213.

38. Kancelaria Jana Marczyńskiego, syg. 34, mf. S-140, no. 6956/321, APWa, 805–808; Kancelaria Jana Wincentego Bandtkie, syg. 30a, no. 2944, APWa, 173–176. Numerous notarial documents from 1817 describe Berek Szmul as feeble and sick in his body, though not his mind. These notarial documents were signed in his house. Kancelaria Andrzeja Kalinowskiego, syg. 14, mf. S-971, no. 4017/1134, APWa, 916–917.

39. Kosim, *Losy pewnej fortuny*, 88–110.

40. Kancelaria Walentego Skorochód-Majewskiego, syg. 95, mf. S-142, no. 8369/2, 189–195; no. 8394/27, 266–267, APWa. In 1820, Berek Szmul and Ignacy Neumark issued power of attorney to Salomon Neumark and Berek's son, Gabriel Bereksohn, to sell salt in the free city of Cracow. Cracow fell to the Habsburg Empire in the third partition of Poland 1795 and was part of the Duchy of Warsaw from 1809 to 1815. After the Congress of Vienna, the Republic of Cracow was established as a protectorate of the three partitioning parties. Kancelaria Jana Wincentego Bandtkie, syg. 30a, no. 2950, APWa, 197–202v.

41. Kancelaria Jana Wincentego Bandtkie, syg. 41a, no. 4044/98, APWa, 120–122.

42. Kosim, *Losy pewnej fortuny*, 216–219. Although Kosim suggests that the attempted arrest of Frankel served the interests of his competitors Berek Szmul and Ignacy Neumark, he does not provide any evidence that they were involved directly in some kind of intrigue against Frankel. Eventually, Neumark resigned from the business and focused exclusively on army supplying. Kołodziejczyk, *Piotr Steinkeller*, 38.

43. Karp, *The Politics of Jewish Commerce*, 202–203.

44. Dynner, *Men of Silk*, 89–116.

45. Ibid., 89, 95–99; Bergman, "Nie masz bóżnicy powszechnej, 162–163.

46. Dynner, *Men of Silk*, 99.

47. Atalia, the daughter from Szmul's second marriage, was first married to Haim Lasker from the Polish town Wyszogród. After her husband passed away few years into their marriage, she remarried Samuel Antoni Frankel of Prussia; both converted to Catholicism in 1806. Judyta's daughter Marianna Barbara Bona (1780–1830) was married to Leib (Ludwik) Oesterreicher, who hailed from Habsburg lands. The second daughter, Ludwika Rebekka (b. 1781), married Itzig Jacob. The third daughter, Anna (1788–1828), was first married to Lazarus Tischler, a Jewish merchant from Warsaw. Certainly, his name also suggests that he emigrated from German-speaking lands. After his death and her conversion in 1813, she married Jozef Aleksander Morawski, a member of the Polish government in the Kingdom of Poland. Reychman, *Szkice genealogiczne*, 18, 73. Eisenbach and Kosim, "Akt masy spadkowej Judyty Jakubowiczowej," 97–98.

48. On Jewish women and their economic activities in the early modern period, see Rosman, "The History of Jewish Women in Early Modern Poland," 25–56; Toch, "Jewish Women Entrepreneurs," 254–263.

49. Acta betr. das Gesuch des jüdischen Handlungs-Bedienten Itzig Jacob, um Bewilligung eines Schutz-Privilegii auf die Stadt Soldau, 1791–1792, II. HA, Abt. 7, II Materien, no. 4717, GStA, 1v.

50. Die Gesuche verschiedener Juden um allgemeine Privilegien und Konzessionen auf Südpreußen, GDDPP I, no. 896, AGAD, 27–29. Another interesting point in the letter is the content which suggests that his daughter decided of her own volition to marry Itzig Jacob, with no reference to her young age. One can speculate that Jakubowiczowa or both of them understood that that sort of formulation would be read positively by the Prussian administration.

51. Kancelaria Jana Wincentego Bandtkie, syg. 35b, no. 3481, APWa, 86–88v. Immovable goods are referred to as *posag* (dowry), whereas *bona paraphernalia* is used for movable goods.

52. Ibid., syg. 50b, no. 4954, 13–17v. The record also contains a listing of movable goods that were primarily household textiles and clothes that Rozalia would bring into her marriage. They were worth 12,150 złoty or 675 thaler.

53. On conversions from Judaism in the Russian Empire and their social implications, see Ellie R. Schainker, *Confessions of the Shtetl*, ch. 3.

54. The portrait of Chajke, the daughter of Abramek of Lwów (1781), painted by court painter Krzysztof Radziwiłłowski and commissioned by the Polish king, makes for an interesting comparison. Chaijke's portrait displays her as a woman of wealth in a sumptuous dress. See Hundert, *Jews in Poland-Lithuania*, jacket, 5–6. The portrait of Feigele is owned by the Toeplitz family and the late Krzysztof Teodor Toeplitz allowed me to see it in 2007. On the back of the portrait a note states that the painting depicts the mother of Judyta Jakubowiczowa and that it was painted in accordance with the original by M[aurycy] Sztencel in 1895. One hint that it really is a copy of a portrait of Jakubowiczowa's mother is the fact that the property list compiled after her death in 1829 lists "a small portrait depicting a woman in muted colors." Eisenbach and Kosim, "Akt masy spadkowej Judyty Jakubowiczowej," 102.

55. It was maybe the Polish-Jewish historian Ignacy Schiper who first claimed the drawing to be a depiction of Judyta and Szmul Jakubowicz. Schiper, *Żydzi w Polsce odrodzonej*, 1:187. See also Shatzky, *Geshikhte fun yidn in Varshe*, vol. 1, 128.

56. Hertz, *Jewish High Society*; Lowenstein, *The Berlin Jewish Community*, 104–110.

57. Lowenstein, *The Berlin Jewish Community*, 91–107, 137–140. Men and women, however, sat separately and most of the service was conducted in Hebrew.

58. According to Frenk, who displays a deep dislike for Judyta, she held a tight reign over the cemetery and designated burial fees, a right she is said to have retained after Szmul's death. Frenk, *Meshumadim in Poilen*, 28.

59. The contract can be found in the *pinkas* of the Praga Ḥevrah Kadisha: Pinkas haḥevrah kadisha de-Praga/Księga Bractwa Pogrzebowego na Pradze 1785–1870, S 63/23, CAHJP, 243–246. The contract is the only existing document Judyta signed with her Jewish name Gittl (wife of Szmul) and in Hebrew characters.

60. The first version is dated February 27 and the second is dated March 5, 1829. The differences are minimal. The copies used here were preserved in the notarial records

Kancelaria Kowalewskiego, syg. 8, no. 675, APWa, 159–163v. A second set of copies seems to exist in the mortgage book of Jakubowiczowa's house in Przejazd Street 643. Ludwig Frenk consulted it in the 1820s. Frenk, "Testament Judyty Zbytkower," 377–382.

61. Her use of the word "Brüderschaft" clearly points to the continued existence of the traditional Ḥevrah Kadisha, despite the fact that it had been officially abolished in 1822.

62. Kancelaria Kowalewskiego, syg. 8, no. 675, APWa, 162v–163. The synagogue was situated in one of the houses that belonged to Jakubowiczowa's property. After her death, it went to her grandsons, Jacob and Stanisław Flatau, on condition that they would provide annually 500 złoty to the poor family members from her husband's side, who lived in the house. Bergman, "Nie masz bóżnicy powszechnej," 102, 106.

63. The Jewish hospital in Warsaw and the Jewish Society for Clothing the Poor received the total sum of 27,000 gulden, whereas three Christian charitable organizations shared 19,000 gulden. Another fund of 2,500 gulden was set aside for the education of children "without regard to religion," but with some preference to be shown to poor members of her family. Kancelaria Kowalewskiego, syg. 8, no. 675, APWa, 160v–161v.

64. See, for example, the mid-seventeenth-century will of the wealthy Cracow merchant David Theodore Kozuchowski, who bequeathed everything in terms of movable and immovable property and business responsibility to his wife Gitel, except for his books, which were inherited by his male children. Rosman, "How Family Wealth and Power Are Organized," 57.

65. Eisenbach and Kosim, "Akt masy spadkowej Judyty Jakubowiczowej," 102, 115.

66. Dynner, *Men of Silk*, 100–103. See also "Akt darowizny bóżnicy przez Berka. Miscellanea," 180–182.

67. Notarialne przejęcie testamentu i jego polskie tłumaczenie, CWW 1012, AGAD, 13–20. Printed in Wodziński, "Legat Berka Sonnenberga," 152–157.

68. Notarialne przejęcie testamentu i jego polskie tłumaczenie," CWW 1012, AGAD, 16.

69. This has been shown in great detail by Wodziński, "Legat Berka Sonnenberga," 141–151. For the correct numbers, see Akta Legatów Staroz. Berka Sonenberga 1824 r., KRWROP 7341, AGAD, 3–5. In toto, 219,000 złoty were to be allocated to Jewish institutions; 20,000 złoty to Christian institutions; and 2,500 złoty to the (Christian) Institute of the Deaf.

70. Dynner, *Men of Silk*, 99–101.

71. Dynner, "Jewish Quarters," 91–92.

72. On the acquisition of houses and the right of settlement in certain parts of Warsaw, see Dynner, *Men of Silk*, 103–104, 106. For the 1815 petition, see KRSW, no. 6628, AGAD, 212.

73. Addresses become easier to trace after 1808, when notarial offices opened. Kancelaria Andrzeja Kalinowskiego, syg. 1, mf. S-957, no. 98, APWa, 265; Kancelaria Jana Wincentego Bandtkie, syg. 4a, no. 332, APWa, 135; Kancelaria Jana Marczyńskiego, syg. 11, mf. S-116, no. 1106/91, APWa, 224.

74. The palace was centrally located right at the southern edge of the Saxon Garden at the corner of Królewska and Marszałkowska streets. Jews had lived there back in the eighteenth century because it was noble land and thus the Warsaw settlement restrictions did not apply. Kancelaria Teodora Czempińskiego, syg. 10, no. 1253, APWa, 443. Zieliński, *Atlas dawnej architektury ulic i placów Warszawy*, vol. 8, 74, 77. Królewska was off-limits only from

Krakowskie Przedmieście to Mazowiecki Street. Kirszrot, *Prawa Żydów*, 99. See also: Bergman, *"Nie masz bóżnicy powszechnej,"* 37, map 3. Sometimes the palace is also called Łubieński Palace. On the acquisition of houses and the right of settlement in certain parts of Warsaw, see also Dynner, *Men of Silk*, 103–104, 106. Kancelaria Walentego Skorochód-Majewskiego, syg. 3, mf. S-320, no. 150, APWa, 110–110v; Kancelaria Przeździeckiego, syg. 7, no. 19, APWa, 27; Kancelaria Jana Wincentego Bandtkie, syg. 11b, no. 1046, 53; syg. 26b, no. 2536, APWa, 1.

75. For the additional streets, see Kirszrot, *Prawa Żydów*, 101. Berek Szmul moved to Orla Street briefly before his death, Posner to Nalewki Street. Kancelaria Jana Wincentego Bandtkie, syg. 41a, no. 4044/98, 120; syg. 48a, no. 4739, APWa, 178.

76. Kancelaria Walentego Skorochód-Majewskiego, syg. 3, mf. S-320, no. 150, APWa, 110–110v; Kancelaria Przeździeckiego, syg. 7, no. 19, APWa, 27; Kancelaria Jana Wincentego Bandtkie, syg. 11b, no. 1046, 53; syg. 26b, no. 2536, APWa, 1. Wodziński, *Haskalah and Hasidism*, 92.

77. Eisenbach, *The Emancipation of the Jews in Poland*, 179, 211, 227, 263, 299. On his role in the Polish uprising of 1830/31, see Gelber, *Hayehudim ve hamered hapolani*.

78. In Warsaw and across all of the Kingdom of Poland, the Imperial Russian state attempted to extend authority over Jewish communities by abolishing the traditional *kahal* as well as all charitable societies in 1822. The *kahal* was replaced by an official synagogue board (*dozór bóżniczy*), although evidence from multiple communities suggests that the former structure continued to exist and the lay leadership successfully retained much of its power. Guesnet, *Polnische Juden im 19. Jahrhundert*, 223–229, 378–379; Bergman, *"Nie masz bóżnicy powszechnej,"* 68. Tugendhold belonged to the community's enlightened establishment, but was also the first *maskil* to defend Hasidism. See Wodziński, *Haskalah and Hasidism*, 142–153.

79. The epitaph is printed in Yevnin, *Sefer naḥalat 'olamim*, 12. The form of an *'ohel* was usually used for tombs of exceptional scholars and rabbis since the beginning of the eighteenth century. Wodziński, "Tombstones," 1887–1891.

80. See Guesnet, *Polnische Juden im 19. Jahrhundert*, 121–122.

81. Dynner, *Men of Silk*, 115–116.

Conclusion

Tracing the paths of three extended Jewish families and their business partners—the Symons of Amsterdam, the Schlesingers of Frankfurt an der Oder and the Jakubowicz family in Warsaw—illuminates the crucial role transcultural and transnational connections played for commerce across the European continent at the transition from the early modern to the modern period. Following these families from west to east, contrary to the more common direction of Jewish migration during the eighteenth century and in later periods, allowed for new insights into the making of a Jewish economic elite in modern Europe. These commercial connections facilitated the provision of credit from Amsterdam to central Europe and from there via Prussian Jewish merchants in general and those in Frankfurt an der Oder in particular to Jewish merchants in Poland. These commercial networks were primarily based on extended families and ethnic belonging, though they obviously operated in the general world of commerce. During my research, family ties provided me with a measure as to whom I ought to include in the story.[1] My work suggests a number of conclusions in three thematic areas: Jewish merchant strategies of creating and maintaining networks; the entry into specific areas of economic activity and adaptation to local economic and legal conditions; and the possible social and cultural implications of these network ties.

At the core of strategies to enhance one's business opportunities was tying the knot. Marriage was the most important means to establish or strengthening ties between Jewish merchants, grow assets, broaden commercial networks geographically, open up new markets, or especially in the case of Prussian Jewry, circumvent legal restrictions. Thus, familial and ethnic ties played a crucial role in establishing and maintaining networks among Ashkenazim who were involved in trade and brokerage across Europe, a feature that distinguished them from their fellow Sephardic merchants. The latter established close ties with non-Jewish business partners, described by Francesca Trivellato. Although members of the Ashkenazic mercantile elite were involved in the wider economy and did business with Christians, the core of their commercial networks centered around family members and other Jewish, though sometimes converted, business partners.

The geographic mobility of Jewish merchants and entrepreneurs was of no less importance than their family ties. Familial and commercial connections were not exceptional in comparison to familial ties in other segments of the Jewish population. These ties are rather one example of the high degree of Jewish mobility in the early modern period in general.[2] Yet these familial and commercial connections were not stagnant over time. Commercial ties shifted and adapted in accordance with economic necessity. In the transitional period between the mid-eighteenth and the early nineteenth centuries, general economic shifts contributed significantly to the disintegration of some networks as well as to the establishment of others.

Looking at the role of Jewish merchants, brokers, and entrepreneurs in the second half of the eighteenth century and at the transition to modernity helps us to understand the rise of a new Jewish economic elite in nineteenth-century Europe. Jews filled certain occupational niches in which they were strongly visible and in numbers—in comparison with their percentage of the overall population—clearly overrepresented.[3] However, they did not belong to the wealthiest strata of the population during the second half of the eighteenth century. And even these successful merchants and entrepreneurs were the exception rather than the rule: A majority of the Ashkenazic population in all of the cities and states examined here remained rather poor in comparison with other urban populations at the time under consideration.

Only a small number of Jews were economically successful. The economic niches filled by Jews differed from place to place and changed over time. In Amsterdam, ordinary merchants and brokers provided credit for Jewish and non-Jewish merchants in central and eastern Europe, but were also involved in the diamond trade and provided smaller credits. In Prussia in general and in Frankfurt an der Oder in particular, Jewish merchants used this credit for their commercial activities. Most of these merchants were heavily involved in textile trade. They functioned as middlemen between east and west in terms of merchandise exchange and in providing credit to Jewish merchants from Poland, especially at the fairs in Frankfurt an der Oder and Leipzig.

In the case of Warsaw, we noted clear patterns in the rise of a new economic elite comprising Jewish traders from the city surroundings and Jewish merchants hailing in the main from the partition territories, Prussia, Silesia, and the Habsburg lands. Most of them had started out rather modestly: they were butchers and traders in meat, merchants in other agricultural goods and holders of the privilege of producing and selling alcohol (*propinacja*) or sub-lessees, and in many cases they were more than one of these in combination. In the years between the partitions of Poland and the Napoleonic Wars, many of them moved into or added army supplying to their sources of income, a pattern that can be seen at other times and places in Jewish economic history as well. Some of them were able to amass quite a fortune in this business, providing food and feed to the Polish, Prussian, Russian, Habsburg, and French armies; and more often than not, one supplier supplied to more than one of these. From this involvement in army supplying it was not such a herculean step to move into financial services and eventually into banking.

The political changes surrounding the partitions of Poland paved the way for new economic avenues. Because of the ever-increasing need to supply the armies of the political powers involved in partitioning Poland, and even more so the outbreak of the Napoleonic Wars, army supplying blossomed into perhaps the most profitable business for Jewish merchants and entrepreneurs. They had certain abilities and experience that made them far more suited to this niche than their average Christian counterparts: they could draw on their transregional networks, their prior expertise in trading agricultural products and textiles, and their willingness to sustain the risk of supplying multiple armies and extend credit to multiple states.

One must keep in mind that the willingness to incur greater risk was often motivated by striving for legal security; this was true in Prussia as well as in Warsaw, the Polish-Prussian borderlands, and nineteenth-century Poland. In those regions, army supplying prepared Jewish entrepreneurs for the move into banking and leasing of state monopolies, a shift that had already begun in the 1790s but grew more pronounced after the end of the Napoleonic Wars, as demand for military supplies receded. These changes facilitated the rise of a new banking elite in Warsaw and, more generally, in the Kingdom of Poland, an elite in which Jewish bankers indeed stood out.

The significance of these Jewish commercial networks is to be found not in their alleged contribution to the emergence of, or certain features of, capitalism. Rather, Jewish commercial networks contributed significantly to the flow of credit and goods between Amsterdam in the west and the Polish-Lithuanian Commonwealth in the east. Only toward the end of the eighteenth century, and more clearly after the end of the Napoleonic Wars, did Jewish bankers in Poland and specifically in Warsaw win increasing influence, while Amsterdam lost its important role for commerce in central and eastern Europe. The supply networks proved highly mobile and flexible, and individual merchants actively extended their ties to new markets and sources of supply and adapted themselves to changing economic conditions.

This ability to adjust to new economic conditions, however, does not mean that these Jewish merchants and entrepreneurs were particularly innovative in terms of business practice or fields of business by contemporary European standards. To be sure, they were closely integrated into the general economic realm, and thus it is questionable whether their success can be described as a result of primarily "internal solidarity and external strangeness."[4] Rather, their strength was rooted in filling particular economic niches as part of the general economy, though it is clear that familial and ethnic ties played a vital role.

These familial ties, however, usually did not last over more than two generations. It becomes obvious that there is no clear trajectory from early modern Court

Jews in central Europe to the nineteenth-century banking elite, even if there were a few bankers who as individuals had that sort of family background. The same is true for Poland, where integration into feudal society was crucial for the rise of a new commercial and financial elite in the nineteenth century. However, most of the Jewish entrepreneurs who were part of Warsaw's nineteenth-century elite did not emerge right out of the economically powerful Jewish families of eighteenth-century Poland.

Regarding the third thematic area, the preliminary evidence of the relationship between economic and cultural developments calls into question the allegedly close ties between them.[5] The economic efforts of the Jewish merchants and entrepreneurs scrutinized in this study reflect how closely integrated they were into the general world of eighteenth-century commerce. Yet for all their "commercial cosmopolitanism," they were most certainly not "citizens of the world."[6] Their far-flung connections were not driven by ideological conviction. They maintained numerous connections across continental Europe with Jewish and non-Jewish merchants alike. Interacting with non-Jewish business partners, clients, and state officials was part and parcel of the commercial undertakings of Jewish merchants and entrepreneurs. Yet these ties did not imply the removal of social and legal limitations; Jewish merchants continued to face, to varying degrees, legal restrictions on settlement, access to trade in specific commodities, higher taxes, and fees at fairs. Some of these Jewish merchants enjoyed close ties to Jews with different religious outlooks and cooperated economically with Jewish converts to Christianity as well as with Christians, but there is little evidence that these commercial encounters significantly altered their religious attitudes and forms of social practice.

The Nineteenth Century: Private Banking and Industrialization

Looking out to the historical landscape of nineteenth-century Warsaw, the picture changes considerably. Around the mid-eighteenth century, Jews enjoyed more rights in the Polish-Lithuanian Commonwealth than in central Europe; still, in Warsaw, they remained a legally excluded group. Even by the late eighteenth century, there was no established Jewish community in Warsaw, due to the formal ban on Jewish settlement. This was the policy, despite the fact that thousands of Jews did actually live in Warsaw at the time. Jews' economic activity around the mid-eighteenth century—primarily retail trade, leaseholding, artisanry, and some wholesale trade—was crucial for supplying the local population, including poor nobles, wealthier peasants and burghers. Jewish economic endeavors translated into being deeply ingrained in the Polish-Lithuanian Commonwealth's feudal society.

However, a century later, Jews had risen to prominence in banking and entrepreneurship; they had done so throughout Poland, then the Kingdom of Poland under Russian rule, and in Warsaw in particular. This development went along with an increasing urbanization of the Jewish population across the Kingdom of Poland, which began already in the first quarter of the nineteenth century and intensified in the following decades. In Warsaw, one of the most important centers of migration, the number of Jewish inhabitants grew from about 15,000 in 1816 (about 19 percent of Warsaw's population) to about 49,000 in 1864, the year of the abolishment of peasants' serfdom, and close to 220,000 in 1897, when 32 percent of Warsaw's population was Jewish. Most of these Jewish immigrants, however, were rather poor and remained poor in the Polish capital. Thus, they constituted a strong contrast to the Jewish merchants, army suppliers, and bankers, who eventually became successful figures as the city turned into a (Jewish) metropolis.[7]

Whereas until the last decade of the eighteenth century major banking houses in Warsaw were owned by Protestants of German descent, half a century later most important banks in Warsaw belonged to Jews or Jewish converts to Christianity. This development was linked in part to specific conditions in the Polish Kingdom: the continued rejection of involvement into commerce, finance, and industry among most Polish nobles; a weak Polish burgher's estate; and the continuing existence of strict estate boundaries until at least the abolishment of peasants' serfdom in 1864.

Like elsewhere in central and eastern Europe, private banks assumed a central role in the process of industrialization. The state-run Polish national bank (Bank Polski) financed only a small number of state-run factories, while the assets of the private bankers contributed greatly to the beginning industrialization of the Polish capital. Though we find few financiers with a German background or from the Polish nobility, Jews, including some who converted to Christianity under the unsatisfactory legal conditions of the Kingdom, constituted the majority of figures in those circles. They continued the investments of the earlier generations, described in this book, as bankers and industrialists, investing in state monopolies, such as tobacco, and new industrial undertakings like railway construction. One often-overlooked factor in the move into investment in industry, infrastructure, and agricultural modernization is the constant in-flow of cash from the state's repaying state loans.[8]

Numerous descendants of those army suppliers and entrepreneurs, whom we have encountered at the turn of the century, were among those leading Jewish bankers in Warsaw and later industrialists in the second and third quarter of the nineteenth century. These bankers and entrepreneurs included Gabriel Bergson/Bereksohn (1790–1844, the son of Berek Szmul), Leopold Kronenberg (1812–1878), Jan Bloch (1836–1902), Hipolit Wawelberg (1843–1901), Juljusz Jakob Wertheim (1819–1901), Matthias Rosen (1804–1865), and Jakub Epstein (1771–1843) and his four sons: Josef (1795–1876), Adam (1799–1870), Jan (1805–1885), and Herman

(1806–1867). They all became part of the banking and industrial elite of Warsaw in the nineteenth century and successfully invested in industrialization projects.[9]

Yet these entrepreneurs did not operate in an exclusively Polish framework, limited to the Kingdom of Poland or even Imperial Russia. They and their successful rise to a Jewish economic elite of bankers and entrepreneurs were part of a larger development that included a considerable number of Jewish bankers and entrepreneurs, who successfully operated across Europe from the first decades of the nineteenth century. The Rothschild family, whose origins can be found on the Jewish street of Frankfurt am Main, is the most emblematic example of the rise of this new Jewish banking elite across Europe. Though Mayer Amschel Rothschild was a traditional Court Jew at the court of the elector of Hesse and active in trade and moneylending, he only moved into banking proper around the turn of the century. His sons founded new branches of the house of Rothschild across Europe: in London, Vienna, Naples, and Paris. They extended their business into most European countries by providing government loans, especially during the Napoleonic Wars, and by investing in industrialization projects and the development of transportation.[10] The rise of the Rothschild family was typical for the development of Jewish private banking in late-eighteenth and early-nineteenth-century Europe, though their business was exceptional in size with its multiple branches and agents across and beyond Europe.

The origin of most of these nineteenth-century private bankers can be found in commerce and the trade in bills of exchange; only some like Rothschild already had a previous career as Court Jews. Their rising importance was closely linked to industrialization and the increased need for capital to finance industrial undertakings, railway construction, and similar endeavors.[11] With London established as the most important center for private banking in Europe, other important banking houses were located in Paris, Frankfurt am Main, Cologne, and Hamburg. In Paris, Protestant banking houses flourished alongside the banking houses of the Rothschilds and of the Sephardic Pércire brothers. In German centers of private banking, Protestant houses also dominated the scene alongside Jewish bankers. Berlin only rose to international importance in the 1860s. Nevertheless, the banking houses of Joseph and Abraham Mendelssohn (founded in 1795), of Samuel Bleichröder (founded in 1803), and of F. Martin Magnus (founded 1821) already played a central role in the business undertakings of Warsaw bankers during the first half of the nineteenth century. In Vienna, the Arnstein and Eskeles families founded influential banking houses; banks were also founded and run by Jews in Hungary, Sweden, Denmark, Belgium, the Netherlands, and Switzerland. Most were involved in state loans and in financing industry and transport infrastructure. In most cases, private bankers invested jointly in those sorts of projects to cover the substantial amount of capital and share the risk. Although large banking houses like the Rothschilds were often involved in state loans, a large number of smaller private banks of local or regional importance invested in new industrial undertakings. It was only in the second half of the nineteenth century that these private banks were increasingly replaced by newly emerging joint-stock banks.[12]

As was the case in western and central Europe, the new commercial and financial elite in Warsaw assumed an equal role in these developments, even though the industrial revolution took off in Warsaw and the Kingdom of Poland decades later than in parts of western and central Europe. What facilitated the acceleration of the industrial revolution was an intersection of events: The beginning of railway construction opened the Russian markets in the early 1840s, and the abolition of serfdom in the Kingdom of Poland in 1864 made a larger workforce available. The advance of the industrialization also opened new fields of entrepreneurship for bankers in Warsaw and the Kingdom of Poland.

In Russia, where private banking houses emerged only from the 1860s on, Evzel' Gintsburg (1812–1878), his son Horace (1833–1909), and the Poliakov brothers rose to prominence as private bankers and financiers of railroad development and other infrastructural projects.[13] All of these banking houses invested heavily in infrastructure and industrial projects. They were also active in leasing fiscal revenues, including the tobacco monopoly and lottery, and, in the case of the Gintsburgs, the traditional field of leasing the rights to produce and sell alcohol.

These bankers, entrepreneurs, and industrialists had much in common with members of the Jewish commercial and financial elite elsewhere in Europe, and were thus closely connected to them. Polish Jewish bankers sent family members abroad for occupational training, such as Leopold Kronenberg, who lived abroad from 1829 until 1832, where he was trained at the banking house of Salomon Heine (1767–1844) in Hamburg.[14] Hipolit Wawelberg received his professional training at his father's bank in Warsaw and Berlin before he founded his own banking house in St. Petersburg. Juljusz Jakob Wertheim was trained in Warsaw and Dresden, among others in the trading house of Piotr Steinkeller, one of the outstanding Christian entrepreneurs in Warsaw.[15] The Epstein family was equally well linked to foreign banking houses. Jan Epstein was trained at various European banking houses, while his nephew Mieczysław Epstein (son of Hermann Epstein) was trained in Berlin and Paris as well as at the office of the House of Rothschild in Brussels, after his father Hermann Epstein had brokered loans in earlier years from the Rothschilds in Frankfurt am Main.[16]

On the matter of business practice, Polish Jewish bankers did not differ greatly from Jewish and non-Jewish private bankers across Europe. They were most likely to establish and use connections with foreign banking houses in two particular fields of business: state loans and investments into railway construction. The business of state loans was usually taken over by English, French, and German banking houses, either with or without Jewish owners, who possessed the necessary capital.[17] Compared to the large loans provided by the Rothschilds and others to the governments of England, France, or Russia, the loans provided to the government of the Kingdom of Poland were rather minor. Nevertheless, they were too large to be taken on by Polish-Jewish bankers alone. In the late 1820s and the 1830s, S. A. Frankel's banking house brokered large loans for the Polish national bank and the Polish government from bankers in Berlin; Hermann Epstein brokered loans from the Rothschilds in Frankfurt am Main.[18]

In many ways, we see some continuation of business operations of the eighteenth century, when Amsterdam served as the center for the provision of credit to central and eastern Europe. Though Jewish merchant-bankers in Amsterdam did themselves provide small credits, many were rather involved in the brokerage of credit from larger Christian banking houses. With the decline of Amsterdam's importance as a financial center and the rise of a new banking elite in Warsaw, the coordinates of the provision of credit changed; Jewish banking houses in Warsaw took over the brokers' role.

After 1830 the financing of railway construction across Europe turned into one of the largest business fields of European private bankers, with strong involvement on the part of the various branches of the Rothschilds. In the Kingdom of Poland and the Russian Empire, Jewish financiers played a similar role; they were willing to assume the financial risk linked with this investment. The financing of Russian and eventually Polish railways also shows that the funds that Polish Jewish bankers could contribute were rather limited; similar to state loans, these projects needed transnational financing.[19]

Transnational connections and business operations turned these Polish Jewish bankers into European economic players like their fellow Jewish or converted bankers and entrepreneurs across Europe. This transnational activity does not mean, however, that these bankers were not also Polish patriots and advocates for the Polish and often equally for the Jewish case. Members of the new Jewish mercantile elite in Warsaw were involved in the Polish uprising of 1830/31, which led to severe restrictions on the autonomous status of the Kingdom of Poland. Among those who tried to join the "National Guard," which was organized to maintain order in the wake of the uprising, were a number of acculturated Jewish intellectuals and members of the economic elite, including Samuel Kronenberg, Jakub Epstein, and members of the Toeplitz family.[20] In their economic activities, many of these entrepreneurs involved in industrialization projects and later railway building had to maneuver between their loyalty to the Polish nation and their sometimes close relationship to the Russian tsarist government.

Despite the prominent number of converts among the wealthiest bankers, it appears that their conversion did not play a significant role in the business world.[21]

The situation was similar to that explored during the early decades of the nineteenth century; just as Judyta Jakubowiczowa worked closely with her converted son-in-law, Samuel Antoni Frankel, who enjoyed equally close business relations with his Hasidic relative Berek Szmul, a change in religion or an individual's religious or cultural sense of belonging did not significantly impact upon their business connections. Jewish bankers and entrepreneurs (and those of Jewish origin) in Warsaw had become part of a Jewish economic elite that at the very same time was able to act locally, transregionally, and transnationally.

The Jewish bankers and entrepreneurs of nineteenth-century Warsaw were members of a cosmopolitan elite that identified with a titular nation but felt at the same time unrestricted in forging their international commercial connections. One can assume that their identity as subjects of a nineteenth-century Empire was equally central to their entrepreneurial endeavors. Despite the rise of the modern nation state and the involvement of some of these entrepreneurs in the Polish national cause, the political frame of reference for these entrepreneurs was the Russian Empire. Moreover, Jewish bankers and entrepreneurs across Europe played a crucial role in connecting Europeans to the global economy, whether they were subjects of the British, Ottoman, or Russian empires.[22]

With the exception of outstanding international families such as the Rothschilds, historians of the nineteenth and twentieth centuries have traditionally examined entrepreneurs and bankers and their families in their respective national frameworks. It is only a recent trend in scholarship, including literature that trails transregional and transnational families, Jewish and non-Jewish alike, to look beyond those national frameworks. Such works examine which impact transnational connections, international marriage, multiple citizenships, or property in more than one nation state or empire had on their business strategies and their identity. Such a transnational life can be equally assumed for the case of nineteenth-century Polish Jewish bankers and entrepreneurs and their families in Warsaw and Poland.[23]

The small elite of Jewish or converted bankers and entrepreneurs in Warsaw around the mid-nineteenth century constituted a relatively close-knit web of long-term acquaintances, including marital ties; yet they were also international and indeed cosmopolitan families in many ways. Closely embedded in their Polish environment, often giving their children Polish names, they nevertheless traveled abroad for professional training, marriage, business, and pleasure, and were closely linked to Jewish bankers and entrepreneurs across Europe. They had become part of a larger European circle of private bankers and industrialists of Jewish descent.

Notes

1. See Sabean and Teuscher, "Rethinking European Kinship," 7.

2. Ruderman, *Early Modern Jewry*, 23–55.

3. On the question of overrepresentation and the need of its explanation out of the contemporary conditions, see Hollinger, "Rich, Powerful, and Smart," 595–602.

4. Slezkine, *The Jewish Century*, 43.

5. Jonathan Israel has linked the economic decline that he detected in the first half of the eighteenth century to a parallel "cultural impoverishment." Israel, *European Jewry*, 216. Francesca Bregoli rejects Israel's argument for the case of Livorno. Bregoli, *Mediterranean Enlightenment*, 241.

6. On these terms and the rise of cosmopolitanism in the early modern period, see Jacob, *Strangers Nowhere in the World*, 1–4. On Jews and cosmopolitanism, see Miller and Ury, "Cosmopolitanism: The End of Jewishness?," 344–352.

7. Guesnet, *Polnische Juden*, 34. See also Garncarska-Kadary, "Hayehudim ve hagormim lehitpathutah vemikumah shel ha-ta'asiyah be-Varshe," 29, 56. On Warsaw as a Jewish metropolis, see Dynner and Guesnet, *Warsaw*, 1–10. On the growing religious, cultural, and eventually political diversity of Warsaw's Jewish inhabitants, see Guesnet, "From Community to Metropolis," 128–153.

8. Garncarska-Kadary, "Hayehudim ve hagormim lehitpathutah vemikumah shel ha-ta'asiyah be-Varshe," 38–41; Garncarska-Kadary, "Hayehudim behitpathutah hakalkalit shel polin ba-me'ah ha-19," 322–326.

9. On the families, see Reychman, *Szkice genealogiczne*, passim. On their economic rise, see Kosim, *Losy pewnej fortuny*; Kołodziejczyk, *Portret warszawskiego milionera*.

10. Among the vast literature on the Rothschilds, see Ferguson, *The House of Rothschild*; Liedtke, *N.M. Rothschild & Sons*; Kaplan, *Nathan Mayer Rothschild*. For more literature, see Aust, "Jewish Economic History," http://www.oxfordbibliographies.com/view/document/obo-9780199840731/obo-9780199840731-0106.xml.

11. Pohl, "Banken und Bankgeschäfte," 197; Liedtke, *N.M. Rothschild & Sons*, 15.

12. Liedtke, *N.M. Rothschild & Sons*, 15–17; Pohl, "Banken und Bankgeschäfte," 198–200; Baron and Kahan, *Economic History of the Jews*, 218–222.

13. Guesnet, "Banking"; Baron and Kahan, *Economic History of the Jews*, 221.

14. Kosim, *Losy pewnej fortuny*, 264; Kołodziejczyk, *Portret warszawskiego milionera*, 10.

15. Schiper, *Dzieje handlu żydowskiego*, 480.

16. *Polski słownik biograficzny*, 6:283–284. Mieczysław Epstein married Leonide Lambert in 1855. She was the daughter of Samuel Lambert, who provided services for the Rothschilds in Antwerp before he assumed representation of the banking house in Brussels in 1853 and ran his own private bank. On the connection between the Lambert family and the Rothschilds, see Liedtke, *N.M. Rothschild & Sons*, 53, 113–114.

17. Pohl, "Banken und Bankgeschäfte," 201.

18. Kołodziejczyk, *Portret warszawskiego milionera*, 107, 111–112. Kołodzieczyk states that despite this influx of capital, the important Polish financiers and industrialists rose to power not due to foreign capital but due to the exploitation of Polish peasants, artisans, and

workers. Although this is on the whole probably true, it applies equally to both Jewish and Christian entrepreneurs during that time.

19. Baron and Kahan, *Economic History of the Jews*, 184.

20. Toeplitz, *Rodzina Toeplitzów*, 68–72; Kieniewicz, "The Jews of Warsaw," 160.

21. On the conversion of Jews in general and members of the economic elite in Warsaw in particular, see Endelman, "Jewish Converts in Nineteenth-Century Warsaw," 28–59.

22. On the nineteenth century as the century of empires, see Osterhammel, *Die Verwandlung der Welt*, 606, 1031. On Jewish merchants in the nineteenth-century British Empire, see Mendelsohn, *The Rag Race*, 207–228. On the integration of Jews in the nineteenth-century Ottoman Empire, see Cohen, *Becoming Ottomans*, 19–44, 132–142.

23. For a recent exemplary study of a German industrialist family, see Derix, *Die Thyssens*, 107–232; Derix, "Transnationale Familien," 335–351. One attempt in this direction for Polish-Jewish entrepreneurs is Bauer, "Jan Gottlieb Bloch," 415–429.

ABBREVIATIONS

AGAD	Archiwum Główne Akt Dawnych
AGW	Archiwum Gospodarcze Wilanowskie
AKP	Archiwum Królestwa Polskiego
APG	Archiwum Państwowe w Gdańsku
APP	Archiwum Publiczne Potockich
APW	Archiwum Państwowe we Wrocławiu
APWa	Archiwum Państwowe w Warszawie
ASK	Archiwum Skarbu Koronnego
BLHA	Brandenburgisches Landeshauptarchiv
BŻIH	Biuletyn Żydowskiego Instytutu Historycznego
CAHJP	Central Archives for the History of the Jewish People
CJB	Centrum Judaicum Berlin
CWW	Centralne Władze Wyznaniowe
Fasz.	Faszikel
GDDPP	Generalne Dyrektorium, Departament Prus Południowych
GStA	Geheimes Preußisches Staatsarchiv
HA	Hauptabteilung
KK	Księga Kancelarskie
KPŻP	Kwartalnik poświęcony przeszłości Żydów w Polsce
KRSW	Kommissya Rządowa Spraw Wewnętrznych i Policyi
KRWROP	Kommissya Rządowa Wyznań Religijnych i Oświecenia Publicznego
LOMKD	Landes-, Ökonomie-, Manufaktur- und Kommerziendeputation
mf.	microfilm
MK	Metryka Koronna
ML TA	Maimonides Library, Tel Aviv
NAA	Notarielle Archieven van Amsterdam
Rep.	Repositur
RMKW	Rada Ministrów Księstwa Warszawskiego
SHstA DD	Sächsisches Hauptstaatsarchiv Dresden
StAA	Stadsarchief Amsterdam (Amsterdam City Archives)
StAF	Stadtarchiv Frankfurt an der Oder
StAL	Stadtarchiv Leipzig
syg	sygnatura (file number)

BIBLIOGRAPHY

Primary Sources

ARCHIWUM GŁÓWNE AKT DAWNYCH, WARSAW (AGAD)
Archiwum Gospodarcze Wilanowskie (AGW): Dział Archiwum Główne Potockich zesp.
   342/II; Anteriora zesp. 342, syg. 221
Archiwum Królestwa Polskiego (AKP): 206, 241, 254, 255, 257, 285, 289, 323, 354, 357, 363
Archiwum Potockich z Jabłonny (APJ): 47
Archiwum Publiczne Potockich (APP): 93
Archiwum Skarbu Koronnego (ASK): 237
Centralne Władze Wyznaniowe (CWW): 1012
Generalne Dyrektorium. Departament Prus Południowych (GDDPP): I–884, 896, 1025, 1028;
   VI–3361, 3565, 3566, 3399; IX–256, 257
Kommissya Rządowa Spraw Wewnętrznych i Policyi (KRSW): 6628
Kommissya Rządowa Wyznań Religiynich i Oświecenia Publicznego (KRW): 7341
Korespondencja Stanisława Augusta 1792–1797 (KSA)
Metryka Koronna (MK): 283, 284, 286, 297, 299, 300, 301
Metryka Koronna, Księga Kancelarskie (KK): 18, 90
Rada Ministrów Księstwa Warszawskiego (RMKW): serja 2-go, 115
Stara Warszawa (SW): 283

ARCHIWUM PAŃSTWOWE W GDAŃSKU (APG)
Urząd Sędziego/ Stadtrichter: 300, 6
Weta/Wettgericht: 300, 58

ARCHIWUM PAŃSTWOWE W WARSZAWIE (APWa)
Kancelaria Alexandra Engelke
Kancelaria Andrzeja Kalinowskiego
Kancelaria Jana Marczyńskiego
Kancelaria Jana Wincentego Bandtkie
Kancelaria Kowalewskiego
Kancelaria Przeździeckiego
Kancelaria Teodora Czempińskiego
Kancelaria Walentego Skorochód-Majewskiego

ARCHIWUM PAŃSTWOWE WE WROCŁAWIU (APW)
Oddział Kamieniec Ząbkowicki, Dom Bankowy Eichborn

GEHEIMES PREUßISCHES STAATSARCHIV, BERLIN (GStA)
I. Hauptabteilung (HA)

Rep. 7: no. 106i, Fasz. 62
Rep. 7A: no. 1894
Rep. 7C: no. 34g, Fasz. 367; no. 6 N 10, Fasz. 16
Rep. 9 (Allgemeine Verwaltung): Y2, Fasz. 123; C6 a2, Fasz 5
Rep. 9 (Polen): no. 28-7C, no. 28-12B
Rep. 11: no. 279, Fasz. 361; 171–175, Rußland D, 1775–1780, 1796–1797
Rep. 46B: no. 203a (Pk. 1); no. 37, Fasz. 1 (1745–1781)
Rep. 49: Lit. K, 1759–1769, no. 16213
Rep. 151: M (IA), no. 5146

II. Hauptabteilung (HA)

Abt. 7 (General Direktorium): Ostpreußen und Litauen, II Materien, no. 4545, 4551, 4677, 4709, 4712, 4717, 4740, 4767
Abt. 9 (General Direktorium): Westpreußen und Netzedistrikt, Stadt Flatow, Sekt. 4, no. 1, 13
Abt. 24, Generalakzise- und Zolldepartement: B2, Tit. 24, no. 1
Abt. 25: Tit. XXXII, no. 2 (vol. 45)

XX. Hauptabteilung (HA)

Etats-Ministerium (EM): Tit. 97j, no. 37; Tit. 111j, no. 526

BRANDENBURGISCHES LANDESHAUPTARCHIV, POTSDAM (BLHA)
Rep. 2: S 4221, S 4232, S 4233, S 4287, S 4449
Rep. 19: 275

SÄCHSISCHES HAUPTSTAATSARCHIV, DRESDEN (SHStA DD)
10024 Geheimer Rat (Geheimes Archiv): Loc. 9482/3–4
10025 Geheimes Konsilium: Loc. 5286, Loc. 5409
10026 Geheimes Kabinett: Loc. 2360/3
10036 Finanzarchiv: Loc. 33709
Landes-, Ökonomie-, Manufaktur- und Kommerziendeputation (LOMKD): no. 803

STADTARCHIV FRANKFURT AN DER ODER (StaF)
Abteilung 1: VII: 107, 108, 437; X: 220, 224
Register von denjenigen Kauffleuten welche die Meßen zu Frankfurth an der Oder besuchen . . . , Franckfurth an der Oder Anno 1756, Druck

STADTARCHIV LEIPZIG (StAL)
Titelakten (Tit.)—Juden (LI): 12a, 12b, 18

Bibliography

CENTRUM JUDAICUM, BERLIN (CJB)
Familienpapiere Schlesinger/Fersenheim, Frankfurt an der Oder: 1795–1875, 1, 75 E, no. 587

STADSARCHIEF AMSTERDAM (StAA, AMSTERDAM CITY ARCHIVES)
Archief van de Firma Hope & Co., file 103
D.T.P. Ondertrouwen
Notarielle Archieven van Amsterdam (NAA), no. *5075:* Notariat C. van Homrigh, Notariat D. Geniets, Notariat Daniel Brink, Notariat Gerrit Bouman, Notariat N. Wilthuyzen, Notariat R. van Eibergen, Notariat Salomon Dorper

CENTRAL ARCHIVES FOR THE HISTORY OF THE JEWISH PEOPLE, JERUSALEM (CAHJP)
Synagogengemeinde Frankfurt/Oder: D/Fr 1/ 30, 93; G5/896
Księga Bractwa Pogrzebowego na Pradze 1785-1870/ Pinkas ha-ḥevrah kadisha de-Praga: S 63/23

MAIMONIDES LIBRARY, TEL AVIV (ML TA)
Pinkas Kehilat Frankfurt an der Oder: MS 19

Printed Primary Sources

Der Anzeiger. Ein Tagblatt zum Behuf der Justiz, der Polizey und aller bürgerlichen Gewerbe . . . , Kaiserliches Reichs-Post Amt, 1791.
Bulletin National Hebdomadaire, Warsaw, 1793–1794.
Cohen, Mori. *Zikaron besefer.* Frankfurt a.O., 1796.
Dohm, Christian Wilhelm von. *Über die bürgerliche Verbesserung der Juden.* 2 vols. Berlin: F. Nicolai, 1781.
Gazeta Rządowa, Warsaw, 1794.
Gazeta Warszawska, Warsaw, 1789, 1792, 1795, 1801.
Gazeta Wolney Warszawskiey, Warsaw, 1794.
Goldbeck, Johann Friedrich. *Vollständige Topographie des Königreichs Preußen,* vol. 2. Marienwerder, 1789.
Hannover, Nathan Nata, and Abraham J. Mesch, ed. *Abyss of Despair (Yeven metzulah): The Famous 17th Century Chronicle Depicting Jewish Life in Russia and Poland During the Chmielnicki Massacres of 1648–1649.* New Brunswick, NJ: Transaction Books, 1983.
Herz, Marcus. *Über die frühe Beerdigung der Juden.* Berlin: Christian Friedrich Voss und Sohn, 1788.
Katz, Naphtali Herz ben Mori. *She'elat ḥakham.* Frankfurt a.O., 1797.
Korrespondent—Kraiowy y zagraniczny (Korrespondent Warszawski), Warsaw, 1793.
Korrespondent Narodowego y Zagranicznego, Warsaw, 1794.
Krünitz, Johann Georg. *Oekonomische Encyclopaedie oder Allgemeines System der Staats-, Stadt-, Haus- u. Landwirthschaft.* 242 vols. Berlin: Pauli, 1773–1858. http://www.kruenitz1.uni-trier.de.
LeLong, Isaac. *De koophandel van Amsterdam.* Rotterdam, 1753.

Ludovici, Carl Günther. *Eröffnete Akademie der Kaufleute, oder vollständiges Kaufmanns-Lexicon.* 5 vols. 2nd ed. Leipzig: Bernhard Christoph Breitkopf und Sohn, 1767.

———. *Grundriß eines vollständigen Kaufmanns-Systems, nebst den Anfangsgründen der Handlungswissenschaft, und angehängter kurzen Geschichte der Handlung zu Wasser und zu Lande.* 2nd ed. Leipzig: Bernhard Christoph Breitkopf und Sohn, 1768.

Püttmann, Josias Ludwig Ernst. *Die Leipziger Wechselordnung mit Anmerkungen und Beilagen versehen.* Leipzig: J.S. Heinsius, 1787.

Rönne, Ludwig von, and Heinrich Simon. *Die früheren und gegenwärtigen Verhältnisse der Juden in den sämmtlichen Landestheilen des Preußischen Staates. Eine Darstellung und Revision der gesetzlichen Bestimmungen über ihre Staats- und privatrechtlichen Zustände.* Breslau: Aderholz, 1843.

Satanow, Isaac. *Sefer hagedarim.* Berlin: Ḥinukh Neʻarim, 1798.

Secondary Sources

Ajzensztejn, Andrea. "Der Aufstieg der jüdischen Familie Friedländer in Königsberg." In *Zur Geschichte und Kultur der Juden in Ost- und Westpreußen,* edited by Michael Brocke, Margret Heitmann, and Harald Lordick, 377–396. Hildesheim: Georg Olms, 2000.

"Akt darowizny bóżnicy przez Berka. Miscellanea." *KPŻP* 1 (1912): 180–182.

Ariès, Philippe. *The Hour of Our Death.* New York: Oxford University Press, 1991.

Arkush, Allan. *Moses Mendelssohn and the Enlightenment.* Albany: State University of New York Press, 1994.

Aslanian, Sebouh David. *From the Indian Ocean to the Mediterranean: The Global Trade Networks of Armenian Merchants from New Julfa.* Berkeley: University of California Press, 2011.

Aust, Cornelia. "Conflicting Authorities: Rabbis, Physicians, Lay Leaders and the Question of Burial." In *Meditations on Authority,* edited by David Shulman, 87–100. Jerusalem: Hebrew University Magnes Press, 2013.

———. "Daily Business or an Affair of Consequence? Credit, Reputation, and Bankruptcy among Jewish Merchants in Eighteenth-Century Central Europe." In *Purchasing Power: The Economics of Jewish History,* edited by Rebecca Kobrin and Adam Teller, 71–90. Philadelphia: University of Pennsylvania Press, 2015.

———. "Jewish Economic History." In *Oxford Bibliographies.* http://www.oxfordbibliographies.com/view/document/obo-9780199840731/obo-9780199840731-0106.xml.

———. "Kontinuität und Wandel in den jüdischen Gemeinden Berlins und Warschaus im Übergang vom 18. zum 19. Jahrhundert. Ein kontrastierender Vergleich am Beispiel der Beerdigungsbruderschaften (Chewrot Kadischa)." MA thesis, Freie Universität Berlin, 2003.

Bałaban, Majer. *Historja i literatura żydowska, ze szczególnem uwzględnieniem historji Żydów w Polsce.* Lwów: Zakład Narodowy im. Ossolińskich, 1916.

Barber, Peter. "Isaac Bernard: Prague Jew, Jeweller, Mintmaster and Spy." *British Library Journal* 16, no. 2 (1990): 131–150.

Baron, Salo W., and Arcadius Kahan. *Economic History of the Jews.* Jerusalem: Keter, 1975.

Bibliography

Bartal, Israel. "From Corporation to Nation: Jewish Autonomy in Eastern Europe, 1772–1881." *Simon Dubnow Institute Yearbook* 5 (2006): 17–31.

———. *The Jews of Eastern Europe, 1772–1881*. Philadelphia: University of Pennsylvania Press, 2005.

Bauer, Ela. "Jan Gottlieb Bloch: Polish Cosmopolitanism Versus Jewish Universalism." *European Review of History—Revue européenne d'histoire* 17, no. 3 (2010): 415–429.

Beachy, Robert. "Fernhandel und Krämergeist. Die Leipziger Handelsdeputierten und die Einführung der sächsischen Wechselordnung 1682." In *Leipzigs Messen 1497–1997*, edited by Hartmut Zwahr, Thomas Topfstedt, and Günter Bentele, 135–147. Cologne: Böhlau, 1999.

———. *The Soul of Commerce: Credit, Property, and Politics in Leipzig, 1750–1840*. Leiden and Boston: Brill, 2005.

Berger, Shlomo. *Producing Redemption in Amsterdam: Early Modern Yiddish Books in Paratextual Perspective*. Leiden and Boston: Brill, 2013.

Bergman, Eleonora. *"Nie masz bóżnicy powszechnej": Synagogi i domy modlitwy w Warszawie od końca XVIII do początku XXI wieku*. Warsaw: DiG, 2007.

———. "Synagoga na Daniłowiczowskiej 1800–1878—próba rekonstrukcji." In *Rozdział wspólnej historii. Studia z dziejów Żydów w Polsce ofiarowane profesorowi Jerzemu Tomaszewskiemu w siedemdziesiątą rocznicę urodzin*, edited by Jolanta Żyndul, 113–128. Warsaw: Cyklady, 2001.

Bloch, Philipp. "Der Mamran (ממרן), der jüdisch-polnische Wechselbrief." In *Festschrift zum siebzigsten Geburtstage A. Berliner's*, edited by A. Freimann and M. Hildesheimer, 50–63. Frankfurt a.M.: J. Kauffmann, 1903.

Bloom, Herbert Ivan. *The Economic Activities of the Jews in Amsterdam in the Seventeenth and Eighteenth Centuries*. Williamsport, PA: Bayard Press, 1937.

Bodian, Miriam. *Hebrews of the Portuguese Nation: Conversos and Community in Early Modern Amsterdam*. Bloomington: Indiana University Press, 1997.

Bogucka, Maria. "Dutch Merchants' Activities in Gdańsk in the First Half of the 17th Century." In *Baltic Commerce and Urban Society, 1500–1700: Gdańsk/Danzig and Its Polish Context*, edited by Maria Bogucka, 19–32. Burlington, VT: Ashgate, 2003.

———. "Jewish Merchants in Gdańsk in the 16th–17th Centuries: A Policy of Toleration or Discrimination?" *Acta Poloniae Historica* 65 (1992): 47–57.

Bömelburg, Hans-Jürgen. *Zwischen polnischer Ständegesellschaft und preußischem Obrigkeitsstaat. Vom Königlichen Preußen zu Westpreußen (1756–1806)*. Munich: R. Oldenbourg, 1995.

Brann, Marcus. "Die schlesische Judenheit vor und nach dem Edikt vom 11. März 1812." *Jahres-Bericht des jüdisch-theologischen Seminars Fraenckel'scher Stiftung für das Jahr 1912* (1913): 3–44.

Bregoli, Francesca. *Mediterranean Enlightenment: Livornese Jews, Tuscan Culture, and Eighteenth-Century Reform*. Stanford, CA: Stanford University Press, 2014.

Breuer, Mordechai, and Michael Graetz. *Tradition and Enlightenment, 1600–1780*. German-Jewish History in Modern Times, edited by Michael A. Meyer, vol. 1. New York: Columbia University Press, 1996.

Brocke, Michael, Julius Carlebach, and Carsten Wilke. *Biographisches Handbuch der Rabbiner. Teil 1: Die Rabbiner der Emanzipationszeit in den deutschen, böhmischen, und großpolnischen Ländern, 1781–1871*. 2 vols. Munich: K.G. Saur, 2004.

Bruer, Albert A. *Geschichte der Juden in Preußen (1750–1820)*. Frankfurt a.M. and New York: Campus, 1991.

Buist, Marten G. *At spes non fracta: Hope & Co. 1770–1817: Merchant Bankers and Diplomats at Work*. The Hague: Nijhoff, 1974.

Bull, Ida. "Merchant Households and Their Networks in Eighteenth-Century Trondheim." *Continuity and Change* 17, no. 2 (2002): 213–231.

Butterwick, Richard. "The Enlightened Monarchy of Stanisław August Poniatowski (1764–1795)." In *The Polish-Lithuanian Monarchy in European Context, c. 1500–1795*, edited by Richard Butterwick, 193–218. New York: Palgrave, 2001.

Cassis, Youssef. *Capitals of Capital: A History of International Financial Centres, 1780–2005*. Cambridge: Cambridge University Press, 2006.

Cohen, Abner. "Cultural Strategies in the Organization of Trading Diasporas." In *The Development of Indigenous Trade and Markets in West Africa*, edited by Claude Meillassoux, 266–281. Oxford: Oxford University Press, 1971.

Cohen, Julia Phillips. *Becoming Ottomans: Sephardi Jews and Imperial Citizenship in the Modern Era*. Oxford and New York: Oxford University Press, 2014.

Craswell, Richard. "On the Uses of 'Trust': Comment on Williamson, 'Calculativeness, Trust, and Economic Organization.'" *Journal of Law and Economics* 36, no. 1 (1993): 487–500.

Curtin, Philip D. *Cross-Cultural Trade in World History*. Cambridge and New York: Cambridge University Press, 1984.

Czubaty, Jarosław. *The Duchy of Warsaw, 1807–1815: A Napoleonic Outpost in Central Europe*. London: Bloomsbury Academic, 2016.

Dahl, Gunnar. *Trade, Trust, and Networks: Commercial Culture in Late Medieval Italy*. Lund: Nordic Academic Press, 1998.

Davern, Michael. "Social Networks and Economic Sociology: A Proposed Research Agenda for a More Complete Social Science." *American Journal of Economics and Sociology* 56, no. 3 (1997): 287–302.

Davies, Martin L. *Identity or History? Marcus Herz and the End of the Enlightenment*. Detroit: Wayne State University Press, 1995.

Denzel, Markus A., ed. *Geld- und Wechselkurse der deutschen Messeplätze Leipzig und Braunschweig (18. Jahrhundert bis 1823)*. Stuttgart: Steiner, 1994.

———. "Die Integration Deutschlands in das internationale Zahlungsverkehrssystem im 17. und 18. Jahrhundert." *Vierteljahresschrift für Sozial- und Wirtschaftsgeschichte, Beihefte* 128 (1996): 58–109.

———. "Zahlungsverkehr auf den Leipziger Messen vom 17. bis zum 19. Jahrhundert." In *Leipzigs Messen 1497–1997. Gestaltwandel—Umbrüche—Neubeginn. Teilband 1: 1497–1914*, edited by Hartmut Zwahr, Thomas Topfstedt, and Günter Bentele, 149–165. Cologne: Böhlau, 1999.

Derix, Simone. *Die Thyssens. Familie und Vermögen*. Paderborn: Ferdinand Schöningh, 2016.

———. "Transnationale Familien." In *Dimensionen internationaler Geschichte*, edited by Jost Dülffer and Wilfried Loth. Munich: Oldenbourg Verlag, 2012, 335–351.

De Roover, Raymond. *L'Evolution de la Lettre de Change XIVe-XVIIIe siècles*. Paris: Librairie Armand Colin, 1953.

De Vries, Jan, and A. M. van der Woude. *The First Modern Economy: Success, Failure, and Perseverance of the Dutch Economy, 1500–1815*. Cambridge, New York: Cambridge University Press, 1997.

Diekmann, Irene. *Das Emanzipationsedikt von 1812 in Preußen: Der lange Weg der Juden zu "Einländern" und "preußischen Staatsbürgern."* Berlin and Boston: De Gruyter, 2013.

Dynner, Glenn. "Jewish Quarters: The Economics of Segregation in the Kingdom of Poland." In *Purchasing Power. The Economics of Modern Jewish History*, edited by Rebecca Kobrin and Adam Teller, 91–111. Philadelphia: University of Pennsylvania Press, 2015.

———. *Men of Silk: The Hasidic Conquest of Polish Jewish Society*. Oxford and New York: Oxford University Press, 2006.

———. *Yankel's Tavern. Jews, Liquor, and Life in the Kingdom of Poland*. Oxford: Oxford University Press, 2014.

Dynner, Glenn, and François Guesnet, eds. *Warsaw. The Jewish Metropolis: Essays in Honor of the 75th Birthday of Professor Antony Polonsky*. Leiden: Brill, 2015.

Echt, Samuel. *Die Geschichte der Juden in Danzig*. Leer: Rautenberg, 1972.

Eile, Płk. H. "Liweranci." *Przegląd Intendencki* 1, no. 1 (1926): 32–41.

Eisenbach, Artur. *The Emancipation of the Jews in Poland, 1780–1870*. Oxford: Blackwell, 1991.

———. "The Jewish Population in Warsaw at the Turn of the Eighteenth Century." *Polin* 3 (1988): 46–77.

———. "Status prawny ludności żydowskiej w Warszawie w końcu XVIII i na początku XIX wieku." *BŻIH* 39 (1961): 3–16.

———. "Żydzi warszawscy i sprawa żydowska w XVIII w." *Nadbitka* 3 (1975): 229–298.

Eisenbach, Artur, and Jan Kosim. "Akt masy spadkowej Judyty Jakubowiczowej." *BŻIH* 39 (1961): 88–143.

Eisenbach, Artur, Jerzy Michalski, Emanuel Rostworowski, and Janusz Woliński, eds. *Materiały do dziejów sejmu czteroletniego*, vol. 6. Wrocław: Zakład Narodowy im. Ossolińskich, 1969.

Elon, Menachem. *The Principles of Jewish Law*. Jerusalem: Keter Publishing House, 1975.

Endelman, Todd M. "Jewish Converts in Nineteenth-Century Warsaw: A Quantitative Analysis." *Jewish Social Studies* 4, no. 1 (1997): 28–59.

Epstein, Louis M. *The Jewish Marriage Contract: A Study in the Status of the Woman in Jewish Law*. New York: Arno Press, 1973.

Feiner, Shmuel. "Haskalah." In *Enzyklopädie jüdischer Geschichte und Kultur*, edited by Dan Diner, 544–554. Stuttgart and Weimar: J. B. Metzler, 2012.

———. *The Jewish Enlightenment*. Philadelphia: University of Pennsylvania Press, 2004.

Feiner, Shmuel, and David Sorkin, eds. *New Perspectives on the Haskalah*. London and Portland, OR: Littman Library of Jewish Civilization, 2001.

Ferguson, Niall. *The House of Rothschild*. 2 vols. New York: Viking, 1998.

Fram, Edward. *Ideals Face Reality: Jewish Law and Life in Poland, 1550–1655*. Cincinnati: Hebrew Union College Press, 1997.

Freeze, ChaeRan Y. *Jewish Marriage and Divorce in Imperial Russia*. Hanover, NH: Brandeis University Press, 2002.

Frenk, Ezriel N. *Meshumadim in Poilen in 19ten yohrhundert*. Warsaw: M. I. Freid, 1923.

Frenk, Ludwik. "Testament Judyty Zbytkower." *Nowe Życie. Miesięcznik poświęcony nauce, literaturze i sztuce żydowskiej* 1, no. 3 (1924): 377–382.

Freudenthal, Max. *Leipziger Messgäste. Die jüdischen Besucher der Leipziger Messen in den Jahren 1675 bis 1764*. Frankfurt a.M.: J. Kauffmann, 1928.

Freund, Ismar. *Die Emanzipation der Juden in Preußen unter besonderer Berücksichtigung des Gesetzes vom 11. März 1812. Ein Beitrag zur Rechtsgeschichte der Juden in Preußen*. 2 vols. Berlin: M. Poppelauer, 1912.

Fuks-Mansfeld, R. G. "Enlightenment and Emancipation, from c. 1750 to 1814." In *The History of the Jews in the Netherlands*, edited by J. C. H. Blom, R. G. Fuks-Mansfeld and I. Schöffer, 164–191. Oxford and Portland, OR: Littman Library of Jewish Civilization, 2007.

Garncarska-Kadary, Bina. "Ha-yehudim be-hitpatḥutah ha-kalkalit shel polin ba-me'ah ha-19." In *Kiyum va-shever: Yehude Polin le-dorotehem*, edited by Israel Bartal and Israel Gutman, 315–336. Jerusalem: Zalman Shazar Center, 1997.

———. "Ha-yehudim ve ha-gormim le-hitpatḥutah ve-mikumah shel ha-ta'asiyah be-Varshe." *Gal-Ed* 2 (1975): 25–58.

Gelber, N. M. *Ha-Yehudim ve ha-mered ha-Polani: Zikhronotav shel Ya'akov ha-Levi Levin mi-yeme ha-mered ha-Polani bi-shenat 1830–1831*. Jerusalem: Mosad Bialik, 1953.

———. "Żydzi a zagadnienie reformy Żydów na Sejmie Czteroletnim." *Miesięcznik Żydowski* 1, no. 10 (1931): 326–344; no. 11 (1931): 429–440.

Gelderblom, Oscar. *Cities of Commerce. The Institutional Foundations of International Trade in the Low Countries, 1250–1650*. Princeton, NJ, and Oxford: Princeton University Press, 2013.

Goldberg, Jacob. "Jewish Marriage in Eighteenth-Century Poland." *Polin* 10 (1997): 3–31.

———. *Jewish Privileges in the Polish Commonwealth: Charters of Rights Granted to Jewish Communities in Poland-Lithuania in the Sixteenth to Eighteenth Centuries. Critical Edition of Original Latin and Polish Documents with English Introductions and Notes*. Jerusalem: Israel Academy of Sciences and Humanities, 1985.

———. "The Jewish Sejm: Its Origins and Functions." In *The Jews in Old Poland, 1000–1795*, edited by Antony Polonsky, Jakub Basista, and Andrzej Link-Lenczowski, 147–165. London: I. B. Tauris, 1993.

———. "Pierwszy ruch polityczny wśród Żydów polskich plenipotenci żydowscy w dobie Sejmu Czteroletniego." In *Lud Żydowski w Narodzie Polskim. Materiały sesji naukowej w Warszawie 15–16 wresień 1992*, edited by Jerzy Michalski, 45–63. Warsaw: Instytut Historii PAN, 1994.

Gömmel, Rainer. *Die Entwicklung der Wirtschaft im Zeitalter des Merkantilismus 1620–1800*. Munich: R. Oldenbourg, 1998.

Gotzmann, Andreas. *Jüdisches Recht im kulturellen Prozess: Die Wahrnehmung der Halacha im Deutschland des 19. Jahrhunderts*. Tübingen: M. Siebeck, 1997.

Graetz, Michael. "'Aliyato ve-shkiato shel sapak ha-tsava ha-yehudi: Kalkalah yehudit be-'etot milḥamah." *Zion* 56 (1991): 255–273.

———. "Court Jews in Economics and Politics." In *From Court Jews to the Rothschilds. Art, Patronage and Power, 1600–1800*, edited by Vivian B. Mann and Richard I. Cohen, 27–43. Munich and New York: Prestel, 1996.

Grochulska, Barbara. "Échos de la faillite des banques de Varsovie." *Annales historiques de la Révolution française* 53, no. 4 (1981): 529–540.

———. *Warszawa na mapie Polski "stanisławskiej."* Warsaw: Wydawnictwo Uniwersytetu Warszawskiego, 1980.

Grünhagen, Colmar. "Eine südpreußische Kriegslieferung von 1794." *Zeitschrift der Historischen Gesellschaft für die Provinz Posen* 12 (1897): 53–60.

Grunwald, Max. *Hamburgs deutsche Juden bis zur Auflösung der Dreigemeinden 1811*. Hamburg: Alfred Janssen, 1904.

Guesnet, François. "Banking." In *The YIVO Encyclopedia of Jews in Eastern Europe*, edited by Gershon Hundert, 119–122. New Haven, CT, and London: Yale University Press, 2008.

———. "From Community to Metropolis: The Jews of Warsaw, 1850–1880." In *Warsaw. The Jewish Metropolis: Essays in Honor of the 75th Birthday of Professor Antony Polonsky*, edited by Glenn Dynner and François Guesnet, 128–153. Leiden and Boston: Brill, 2015.

———. "Geschichte fürs jüdische Volk. Ein vorläufiges Porträt des Historikers Ezriel Natan Frenk." In *Zwischen Graetz und Dubnow: Jüdische Historiographie in Ostmitteleuropa im 19. und 20. Jahrhundert*, edited by François Guesnet, 119–145. Leipzig: Akademische Verlagsanstalt, 2009.

———. "Politik der Vormoderne - Shtadlanuth am Vorabend der polnischen Teilungen." *Jahrbuch des Simon-Dubnow-Instituts* 1 (2002): 235–255.

———. *Polnische Juden im 19. Jahrhundert: Lebensbedingungen, Rechtsnormen und Organisation im Wandel*. Cologne: Böhlau, 1998.

Guldon, Zenon. "Źródła i metody szacunków liczebności ludności żydowskiej w Polsce w XVI-XVIII wieku." *Kwartalnik Historii Kultury Materialnej* 34, no. 2 (1986): 249–262.

Hasse, Ernst. *Geschichte der Leipziger Messen*. Leipzig: S. Hirzel, 1885 [reprint: Leipzig, 1963].

Hensel, Jürgen. "Polnische Adelsnation und jüdische Vermittler 1815–1830. Über den vergeblichen Versuch einer Judenemanzipation in einer nicht emanzipierten Gesellschaft." *Forschungen zur Osteuropäischen Geschichte* 23 (1983): 7–227.

———. "Wie 'deutsch' war die 'fortschrittliche' jüdische Bourgeoisie im Königreich Polen?" In *Symbiose und Traditionsbruch. Deutsch-jüdische Wechselbeziehungen in Ostmittel- und Südosteuropa (19. und 20. Jahrhundert)*, edited by Hans Hecker and Walter Engel, 135–172. Essen: Klartext, 2003.

Hertz, Deborah. *Jewish High Society in Old Regime Berlin*. New Haven, CT: Yale University Press, 1988.

Heyde, Jürgen. "Zwischen Polen und Preußen—Die jüdische Bevölkerung in der Zeit der Teilungen Polens." In *Fremde Herrscher—fremdes Volk. Inklusions- und Exklusionsfiguren* bei Herrschaftswechseln in Europa, edited by Helga Schnabel-Schüle and Andreas Gestrich, 297–332. Frankfurt a.M.: Peter Lang, 2006.

Hollinger, David A. "Rich, Powerful, and Smart: Jewish Overrepresentation Should Be Explained Instead of Avoided or Mystified." The Jewish Quarterly Review 94, no. 4 (2004): 595–602.

Horn, Maurycy. Regesty dokumentów i ekscerpty z Metryki Koronnej do historii Żydów w Polsce, 1697–1795. Wrocław: Zakład Narodowy im. Ossolińskich, 1984.

Hundert, Gershon. "Approaches to the History of the Jewish Family in Early Modern Poland-Lithuania." In The Jewish Family. Myth and Reality, edited by Steven M. Cohen and Paula Hyman, 17–28. New York: Holmes & Meier, 1986.

———. The Jews in a Polish Private Town: The Case of Opatów in the Eighteenth Century. Baltimore: Johns Hopkins University Press, 1992.

———. Jews in Poland-Lithuania in the Eighteenth Century: A Genealogy of Modernity. Berkeley: University of California Press, 2004.

———. "Re(de)fining Modernity in Jewish History." In Rethinking European Jewish History, edited by Jeremy Cohen and Moshe Rosman, 133–145. Oxford and Portland, OR: Littmann Library of Jewish Civilization, 2009.

———. "The Role of the Jews in Commerce in Early Modern Poland-Lithuania." Journal of European Economic History 16, no. 2 (1987): 245–275.

———. "Was There an East European Analogue to Court Jews?" In The Jews in Poland, edited by Andrzej K. Paluch, 67–75. Kraków: Jagiellonian University, 1992.

Israel, Jonathan. European Jewry in the Age of Mercantilism, 1550–1750. 3rd ed. London and Portland, OR: Littman Library of Jewish Civilization, 1998.

———. "The Republic of the United Netherlands until about 1750: Demography and Economic Activity." In The History of the Jews in the Netherlands, edited by J. C. H. Blom, R. G. Fuks-Mansfeld, and I. Schöffer, 85–115. Oxford and Portland, OR: Littman Library of Jewish Civilization, 2007.

Jacob, Margaret C. Strangers Nowhere in the World. The Rise of Cosmopolitanism in Early Modern Europe. Philadelphia: University of Pennsylvania Press, 2006.

Jagodzińska, Agnieszka. Pomiędzy. Akulturacja Żydów Warszawy w drugiej połowie XIX wieku. Wrocław: Wydawnictwo Uniwersytetu Wrocławskiego, 2008.

Jehle, Manfred. "'Relocations' in South Prussia and New East Prussia: Prussia's Demographic Policy towards the Jews in Occupied Poland 1772–1806." Leo Baeck Institute Year Book 52 (2007): 23–47.

Jersch-Wenzel, Steffi. Juden und "Franzosen" in der Wirtschaft des Raumes Berlin-Brandenburg zur Zeit des Merkantilismus. Berlin: Colloquium, 1978.

———, ed. Die Memoiren des Moses Wasserzug. Leipzig: Leipziger Universitätsverlag, 1999.

Kagan, Berl. Sefer ha-prenumerantn. New York: Jewish Theological Seminary and Ktav Publishing House, 1975.

Kalik, Judith. "Leaseholding." In The YIVO Encyclopedia of Jews in Eastern Europe, edited by Gershon Hundert, 1001–1003. New Haven, CT, and London: Yale University Press, 2008.

Kaplan, Herbert H. Nathan Mayer Rothschild and the Creation of a Dynasty: The Critical Years, 1806–1816. Stanford, CA: Stanford University Press, 2006.

Kaplan, Yosef. *An Alternative Path to Modernity: The Sephardi Diaspora in Western Europe.* Leiden and Boston: Brill, 2000.

———. "Amsterdam and Ashkenazic Migration in the Seventeenth Century." *Studia Rosenthaliana* 23, no. 2 (1989): 22–44.

———. "Court Jews before the Hofjuden." In *From Court Jews to the Rothschilds. Art, Patronage and Power, 1600–1800,* edited by Vivian B. Mann and Richard I. Cohen, 11–25. Munich and New York: Prestel, 1996.

———. "The Jews in the Republic until about 1750: Religious, Cultural, and Social Life." In *The History of the Jews in the Netherlands,* edited by J. C. H. Blom, R. G. Fuks-Mansfeld, and I. Schöffer, 116–163. Oxford and Portland, OR: Littman Library of Jewish Civilization, 2007.

———. "The Self-Definition of the Sephardic Jews of Western Europe and Their Relation to the Alien and the Stranger." In *Crisis and Creativity in the Sephardic World, 1391–1648,* edited by Benjamin R. Gampel, 121–145. New York: Columbia University Press, 1997.

Karniel, Josef. "David Michael Levy. Ein jüdischer Agent der habsburgischen Gegenspionage zur Zeit Kaiser Josephs II." *Jahrbuch des Instituts für Deutsche Geschichte* 15 (1986): 117–138.

———. "Heymann Kiewe. Ein jüdischer Agent der habsburgischen Gegenspionage zur Zeit Kaiser Josephs II." *Jahrbuch des Instituts für Deutsche Geschichte* 14 (1985): 29–74.

Karp, Jonathan. "Economic History and Jewish Modernity—Ideological versus Structural Change." *Simon Dubnow Institute Yearbook* 6 (2007): 249–266.

———. "It's the Economy, Shmendrick! An 'Economic Turn' in Jewish Studies?" *AJS Perspectives* (Fall 2009): 8–11.

———. *The Politics of Jewish Commerce: Economic Thought and Emancipation in Europe, 1638–1848.* Cambridge and New York: Cambridge University Press, 2008.

Kaskel, Joachim Felix. "Vom Hoffaktor zur Dresdner Bank. Die Unternehmerfamilie Kaskel im 18. und 19. Jahrhundert." *Zeitschrift für Unternehmensgeschichte* 28, no. 3 (1983): 159–187.

Kaufhold, Karl Heinrich. "Preußische Staatswirtschaft: Konzepte und Realität, 1640–1806." *Jahrbuch für Wirtschaftsgeschichte* 35, no. 2 (1994): 33–70.

———. "'Wirtschaftswissenschaften' und Wirtschaftspolitik in Preußen von um 1650 bis um 1800." In *Wirtschaft, Wissenschaft und Bildung in Preußen. Zur Wirtschafts- und Sozialgeschichte Preußens vom 18. bis zum 20. Jahrhundert,* edited by Karl Heinrich Kaufhold and Bernd Sösemann, 51–72. Stuttgart: Franz Steiner, 1998.

Keep, John L. H. "The Russian Army in the Seven Years War." In *The Military and Society in Russia, 1450–1917,* edited by Eric Lohr and Marshall Poe, 24–44. Leiden: Brill, 2002.

Kieniewicz, Stefan. "The Jews of Warsaw, Polish Society and the Partitioning Powers, 1795–1861." *Polin* 3 (1988): 102–121.

Kirszenbaum, H. "Bractwo pogrzebowe na Pradze." *KPŻP* 3 (1913): 133–146.

Kirszrot, Jakób. *Prawa Żydów w Królestwie Polskiem. Zarys historyczny.* Warsaw: Nakład Zarządu Warszawskiej Gminy Starozakonnych, 1917.

Klein, Birgit E. "Das jüdische Ehegüter- und Erbrecht der Frühneuzeit. Entwicklung seit der Antike und Auswirkung auf das Verhältnis der Geschlechter und zur nichtjüdischen

Gesellschaft." Habilitation, Freie Universität Berlin, 2016. http://www.diss.fu-berlin.de/diss/receive/FUDISS_thesis_000000101742.

Kobrin, Rebecca, and Adam Teller, eds. *Purchasing Power: The Economics of Modern Jewish History*. Philadelphia: University of Pennsylvania Press, 2015.

Kołodziejczyk, Ryszard. *Piotr Steinkeller. Kupiec i Przemysłowiec 1799–1854*. Warsaw: Państwowe Wydawnictwo Naukowe, 1963.

———. *Portret warszawskiego milionera*. Warsaw: Książka i Wiedza, 1968.

Korzon, Tadeusz. *Wewnętrzne dzieje polski za Stanisława Augusta (1764–1794). Badania historyczne ze stanowiska ekonomicznego i administracyjnego*, vol. 1. Kraków: Wydanie akademii umiejętności, 1882.

Kosim, Jan. *Losy pewnej fortuny. Z dziejów burżuazji warszawskiej w latach 1807–1830*. Wrocław: Zakład Narodowy im. Ossolińskich, 1972.

Kossert, Andreas. "Die jüdische Gemeinde Ortelsburg. Ein Beitrag zur Geschichte der Juden in Masuren." In *Zur Geschichte und Kultur der Juden in Ost- und Westpreußen*, edited by Michael Brocke, Margret Heitmann, and Harald Lordick, 87–124. Hildesheim: Georg Olms, 2000.

Kraft, Claudia. "Polnische militärische Eliten in gesellschaftlichen und politischen Umbruchsprozessen 1772–1831." In *Fremde Herrscher—fremdes Volk. Inklusions- und Exklusionsfiguren bei Herrschaftswechseln in Europa*, edited by Helga Schnabel-Schüle and Andreas Gestrich, 271–295. Frankfurt a.M.: Peter Lang, 2006.

Krochmalnik, Daniel. "Scheintod und Emanzipation. Der Beerdigungsstreit in seinem historischen Kontext." *Trumah* 6 (1997): 107–149.

Krüger, Hans-Jürgen. *Die Judenschaft von Königsberg in Preußen 1700–1812*. Marburg: Johann Gottfried Herder Institut, 1966.

Landes, David S. *Dynasties: Fortunes and Misfortunes of the World's Great Family Businesses*. New York: Viking, 2006.

Laux, Stephan. "'Ich bin der Historiker der Hoffaktoren': Zur antisemitischen Forschung von Heinrich Schnee (1895–1968)." *Jahrbuch des Simon-Dubnow-Instituts* 5 (2006): 485–513.

———. "Zwischen Anonymität und amtlicher Erfassung. Herrschaftliche Rahmenbedingungen jüdischen Lebens in den rheinischen Territorialstaaten vom 16. Jahrhundert bis zum Beginn der 'Emanzipationszeit.'" In *Jüdisches Leben im Rheinland. Vom Mittelalter bis zur Gegenwart*, edited by Monika Grübel and Georg Mölich, 79–110. Cologne: Böhlau, 2005.

Léon, Abraham. *Judenfrage & Kapitalismus*. Munich: Trikont, 1971.

Levie Bernfeld, Tirtsah. *Poverty and Welfare among the Portuguese Jews in Early Modern Amsterdam*. London and Portland, OR: Littman Library of Jewish Civilization, 2012.

Lewin, Louis. "Jüdische Studenten der Universität Frankfurt a.O." *Jahrbuch der Jüdisch-Literarischen Gesellschaft* 14 (1921): 217–238; 15 (1923): 59–96; 16 (1924): 43–86.

Liedtke, Rainer. *N.M. Rothschild & Sons: Kommunikationswege im europäischen Bankenwesen im 19. Jahrhundert*. Cologne: Böhlau, 2006.

Light, Ivan Hubert, and Steven J. Gold. *Ethnic Economies*. San Diego: Academic Press, 2000.

Loewe, Heinrich. "Memoiren eines polnischen Juden." *Jahrbuch der Jüdisch-Literarischen Gesellschaft* 8 (1910): 87–114 (Hebräische Abteilung), 440–446.

Bibliography

Löwenstein, Leopold. *Beiträge zur Geschichte der Juden in Deutschland. I. Geschichte der Juden in der Kurpfalz.* 2 vols. Frankfurt a.M.: J. Kaufmann, 1895.

Lowenstein, Steven M. *The Berlin Jewish Community: Enlightenment, Family, and Crisis, 1770–1830.* New York: Oxford University Press, 1994.

Lukowski, Jerzy. *Liberty's Folly. The Polish-Lithuanian Commonwealth in the Eighteenth Century, 1697–1795.* London and New York: Routledge, 1991.

Mahler, Raphael. *A History of Modern Jewry.* New York: Schocken Books, 1971.

———. *Yidn in amolikn Poyln in likht fun tsifern: di demografishe un sotsyal-ekonomishe struktur fun Yidn in Kroyn-Poyln in akhtsentn yorhundert.* Warsaw: Yiddish bukh, 1958.

Marcus, Jacob Rader, and Marc Saperstein. *The Jew in the Medieval World: A Source Book, 315–1791.* Cincinnati: Hebrew Union College Press, 1999.

Markgraf, Richard. *Zur Geschichte der Juden auf den Messen in Leipzig von 1664–1839.* Bischofswerda: Friedrich May, 1894.

Martyn, Peter M. "The Undefined Town within a Town. A History of Jewish Settlement in the Western Districts of Warsaw." *Polin* 3 (1988): 17–45.

Marwedel, Günter. "Die aschkenasischen Juden im Hamburger Raum (bis 1780)." In *Die Juden in Hamburg 1590–1990*, edited by Arno Herzig, 41–60. Hamburg: Dölling und Galitz, 1991.

McCabe, Ina Baghdiantz, Gelina Harlaftis, and Ioanna Pepelasíe Minoglou, eds. *Diaspora Entrepreneurial Networks: Four Centuries of History.* Oxford and New York: Berg, 2005.

Meier, Brigitte. "Die jüdische Gemeinde in Frankfurt an der Oder auf dem Weg in die Moderne 1750–1850. Eine sozialhistorische Mikrostudie." *Jahrbuch für Brandenburgische Landesgeschichte* 46 (1995): 111–128.

Meisl, Josef, ed. *Pinkas Kehilat Berlin, 483–614 (1723–1854).* Jerusalem: R. Mas, 1962.

Menda-Levy, Oded. "Kaminka, Aharon." In *The YIVO Encyclopedia of Jews in Eastern Europe*, edited by Gershon Hundert, 855. New Haven, CT, and London: Yale University Press, 2008.

Mendelsohn, Adam. *The Rag Race: How Jews Sewed Their Way to Success in America and the British Empire.* New York and London: New York University Press, 2015.

Michałowska, Anna. "Szmul Jakubowicz Zbytkower." *BŻIH* 162–163 (1992): 79–90.

Michałowska-Mycielska, Anna. "Jewish Family Structure in the Polish-Lithuanian Commonwealth at the End of the 18th Century: The Case of Radoszkowice." *Acta Poloniae Historica* 94 (2006): 153–164.

Michalski, Jerzy. "Sejmowe Projekty Reformy Położenia Ludności Żydowskiej w Polsce w Latach 1789–1792." In *Lud Żydowski w Narodzie Polskim. Materiały sesji naukowej w Warszawie 15–16 wresień 1992*, edited by Jerzy Michalski, 20–44. Warsaw: Instytut Historii PAN, 1994.

Miller, Michael L., and Scott Ury. "Cosmopolitanism: The End of Jewishness?" *European Review of History—Revue européenne d'histoire* 17, no. 3 (2010): 337–359.

Muller, Jerry Z. *Capitalism and the Jews.* Princeton, NJ: Princeton University Press, 2010.

Müller, Leos. *The Merchant Houses of Stockholm, c. 1640–1800. A Comparative Study of Early Modern Entrepreneurial Behaviour.* Uppsala: Acta Universitatis Upsaliensis, 1998.

Murdoch, Steve. *Network North: Scottish Kin, Commercial and Covert Associations in Northern Europe, 1603–1746.* Leiden and Boston: Brill, 2006.

North, Douglass Cecil. *Institutions, Institutional Change and Economic Performance*. Cambridge: Cambridge University Press, 1990.

Nussbaum, Hilary. *Szkice historyczne z życia Żydów w Warszawie od pierwszych śladów pobytu ich w tem mieście do chwili obecnej*. Warsaw: Druk K. Kowalewskiego, 1881.

Oliel-Grausz, Evelyne. "Networks and Communication in the Sephardi Diaspora. An Added Dimension to the Concept of Port Jews and Port Jewries." *Jewish Culture and History* 7, nos. 1–2 (2004): 61–76.

Osterhammel, Jürgen. *Die Verwandlung der Welt. Eine Geschichte des 19. Jahrhunderts*. Munich: C.H. Beck, 2009.

Ostrowski, Teodor. *Poufne wieści z oświeconej Warszawy. Gazetki pisane z roku 1782*. Wrocław: Zakład Narodowy im. Osslińskich, 1972.

Padgett, John F., and Christopher K. Ansell. "Robust Action and the Rise of the Medici, 1400–1434." *The American Journal of Sociology* 98, no. 6 (1993): 1259–1319.

Panitz, Michael Edward. "Modernity and Mortality: The Transformation of Central European Jewish Responses to Death, 1750–1850." PhD diss., Jewish Theological Seminary of America, 1989.

Pannwitz, Kurt von. *Die Entstehung der Allgemeinen Deutschen Wechselordnung. Ein Beitrag zur Geschichte der Vereinheitlichung des deutschen Zivilrechts im 19. Jahrhundert*. Frankfurt a.M.: Peter Lang, 1999.

Pawłowski, Bronisław, ed. *Protokoły Rady Stanu Księstwa Warszawskiego*, vol. 1, pt. 1. Toruń: Towarzystwo naukowe w Toruniu, 1960.

———, ed. *Protokoły Rady Stanu Księstwa Warszawskiego*, vol. 1, pt. 2. Toruń: Towarzystwo naukowe w Toruniu, 1962.

Pawłowski, Bronisław, and Tadeusz Mencel, eds. *Protokoły Rady Stanu Księstwa Warszawskiego*, vol. 2, pt. 1. Toruń: Towarzystwo naukowe w Toruniu, 1965.

———, eds. *Protokoły Rady Stanu Księstwa Warszawskiego*, vol. 2, pt. 2. Toruń: Towarzystwo naukow w Toruniu, 1968.

Penslar, Derek Jonathan. *Shylock's Children: Economics and Jewish Identity in Modern Europe*. Berkeley: University of California Press, 2001.

Peri, Anat. "Pe'ilutam shel safke tsava yehudim be-mamlekhet hungarit be-maḥtsit ha-rishonah shel ha-me'ah ha-18." *Zion* 57, no. 2 (1992): 135–174.

Philippi, Eduard. *Die Messen der Stadt Frankfurt an der Oder*. Frankfurt a.O.: Gustav Harnecker & Comp., 1877.

Pohl, Hans. "Banken und Bankgeschäfte bis zur Mitte des 19. Jahrhunderts." In *Europäische Bankengeschichte*, edited by Hans Pohl, 196–217. Frankfurt a.M.: Fritz Knapp, 1993.

Pohorille, Wilhelm. "Dostawy wojskowe Szmula Jakubowicza Zbytkowera w latach 1792–94." In *Księga pamiątkowa (album) ku czci Berka Joselewicza*, edited by Majer Bałaban, 125–135. Warsaw: Pułkownika, 1934.

Radtke, Wolfgang. "Preußischer Merkantilismus/ Kameralismus. Dargestellt am Beispiel der Kurmark Brandenburg." *Jahrbuch für Brandenburgische Landesgeschichte* 46 (1995): 94–110.

Rakover, Nahum. "Amsterdam and Sulzbach: A Conflict of Printer-Publishers." *Dutch Jewish History* 2 (1989): 167–175.

Bibliography

Reinhold, Josef. "Die Leipziger Messen und die Rzeczpospolita in der zweiten Hälfte des 18. Jahrhunderts." *Sächsische Heimatblätter* 2 (1962): 80–86.

Reinke, Andreas. *Judentum und Wohlfahrtspflege in Deutschland. Das jüdische Krankenhaus in Breslau 1726–1944.* Hannover: Hahnsche Buchhandlung, 1999.

Reuveni, Gideon, and Sarah Wobick-Segev, eds. *The Economy in Jewish History: New Perspectives on the Interrelationship between Ethnicity and Economic Life.* New York: Berghahn Books, 2010.

Reychman, Kazimierz. *Szkice genealogiczne.* Warsaw: F. Hoesick, 1936.

Richarz, Monika. *Der Eintritt der Juden in die akademischen Berufe: Jüdische Studenten und Akademiker in Deutschland 1678–1848.* Tübingen: J. C. B. Mohr, 1974.

Ries, Rotraud. "Hofjuden—Funktionsträger des absolutistischen Territorialstaates und Teil der jüdischen Gesellschaft. Eine einführende Positionsbestimmung." In *Hofjuden— Ökonomie und Interkulturalität. Die jüdische Wirtschaftselite im 18. Jahrhundert*, edited by Rotraud Ries and Friedrich J. Battenberg, 11–39. Hamburg: Christians, 2002.

Riley, James C. *International Government Finance and the Amsterdam Capital Market, 1740–1815.* Cambridge and New York: Cambridge University Press, 1979.

Ringelblum, Emanuel. "Dzieje zewnętrzne Żydów w dawnej Rzeczypospolitej." In *Żydzi w Polsce odrodzonej. Działalność społeczna, gospodarcza, oświatowa i kulturalna*, edited by Ignacy Schiper, vol. 1, 37–80. Warsaw: Wydawnictwo "Żydzi w Polsce Odrodzonej," 1932.

———. "Szmul Zbytkower." *Zion* 3, no. 3 (1938): 246–266; no. 4 (1938): 337–355.

———. *Żydzi w powstaniu kościuszkowskiem.* Warsaw: Księgarnia Popularna, 1938.

———. "Żydzi w świetle prasy warszawskiej wieku XVIII-go." *Miesięcznik Żydowski* 2, no. 1 (1932): 489–518; 2, no. 2 (1932): 42–85, 299–317.

———. *Żydzi w Warsawie, I: Od czasów najdawniejszych do ostatniego wygnania w.r. 1527.* Warsaw: Towarzystwo Miłośników Historji, 1932.

Rohrbacher, Stefan. "Die Drei Gemeinden Altona, Hamburg, Wandsbek zur Zeit der Glikl." *Aschkenas* 8, no. 1 (1998): 105–124.

Roitman, Jessica V. *The Same But Different? Inter-Cultural Trade and the Sephardim, 1595–1640.* Leiden and Boston: Brill, 2011.

Rosman, Moshe. "Ḥelkam shel ha-yehudim ba-misḥar ha-shayit mi-drom mizraḥ Polin le-Gdansk 1695–1726." *Gal-Ed* 7–8 (1985): 70–83.

———. "The History of Jewish Women in Early Modern Poland: An Assessment." *Polin* 18 (2005): 25–56.

———. "How Family Wealth and Power Are Organized." In *Early Modern Workshop: Jewish History Resources.* Vol. 3: *Gender, Family, and Social Structure.* Wesleyan University, Middletown, CT, 2006. http://fordham.bepress.com/cgi/viewcontent.cgi?article=1036&context=emw.

———. "Izrael Rubinowicz: Żyd w służbie polskich magnatów w XVIII w." *Sobótka* 3–4 (1982): 497–507.

———. "Jewish History across Borders." In *Rethinking European Jewish History*, edited by Jeremy Cohen and Moshe Rosman, 15–29. Oxford and Portland, OR: Littman Library of Jewish Civilization, 2009.

———. *The Lords' Jews: Magnate-Jewish Relations in the Polish-Lithuanian Commonwealth During the Eighteenth Century.* Cambridge, MA: Harvard University, Harvard Ukrainian Research Institute and the Center for Jewish Studies, 1990.

———. "Polish Jews in the Gdańsk Trade in the Late Seventeenth and Early Eigtheenth Centuries." In *Danzig between East and West: Aspects of Modern Jewish History,* edited by Isadore Twersky, 111–120. Cambridge, MA: Harvard University, Center for Jewish Studies and the Harvard Semitic Museum, 1985.

Rostworowski, Emanuel, ed. *Polski słownik biograficzny,* vol. 6. Wrocław: Zakład Narodowy im. Ossolińskich, 1948.

Rostworowski, Michał, ed. *Materiały do dziejów Komisyi Rządzącej z roku 1807.* Kraków: Akademia Umiejętności, 1918.

Ruderman, David B. *Early Modern Jewry. A New Cultural History.* Princeton, NJ, and Oxford: Princeton University Press, 2010.

———. *Jewish Thought and Scientific Discovery in Early Modern Europe.* New Haven, CT: Yale University Press, 1995.

———. "Review: Israel's "European Jewry in the Age of Mercantilism." *Jewish Quarterly Review* 78, nos. 1–2 (1987): 154–159.

Sabean, David Warren, and Simon Teuscher. "Rethinking European Kinship: Transregional and Transnational Families." In *Transregional and Transnational Families in Europe and Beyond. Experiences Since the Middle Ages,* edited by Christopher H. Johnson, David Warren Sabean, Simon Teuscher, and Francesca Trivellato, 1–21. New York and Oxford: Berghahn Books, 2011.

Samet, Moshe. "Halanat metim: Le-toldot ha-pulmus al kvi'at zman ha-mavet." *Asufot* 4 (1989): 413–465.

Santarosa, Veronica Aoki. "Financing Long-Distance Trade: The Joint Liability Rule and Bills of Exchange in Eighteenth-Century France." *Journal of Economic History* 75, no. 3 (2015): 690–719.

Saperstein, Marc. *Exile in Amsterdam: Saul Levi Morteira's Sermons to a Congregation of "New Jews."* Cincinnati: Hebrew Union College Press, 2005.

Schainker, Ellie R. *Confessions of the Shtetl. Converts from Judaism in Imperial Russia, 1817–1906.* Stanford, CA: Stanford University Press, 2016.

Schenk, Tobias. *Wegbereiter der Emanzipation? Studien zur Judenpolitik des "Aufgeklärten Absolutismus" in Preußen (1763–1812).* Berlin: Duncker & Humblot, 2010.

Schiper, Ignacy. *Dzieje handlu żydowskiego na ziemiach polskich.* Warsaw: Nakładem Centrali Związku Kupców, 1937 [reprint: Kraków, 1990].

———. *Onhoyb fun kapitalizm bey yuden in mayrev Eyrope.* Warsaw: Arbeyter Heym, 1920.

———, ed. *Żydzi w Polsce odrodzonej. Działność społeczna, gospodarcza, oświatowa i kulturalna.* 2 vols. Warsaw: Wydawnictwo "Żydzi w Polsce Odrodzonej," 1932–1933.

Schnabel, Isabel, and Hyun Song Shin. "Liquidity and Contagion: The Crisis of 1763." *Journal of the European Economic Association* 2, no. 6 (2004): 929–968.

Schnabel-Schüle, Helga. "Herrschaftswechsel—zum Potential einer Forschungskategorie." In *Fremde Herrscher—fremdes Volk: Inklusions- und Exklusionsfiguren bei Herrschaftswech-*

seln in Europa, edited by Helga Schnabel-Schüle and Andreas Gestrich, 5–20. Frankfurt a.M.: P. Lang, 2006.

Schnee, Heinrich. *Die Hoffinanz und der moderne Staat: Geschichte und System der Hoffaktoren an deutschen Fürstenhöfen im Zeitalter des Absolutismus. Nach archivalischen Quellen.* Berlin: Duncker & Humblot, 1953.

Schneider, Jürgen. "Messen, Banken und Börsen (15.–18. Jahrhundert)." *Banchi pubblici, banchi privati e monti di pietà nell' Europa preindustriale* 31, no. 1 (1990): 135–169.

Shatzky, Jacob. *Geshikhte fun Yidn in Varshe*, vol. 1. New York: Yidisher Visnshaftlekher Institut, Historishe Sektsye, 1947.

Sheffer, Gabriel. "A Profile of Ethno-National Diasporas." In *Diaspora Entrepreneurial Networks: Four Centuries of History*, edited by Ina Baghdiantz McCabe, Gelina Harlaftis, and Iloanna Pepelasíe Minoglou. Oxford and New York: Berg, 2005, 359–370.

Shmeruk, Chone. "Ha-ḥasidut ve-'iske haḥakhirot." *Zion* 35 (1970): 182–192.

Shulvass, Moses A. *From East to West: The Westward Migration of Jews from Eastern Europe during the Seventeenth and Eighteenth Centuries.* Detroit: Wayne State University Press, 1971.

Simsch, Adelheid. *Die Wirtschaftspolitik des preußischen Staates in der Provinz Südpreußen 1793–1806/07.* Berlin: Duncker & Humblot, 1983.

Skalweit, August. *Die Getreidehandelspolitik und Kriegsmagazinverwaltung Preußens 1756–1806.* Berlin: Paul Parey, 1931.

Slezkine, Yuri. *The Jewish Century.* Princeton, NJ: Princeton University Press, 2004.

Sombart, Werner. *Die Juden und das Wirtschaftsleben.* Leipzig: Duncker & Humblot, 1911.

Sonnenberg-Stern, Karina. *Emancipation and Poverty: The Ashkenazi Jews of Amsterdam, 1796–1850.* New York: St. Martin's Press, 2000.

Sorkin, David. "Beyond the East-West Divide: Rethinking the Narrative of the Jews' Political Status in Europe, 1600–1750." *Jewish History* 24 (2010): 247–256.

———. *Moses Mendelssohn and the Religious Enlightenment.* Berkeley: University of California Press, 1996.

Spalding, Almut. *Elise Reimarus (1735–1805): The Muse of Hamburg. A Woman of the German Enlightenment.* Würzburg: Königshausen & Neumann, 2005.

Spufford, Peter. "From Antwerp and Amsterdam to London: The Decline of Financial Centres in Europe." *De Economist* 154 (2006): 143–175.

Steele, Mark. "Bankruptcy and Insolvency: Bank Failure and Its Control in Preindustrial Europe." *Banchi pubblici, banchi privati e monti di pietà nell'Europa preindustriale* 31, no. 15 (1991): 181–204.

Stern, Selma. *The Court Jew: A Contribution to the History of the Period of Absolutism in Central Europe.* Philadelphia: Jewish Publication Society of America, 1950.

———. *Der Preußische Staat und die Juden. Dritter Teil: Die Zeit Friedrichs des Großen.* 2 vols. Tübingen: J. C. Mohr (Paul Siebeck), 1971.

Stow, Kenneth R. *Theater of Acculturation: The Roman Ghetto in the Sixteenth Century.* Seattle: University of Washington Press, 2001.

Straubel, Rolf. *Frankfurt (Oder) und Potsdam am Ende des Alten Reiches. Studien zur städtischen Wirtschafts- und Sozialstruktur.* Potsdam: Verlag für Berlin-Brandenburg, 1995.

———. *Die Handelsstädte Königsberg und Memel in friderizianischer Zeit. Ein Beitrag zur Geschichte des ost- und gesamtpreußischen "Commerciums" sowie seiner sozialen Träger (1763–1806/15)*. Berlin: Berliner Wissenschaftsverlag, 2003.

———. *Kaufleute und Manufakturunternehmer. Eine empirische Untersuchung über die sozialen Träger von Handel und Großgewerbe in den mittleren preußischen Provinzen (1763–1815)*. Stuttgart: Franz Steiner, 1995.

Struck, Bernhard. "Vom offenen Raum zum nationalen Territorium. Wahrnehmung, Erfindung und Historizität von Grenzen in der deutschen Reiseliteratur über Polen und Frankreich um 1800." In *Die Grenze als Raum, Erfahrung und Konstruktion. Deutschland, Frankreich und Polen vom 17. bis zum 20. Jahrhundert*, edited by Etienne François, Jörg Seifarth, and Bernhard Struck, 77–104. Frankfurt a.M. and New York: Campus, 2007.

Swetschinski, Daniel. "From the Middle Ages to the Golden Age, 1516–1621." In *The History of the Jews in the Netherlands*, edited by J. C. H. Blom, R. G. Fuks-Mansfeld, and I. Schöffer, 44–84. Oxford and Portland, OR: Littman Library of Jewish Civilization, 2007.

———. *Reluctant Cosmopolitans: The Portuguese Jews of Seventeenth-Century Amsterdam*. London and Portland, OR: Littman Library of Jewish Civilization, 2000.

Szaja, Wiesław. "Sprawy żydowskie przed komisjami porządkowymi cywilno-wojskowymi na pograniczu wielkopolski i Śląska w latach 1789–1792." *Acta Universitatis Wratislaviensis* 84 (1991): 171–180.

Tal, Elchanan, ed. *The Ashkenazi Community of Amsterdam in the Eighteenth Century*. Jerusalem: Zalman Shazar Center for Jewish History, 2010.

Targiel, Ralf-Rüdiger. "Gedruckt mit den Typen von Amsterdam. Hebräischer Buchdruck in Frankfurt an der Oder." In *Jüdisches Brandenburg. Geschichte und Gegenwart*, edited by Irene A. Diekmann, 450–481. Berlin: Verlag für Berlin-Brandenburg, 2008.

Teller, Adam. *Kesef, koah, vehashpa'ah: Ha-yehudim ba-ahuzot bet Radzivil be-Lita ba-me'ah ha-18*. Jerusalem: Merkaz Zalman Shazar le-Toldot Yisrael, 2006.

———. "The Legal Status of the Jews on the Magnate Estates of Poland-Lithuania in the Eighteenth Century." *Gal-Ed* 15–16 (1997): 41–63.

———. *Money, Power, and Influence in Eighteenth-Century Lithuania. The Jews on the Radziwiłł Estates*. Stanford, CA: Stanford University Press, 2016.

———. "Telling the Difference: Some Comparative Perspectives on the Jews' Legal Status in the Polish-Lithuanian Commonwealth and the Holy Roman Empire." *Polin* 22 (2009): 109–141.

Tiggemann, Daniela. "Familiensolidarität, Leistung und Luxus. Familien der Hamburger jüdischen Oberschicht im 19. Jahrhundert." In *Die Juden in Hamburg 1590–1990*, edited by Arno Herzig, 419–430. Hamburg: Dölling und Galitz, 1991.

Toch, Michael. "Jewish Women Entrepreneurs in the 16th and 17th Century Economics and Family Structure." *Jahrbuch für Fränkische Landesforschung* 60 (2000): 254–263.

Toeplitz, Krzysztof Teodor. *Rodzina Toeplitzów. Książka mojego ojca*. Warsaw: Wydawnictwo ISKRY, 2004.

Tokarz, Wacław. *Warszawa przed wybuchem powstania 17. Kwietnia 1794 roku*. Kraków: Nakład Funduszu Nestora Bucewicza, 1911.

Tribe, Keith. *Governing Economy: The Reformation of German Economic Discourse, 1750–1840*. Cambridge and New York: Cambridge University Press, 1988.

Trivellato, Francesca. *The Familiarity of Strangers: The Sephardic Diaspora, Livorno, and Cross-cultural Trade in the Early Modern Period*. New Haven, CT: Yale University Press, 2009.

———. "The Port Jews of Livorno and Their Global Networks of Trade in the Early Modern Period." *Jewish Culture and History* 7, nos. 1–2 (2004): 31–48.

Turniansky, Chava, ed. *Glikl: Zikhronot, 1691–1719*. Jerusalem: Merkaz Zalman Shazar le-toldot Yisrael, 2006.

Ury, Scott. "The *Shtadlan* of the Polish-Lithuanian Commonwealth: Noble Advocate or Unbridled Opportunist?" *Polin* 15 (2002): 267–299.

Van der Wee, Herman. "Monetary, Credit, and Banking Systems." In *The Cambridge Economic History of Europe*, edited by M. M. Postan and H. J. Habakkuk, 291–392. Cambridge: Cambridge University Press, 1977.

Van Rahden, Till. *Jews and Other Germans: Civil Society, Religious Diversity, and Urban Politics in Breslau, 1860–1925*. Madison: University of Wisconsin Press, 2008.

Van Straten, Jits, ed. *De begraafboeken van Muiderberg 1669–1811. Indexen van personen begraven op de joodse begraafplaats Muiderberg vanaf 12 januari 1699 tot 21 juli 1811*. Amsterdam: Stichting Bevordering Onderzoek Joodse Historische Bronnen, 2000.

Van Wie, Paul D. *Image, History, and Politics: The Coinage of Modern Europe*. Lanham, MD: University Press of America, 1999.

Veluwenkamp, Jan Willem. "Familienetwerken binnen de Nederlandse koopliedengemeenschap van Archangel in de eerste helft van de achttiende eeuw." *Bijdragen en Mededelingen betreffende de Geschiedenis der Nederlanden* 108, no. 4 (1993): 655–672.

Verdooner, Dave, and Harmen Snel. *Trouwen in Mokum: Jewish Marriage in Amsterdam*, 2 vols. Gravenhage: Warray, 1992.

Vogel, Jakob. *Ein schillerndes Kristall: Eine Wissensgeschichte des Salzes zwischen Früher Neuzeit und Moderne*. Cologne: Böhlau, 2008.

Vries, B. W. de. *From Pedlars to Textile Barons: The Economic Development of a Jewish Minority Group in the Netherlands*. Amsterdam and New York: North Holland, 1989.

Walker, Jonathan, Filippo de Vivo, and James Shaw. "A Dialogue on Spying in 17th-Century Venice." *Rethinking History* 10, no. 3 (2006): 323–344.

Wasserman, Stanley, and Katherine Faust. *Social Network Analysis: Methods and Applications*. Cambridge and New York: Cambridge University Press, 1994.

Weber, Max. "Die protestantische Ethik und der Geist des Kapitalismus." *Archiv für Sozialwissenschaft und Sozialpolitik* 20 (1904): 1–54; 21 (1905): 1–110.

Węgrzynek, Hanna. "Illegal Immigrants: The Jews of Warsaw, 1527–1792." In *Warsaw. The Jewish Metropolis. Essays in Honor of the 75th Birthday of Professor Antony Polonsky*, edited by Glenn Dynner and François Guesnet, 19–41. Leiden and Boston: Brill, 2015.

Weinryb, Bernard D. *Neueste Wirtschaftsgeschichte der Juden in Russland und Polen; von der 1. Polnischen Teilung bis zum Tode Alexanders II. (1172–1881)*. 2nd ed. Hildesheim and New York: G. Olms, 1972.

———. "Yehude Polin ve-Lita ve-yaḥasehem le-Breslau." In *Meḥkarim u-mekorot le-toldot Yisra'el ba-'et ha-ḥadashah*, edited by Bernard D. Weinryb, 25–67. Jerusalem: Makor, 1975.

Wellman, Barry, and Charles Wetherell. "Social Network Analysis of Historical Communities: Some Questions from the Present for the Past." *History of the Family* 1, no. 1 (1996): 97–121.

Wiesemann, Falk. "Jewish Burials in Germany: Between Tradition, the Enlightenment, and the Authorities." *Leo Baeck Institute Year Book* 37 (1992): 17–31.

Williamson, Oliver E. "Calculativeness, Trust, and Economic Organization." *Journal of Law and Economics* 36, no. 1 (1993): 453–486.

Wodziński, Marcin. *Haskalah and Hasidism in the Kingdom of Poland: A History of Conflict*. Oxford and Portland, OR: Littman Library of Jewish Civilization, 2005.

———. "Legat Berka Sonnenberga czyli o zaskakującej karierze mimowolnego dobroczyńcy." *Studia Judaica* 7, no. 1 (2004): 139–162.

———. "Tombstones." In *The YIVO Encyclopedia of Jews in Eastern Europe*, edited by Gershon Hundert. New Haven, CT, and London: Yale University Press, 2008, 1887–1891.

Yevnin, Shmuel. *Sefer Naḥalat 'Olamim*. Warsaw: Yitsḥak Goldman, 1882.

Yogev, Gedalia. *Diamonds and Coral: Anglo-Dutch Jews and Eighteenth-Century Trade*. New York: Holmes & Meier, 1978.

Zieliński, Jarosław. *Atlas dawnej architektury ulic i placów Warszawy: Śródmieście historyczne*. Vol. 8: *Pl. Krasińskich—Kwiatowa*. Warsaw: TOnZ, 2002.

Zieńkowska, Krystyna. "Spór o Nową Jerozolimę." *Kwartalnik Historyczny* 93, no. 2 (1986): 351–376.

INDEX

acculturation, 156–57, 160–69, 161–62f5.2–3, 179, 183–84. *See also* integration
agriculture: modernization of, 180; trade in and army supplying, 92–93, 95, 115, 119–22, 146–47, 148, 178
alcohol monopolies *(propinacja)*, 100, 121, 150, 171n24, 177, 182
Allenstein, 88–89
Altona rabbinate, 45–46
Amsterdam: Ashkenazic community in, 2–5, 29; in banking, 2, 183; bankruptcies in, 25–27, 58; in brokerage of bills of exchange, 1–2, 4, 8–9, 10–15, 14t1.1, 15; in brokerage of credit, 2, 5–6, 23–29; as a commercial and financial center, xxiii, 1, 29, 99; economic decline of, 27–29, 149, 183; legal equality in, 30; Schlesinger family ties to, 22–23
anti-Jewish argumentation, xvi–xvii
army suppliers/supplying: agriculture trade in, 92–93, 95, 115, 119–22, 146–47, 148, 178; in Berlin, 69; in the borderlands, 80–81, 83, 91–95; in gaining privileges, 91; during the Kościuszko uprising, 123–24; monopolies in, 133n31; to multiple powers, 122–26; in the Napoleonic Wars, 138–48; as new opportunity, 60–61, 89; on the Polish-Prussian border, xxv, 81, 83, 91–95; in Praga, 119–22; and private banking, 180–81; in Prussia policy, 39–40, 85, 92, 93–94, 95; state obligations in, 140–41, 142–43t5.1; in the Thirty Years' War, xviii, 39–40, 91–92; in Warsaw, 99, 100–101, 125–26, 140–41, 142–45t5.1–2, 177–78

Ashkenazim, xx–xxiii, xxvi, 2–5, 15–27, 29–30, 45–46, 176
attire in acculturation, 160–62, 161–62f5.2–3, 166
Austria, 150–52
autonomy, 83, 84–85, 127–28, 129. *See also* freedom; *kahal* (communal self-government)

bankers/banking: in Amsterdam, 1, 2, 183; in Berlin, 60, 69; and bills of exchange, 24; century of, xvii–xviii; in industrialization, 179–84; and legal security, 178; stability in, 148; in Warsaw and Poland, xxvi, 98–101, 137–38, 148–49, 171n22, 178–84
bankruptcies, 25–27, 37, 58, 98–99
Bavarian War of Succession, 92
Beer, Jacob Herz, 60, 94–95, 139–40, 149, 163
Beer, Juda Herz, 52, 58, 60
Benjamin, Joseph, 26–27
Benjamin & Samuel Symons & Sons, 5, 20–21, 27–29. *See also* Symons family
Benoît, Gideon, 125
Bereksohn, Gabriel, 155
Berek Szmul, xxvi, 120–21f4.2–3, 138–48, 150–56, 165–68
Berlin, 60, 69, 181
Berlin, Saul Levin: *Ktav yosher*, 54–55
Berlin Haskalah, 54–55
Bethel, W. Mauricio, 159–60
Bibikov, Alexander, 125
Bielinski Palace, 166–67
bills of exchange: Amsterdam in trade of, 1–2, 4, 8–9, 10–15, 14t1.1; in central European commerce, 2, 5–10, 6–7f1.1–2; commercial law on, 6, 8; in

bills of exchange (*cont.*)
credit, 5–6, 24–26; "in honor" acceptance of, 25–26; networks in trade of, 1–2, 10, 15; in private banking, 181; protest of, 7–9, 10–12, 13*f1.4*, 24–27, 32n39; Symons family brokerage of, 10–15, 12–13*f1.3–4*, 14*t1.1*, 16–17*t1.2*, 26
Bleichröder, Samuel, 181
Boas, Hyman, 19
Boas, Moses, 29, 99
Boas, Tobias, 19
Boas family, 14*t1.1*, 19–20, 20*f1.5*
borderlands. *See* Polish-Prussian borderlands
boundary crossing, 91–92, 122–23, 127
brokers/brokerage: of bills of exchange, 1–2, 4, 8–9, 10–15, 12–13*f1.3–4*, 14*t1.1*, 16–17*t1.2*, 23, 26; in commerce, 30; of credit, 130
Buko, Elias, 56, 60, 70, 138–39
Buko, Levin, 40, 45, 52, 70
burial societies, 118, 131n10, 163–64
butchers, Jewish, 85, 89, 141

Cameralism, 72n7, 77–78n68, 150–51
capital, financial: in commercial networks, xxi; credit in raising, 23–24; in industrialization, 181–83; marriage in raising of, 18, 19, 21–23, 160
capital, social, xxi, xxii–xxiii
capitalism: Court Jews in, xv, xviii–xix; integration into, 168; and Jewish autonomy, 127–28; Jewish economic actors in, xv–xvii
Chemiak, Baruch, 89–90, 101
Christian banking houses, 26–28, 60, 69, 98–99, 171n22, 183
Christians: in army supplying, 139–40, 146; assets of, 43–44, 44*t2.1*; and bills of exchange, 9–10, 15, 20; in commercial networks, xxii–xxiii, 16, 18, 45, 49–51; family ties of, 15, 18; and settlement rights, 88, 112–13. *See also* non-Jews

commerce: bills of exchange in, 2, 4, 5–10, 6–7*f1.1–2*; changing political powers in, 122–24; family and ethnic networks in, 15–27; importance of Jewish brokers to, 30; local and regional in the borderlands, 84; shift to banking from, 60, 69; transcultural, xvi, xvii, xxii, 176; transnational, xvi, xvii, 51
Commerce of Amsterdam (LeLong), 4
commercial courts, 8, 27
communal leadership: alternatives to, 168–69; assets of, 58; in the emancipation debates, 129; in Frankfurt an der Oder, 39, 52–56; in Praga, 117–18; tax paying role of, 102, 109n73, 117–18, 130; in Warsaw, 167. *See also* autonomy; *kahal* (communal self-government)
competition, 88, 94–95, 112, 141, 147, 155–56
conservatism, 56–57, 128, 161–62
contracts: in army supplying, 92–94; in leaseholding monopolies, 151–52, 153; of marriage, 21–22, 159–60
converts and conversion to Christianity: and acculturation, 163–64, 168; in banking and industrialization, 180, 183–84; in leaseholding, 155–56; Portugese, 2–3; and religious attitudes, 159–60, 179; in Warsaw, 137, 149, 168
cosmopolitanism, xvi–xvii, 184
Council of the Four Lands, 127–28
Court Jews, xv, xvi, xviii–xix, 18–19, 39–40, 92, 181
Cracow Palace, 98
credit: in army supplying, 140–41, 178; Ashkenazim in brokering, 2, 29–30; and banking in Warsaw, 98–99; bills of exchange in, 5–6, 24–26; in economic success, 177; in supply networks, 178; in textile trading, 38
cross-border connections, 122–25, 126, 138–39, 152

culture: across political borders, 122; and economic success, xxvi; fluidity of, 81, 138; rabbinic, in enlightenment thought, 56–57; in Warsaw, 156–57, 166–67, 168. *See also* acculturation

Danzig, 50–51
debt, 26–27, 98–99
development: economic, 71–72, 98, 111, 113, 179–80; industrial, 168, 179–84
diamond trade, 28
diaspora, xvi, xx, xxii–xxiii
disloyalty, alleged, 122, 133n33
Dohm, Christian Wilhelm, 127
dowries, 18, 21–22, 159–60
Duchy of Warsaw, 140–41, *142–45t5.1–2*, 150–55, 166–67, 169–70n9. *See also* Warsaw
Dutch Republic, 2–3. *See also* Amsterdam
Dynner, Glenn, 118, 156

economic decline: in Amsterdam, 27–29, 149, 183; and cultural impoverishment, 185n5; in Frankfurt an der Oder, 38–39, 57–60, 71–72; political and economic context of, xviii
economy, global, 184
Edict of Potsdam, 39
Eisenbach, Artur, 129
emancipation: debate over, xxv–xxvi, 110–11, 127–30; by the Dutch National Assembly, 30; and occupational structure, xxixn30; Prussian edict of, 96, 139
emigration/emigrants. *See* migration/migrants
emphiteutic law, 133n30
endorsement system, 5–6, *6f1.2*, 27
Enlightenment, Jewish, 39, 54–57, 72, 127–28, 156
entrepreneurs/entrepreneurship: in banking and industrialization, 100–101, 181; competition among, 155–56; in historiography, xviii–xix; moratoria for, 125–26, 135n46; in resisting restrictions, 103; in Warsaw, 100–101, 137–38; women as, 157, 159

Epstein family, 182
estates, 95, 100, 121–22, *121f4.3*, 150
ethnicity, xx–xxiii, 70, 152–53, 155–56
expulsion of Jews, 86, 88–89, 97–98, 103, 105n41, 112–13

fairs: discrimination at, 179; in Frankfurt an der Oder, 42–43, 57–58, 69; in Leipzig, 8, 23, 49–50; in networks, 18–19, 23, 43, 45, 48–50; in trade of bills of exchange, 8–9
feudal system/economy, xix, xxv–xxvi, 83, 110, 119, 150, 168, 178–79
finance, international, 4–5, 181–82, 185–86n18
financial crisis of 1763, 25–26, 98–99
Flatau, Felicya, 159
Flatau, Izaak. *See* Itzig Jacob
Flatow, 83–84, 86
Four Year Sejm (1788–1792), xx, 97, 110–11, 127, 129–30
Frankel, Samuel Antoni, 149, 154, 155
Frankfurt an der Oder: assets of Jews in, 44–45, *44t2.1*, *61–62t2.3*, *63–68t2.4*; as a commercial hub, xxiii, 41–43; decline of, 38–39, 57–60, 71–72; economic success in, 177; enlightenment thought in, 54–57; Jewish community in, 40, 52–54, *53t2.2*, 74n22; socioeconomic status of Jews in, 43–44, 52
Frederick the Great, King of Prussia, 52–53
Frederick William, King of Prussia, 40
Frederick William II, King of Prussia, 57–58
freedom, 2–3, 40, 83–85, 96, 101–2. *See also* autonomy
Fürstenberg, Hiel, 147, 167
Fürstenberg, Moses Aron, 97, 98, 146–47, 167

Galicia, 151, 154
Gazeta Rządowa (Warsaw), 126
geography: in commercial ties, xviii, 19; and economic opportunities, 60, 69–70; in immigration to Warsaw, 112; and marriages, 59–60. *See also* mobility, geographic

Glikl bas Juda Leib, 1, 18, 19
grain trade, 85, 92–93, 100, 119–20, 146–47

Habsburg Empire, 150–52
Hamburg, 6, 23–24, 45–46, 58
Hasidic movement, 118, 138, 156, 165–66, 168–69
Haskalah. *See* Enlightenment, Jewish
Heineccius, J. G., 9
Ḥevrah Kadisha (Jewish burial society), 118, 131n10, 163–64
Heymann, Moses, 113–14, 116–17, 125
Heymann, Wolfgang, 112, 114, 124–26, 135, 135n46
home ownership, 59, 86, 105n19
Hope & Co, 26, 35n71
Hoym, Karl Georg Heinrich von, 92–93

immigration/immigrants. *See* migration/migrants
industrialization, 168, 179–84
infrastructure, 113, 180, 181–82
integration: and economic success, 80, 156–60, 178; into feudal society and economy, xxv–xxvi, 110, 119, 150, 168, 178–79; of markets, 1, 2; of non-Jews into Jewish networks, xxii, 51, 71, 138–39; and religious attitudes, 156; social, in Warsaw, 164–65. *See also* acculturation
Israel, Jonathan, xvi, 29, 72n6, 92; *European Jewry,* xxviin6
Itzig Jacob: in army supplying, 93–95, 100–101; in banking, 99–101; in espionage, 122; migration and career of, xxv; rise of, 80–81; search for settlement rights and opportunities, 87–91, 103; stations of life in West Prussia, 90f3.2; strategies of in personal success, 81, 83, 87; in Warsaw, 95–98, 99–102

Jakubowicz, Szmul: in army supplying, 89, 91, 93, 115, 119–24; early years of in Praga, 115–18; economic rise of, 112; estate of in Targówek, 121–22, 121f4.3; family tree of, 158f5.1; Hasidism of, 156–57; marriage of to Judyta, 118–19, 156–57; and Moses Heymann, 125; wealth and influence of, 114
Jakubowiczowa, Judyta: acculturation and traditional values of, 160–68; in army supplying, 89, 91, 119–22, 138–48; in banking, xxvi, 148–49; estate of in Targówek, 121–22, 121f4.3; and the Ḥevrah Kadisha in Praga, 163–64; marriage of, 115–16, 156–57; mother of, 160–61, 161f5.2, 173n54; painting of, 161–62, 162f5.3; religious attitude of, 156–60; role of in business, 118–19
joint liability rule, 6, 8, 27
joint-stock banks, 182
Judenordnung (regulations concerning Jews), 8–9

kahal (communal self-government), 127–28, 167, 175n78. *See also* autonomy; communal leadership
Kaskel, Jacob, 69–70
kinship, xx–xxiii, xxvi, 15–27, 71. *See also* networks, family
Königsberg, 46–47, 48
Königsberger, David, 128–29, 134n37
Kościuszko, Tadeusz, 123
Kościuszko uprising of 1794, 93, 99, 122–24
kosher meat taxes *(korobka),* 102
Kosim, Jan, 138
Ktav yosher (Berlin), 54–55

Landes, David, xx
leaseholding: competition in, 95; in emphiteutic law, 133n30; and legal security, 178; in Warsaw and Poland, xxvi, 100, 137–38, 149–56
legal status of Jews: and banking in Warsaw, 100–101; in the emancipation debate, 127; in the Polish-Lithuanian Commonwealth, 110–11; in the Polish-Prussian borderlands, 102–103; as "privileged

protected Jew," 89; in the Prussian occupation, 83–84
legislation and policy: on Jews in Prussia, 38, 39–41, 46–48, 96; in Leipzig, 49
Leipzig, 6, 8–9, 49–50, 69–70
LeLong, Isaac: *Commerce of Amsterdam,* 4
Lesser, Aleksander: "Jewish couple," 162f5.3
Levi, Baruch Aron, 26–27
Levin, Mendel, 47–48
local policies, 86, 89, 94, 102–103
loyalty, 87, 124, 165

Magnus, F. Martin, 181
manufactured goods, Prussian: in economic policy, 57–58, 85, 102–103; export of, 47, 52–53, 88–89; Jews in trade of, 43; trade in at fairs, 49–50
markets: bills of exchange in, 8; credit, 19, 22–23, 71; financial, 98–99; integration of, 1, 2; for manufactured goods, 85; railways in opening of, 182
marriages: in commercial networks, 15, 16, 18–23, 176; contracts in, 21–22, 159–60; in creating community ties, 115–16; in family connections, 15, 46–48; in Jewish tradition, 131–32n14; in legal status on the borderlands, 89, 91; public announcement of, 34n52; religion and lifestyle in, 156–57, 159; of the Schlesinger family, 59–60; settlement rights in, 87; of the Symons and Boas families, 19–20, 20f1.5
maskilim (enlighteners), 54–55, 57
meat supplying, 133n31, 140, 141
membrana/mamran (debt bill), 9
Mendelssohn, Joseph and Abraham, 181
Mendelssohn, Moses, 56–57
merchants: assets of, 44–45, 44t2.1, 58, 59, 61–62t2.3; discrimination against, 8–9; in family and ethnic networks, 1–2, 18–19; in Frankfurt an der Oder, 42–43; in historiography, xviii–xix; in trade of bills of exchange, 1–2, 4; women as, 157, 159

middlemen, Central European: change in fortunes of, 60–70; in East/West trade, 177; and Enlightenment thought, 54–57; family and commercial networks of, 24, 37–39, 43–51, 53–54, 55–56, 60, 70–71; in Frankfurt an der Oder, 41–43, 52–54; and Prussian policy, 39–41
migration/migrants: in Amsterdam, 2–3; in banking and industrialization, 168; economic success of, xv, 28, 81, 83, 100–101; in network building, 46–47; in new opportunities, 69, 70, 71–72, 81, 83; to Prussia, 39–40, 57, 60–61; and societal integration, 156; in transnational and transcultural commerce, xvi; to Warsaw and Praga, 112–13, 114, 127–30, 180
mobility, geographic: in army supplying, 93–94, 95; and commercial networks, 176–77; in economic opportunities, 60, 69, 89; marriages in, 18, 47; in Polish-Prussian borderlands, 80–81
monopolies: on alcohol *(propinacja),* 115, 150, 171n24; and legal security, 178; in meat supplying, 133n31; in Russia, 182; on salt, xxvi, 149–56

Napoleonic Wars, 138–48, 177–78
networks, commercial: in army supplying, xviii, 93, 94–95, 119, 138–40, 147, 178; Ashkenazic, xx–xxiii, xxvi, 15–27, 45–46, 176; in banking and industrialization, 100–101, 178–79, 182; in the borderlands, 89–90, 93, 94–96; in the emancipation debate, 129–30; fairs in, 18–19, 23, 43, 45, 46–47, 48–50; in the flow of credit and goods, 178; geographic mobility in, 176–77; of middlemen, 24, 37–39, 43–51, 53–54, 55–56, 60, 70–71; religion in, xx, 137, 160, 179, 184; and state privileges, 117–18; transnational, xxii, 176, 183; and *yeshivah* studies, 55–56
networks, ethnic: in brokerage of bills of exchange, 1–2, 10; in commercial

networks, ethnic (*cont.*)
  networks, xx–xxi, 15–27, 176; in leaseholding, 152, 153; merchants' reliance on, 71; in new opportunities, 69; in Warsaw, 137
networks, family: in banking, 178–79; in borderland opportunities, 89–90; in brokerage of bills of exchange, 1–2, 10, 15; in commercial networks, 15–27, 176; in leaseholding monopolies, 155–56; of middlemen, 37–38, 43–51, 70–71; in payment of Prussian taxes, 54; religion in, 137, 160; in Warsaw, 137, 138–39
networks, transregional: and banking, 100–101; in leaseholding monopolies, 150, 155–56; of the new Jewish elite, 130; in the Polish-Prussian borderlands, 80–81, 89, 103
Netze district, 84–86
Neumann, Salomon, 94
Neumark, Ignacy, 147, 155
Nijmegen, Elias Moses Daniel, 26–27
Nijmegen family, *14t1.1, 22f1.6,* 26, 28
nobility, Polish: as banking clients, 99–100, 149; connections to, 115, 120–21, 168; in the emancipation debates, 129; and leaseholding, xix, 150
non-Jewish authorities, 102, 117–18, 163, 166
non-Jews: in Jewish networks, xx, xxi–xxiii, 16, 18, 45, 50–51, 71, 138–40, 176, 179; socialization with at salons, 162–63. *See also* Christians
notaries, 9, 11, *14f1.4,* 15, 32n38
Nussbaum, Hilary, 80, 101

occupations/occupational structure: in Amsterdam, 3–4; in banking and industrialization, 182; debates on in the enlightenment, 54–55, 57, 72, 156; in the emancipation debates, 127, 129, xxixn30; flexibility in, xv, xix, xxv–xxvi, 60, 80, 81, 83, 130; monopoly leasing, 150; niches in, 177; in the Prussian General Code for the Jews, 96
Oesterreicher, Leib, 97–98, 100, 146–47, 151

Oesterreicher, Rozalia Konstancya Jozefa, 159–60
opportunities: migration in, 69, 70, 71–72, 81, 83; in the Polish-Lithuanian Commonwealth, 110–11; in the Polish-Prussian borderlands, 84, 87–91; in Warsaw, 110, 137–38

petitions, 88–89, 102–103, 116–18, 128, 166
pinkassim (record books), 52, 75–76nn47–48, 131n10
Poland (Polish-Lithuanian Commonwealth): age at marriage in, 132–33n14; army supplying in, xviii, 58, 81, 83, 92, 147–48, 177–78; autonomy in, 83–85, 127–28; banking in, 148–49, 171n22, 178, 179–84; bourgeois society in, 138; distribution of Jews in, 111–12; elites' success in, xxv–xxvi; emancipation debate in, 127–30; feudal economy of, xix, 83, 110; Hasidic movement in, 138, 156, 165–66, 168–69; industrialization in, 179–84; Jewish relations with the state in, 115–18; leaseholding in, 95, 150, 153–54; *membrany* and bills of exchange in, 9–10; opportunities in, 110–11; partitions of, xviii, 58, 81, *82f3.1,* 83–84, 92, 99, 122–23, 177–78; in trade of raw materials and agricultural products, 119–20. *See also* Warsaw
Polish-Jewish historians, xix
Polish Jews: in historiography, xix–xx; influence of on fairs, 42; legal and economic position of, 110–11; in Leipzig, 69–70; main goods traded by, 119–20; as new mercantile elite, xxv; patriotism of, 183; and private prayer houses, 101–102; in textile trading, 43; urbanization of, 115. *See also* Poland
Polish-Prussian borderlands: army supplying in, xxv, 81, 83, 91–95; insecurity in, 95–98; settlement restrictions in, 80–81, 86, 87–92, 97;

transition of from Poland to Prussia, 83–86. *See also* Warsaw
Polish uprising of 1830/31, 183
political context: of army supplying, 95, 178; in economic activity, xviii; in Warsaw, 95–96, 98–99
Poniatowski, Stanisław August, King of Poland, xxv, 83, 113, 116–17, 123–24, 127–29
population, Jewish: in Amsterdam, 2–3; army supplying in growth of, 91–92; in Frankfurt an der Oder, 74n22; limitations on, 46; in the Polish-Lithuanian Commonwealth, 111–12; in Polish-Prussian borderlands, 83–84, 86; in Praga, 112–13; in Prussia, 96; in Warsaw, 112–13, 130n2, 180
Portugese Jewish immigrants, 2–3
Posner, Salomon Markus, 151–52, 153, 154–55, 167
Potocki, Antoni and Ignacy, 28–29
poverty, 3–4, 177, 180
Praga: and army supplying, 119–22; on Berek Szmul's tombstone, 120–21f4.2–3, 167–68; economic elite in, xxv–xxvi; Jewish cemetery of, 120f4.2, 163–64; in the Kościuszko uprising, 122–24; opportunities in, 110, 112; restricted settlement in, 97, 112–13, 114, 180
Prager, house of, 28
prayer houses, private, 101–102
printing press, Hebrew, 42–43
privileges: and acculturation, 166–67; commercial networks in, 117–18; *de non tolerandis judaeis*, 96, 110; general, 97, 114; in the Polish-Lithuanian Commonwealth, 111–12; in Praga and Warsaw, 112, 116–17; "privileged protected Jews," 40, 46, 89, 91; in Prussia, 132n19
Proops printers, 55, 76n57
protection money, 52–53
Protestant banking networks, 98, 181
Prussia: army supplying in, 39–40, 85, 92, 93–94, 95; bills of exchange and credit in, 24, 177; Cameralism in, 72n7; economic policies of, 57–58, 69, 85; and emancipation, 96, 130, 139; in the Kościuszko uprising, 123–24; migration to, 39–40, 57, 60–61; and occupied Poland, 83–86, 95–96; policies toward Jews in, 38, 39–41, 46–47, 52–54, 96; privileges in, 132n19; readmission of Jews to, xxiii, xxv; reforms of 1812, 168; and the Seven Years' War, 72

railway construction, 180, 182–83
Rapoport, Izaak Wolff, 151, 152, 154–55
raw materials, 102–103, 119–20
regulations/restrictions: and acculturation, 166–67; of bills of exchange, 6, 8–9; in Danzig, 50–51; in Leipzig, 49–50; on marriage of Jews, 46–48, 74–75n34; in the Polish-Prussian borderlands, 80–81, 83–86, 87–92, 97, 102–103; in Prussia, 38, 39–41, 46–47, 52–54, 57–58, 60, 103; in Warsaw, 96, 110, 166–67
reliability, 24–25
religion: in commercial networks, xx, 179, 184; in family and ethnic networks, 137, 160; in Warsaw, 138, 156–68
religious reform movement, 163, 165
reputation: in cross-border connections, 124–25, 126; family networks in preserving, 25–26; and the joint liability rule, 6, 8
resettlement/readmission, xxiii, xxv, 39–40, 91, 128, xxviin6
Retailer's Guild (Leipzig), 69–70
retail trade, 43–44, 58, 71, 179
Revised General Code of 1750 (Prussia), 40–41, 84–85, 96
Ringelblum, Emmanuel, 115, 126
Rintel, Herz, 54
risk, entrepreneurial: in army supplying, 95, 178; and banking in Warsaw, 100–101; in commercial networks, xxi; and economic utility, 103; and Jewish success, xxv–xxvi; and the

risk, entrepreneurial (*cont.*)
    new Jewish elite, 130; in the
    Polish-Prussian borderlands, 80
Rothschild family, 181, 183
royal privileges, 111–12
Russia, 123–24, 132–33n14, 175n78, 182, 183, 184

salt monopolies, xxvi, 149–56
Santarosa, Veronica Aoki, 6, 32n39
Saxon Deputation of Commerce, 49, 69–70
Schlesinger, Abraham Pincus, 46–47
Schlesinger, Adolph, 69–70
Schlesinger, Alexander Pincus, 46–47, 48
Schlesinger, David Pincus, 48, 74–75n34
Schlesinger, Feibisch, 46
Schlesinger, Herz Marcus, 55–57
Schlesinger, Jacob Moses, 46, 53–54
Schlesinger, Leib, 46
Schlesinger, Levin Marcus, 59
Schlesinger, Levin Pincus, 11, 15, 26–27, 37, 38, 49–50, 58–59
Schlesinger, Marcus Moses, 41, 46, 51, 58
Schlesinger, Pincus Moses, 11, 15, 23, 37, 41, 47–49, 51, 58–59
Schlesinger family: in brokerage of bills of exchange, *14t1.1*, 26; commercial misfortunes of, 57–60; connections and networks of, *22f1.6*, 38, 43–51, 59–60, 70–71; in the credit business, 24–25; decline of, 38–39; and enlightenment thought, 55–57; in Frankfurt an der Oder, 40–41, *41f2.1*, 43–45, 71–72; as middlemen, 37–38, 45; new opportunities for, 60, 69–70; subscriptions of, 56, 77n65; wealth and status of, 39, 43–45
Schlesinger/Schlesier, Moses Jacob, 40
Schutz-Jude (privileged protected Jew), 40, 46, 89, 91
Schwartzmann, Josef, 152
Seeligmann, Abraham, 47
Sephardim, xxii–xxiii, 3–4, 18, 21
settlement rights/restrictions: and acculturation, 166–67; and army supplying, xxviii, 139; and economic utility, 53, 87, 88, 91, 103, 128–29;

and fairs, 49–50; in the *Judenordnung*, 8–9; networks in, xxi–xxii, 179; and non-Jewish connections, 45, 50–51, 71; in the Polish-Lithuanian Commonwealth, 111–12; in the Polish-Prussian borderlands, 80–81, 86, 87–92, 97; in Praga and Warsaw, 110, 112–13, 117–18, 128–29, 179–80
Seven Years' War, xviii, xxiii, 25, 72, 92
shoḥet (Jewish butchers), 85, 89, 141
Silesia, 92–93
Simpson, Johann, 139
socio-religious backgrounds, 156
Soermann, Heinrich, 51
Soldau, 88
solidarity, ethnic, xx–xxi, xxii–xxiii, 94. *See also* networks, ethnic
Sombart, Werner, xvi–xvii
Southern Salt Trade Company, 152–53
state loans and financing, 27–28, 180, 181–83
status, socioeconomic, xxii, 18–19, 43–44, 52, 112
Steinhardt, Jozef, 154–55
Stern, Selma, xviii
Symons, Abraham, 5, 29
Symons, Benjamin, 4–5, 23
Symons, Emanuel, 5
Symons, Samuel, 4, 5, 23, 26–27
Symons, Simon, 10, 26–27, 28–29, 37, 38, 99, 128–29
Symons family: in Amsterdam's Ashkenazic community, 4–5; in brokerage of bills of exchange, 10–15, *12–13f1.3–4*, *14t1.1*, *16–17t1.2*, 26; connections and networks of, xxiii, 15, 18–27, *20f1.5*, *22f1.6*; in the credit business, 24–25; decline of business of, 27–29

tariffs, 57, 85, 102–103
taxation/taxpayers: avoidance of, 51; community leadership and organizations in, 102, 109n73, 117–18, 130; discriminatory rates of, 8, 179; in Frankfurt an der Oder, *53t2.2*, 60, *63–68t2.4*; of meat, 85; poll

taxes, 49, 127–28; in Praga, 113, 117–18; of Prussian Jews, 52–54; in Warsaw, 97, 102, 130
Tepper banking house, 29, 98–99
textiles: and army supplying, 147; Frankfurt an der Oder in export of, 42, 43; trade in, 38, 43, 47, 49, 87
The Hague, 19
Thirty Years' War, xviii, 39–40, 91–92
trade: agricultural, 85, 95, 115, 119–22, 148, 178; and army supplying, 95, 115, 119–22, 146–47, 148, 178; in commodities, 2, 8, 14–15, 42, 49, 179; ethnic solidarity in, xx; expansion of, 2; long-distance, 4–6, 27; regulation of, 8–9; in textiles, 38, 43, 47, 49, 87; wholesale, xxiii, xxv, 43–44
tradition, 54, 160–68
transportation infrastructure. *See* railway construction
Trivellato, Francesca, xxi, 1–2
trust, mutual, xx–xxi, xxii, 24–25, 69, 137, 168

University of Frankfurt an der Oder, 42–43, 55–56
urbanization, 115, 180
utility: economic, 87, 88, 91, 103, 128–29; personal, 89, 91, 124, 127, 128–29

Vienna, banking in, 181

war financing, 91, 148
Warsaw: 1779 map of, *111f4.1*; acculturation in, 156–57, 160–68; accusations of espionage in, 126, 133n33; army supplying in, 99, 100–101, 125–26, 138–48, *142–45t5*.

1–2, 177–78; banking in, 98–101, 148–49, 171n22, 179–84; bourgeois society in, 138, 157, 159, 162–63, 165, 168; economic elite in, xxv–xxvi; and the emancipation debate, 127–30; entrepreneurs in, 100–101, 137–38; "German" synagogue in, 101–102; insecurity in, 95–98; Jewish population in, 112–13, 130n2, 137, 180; in the Kościuszko uprising, 122–24; leaseholding in, 149–56; migration to, 112, 127–30; opportunities in, 110, 137–38; political conditions and instability in, 95–98; religious attitudes in, 156–60; restrictions in, 96, 110; taxation in, 97, 102, 130. *See also* Duchy of Warsaw; Poland; Polish-Prussian borderlands
Wasserzug, Moses, 42, 81, 85, 96
wealth, 3–4, 43–45, 52, 58, 59, 114
weavers' guilds, 89
Weber, Max, xvi
West Prussia, 84–89, *90f3.2*, 96
wills, 163–65, 165–66
women: in commercial networks, 15, 18; as merchants and entrepreneurs, 157, 159; salons held by, 162–63; in Warsaw banking, xxvi
wool trade, 88–89
Wulfowicz, Mendel, 119, 121–22

yeshivah studies, 55–56

Zbytkower, Szmul Jakubowicz. *See* Jakubowicz, Szmul
Zuker, Lazer, 152

ABOUT THE AUTHOR

Cornelia Aust is a research associate at the Leibniz Institute of European History in Mainz, Germany. She specializes in the history of Jewish communities in Poland and German-speaking lands from the seventeenth to the nineteenth century.